Contemporary Europe

Third Edition

Edited by

RICHARD SAKWA

and

ANNE STEVENS

palgrave
macmillan

First edition 2000
Second edition 2006

This edition published 2012 by
PALGRAVE MACMILLAN

Palgrave Macmillan in the UK is an imprint of Macmillan Publishers Limited, registered in England, company number 785998, of Houndmills, Basingstoke, Hampshire RG21 6XS.

Palgrave Macmillan in the US is a division of St Martin's Press LLC, 175 Fifth Avenue, New York, NY 10010.

Palgrave Macmillan is the global academic imprint of the above companies and has companies and representatives throughout the world.

Palgrave® and Macmillan® are registered trademarks in the United States, the United Kingdom, Europe and other countries

ISBN 978–0–230–28289–6   paperback

This book is printed on paper suitable for recycling and made from fully managed and sustained forest sources. Logging, pulping and manufacturing processes are expected to conform to the environmental regulations of the country of origin.

A catalogue record for this book is available from the British Library.

A catalog record for this book is available from the Library of Congress.

10 9 8 7 6 5 4 3 2 1
21 20 19 18 17 16 15 14 13 12

Printed in China

Contents

List of Illustrative Material

Tables

Boxes

Key Figures

Preface

Much has changed since the first edition of this book appeared in 2000. The process of NATO enlargement accelerated, and with the accessions of 2004 much of the former communist world was encompassed within the alliance. However, while some more countries are set to join in the next few years, notably in the Western Balkans, the process in the former Soviet space encountered strong Russian resistance and has now faltered. The Russo-Georgian War of August 2008 could be called a 'war of NATO enlargement', and further enlargement in the region is now on hold. Instead, Russia has countered with plans for a new 'European Security Treaty' rethinking the foundations of European security. The enlargement of the European Union (EU) is also slowing down. On 1 May 2004 the EU welcomed ten new members, eight of them former communist states, and on 1 January 2007 Bulgaria and Romania joined. The process of enlargement is not over, with several Western Balkan countries in varying stages of accession, but the door remains closed despite Turkey's insistent knocking. Ukraine, after its 'orange' revolution of late 2004, in which attempts to rig the presidential election were thwarted by a mass movement that for several weeks saw three-quarters of a million people occupying the centre of Kiev, sought an accelerated timetable for integration in the accession process, but with the election of a new president in early 2010 its enthusiasm waned.

The EU itself has been undergoing a period of intensive change, culminating in the struggle to adopt a new constitution. In the event, the Lisbon Treaty was adopted as the lowest common denomi-

nator. Pan-European institutions such as the Organization for Security and Cooperation in Europe (OSCE) and the Council of Europe have come up against the stubborn assertiveness of nation-states. These countries have faced major challenges and live in a different security environment following the destruction of the World Trade Center in New York on 11 September 2001. Russia remains caught up in its transformation process that may or may not result in the consolidation of democracy. France and Germany found themselves divided from their American ally during the Iraq War of 2003, and each in their own way faces the problem of economic competitiveness and social change. The UK, especially with a Conservative–Liberal Democrat coalition in power from May 2010, remains unsure whether it is only in Europe but not yet part of it.

This book provides the context for these and many other issues to be understood. The aim has been to provide an accessible introduction to some of the main problems and processes in contemporary European development. The expertise of a broad range of scholars has been drawn on to contribute to the discussion. We have not sought to impose upon the contents of the book, nor upon our contributors, too narrow a vision. The consequence is that some themes and events reappear in a number of places throughout the text, often in a slightly different guise and subject to varying interpretations. We feel that this is appropriate in a work that seeks to illuminate debates and to consider very diverse situations and approaches. We have sought to avoid oversimplification, or reducing complex issues to mere wordbites, but rather to provide throughout an analysis suitable for those coming to the field for the first time. We believe that even an introductory text like this has a responsibility to challenge and to question, to stretch and to inspire students to go and pursue in greater depth some of the issues raised here. We have sought to provide a nuanced yet accessible text for those new to the field, while providing material for thought for those already familiar with the area.

The first chapter focuses on what may be called the 'civilizational' aspect of the identity of Europe. To what degree is the continent today a separate and distinct civilization with a fundamental unity, crossing the old dividing line of ideological confrontation – the 'iron curtain' – stretching, as Winston Churchill so memorably put it in his Fulton, Missouri, speech on 5 March 1946, 'from Trieste in the Adriatic to Stettin on the Baltic'? Is there something that transcends the individual histories of particular countries and peoples to suggest a coherence drawn from history and the dynamics of modern development? In short, what is specifically European about Europe? It is this question that is addressed in the first chapter and that is touched on and developed at various points in the book.

The second chapter provides a historical survey of political development in Europe in the twentieth century. Following the Second World War, Europe emerged devastated and unable to control its own destiny. Under the umbrella of the superpower rivalry formalized in the conventions of the Cold War, the western part of the continent not only rebuilt its economy but entered into an era of unprecedented prosperity, accompanied by the creation of what was to become the European Union. The Eastern part of the continent, however, was wracked by sporadic attempts to reform the Soviet-type systems imposed after 1945. Only after 1989 could the two parts of the continent begin to come together, a process that will stretch well into the twenty-first century.

The third chapter focuses precisely on the question of pan-European integration since the fall of communism in 1989–91. One of the conditions for Europe to come together is a shared normative vison of what it means to be European. At the heart of this vision is a common set of democratic principles. The struggle for these principles to be imple-

mented in the post-communist world has been the main drama in the recent period. This chapter notes the divergent patterns that have emerged, with the East-Central European and Baltic states having made adequate progress to be accepted in the EU, whereas in most other countries the struggle to establish accountable democratic systems continues. Chapter 4 examines Europe's institutional identity, and in particular the development of the EU. The intensification of European integration is analysed, together with the dilemmas facing the EU today. The failure to adopt the new constitution is discussed, but the stress is on the new institutional framework emerging out of the Lisbon Treaty. The 'European project', of which the development of the EU is the most vivid and intense manifestation, is far from complete.

In Chapter 5 the focus is more narrowly political. Thomas Saalfeld examines questions of contemporary political organization, looking at ways in which the people can influence and control governments. As the experience of many post-communist countries has demonstrated, adopting the formal institutions of democracy is the easy part; much harder is ensuring governmental accountability to the people and its representatives in parliament and elsewhere. Rich experience in the mechanisms of accountability and their comparative effectiveness are reviewed, including types of voting and electoral systems, the continuing debate over the relative advantages of presidential versus parliamentary systems mechanism, and other aspects of institutional design.

Dieter Rucht takes up some of the issues raised in the previous chapter to examine the way that political participation in society is organized. The politics of protest and the new social movements are deeply rooted in the main social and cultural developments in society. The role and types of political parties, the variety of interest groups, various types of protest movements and the role of the media are discussed. Ultimately, this is a chapter about the quality of democracy – about the extent to which citizens are active in the public sphere. In Chapter 7 William Outhwaite focuses on the theme of European identity in relation to social structures and social change. The major categories and processes of modernity are assessed: capitalism, constitutionalism, rationalization and individualism, together with issues such as social mobility and social identity. Some of the themes in this chapter are picked up by Vivien A. Schmidt, who looks at development in European political economy in recent decades. The phenomenal economic development of the early post-war years has now created mature economies and mature societies that are faced with the problems spawned by the earlier process of modernization.

The traditional notion of the undiluted sovereignty of the nation-state is under challenge from above, as Anne Stevens notes in her discussion of the development of the EU, but it is also challenged from below by the rise of regionalism. In Chapter 9 Jörg Mathias examines the territorial organization of European space and above all the role and meaning of various types of regionalism. Chapter 10, by Mike Bowker, examines some of the questions associated with European security. The shift from the certainties of the Cold War to a much more fluid security environment is discussed, as well as some of the main challenges, notably international terrorism in the post-9/11 world. The chapter by John Coombes analyses some of the cultural movements of our time, suggesting that the tension between modernism and more traditional forms of artistic production is far from resolved by the emerging postmodern trend. Finally, the editors consider some of the possible interpretations of Europe, the nature of its identity and some of the implications of this for the future.

These themes are not separated by iron curtains but weave in and out of the various chapters. Together they constitute the tapestry that is contemporary Europe. The debts of gratitude accumulated in the preparation of a work of this sort can only be acknowledged but not repaid. Above all, we must thank the contributors themselves, who have endured the various tribulations of moulding their individual styles to that required to ensure consistency across the book as the whole. The patience and understanding of our editor at Palgrave Macmillan, Steven Kennedy, has been exemplary, and he provided the encouragement and incentives to see this work to a conclusion. This book is itself a combination of various styles, approaches and themes, and thus reflects in miniature the larger picture that is contemporary Europe. We hope that the portrait that it presents is relatively faithful to the original and, like the great Bayeux tapestry of an earlier age, provides a source of learning and wonderment.

RICHARD SAKWA AND ANNE STEVENS
Canterbury and London, August 2011

Acknowledgements

The author and publishers would like to thank the following who have kindly given permission for the use of pictorial copyright material:

Press Association, pp. 10, 14, 30, 32, 39, 41, 43, 55, 80, 95, 110, 142, 187, 189, 200, 223, 236, 237; Getty Images, pp. 38, 199, 244; Audiovisual Library of the European Commission (© European Union 2011), p. 87.

Every effort has been made to contact all copyright-holders, but if any have been inadvertently omitted the publishers will be pleased to make the necessary arrangement at the earliest opportunity.

List of Acronyms

ACUSE	Action Committee for the United States of Europe
ALDE	Alliance of Liberals and Democrats in Europe
AMS	additional and compensatory member systems
AV	alternative vote
CAP	Common Agricultural Policy
CBSS	Council of the Baltic Sea States
CDC	Convergència Democràtica de Catalunya (Democratic Convergence of Catalonia)
CDU	Christian Democratic Union (Germany)
CEE	Central and East European (states)
CEO	Chief Executive Officer
CFSP	Common Foreign and Security Policy
CIS	Commonwealth of Independent States
CoR	Committee of the Regions
CPMR	Conference of Peripheral Maritime Regions
CPSU	Communist Party of the Soviet Union
CSCE	Conference on Security and Co-operation in Europe
EaP	Eastern Partnership
EBRD	European Bank for Reconstruction and Development
EC	European Community
ECHR	European Convention on Human Rights
ECJ	European Court of Justice
ECtHR	European Court of Human Rights
ECSC	European Coal and Steel Community
EEA	European Economic Area
EEC	European Economic Community
EFSF	European Financial Stability Facility
EFTA	European Free Trade Association
EMU	Economic and Monetary Union
ENP	European Neighbourhood Policy
EPP	European People's Party
ERDF	European Regional Development Fund
ERM	Exchange Rate Mechanism
ESDP	European Security and Defence Policy
ETA	Euskadi Ta Askatasuna
EU	European Union
EURATOM	European Atomic Energy Community
EUREGIO	European Region
FDP	Free Democratic Party (Germany)
FRG	Federal Republic of Germany
FRY	Federal Republic of Yugoslavia
FYROM	Former Yugoslav Republic of Macedonia
GATT	General Agreement on Tariffs and Trade
GDP	gross domestic product
GDR	German Democratic Republic
GNP	gross national product
IMF	International Monetary Fund
KGB	Committee for State Security (Russia)

MAD	Mutually Assured Destruction	RDA	Regional Development Agency
MEP	Member of the European Parliament	RETI	Association of European Regions of Industrial Technology
MP	Member of Parliament		
NATO	North Atlantic Treaty Organization	RPR	Rassemblement pour la République (France)
NGO	non-governmental organization		
NRC	NATO–Russia Council	SED	East German Communist Party
ODS	Civil Democratic Party (Czech Republic)	SNP	Scottish Nationalist Party
		SPD	Social Democratic Party (Germany)
OECD	Organization for Economic Cooperation and Development	START	Strategic Arms Reduction Treaty
		STV	single transferable vote
OPEC	Organization of the Petroleum Exporting Countries	TEU	Treaty on European Union
		UEN-EA	Union for Europe of the Nations–European Alliance
OSCE	Organization for Security and Co-operation in Europe		
		UKIP	United Kingdom Independence Party
PACE	Parliamentary Assembly (Council of Europe)		
		UN	United Nations
PES	Party of European Socialists	UMP	Union pour un Mouvement Populaire (France)
PJC	Permanent Joint Council (Russia–NATO)		
		USSR	Union of Soviet Socialist Republics
PR	proportional representation	WHO	World Health Organization
QMV	qualified majority voting	WTO	World Trade Organization

Notes on the Contributors

Mike Bowker is Senior Lecturer in Politics at the University of East Anglia, Norwich. His current research interests are Russian foreign policy and the nature of the Cold War and post-Cold War worlds. His most recent monograph is *Russia, America and the Islamic World* (2007).

John Coombes writes on comparative literature and culture, having retired from the Department of Literature at the University of Essex. He has taught and lectured extensively abroad, including Paris, East Berlin, Katowice, Tokyo, Albuquerque and Las Vegas. His principal field of interest is the relationship between literature, politics and society in modern Europe (including England), and he is also interested in comparisons of Japanese and European literature. He is the author of *Writing from the Left; Socialism, Liberalism and the Popular Front* (1989) and of numerous articles on English, French and comparative literature since 1600.

Jackie Gower is a Teaching Fellow in the Department of War Studies, King's College London. She has worked on EU and British government projects in Poland, Hungary, Lithuania, Croatia, Ukraine and Russia, and was the specialist adviser to the House of Lords European Communities Committee for its report *Enlargement of the EU: Progress and Problems* (1999). She is currently working on EU–Russian relations and is a coordinator of the EU–Russia Research Network supported by UACES and BASEES.

Robert Ladrech is Professor of European Politics at the University of Keele. His most recent publications are *Europeanization and National Politics* (Palgrave Macmillan, 2010) and *The Europeanization of National Political Parties* (2007; co-editor). He has also recently completed a British Academy-funded project on social democratic parties and climate change.

Jörg Mathias is Senior Lecturer in Politics at the University of Aston, Birmingham. His main research interests include comparative regional studies, regional economic and social development policy, devolution and federalism. He is the author of *Regional Interests in Europe* (2003) and various articles on regional politics and policy. Up to 2011 he was Associate Dean of Undergraduate Programmes at Aston's School of Languages and Social Sciences.

William Outhwaite is Professor of Sociology at the University of Newcastle. He is the author of *European Society* (2008) and *Contemporary Europe* (2012) and (with Larry Ray) of *Social Theory and Postcommunism* (2005).

Dieter Rucht is Honorary Professor of Sociology at the Free University of Berlin and co-director of the research group 'Civil Society, Citizenship and Political Mobilization in Europe' at the Social Science Centre, Berlin. His research interests include political participation, social movements and political protest. Currently he is working on global justice movements.

Thomas Saalfeld is Professor of Political Science at the University of Bamberg, Germany. His research focuses on comparative legislatures, cabinet stability and the representation of immigrants and ethnic minorities in liberal democracies. His recent publications include *The Political Representation of Immigrants and Minorities: Voters, Parties and Parliaments in Liberal Democracies* (joint editor with Karen Bird and Andreas M. Wuest, 2011); and *Parteien und Wahlen* (in German, 2007).

Richard Sakwa is Professor of Russian and European Politics at the University of Kent and an Associate Fellow of the Russia and Eurasia Programme at the Royal Institute of International Affairs, Chatham House. He has published widely on Soviet, Russian and post-communist affairs. Recent books include *Russian Politics and Society* (4th edn, 2008), and *Putin: Russia's Choice* (2nd edn, 2008). His book on *The Quality of Freedom: Khodorkovsky, Putin and the Yukos Affair* came out in 2009, and his study *The Crisis of Russian Democracy: The Dual State, Factionalism, and the Medvedev Succession* was published in 2011.

Vivien A. Schmidt is Jean Monnet Chair of European Integration, Professor of International Relations and Political Science, and Founding Director of the Center for the Study of Europe at the University of Boston. Her books include *Debating Political Identity and Legitimacy in the European Union* (co-edited with S. Lucarelli and F. Cerutti, 2011), *Democracy in Europe* (2006) and *The Futures of European Capitalism* (2002). Her current work focuses on the impact of the economic crisis on European political economy and democracy.

Anne Stevens is Emeritus Professor of European Studies in the School of Languages and Social Sciences at the University of Aston, Birmingham. She has a particular interest in administrative structures in France and in the institutions of the EU, and is the author of *Brussels Bureaucrats? The Administrative Services of the European Union* (2001) and *The Government and Politics of France* (3rd edn, 2003). She also writes about women and politics and published *Women, Power and Politics* in 2007.

CHAPTER 1

Introduction: the Many Dimensions of Europe

RICHARD SAKWA

Europe, the homeland of my heart's choice, is lost to me, since it has torn itself apart suicidally a second time in a war of brother against brother . . . . I have seen the great mass ideologies grow and spread before my eyes – Fascism in Italy, National Socialism in Germany, Bolshevism in Russia and above all else that arch-plague nationalism which has poisoned the flower of our European culture. . . . It was reserved for us, after centuries, again to see wars without declarations of war, concentration camps, persecution, mass robbery, bombing attacks on helpless cities, all bestialities unknown to the last fifty generations, things which future generations, it is hoped, will not allow to happen. But paradoxically, in the same era when our world fell back morally a thousand years, I have seen that same humankind lift itself, in technical and intellectual matters, to unheard-of deeds, surpassing the achievement of a million years with a single beat of wings. . . . Not until our time has mankind as a whole behaved so infernally, and never before has it accomplished so much that is godlike.

STEFAN ZWEIG, *The World of Yesterday* (1943), pp. 7–8

As one chapter in Europe's tumultuous history closed in 1989 with the fall of the communist regimes of Eastern Europe, a new era began in which we are now embroiled. What are the main patterns and challenges of this new episode in the European saga? What is it in any case that is distinctively 'European' about Europe? We will examine these questions in this chapter, indicating some of the themes that will be developed later.

The idea of Europe is of relatively recent provenance. Until the modern period the notion of Christendom was predominant, and only from the eighteenth century did the geographical expression become more settled as a term to describe the region. European predominance as the source of power and ideas became established, and for the next three centuries the continent went on to assert its primacy in the rest of the world. The European powers created colonial empires, and insisted that its culture was the measure of global civilization. However, even as Europe reached the height of its power, backed up by relative technological superiority, its claims were challenged externally and weakened by internal divisions. Philosophers and political leaders in the Arab, Chinese, Japanese and Indian worlds, to list just a few, challenged Europe's ambitions. As for internal fragmentation, the European model of development was always subject to question, notably by Karl Marx (1818–83) and his followers, and the tensions arising from the competitive European state system ultimately provoked the Great War (1914–1918) and the era of revolutions in its wake that destroyed the Russian, German, Austro-Hungarian and Ottoman empires. Only after yet another bout of blood-letting in the Second World War (1939–45) did Europe embark on a new era of decolonization, internal unification, and a more modest appreciation of its place in the world. The features of this post-war period are the subject of the bulk of this book.

With the rise of new powers in America, China, and potentially in India, Africa and Latin America, Europe as a continent has lost its former pre-eminence. In contemporary Europe the former great powers of France, Germany, Italy and the UK have pooled some of their resources in the European Union (EU), while Russia remains outside this endeavour and strives to remain a great power on its own. Even from its reduced status Europe can look back at a history that shaped a large part of the world for 2000 years. The birth of democracy in the Greek **polis** in the fifth century BCE; the challenge of Christianity and its stress on the value of each individual as a moral being with the ability to choose between good and evil; the articulation of the fundamental concepts of **Roman law** that remain the cornerstone of modern concepts of law to this day; the anguished debates over individual responsibility, conscience and the relationship between church and state that accompanied the development of Christendom into the modern era; and the rebirth of classical **humanism** accompanied by the rebirth of the concept of politics as a sphere of autonomous decision-making in the **Renaissance** of the fifteenth century, have all shaped the modern world. It was in Europe that the main movements of **modernity** took shape. These include the individualism associated with the Protestant **Reformation**, the questioning spirit of the eighteenth-century **Enlightenment**, and then the triumph of the idea of progress in the nineteenth century, accompanied by the emergence of the world's first industrial civilizations and liberal democracies. It was here, too, that Europe's restless energy gave birth to overseas expansion and the creation of the European empires. It is against this background that we examine contemporary problems.

The central point here and in later contributions is that these questions can only be understood in the context of the long-term development of Europe; hence we will begin by examining some of the patterns in European history before discussing contemporary European challenges. The central notion will be the concept of modernity. Something unique happened in Europe as it left the Middle Ages, with roots in antiquity and ancient Greece but given new force by intellectual, socio-economic and political developments at this time. The new element was a questing spirit that repudiated the authority of tradition and instead sought to place the individual and his or her conscience and intellect at the heart of the new world. While the traditional authority structures continued, in the form of institutions like the Roman Catholic Church, aristocracies and the family, their authority was challenged by a sense that the past could no longer define the future. Thus the short answer to the question of 'What is Europe?' is that it is a society turned to the future. By the late eighteenth and early nineteenth centuries this dynamic future-oriented world-view gave the continent a pre-eminent economic and military role in the world, and this gave birth to the idea of Europe as a civilization.

In the twentieth century, however, Europe's dominance was challenged by outside powers (above all, the USA), by its own 'civil wars', including two world wars, and by alarm at the darker side of its civilization. The Russian Revolution in October 1917 gave birth to the world's first self-proclaimed communist system on a national scale, accompanied by the abolition of the market and

---

● **Polis**: The Greek word for a city state. Used to denote a complete set of political arrangements, usually with the implication that the existence of such arrangements is desirable.

● **Roman law**: The legal system in operation in ancient Rome, lasting up to the seventh century and dating back over a thousand years, to the Twelve Tables of around 439 BC. The experience of Roman jurisprudence was formulated during the reign of the emperor Justinian I in the *corpus Juris Civilis* (AD 528–35). Roman law laid the foundations of much of continental European civil law.

● **Humanism**: A system of thought and belief which rejects dependence upon the notion of the existence of God as the source of values and ethics and sees human beings as containing within themselves the highest values.

● **Renaissance**: The historical period during the fifteenth and sixteenth centuries which saw the rediscovery of Classical literature and thought, and the development of new forms of art, music, architecture and literature.

● **Modernity**: An attitude to historical time that encompasses the notions of change and progress, and thus a questioning stance towards tradition and given authority. Modernity is often seen as the era succeeding the medieval epoch, characterised by secularism, capitalism, industrialisation, rationality and the nation-state.

● **Reformation**: The historical period during the sixteenth century which saw the emergence in Western Europe of Christian denominations, most of them described as 'Protestant', which broke away from the leadership of the papacy and rejected what they saw as the excesses, abuses and errors of the Roman Catholic Church.

● **Enlightenment**: The name given to a period of intellectual history during the eighteenth century when philosophers and other thinkers stressed the importance of reason, of freedom of thought and of proceeding by observation and deduction.

the repudiation of **liberal democracy**. The attempt to create an alternative form of modernity in the Union of Soviet Socialist Republics (USSR) was extended to large parts of Eastern Europe after 1945, but increasingly suffered from a lack of intellectual, economic and technological dynamism. Various campaigns to reform the system in the late 1980s provoked not only the dissolution of the communist order but also the disintegration of the Soviet Union. Effectively, the fall of the Eastern European regimes in 1989–91 put an end to the greatest future-oriented ideology of all, communism, whose dark side had by then become apparent to all. In a paradoxical way, however, Europe is now living without a future, in the sense of a clearly formulated set of aspirations, but is trying to find a compass to determine its own fate and its place in the world. One of these directions is the emergence of the EU, not only as an economic project but also as a normative power embodying a set of values, above all the transcendence of national conflicts that have plagued the continent since the beginning, which represents one of the great contemporary schemes to find a way of overcoming the past and devising a new human community (see Chapters 3 and 4). Europe remains a community turned to the future, but the nature of the desired outcome is increasingly unclear. Thus 'reform' and permanent change remain central to Europe's identity, but the meaning and purpose of this 'permanent revolution' are blurred.

What is Europe?

It was in Europe that the great movements of our time were forged and, indeed, the very notion of modernity was first given form. This theme recurs in Chapter 7. By 'modernity' we mean, to borrow Therborn's succinct definition, 'an epoch turned to the future' (Therborn, 1995, p. 4). From this perspective the present is no more than the preparation for a future that is perceived to be something better than what exists now, while the present itself is considered to be only a leftover from the backwardness of the past. Thus modernity is a future-

oriented striving for a better future based on notions of progress and development. Modernity is accompanied by notions of modernization and reform, together with the idea of revolution as a way of breaking with the past to usher in a radiant future. The idea of reform was well represented in European modernity and, among other things, gave rise to the powerful current of social reformism known as social democracy. The idea of progress had by the nineteenth century seized the European imagination, reflecting Europe's striving to move out of the alleged darkness and limitations of the past and to build a better world based on science and human reason. Europe was, indeed, in Therborn's words, 'the pioneer of modernity and the centre of it' (Therborn, 1995, p. 19). There was, however, a darker side to modernity's aspiration to dispense with the past. By focusing on the future, the present becomes no more than the brushwood to be cleared as the foundations of the future are laid. This was the basis for various revolutionary ideologies (including fascism and communism) that took shape in Europe, launching destructive programmes for the establishment of a better future world by destroying aspects of the present one. It is these ambiguities in Europe's civilizational identity that we explore in this chapter.

Europe can be studied through the examination of specific countries or the trajectories of particular movements and ideas. Our focus here, however, is on Europe as a civilization, that is, as a distinctive arena of social, political and intellectual interaction. The histories of countries, movements and ideas weave together to create an entity that differs from other civilizations. Above all, European civilization has tended to be dynamic and expansive, whereas comparable civilizations, like that of the Chinese, valued stability and introspection, while Japan cut itself off from the rest of the world for three centuries until forced to open again by the Americans in the 1850s. Europe's dynamism has come from conflict and divisions, in part derived from its geography and ethnography (Diamond, 1997). Peninsular Europe in particular, jutting out into the Atlantic with its outlying islands of Britain, Ireland, Iceland and some others, is divided by high mountain ranges, broad rivers, sea channels and a highly indented coastline (see Maps 1.1 and 1.2). It has been peopled by successive waves of invasions

---

● **Liberal democracy**: A form of democracy which incorporates limited government, accountability of government to the legislature and the people, and a system of regular and competitive elections.

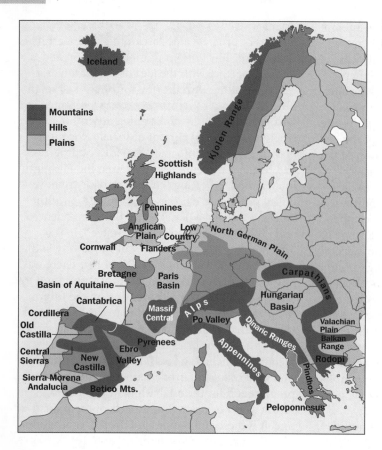

Map 1.1   Physical geography of Europe

and settlement, and it still remains possible to talk of the tribes of Europe. There remain at least 225 autochthonous (indigenous) languages in Europe, joined now by dozens more as new migrant communities become established. At the same time, states cannot be simply mapped onto nations. In the EU, out of a total population of 500 million, at least 70 million speak a language other than the official language of the state in which they live. With successive enlargements, notably in 2004 and 2007 to bring in much of post-communist Eastern Europe (see Chapter 3), the 27-member EU hosted a large community of Turks as its single largest non-indigenous minority group, but Russians now became the second largest. The fundamental drive of the EU, however, is to combine a cosmopolitan political ethos while ensuring the rights of all of its peoples. The fundamental dynamic of the EU is opposed to the basic principle of nationalism that the borders of the nation and the state should coincide (Gellner, 1983), although it is certainly not incompatible with patriotic sentiments and the civic affirmation of nations.

Unlike the Confucian civilizations of Asia, whose underlying principle is *fusion*, the European model, like a nuclear reactor, has historically been based on *fission*, generating an extraordinary creativity, accompanied typically by intense violence. The following tensions and divisions have been particularly important:

1   The separation of religious and political authority

Determining where the dividing line between church and state should be drawn has produced a tension that for most of the last millennium in Western Europe was the source of a rich debate over the proper relationship between temporal and secular authority. At the social level the tension is still far from over, as in the continuing struggle over laicism (*laïcité* in French, a concept of a secular society, connoting the absence of religious

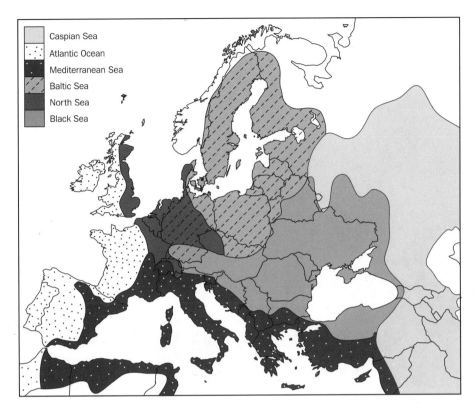

Map 1.2 Watersheds and drainage

Caspian Sea
Atlantic Ocean
Mediterranean Sea
Baltic Sea
North Sea
Black Sea

involvement in government affairs as well as the absence of government involvement in religious affairs), and in general the limits of secular governmental authority to regulate the life of religious institutions. While Islamic political philosophy tends to stress theocracy, the fusion of religious and spiritual authority, the Christian view of 'rendering unto Caesar what is Caesar's, and unto the Lord what is the Lord's' encouraged a far more conflictual relationship.

2 The division between Byzantine and Catholic Christianity

In 1054 the Western half of Christendom, headed by the Pope, based in Rome, separated from the Eastern half under the authority of the patriarch based in Constantinople (today Istanbul) and practising the Eastern (Orthodox) form of Christianity. Relations between the two halves were strained to the degree that in 1204 the Fourth Crusade sacked and looted Constantinople. The crusades, with the first from 1096 to 1099 at the behest of Pope Urban II, sought to recapture the Holy Land from Islam

and transformed Western Christianity into a more militant and worldly institution, whereas Orthodoxy tended to be more contemplative, mystical and devotional, although less independent from the secular authorities. The Orthodox churches derived from Byzantium were historically more closely identified with their princes and states, an ideal of fusion and 'symphonia' that deprived these countries of one of the sources of dynamism that characterized the Western part of the continent. The idea of *sobornost* (conciliarity or collegial government) stresses the unity of spiritual and secular authority and collective forms of decision-making, a principle at odds with the notion of the separations of powers that came to dominate in the West. This historic cultural division has a powerful resonance to this day, with the Orthodox world of Russia, Ukraine, Belarus, Serbia, Montenegro, Macedonia, Greece and Romania sharing a distinctive religious culture and view of political authority that distinguishes them from the rest of Catholic, Protestant, Jewish and Islamic Europe (see Map 1.3).

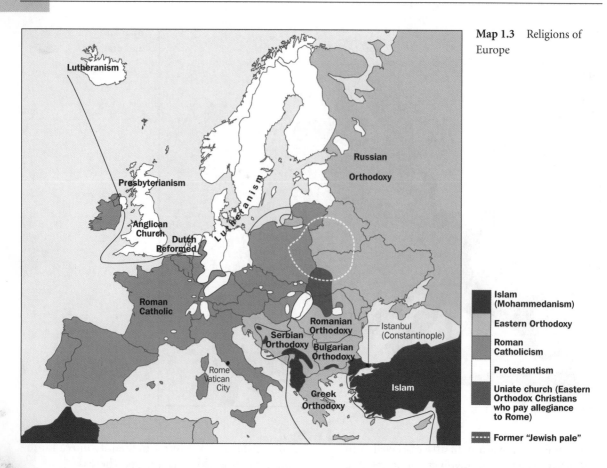

Map 1.3   Religions of Europe

Legend:
- Islam (Mohammedanism)
- Eastern Orthodoxy
- Roman Catholicism
- Protestantism
- Uniate church (Eastern Orthodox Christians who pay allegiance to Rome)
- Former "Jewish pale"

Labels on map: Lutheranism, Presbyterianism, Anglican Church, Dutch Reformed, Roman Catholic, Russian Orthodoxy, Romanian Orthodoxy, Serbian Orthodoxy, Bulgarian Orthodoxy, Greek Orthodoxy, Islam, Istanbul (Constantinople), Rome Vatican City

3   The separation of knowledge and power

Out of the fundamental divide between church and state came the separation of knowledge and power. In the Islamic world, as noted, there is a tendency towards a theocratic fusion of the religious and political worlds. In Western Catholic Europe, already by the twelfth century such a fusion was increasingly challenged. The growing gulf between secular and temporal power created space for the development not only of science but also of independent political philosophy and, ultimately, the critique of authority that lay at the heart of Enlightenment thinking (see Map 1.4).

4   States versus empires

The division of Europe's territory between small states struggling for survival and supremacy among themselves and against the supra-national ambitions of empires was something that distinguished Europe from, for example, China, where the authority of the emperor (despite numerous inva-

sions, rebellions and secessions) had, since the unification of the most productive parts in 221 BCE, extended for thousands of miles without interruption, united by a single written form of a unique dominant language. By contrast, Europe in the fourteenth century was fragmented into over a thousand independent principalities, a total reduced by half by 1500. The number fell steadily to reach a low point of 33 in the 1970s, only to start increasing again after the fall of communism as Europe once again fragmented into smaller political units as part of what some have called the 'new medievalism', a patchwork of units with overlapping sovereignty and jurisdictions. The EU in this acts as a new form of the Holy Roman Empire, the loose political body dating from when Charlemagne was crowned emperor of the Romans in 800 AD to its abolition by Napoleon in 1806. The Holy Roman Empire was far from being a centralized state, and instead the emperor shared authority with hundreds of princes, kings, dukes, bishops

Map 1.4   The religious situation in 1560

and other rulers in what by the time of the Thirty Years War (1618–48) had become some 300 *Kleinstaaten* ('little states') in the centre of Europe. The comparison of the modern EU with the earlier body indicates that the nation-state, in Europe at least, is beginning to wane as the unique form of governmental authority (Zielonka, 2006).

The division of Europe into relatively small statelets, something encouraged by its terrain and patterns of settlement, promoted the development not only of the military arts but also of the organizational abilities of states to conduct wars, and above all the development of fiscal systems that could pay for arms and men. Paul Kennedy argued that it was the intense military competition between the relatively small states of Western Europe in early modern times that prompted the creation of highly centralized governments, something that the larger empires of the East (the Russian, Habsburg and Ottoman) did not need to do because their security concerns were less intense and immediate. They were therefore unable to muster the political will for reform (Kennedy, 1987). Concentrated state power

in the West encouraged technological, administrative and economic changes (Tilly, 2004). To paraphrase Tilly, 'States make war and wars make states.' Herein lies the origin of the modern banking system in northern Italy, structured to fund the war needs of princes, followed by the emergence of the Rothschilds and other great banking families. The development of systems of taxation and the struggle to control revenue collection ultimately provoked revolutions in England and France, and of course in America.

The culmination of this long struggle of small states against the power of a supra-national empire was resolved only in the wake of the First World War, when the four great continental empires (German, Russian, Ottoman and Austro-Hungarian) broke up to spawn national states (see Chapter 2). It was at the Paris Peace Conference in 1919 that Woodrow Wilson, who had come to Europe with his 'fourteen points' defending the right of nations to self-determination, was asked: 'Must every little language have a country all its own?' The answer, apparently, was 'Yes', and the

Treaty of Versailles ensured that out of the dissolution of the empires numerous small states were born. The fall of communism in 1989–91 was accompanied once again by a wave of state formation. For some seven decades the USSR represented the last attempt to maintain a supra-national 'empire' on fundamentally new principles, namely working-class solidarity and socialist internationalism, but with its disintegration into 15 separate countries (along with some de facto unrecognized entities) the nation-state became the universal political form in Europe (although challenged, as noted, by the supra-national authority of the EU). The wars of Yugoslav succession in the 1990s, in which the six constiuent republics separated followed by further disintegration, can be seen as part of the long struggle to establish relatively homogeneous nation-states. In this headlong rush the relative advantages of the European multinational 'empires' should not be forgotten. The Austro-Hungarian and Ottoman empires (see Map 2.1) allowed a multiplicity of peoples to live in communion and relative harmony (Lieven, 2003). The wars in the Balkans in the 1990s were far from inevitable, and in any case failed to resolve the issue of how communities fated to live in proximity with each other can coexist.

5   Civil society versus the state

The tension between state and society in Western Europe took diverse forms, but gradually allowed the emergence of civil society, the realm of civic association and conscience. Civil society is the sphere between the state, on the one hand, and the realm of private activity and the family, on the other, and encompasses such bodies as trade unions, voluntary associations and non-governmental organizations. This is the source of the pluralism that is characteristic of European civilization. Civil society is the basis of democratic politics, since without the social hinterland of a critical and active public, organized not only in political parties but also in innumerable interest groups, communities of common concern and local self-government, democracy becomes not only formal and lifeless, but also brittle and vulnerable. The issue of participation will be discussed further in Chapter 6, but it might be noted here that Marx took a far more gloomy view of civil society, considering it the source of egotism, selfishness and economic exploitation. He was quite willing to see the baby of civil society thrown out with the bathwater of capitalist exploitation, but failed to explain how the individual could be defended against the might of the state if all autonomous intermediate institutions had been swept away. It is for this reason that the restoration of civil society became one of the main demands of the anti-communist movements in Eastern Europe from the 1970s onwards. The concept of civil society became the focus of *resistance*, but it was also sometimes seen as the site of a possible future *emancipation* from traditional forms of politics (see Keane, 1988). In the event, it soon became clear that a vibrant partnership between the state and civil society is the most effective basis for democracy.

6   The guild versus market society

Perhaps the most crucial of all these divisions was that between the principle of the guild, the closed corporation that strictly regulated the work of its members, access to the market, and prices, and the development of market-oriented capitalism based on entrepreneurial capital. From its birth in northern Italy in the early modern period, market capitalism has now become the universal principle of economic organization, but it must be stressed that this was by no means a foregone conclusion. In its own way, the state socialism practised in the former Soviet Union represented an attempt to destroy market forces and to regulate economic life in a manner reminiscent of the old guilds, although of course for modern industrial purposes. Today the market is taken for granted not only as the source of wealth but also as the guarantor of freedom (Hayek, 1944), although the debate over the relationship between the two is far from exhausted (Przeworski, 1991). A similar debate rages over the intrusion of the values of the market into spheres that are considered by many not to be its proper concern, giving rise to fears that altruism will give way to the universal imposition of the 'cash nexus', undermining traditional cultures and eroding selfless concern for others (Marquand, 2004).

7   Class struggles versus liberalism

The hierarchical division of society and inequalities of wealth and privilege have been the universal features of all civilizations. What marks Europe out is not the presence of class divisions, but that these have taken on a systematic and theorized form of class *conflict*. During the French Revolution new ideas of social equality emerged, advanced above all by the so-called *sans-culottes* during the period of Jacobin dominance between 1791 and 1794. In 1797 Gracchus Babeuf for the first time advanced the cause of the proletariat, and thus signalled the beginning of the class struggles between labour and capital. But the French Revolution signalled above all the consolidation of the power of what in that context was called the 'Third Estate', otherwise known as the bourgeoisie and now more commonly known as the middle class. Through their striving for individual rights in the sphere of politics and the economy, liberalism was forcefully placed on the European agenda, and the nineteenth and twentieth centuries were, above all, the history of the travails and, from the perspective of the early twenty-first century, the apparent triumph of liberalism. At the heart of traditional liberalism is the defence of private property rights and individual freedom, to which the neo-liberals from the 1970s added concern for the untrammelled exercise of the free market, even in spheres that in welfare states had been taken over by the state, such as health, welfare and nationalized transport, utilities and public services. Many of these have now been privatized. Financial services were increasingly deregulated and cooperative banks demutualized, allowing the financial sector to grow at the expense of traditional manufacturing. In the end the financial bubble burst in 2008, precipitating the worst economic crisis since the crash of 1929. In response, there has been a renewed belief in greater state intervention, although there are few signs of a return to the full-scale collectivism of earlier years.

8   Revolutionary versus evolutionary socialism

We now come to the period that has just ended, the era that can symbolically be considered to have begun in 1848 with the publication by Karl Marx and Friedrich Engels of *The Communist Manifesto*, proclaiming in its opening sentence that 'A spectre is haunting Europe, the spectre of communism.' Systematized by Marx, revolutionary socialism argued against the ameliorative policies of reformists and insisted that only a socialist revolution could put an end to the exploitation of the

working class and, by doing that, put an end to the exploitation of all suffering humanity. Others, however, argued that socialism could exploit the opportunities offered by liberal rights and institutions to advance the interests of the working class and to improve its living conditions through electoral politics and parliamentary parties (Bernstein, [1899] 1961). Socialism thus divided into revolutionary and evolutionary wings, although there were many shades of red in between.

In Russia, where the achievement of liberal rights lagged behind Western Europe, socialism took a radical form. Vladimir Il'ich Lenin ((see Key Figure 1.1) organized a revolutionary wing of social democracy in the form of the **Bolshevik Party**, which seized power in October 1917. The course of twentieth-century European history was changed. Communism was transformed from a spectre into a living political and military force.

Communism claimed to be able to achieve most of what liberalism aspired to, plus a lot more, above all the emancipation of humanity from the thrall of cold economic laws, from the exploitation of workers by capitalists, and above all from the fetishistic alienation of humans from their own true selves, what Marx called 'species being'. In practice the Soviet republic established by the Bolsheviks under Lenin and his successor, Josef Stalin, became a despotic political system. The abolition of the capitalist mode of production did not on its own lead to the end of exploitation, but only replaced one form of exploitation by another, this time based on the political dominance of the Communist Party and its bureaucracy. Stalinism represented a shift towards an economistic type of socialism, where the focus was on the relationship between *things*, whereas for believers in the original emancipatory potential of Marxism the emphasis should be on a humanistic socialism where the quality of the relationship between *people* would be central. Part of the reason for the evolution of the actually existing communist systems towards authoritarianism is that instead of

---

● **Bolshevik Party**: A revolutionary Marxist party which originated from the part of the Russian Social Democratic Labour Party which supported Lenin after 1903. Under Lenin the Bolsheviks seized control of Russia in the October Revolution in 1917. Renamed the Communist Party of the Soviet Union in 1951.

Key Figure 1.1

Vladimir Il'ich Lenin (1870–1924)

Born Vladimir Il'ich Ulyanov of a family of the minor gentry in Simbirsk, he became the major theorist of the practice of revolutionary socialism in the twentieth century. In his seminal work of 1902, *What Is to Be Done?*, Lenin outlined his theory of a tightly knit party of dedicated revolutionaries separate from the working class who would offer leadership. Left to their own devices, in Lenin's view, the working class would develop only a 'trade union' consciousness, devoted only to the improvement of workers' conditions as opposed to dealing with the root cause of deprivation, capitalist exploitation; and therefore a force had to come from outside – the revolutionary party. Lenin's ideas provoked a split in the Russian Social Democratic Labour Party (RSDLP) in 1903, with his radical wing becoming the Bolsheviks, and the moderates the Mensheviks. On his return to Russia from Swiss exile on 4 April 1917 Lenin's April Theses suggested an immediate transition from the first stage of revolution (the 'bourgeois democratic') to the second ('revolutionary socialist'), based on his theory of imperialism: the world capitalist system was marked by the concentration of financial and industrial capital, and it would take only a break of the 'weakest link of the imperialist chain' to bring the whole capitalist world crashing down. Under his leadership the Bolsheviks were able to seize power in October 1917 and thereafter established the first revolutionary communist state in the world. It was this system that disintegrated in 1991.

communism coming *after* capitalism, the revolutionary socialist system acted as the *alternative* to capitalist development, inheriting a relatively backward society. Development thus took the place of emancipation in Soviet thinking. This is, however, only part of the explanation for the authoritarian turn taken by communist regimes everywhere. Marxist–Leninist ideology simply had no role for civil society and the separation of knowledge and power, let alone the market and the state, and thus represented a repudiation of much of what had made Europe *Europe* in the first place while claiming, paradoxically, to be fulfilling European ideals of modernity.

In Western Europe evolutionary socialism in the form of social democracy brought about a veritable revolution of social reform, producing the modern welfare states, as Chapter 2 indicates. In the East, however, revolutionary socialism became exhausted, having proved unable to achieve consistent economic growth and improvements in standards of living and welfare that could match those of the West. In 1989 the communist regimes in Eastern Europe disintegrated, and in August 1991, following a failed coup by hardliners in the Soviet

Union, revolutionary socialism there, too, collapsed. The fall of the revolutionary socialist systems removed any lingering doubts within social democracy over whether it sought to destroy capitalism or to improve it (Sassoon, 1996). One of the first social democratic parties to reject revolutionary socialism was the Social Democratic Party (SPD) in the Federal Republic of Germany (FRG) at its epochal Bad Godesberg conference in 1959, but in Britain the Labour Party remained formally committed to the nationalization of the 'commanding heights' of the economy until 1994. By that time collectivist ideologies calling for the direct state management of the economy had everywhere waned. In the early 1980s the failure of President François Mitterrand's (see Key Figure 2.6) government's attempt at strongly interventionist management of the French economy discredited all future moves in this direction (see Chapter 2).

9   Foreign influences and domestic development

External influences have played an important part in shaping Europe's identity and development. Islamic scholars reintroduced Aristotle to Western intellectual life and provided the bases of algebra, and indeed the very numbers that we use (cf. Lewis, 1982). By the sixteenth century the fear of external conquest had declined, although the Eastern marches of Europe remained under threat from the Ottomans until their defeat at the gates of Vienna in 1683. The Turks remained in control of the Balkans until the First World War, and Turkey still has a foothold in Europe proper in the form of the province of Thrace. The question of Turkish eligibility for EU membership, as we shall see, continues to raise in the sharpest form questions about Europe's self-identity. At various times European culture was swept by enthusiasm for things Turkish, Chinese, Japanese and Indian.

An enduring aspect of Europe's dynamism is the tension between external and domestic European developments. The voyage to America in 1492 by the adventurer Christopher Columbus, in the employ of Ferdinand and Isabella of Spain, marked the beginning of the modern European state system. This was followed soon after, in 1497, by Vasco da Gama's journey round the coast of Africa to the East, establishing contact with India and Japan. Competition and wealth derived from the overseas empires fuelled the competition between states in Europe. Colonial ventures in the Americas, Africa and Asia exported European values and economic organization to new territories, and 'Europeanization' by the nineteenth century had become a synonym for a distinctive type of modernization (see Map 2.2). Today the values that were earlier exported to the rest of the world have come back to Europe in new forms. America took European culture and transformed it to create something new, while in Asia different models of capitalism have been devised that challenge Europe to redefine its own developmental path.

Out of these fissures and processes was generated the energy and dynamism that propelled Europe to the forefront of technological and cultural development. Much no doubt was lost in abandoning the fusion model of society, and the Soviet experiment in a way represented an attempt to recreate old harmonious ideals of social life, but out of these various reactions the sinews of modern development were forged. A distinctive civilization was born with a coherence that transcends the many divisions to which it is prey.

Endings and beginnings

After the Second World War the global struggle between the superpowers and between ideologies was focused on Europe, but at the same time the struggle diminished Europe's standing and ability to play an independent role. Europe was overlain by the struggle of external powers, each representing facets of ideologies (liberalism and communism) that had, ironically, been born in Europe (see Map 1.5). The **Cold War** meant the primacy of military power, but once again, in a curious inversion, this promoted the demilitarization of European international politics. No interstate war was fought in Europe between 1945 and 1991 and instead energies were concentrated on economic development and building what became the EU, although large military establishments were maintained.

The most profound ending on the European continent in our generation was the fall of the communist regimes in Eastern Europe between 1989 and 1991. The extension of communism to Eastern Europe from the Soviet Union in 1944–8 in the wake of the defeat of Nazi Germany initially fulfilled certain national and social developmental tasks, above all, for example, the stabilization of Poland's borders and the shift everywhere from semi-feudal agrarian societies to urban industrial ones. However, by the 1970s it was clear that the Soviet-type systems in Europe were in crisis. Economic growth rates were falling and the allure of socialism was fading. Attempts to renovate socialism from within were stymied by the conservatives in the Soviet Union. The Prague Spring of 1968, when the Czech Communist Party sought to introduce a more humanistic 'socialism with a human face', was crushed by an invasion of Warsaw Pact (see Box 1.1) forces on 21 August 1968. Thereafter oppositional movements no longer sought to 'renew' socialism but to transcend it. The Soviet Union and its communist allies, in their eagerness to achieve the formal ratification of post-war borders and other security and economic advantages contained in the

---

● **Cold War**: A state of hostility, animosity and tension between the communist bloc and the Western World, embodied particularly in the relationship between the USSR and the USA. It lasted from the period soon after the end of the Second World War until the end of the communist regimes in 1989.

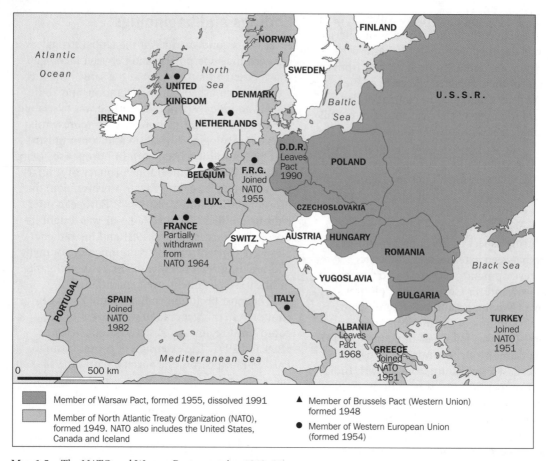

Map 1.5   The NATO and Warsaw Pact countries, 1949–91

first two 'baskets' of the Helsinki Final Act of August 1975, signed up to a third 'basket' dealing with a bundle of issues subsumed under the rubric of human rights (Mastny, 1993, pp. 421–42). This proved one of the more significant catalysts for the fall of the communist systems. It gave the populations a legal document to cite, signed by all the communist states, promising to defend free speech, freedom of movement and many other aspects. Against the background of declining economic performance and concerns over human rights, by 1989 popular support for the communist regimes had largely evaporated. Much of communist officialdom itself realized that the old regimes were exhausted, and prepared for the transition to something new.

With the appointment of Mikhail Gorbachev (see Key Figure 1.2) as leader of the Soviet Union

in March 1985 Soviet history entered its endgame. Beginning with a programme of *perestroika* (restructuring), Gorbachev's policies gradually became more radical as he embraced most of the agenda of the Prague Spring to achieve a renewed democratic socialism. His clear signals that the East European countries could go their own way precipitated the various negotiated revolutions (Poland, Hungary), mass movements (Czechoslovakia, Bulgaria) and popular uprisings (Romania) that put an end to the communist experiment in Central Europe in 1989 and in the USSR itself in 1991. The end of revolutionary socialism raised questions about the role of any sort of socialism in the post-communist world and helped rekindle interest in various 'third-way' projects (between revolutionary socialism and neo-liberal capitalism), particularly in Britain under Tony Blair's New

BOX 1.1
The Warsaw Pact

This military alliance, linking the Soviet Union and its Central and East European satellites, was created in 1955, over and above a series of bilateral treaties between the USSR and its satellites which had allowed for large numbers of Soviet troops to be stationed in those countries. Its creation was primarily, though not solely, a response to the admission of the Federal Republic of Germany to NATO. Its founder members were the USSR, Romania, Poland, Hungary,

Czechoslovakia, Bulgaria and Albania, which ceased participation in 1961 and formally left in 1968. East Germany was admitted in 1956. It was nominally an intergovernmental organization but the military command structure was always under Soviet control. The alliance collapsed with the fall of communism in 1990–91 and its military structure was formally dissolved on 31 March 1991.

Labour after coming to power in May 1997. It also seemed to suggest that a distinctive phase in European modernity had come to an end, including the modernist project in art (see Chapter 11). The idea of never-ending progress, of revolutionary leaps into freedom, and of the liberating effects of science, gave way to fears about emancipatory despotism where the search for liberation leads to suffering and servitude (Scott, 1996) and the risks attendant on scientific development (Beck, 1992).

The end of communism was accompanied by the end of the last multinational 'empires'. The USSR ceased to exist as a state on 31 December 1991, leaving 15 successor republics, including Russia and Ukraine (see Map 2.4). Czechoslovakia underwent a 'velvet divorce' on 1 January 1993 when it divided into the Czech Republic and Slovakia. In contrast, the disintegration of Yugoslavia between 1990 and 1999 provoked bitter warfare (see Chapter 2 and Map 2.5). The process is not yet over. The joint state of Serbia and Montenegro dissolved in June 2006, and following Western intervention in 1999 Serbia's former autonomous province of Kosovo achieved a form of de facto independence, and on 17 February 2008 it declared formal independence. By October 2011, 85 states (including 22 EU member states) had recognized its *de jure* independence, but that number still represented a minority of the UN's 193 member states. Following the Russo-Georgian war of August 2008 Russia recognized the former Georgian

enclaves of Abkhazia and South Ossetia as independent states, but only a handful of states followed its example. The EU insisted on the maintenance of Georgia's territorial integrity, a cardinal principle of the UN Charter; yet this came up against another of its core principles, the right of nations to self-determination. The dilemma ultimately cannot be resolved in the realm of law but is shaped by the strategic interests of the great powers.

The end of the Cold War provided an immediate peace dividend, and most countries slashed their defence budgets. It also ended the continent's subordination to the two contesting blocs, although the Western military alliance was forced to rethink its role. The **Truman Doctrine**, announced in 1947, outlining the principles for the 'containment' of the Soviet threat, provided the rationale for the North Atlantic Treaty Organization (NATO) (see Box 1.2), founded on 4 April 1949, based first in Paris and then, from 1966, in Brussels. The creation of NATO gave Atlanticism concrete form, with Canada and the USA joining with most non-communist West European nations. The existence of NATO demonstrated that security threats were too big for any

---

● **Truman Doctrine**: The ideologically expressed commitment made by US president Truman in 1947 to maintain freedom throughout the world by 'containing' the spread of communism. The Doctrine laid the basis for subsequent US involvement in the Greek civil war, the creation of NATO, and long-term US global military presence.

Key Figure 1.2

Mikhail Sergeevich Gorbachev (1931–)

Born in 1931 and pursuing an orthodox career in the Communist Party of the Soviet Union as local Party leader in Stavropol Krai, in March 1985 he was elected General-Secretary of the CPSU. He immediately launched what he called *perestroika*, the restructuring of the Soviet political system and the economy. This was accompanied by *glasnost*, meaning 'openness', allowing a more critical and truthful discussion of the past – above all, the crimes of Stalin. Initial hopes that some fine-tuning of the Soviet system would allow significant improvements in economic performance were dashed, and instead Gorbachev concentrated on political reform. In March 1990 the CPSU was stripped of its 'leading role' in managing society, but conditions continued to deteriorate. The Baltic republics, forcibly incorporated into the USSR by Stalin in 1940, demanded independence, the working class became more militant, and intellectuals were no longer satisfied with 'socialist' democracy, but simply wanted democracy. By 1991 the accumulation of crises overwhelmed Gorbachev's vision of a reformed, humane and democratic socialism. Following the failed coup of August 1991 the Communist Party in Russia was banned, and in December of that year the USSR itself was abolished. Gorbachev resigned on 25 December 1991, and since then has headed the Gorbachev Foundation, a policy think-tank, in Moscow.

one country on its own, even one as powerful as the USA. In the East the counterpart to NATO, the Warsaw Treaty Organization, established in 1955, was disbanded in 1991.

For the countries involved there was a 'return of history' as the countries could now pursue their own destinies. The enlargement of NATO to the East proved one of the most contentious issues, with Russia resolutely opposed on the grounds that with the end of the communist threat NATO had outlived its usefulness. For the new and aspirant members of NATO, however, membership gave them a sense of security that they had not enjoyed since the end of the First World War. The Atlantic security partnership remains central to post-Cold War security in Europe and represents an obstacle to the re-emergence of balance-of-power politics, a concept that had spawned so many wars in Europe. As we shall see in Chapter 10, however, the relevance of NATO to a world without communism and characterized by the 'asymmetrical warfare' of terrorism has been disputed. One of the superpowers (the USSR) disappeared, while Europe's relationship with the other (the USA) had to be placed on a new footing. Moreover the overlay of the Cold War was withdrawn from

Europe just as global market forces were challenging the very basis of independent political existence (see Chapter 8).

Under these conditions economic transitions in Eastern Europe were achieved. While Poland managed to forge ahead with economic transformation, its economy by the end of the 1990s was still smaller than it had been before the rise of Solidarity in 1980. Slovenia was the only other transition country to restore its 1990 gross domestic product (GDP) level by the end of the decade, with the Czech Republic, Slovakia and Hungary coming up fast. Elsewhere the picture was far gloomier. The Russian economy shrank by some 60 per cent by the end of the decade, leaving the mass of the population worse off than they had been under communism, and with at least a third below the poverty line. The German Democratic Republic (GDR) was united with the Federal Republic of Germany in October 1990 and thus enjoyed exceptional advantages: a sound currency in the form of the Deutschmark (exchanged in 1990 at the very advantageous rate of one-to-one for the communist-era Ostmark), massive budget transfers from the West, billions of Deutschmarks in private direct investment, and the whole panoply of democratic

BOX 1.2

NATO

The North Atlantic Treaty Organization was established in 1949. The previous year Britain, France, the Netherlands, Belgium and Luxembourg had created the Brussels Treaty Organization as a mutual defence organization against the possibility that Germany might once again revive and prove aggressive, and against the menace that the Soviet Union was perceived as constituting. In 1949 these states joined with the United States, Canada, Italy, Portugal, Denmark, Iceland and Norway to sign the North Atlantic Treaty. The intention was to ensure that the USA was firmly committed to the defence of Europe. From this time until the 1990s the Soviet Union was clearly identified as the main threat. Greece and Turkey joined the alliance in 1951. In 1954, following a failed attempt to establish a European Defence Community, the Western European Union was created, superseding the Brussels Treaty Organization, and incorporating West Germany alongside the original members. The Western European Union was first and

foremost a device to enable West Germany to be admitted to NATO, and in 1955 that took place. Spain joined in 1982. Meanwhile, in 1964, General de Gaulle had symbolized his desire to assert French independence from the USA by withdrawing France from NATO's integrated military command, as well as requesting NATO to move its headquarters out of France.

In 1999 the alliance was expanded by the accession of Poland, Hungary and the Czech Republic, in 2004 Estonia, Latvia, Lithuania, Slovakia, Romania, Slovenia and Bulgaria joined, and in 2009 Albania and Croatia acceded, to bring total membership up to 28. The membership of Macedonia is blocked by Greece because of a dispute over the republic's name, while enlargement to include Ukraine and Georgia is bitterly contested by Russia. Defensive throughout the Cold War, its first military action took place in the 1990s in the Balkans and in the 2000s it was involved in policing Afghanistan.

institutions and law (property, commercial, bankruptcy, civil, and so on). However, even here the transition depression was deep, and only in 1999 did the five Eastern *Länder* reach their pre-unification levels of GDP. There remains a gulf between per capita GDP in the East and the West: in the EU the average income in 1999 was $21,600 per head whereas in Poland, one of the most successful transition economies, it was a mere $4096, while in Russia it was just over a thousand US dollars. There has been a gradual convergence as living standards and incomes have risen in the East, although the economic crisis from 2008 dealt a severe blow to countries such as Latvia and Slovakia, which were the most exposed to the global economy.

Wars have been endemic to Europe. Most have been genuine civil wars, in the sense that they were between groups that probably had more in common with each other than with those outside. In the modern period wars were fought within the framework of the balance of power, the attempt to

achieve a rough parity between the European great powers to avoid the dominance of any single power on the continent. The religious wars of the sixteenth century (various types of Protestants against Catholics) and the ideological wars of the twentieth (communism versus capitalism) were the exception. After a period of relative peace in the nineteenth century, Europe's martial traditions took a sharp turn for the worse in the twentieth century, wracked by wars, genocide, mass deportations and ideological hatred. According to Mazower (1998), some 60 million European deaths before 1950 are attributable to war or to violence by the state. As Judt (2005) describes, some 36.5 million Europeans are reckoned to have died between 1939 and 1945 because of the war, and tens of millions more were uprooted by Hitler and Stalin. If democracy is now the universal aspiration, this was far from always being so. Fascism and communism rejected the softness and lack of resolution of 'bourgeois' parliamentarianism, particularly in the interwar years, and to this day nationalist myth-making tears societies apart. While the Western part of the continent might see the second half of the century as one of peace and increasing affluence, the Eastern part was effectively subjugated to an at times murderous but always oppressive social system. The main goal of the Paris Treaty of 18 April 1951 establishing the European Coal and Steel Community (ECSC), inspired by Robert Schuman and Jean Monnet, was to link the economies of France and Germany so that they could never go to war again; and out of this grew the EU of today. The West did little to bring about the end of the Cold War, other than existing as an alternative, and for large parts of the East 1989 represented the triumph not so much of democracy as of capitalism. As Mazower (1998) has vividly argued, Europe is far from being the natural home of liberal democracy, although in the post-Cold War era it appears to have triumphed.

The struggle for unity and its limits

The post-Cold War era in Europe is marked by three main principles: political democracy, economic liberalism, and integration. Although plagued by divisions and wars, the aspiration to European unity is far from new. There have been attempts to unite Europe in the past, and these continue today, although in radically new forms. In the Roman Empire there was one law, one defence system, a road network radiating from Rome, and a single currency for the many peoples sheltering under the *Pax Romana*. This peace lasted until the end of the fourth century when the Goths, Huns and Vandals moved in. The second unificatory project was represented by Christendom, a temporal power that united all of Europe until the fateful split of 1054 between Byzantium and the Roman Catholic Church. In the Western part the popes became the rivals of emperors as the Catholic (or universal) Church emulated the Roman Empire through a system of bishops and monks, with Latin the lingua franca once again of a huge territory. In the Middle Ages neither priests nor scholars recognized frontiers or countries but were part of the single cultural entity of Christendom. The medieval university represented a sphere of knowledge separate from the power of the state.

The third attempt to unite Europe was launched by the crowning of Charlemagne in 800 as Holy Roman Emperor, and the empire as we have seen lasted for just over a thousand years, from 1273 to 1806 in the hands of the Habsburgs, the rulers of the Austrian lands. By the end, of course, not much remained of former glories; Voltaire characterized the remnants as 'neither Holy, Roman, nor an empire'. It was Napoleon who on 6 August 1806 put the empire out of its misery by forcing the abdication of the last emperor, Francis II, but he in turn represented the fourth great unificatory mission. The French Revolution of 1789 brought to the fore-front the two great principles of popular sovereignty (democracy) and self-determination (nationalism), although in the meantime Europe had to endure the Napoleonic empire and the long decay of the other empires. Napoleon built a supra-national empire, but he also represented the principles of the Enlightenment. Even after his final defeat at Waterloo in 1815 **democracy** and **nationalism** thereafter were to go together, since for the people to rule there had to be a limit and definition of who exactly were the people. Europe suffered yet one more military attempt to unite the continent, under Hitler's Germany, before Europe, ruined and overshadowed by the emergent superpowers, embarked on the current, sixth, and far more benign attempt to contain its diversity in a single political form.

Europe's divisions have been a source of dynamism, but they increasingly became a source of weakness. After 1945 it became clear that Europe, devastated by two world wars within a generation, could not continue in the old way. European politics began to move from fission to fusion. Some visionaries began to hark back to the idea of one law and one defence system to cover a larger area of Europe than the Roman Empire. Victory in the Second World War revived hopes for a continent united and at peace. In Zurich on 19

● **Democracy**: Rule by the people. According to Abraham Lincoln in his Gettysburg address in 1864, 'government of the people, by the people and for the people'. Democracy is a much contested concept, subject to many varying interpretations.

● **Nationalism**: A set of beliefs, which may take varied forms, which asserts the primacy of the nation as the source of sovereignty and the main basis for politics and government.

September 1946 Churchill called for 'the re-creation of the European Family, or as much of it as we can, and to provide it with a structure under which it can dwell in peace, in safety and in freedom. We must build a kind of United States of Europe', and he ended with the rousing words: 'Let Europe arise.' He did not propose, however, that Britain would actually be part of this new 'official' Europe. The new Labour government in Britain from July 1945 under Clement Attlee, absorbed by the creation of the welfare state, the defence of the empire (although India and Pakistan were granted independence in 1947), and by its defence ties with the USA, also saw no reason for British involvement in any movement towards European unity. Calls such as Churchill's, however, fell on more receptive ground in Germany (Konrad Adenauer), in France (Jean Monnet and Robert Schuman) and Italy (Alcide De Gasperi). All were devout Catholics, and it is often suggested that some of their commitment to European integration derived from the universalism of the Roman Catholic Church harking back to the unity of Christendom of old. Britain's ambivalence about relations with 'Europe', however, is a pronounced form of a tension now experienced more widely, as the challenges of reconciling national politics with the political expression of aspirations to European unity though the EU become apparent. These themes are further explored in Chapters 3 and 4.

Otto von Bismarck, the 'iron chancellor' who had united Germany through 'blood and iron' in the 1860s, had once dismissed Italy as 'no more than a geographical expression'; yet now, while both Italy and Germany have united, it is Europe that remains a 'geographical expression'. The initial aim of European integration was largely negative, to ensure that never again would war be possible between Germany and France, but a more positive agenda has gradually emerged. This encompasses at the minimum a powerful economic trading bloc that can match the economic power of America and the Far East, but at the maximum there is clearly a dynamic involved that may one day lead to the creation of an integrated state that will supersede the smaller states out of which it is composed.

The process at first was limited to Western Europe but has now encompassed Central Europe and parts of the eastern reaches of the continent.

Further east, disintegration rather than integration remains prevalent. But what are the geographical borders of Europe? What are its limits and how can it be physically defined? Europe's borders are poorly delineated, merging into Asia in the east and separated from Asia by the Hellespont in Turkey, making it no more than a subcontinent jutting out into the Atlantic Ocean. In the discussion that follows, it is clear that geography is never absolute but is politically defined: geography, in short, is politics. Europe remains a geographical expression looking for a political form.

If we look to the West we see the USA, a country of largely European origins and values and one that by 1913 had a gross national product (GNP) that was already nearly three times that of Britain and four times that of Germany. The eclipse of Europe and the shift of the locus of power over the Atlantic was evident in all fields after 1945. The UN, established in San Francisco in April–June 1945, made New York its home, whereas the old and discredited League of Nations was based in Geneva. In the post-war world the fate of Western Europe and North America appeared to be so closely bound together as to have established a single Atlantic community. This, at least, was the traditional British view, but one that was sharply contested by France in particular. The concept of Atlanticism in Britain was sometimes expressed in the form of the notion of the 'special relationship' between the USA and Britain, an idea that was forged in the early post-war years as Britain's growing economic weakness forced it to pass the baton of world leadership to the USA. The special relationship has always been something accorded greater respect in Britain than in America. The Atlantic ideal has been a weak force outside security issues and, except in Britain, was soon overshadowed by the idea of European unity. Even the USA took a positive view of European integration, seeing it as a way of strengthening Europe's economic independence, achieving security against communism and inhibiting a return to the European civil wars of the past. With the end of the Cold War and the tensions generated by the second war in Iraq from 2003 the European and the American worlds appeared to be drifting apart; and Britain found itself uncomfortably in between. The EU today has a total combined GDP equal to that

BOX 1.3
Finlandization

The condition whereby a country loses its freedom of action in foreign policy, but is free to pursue domestic policies of its choice. The term was historically applied to Finland. After 1945 Finland was forced to take into account the wishes of its giant eastern neighbour, the Soviet Union, in external affairs, but internally the country remained capitalist and democratic. Only in 1989, with the fall of communism, did Finland stop being 'Finlandized'.

of the USA ($14.5 trillion), but its lack of political unity means that it lacks a single voice in world affairs.

If we look to the North, the Scandinavian countries during the Cold War espoused the notion of the 'Nordic balance' between the capitalist West and the communist East. Finland found itself in exceptional circumstances, and while internally capitalist, the country accepted some limitations on its freedom of action in foreign policy (a condition known as 'Finlandization'; see Box 1.3). Sweden was the main driving force of neutrality and non-alignment in the region, pursuing social democracy at home and refusing NATO membership overseas. With the end of the Cold War, Sweden and Finland joined the EU but not NATO, while Norway remains a member of NATO but not the EU. Denmark was a member of both organizations, and was always sceptical regarding notions of a Nordic 'Third Way'.

Looking east, the anti-communist revolutions of 1989 represented a long-delayed end to the Second World War, and in a broader sense an end to the division of Europe. The 'iron curtain' had maintained, in Anssi Paasi's words, 'a continual vision of "otherness"' (1996, p. 4). The end of the Cold War tore down the iron curtain but there remains a fundamental division between the prosperity of the west and the travails of transition in the east. The eastern part of the continent is still engaged in the nation-state-building process that is largely complete in the west. With the fall of communism, 24 new nation-states were born, 15 out of the former USSR, seven (so far) out of Yugoslavia, and two out of Czechoslovakia. In the Balkans the

attempt to carve relatively ethnically homogeneous states out of multinational entities was accompanied by forced migration ('ethnic cleansing') on a massive scale. The three Baltic republics (Estonia, Latvia and Lithuania), however, managed to restore their statehood relatively peacefully, although in the first two there were tensions with the large Russian minorities, focusing on issues of citizenship. Membership of the EU and NATO were dependent on resolving theses issues, although as far as Russia is concerned the status of its 'compatriots' in Estonia and Latvia is far from satisfactory. This is now a problem for the EU to feal with. A condition for accession was the resolution of border disputes and the repudiation of territorial claims, something that Latvia did over its claim to territories in Russia. The prospect of EU membership has been an important catalyst in promoting inclusive policies on citizenship and minorities.

As we shall see in Chapter 3, the Central European countries of Poland, Hungary, the Czech Republic, Slovakia and Slovenia were on the fast track for EU membership, and in the event the enlargement of May 2004 also included the Baltic republics of Estonia, Latvia and Lithuania (together with southern Cyprus and Malta), and in 2007 Bulgaria and Romania joined. As for NATO, Poland, the Czech Republic and Hungary joined in March 1999, and in 2004 there was a second 'big-bang' wave of enlargement encompassing Estonia, Latvia, Lithuania, Slovakia, Slovenia, Romania and Bulgaria. But how far to the east? Only in the early eighteenth century did the court of Peter the Great accept the thesis of the Swedish officer, Philipp Johann von Strahlenberg, that the Urals were the border between Europe and Asia, and they only became a significant landmark dividing Europe from Asia in the nineteenth century. There is no real eastern geographical border to Europe, with the Ural mountains a symbolic rather than a physical barrier, and with most of Siberia and the Russian far east as far as the Pacific Ocean brought firmly into the European sphere of civilization by Russian colonization. Europe's southeastern limits, in the borderlands of the Caucasus and the Caspian Sea, provoke even more controversy. The 'Europeanness' of Turkey, as much as that of Armenia, Azerbaijan and Georgia, remains a matter of controversy. All these countries are considered to be marginally European at best. As for the Central Asian states (Kazakhstan, Kyrgyzstan, Tajikistan, Turkmenistan and Uzbekistan), in the period following the end of the Cold War they joined a number of pan-European bodies, but their status on the borderlands of Europe remains contested.

The question of Russia is, as ever, ambivalent. Is it the most western of the Asiatic countries, or the most eastern of the European states? And to what degree can a distinctive Eurasian identity act as a point of reconciliation between the two continents? If Russia's history since the forced 'modernization' of Peter the Great in the early eighteenth century can be described as a 'permanent transition' so, too, we can describe the faultline across Europe as the 'permant border'. Is Russia part of European civilization, or the core of a distinct Eurasian civilization of its own? While Catherine the Great may have issued a famous *ukaz* (decree) declaring that 'Russia is a European nation', the very fact that such a decree was required suggests at least some uncertainty over the issue. These questions came most sharply to the fore when NATO launched its air war against Serbia on 24 March 1999 in response to Serbian repression in Kosovo. The Balkans, as in 1914, provided the spark that brought out the underlying tensions in the post-Cold War order. Russia's role in helping broker peace in Kosovo and in later disputes, however, confirmed that there could be no enduring peace in Europe *without* Russia, however uncomfortable it may be to live *with* Russia. The consolidation of the state under Vladimir Putin between 2000 and 2008 brought new tensions in Russo-Western relations, as the question of democracy came to the fore. From

Moscow's perspective, embattled in the struggle against terrorism emanating from Chechnya, it was not clear whether the West preferred a weak or a strong Russia.

The status of Ukraine is perhaps even more ambivalent. The country was not included in either the fast or slow track of future EU members for two main reasons: the slow pace of its domestic reform; and its identification with Russia, especially through membership of the Commonwealth of Independent States (CIS). Ukraine had done itself no favours under its first post-communist president, Leonid Kravchuk, when it had insisted that Russia was not part of 'Europe', and had thus involuntarily placed itself outside it as well. Under the presidency of Leonid Kuchma from 1994 policy took a rather more pro-Russian turn, although his policy at first proclaimed itself to be 'multi-vectored'. Ukraine declared that its objective was EU and NATO membership, based on the idea of 'integration with Europe, cooperation with the CIS'. Following the appointment of Viktor Yanukovych as prime minister in November 2002 policy came more into line with Russia's, based now on the idea of 'cooperation with Europe, integration with the CIS' until the 'orange revolution' in autumn 2004, in which popular protests forced a re-run of presidential elections to allow the more pro-European candidate, Viktor Yushchenko, to win. Ukraine turned decisively to the West but achieved little to gain entrance to the EU and NATO. When Yanukovych finally won the presidency in Febuary 2010 he once again restored a 'multi-vector' foreign policy.

Finally, the South may well ultimately prove Europe's greatest challenge. Turkey first talked about EU membership in 1978 and put in its official bid in 1987, yet political instability, economic weakness, the role of Islam, the human rights record and ethnic conflict (in particular in the Kurdish areas of Eastern Anatolia) meant that its application was shelved. The December 2004 European Council meeting finally opened the way for negotiations, but already earlier that year Turkey almost broke off negotiations since it felt it was being treated differently from the other candidate countries. Accession negotiations started properly in October 2005, but thereafter work on the 35 EU accession chapters dragged on with painful slowness. In its debate on 11 February 2009 the European Parliament's foreign affairs committee expressed concern about the degeneration of constitutional reform into a debate on the head-scarf issue, quite apart from concerns over freedom of expression. The EU required Turkey to amend Article 301 of the Turkish penal code, grant more freedom to the media, improve religious tolerance, modify the laws on parties and labour unions, and open its ports to Greek shipping and airlines. The constitutional reform is ultimately designed to remove the military's guardianship role over Turkish politics. The Cyprus issue became an insuperable stumbling block on Turkey's road to EU membership. The EU set a December 2009 deadline for Turkey to open its ports and airports to Greek Cypriots, threatening that failure to comply could lead to the suspension of membership talks. The EU insisted on Turkey's full compliance with the Ankara Protocol of 2005, in which Turkey had indirectly recognized Greek Cyprus as the 'Republic of Cyprus', and on that basis the Greek Cypriots insisted that Turkey open up its ports.

The European south (Portugal, Spain, Italy, Greece, Cyprus and Malta) has joined 'official' Europe. For centuries under the Greeks and the Romans, and indeed for Napoleon and Hitler, the Mediterranean was the centre of a civilization that extended into the Levant and North Africa. The capture of Granada and the destruction of the Islamic civilization of Andalusia in the 1490s secured (in strictly Euro-nationalistic terms) the southern border of Western Europe. Today the Maghreb (stretching from Morocco to Egypt) is firmly on the further shore, and for most European policy-makers the continent ends on the sea's northern strand. The Mediterranean most sharply delineates Europe's zone of prosperity from the south, where various struggles for development, democracy and survival are being waged. The northern shore of Africa is part of the EU's European Neighbourhood Policy, and the object of special Mediterranean programmes.

Mention of Europe's Islamic and southern neighbours draws attention to the contradictory process of European border formation. Just as the external borders are taking on a harder character, migration has brought non-European cultures into the heart of Europe. The retreat from empire gave rise to a reverse flow of former colonial peoples into Europe to work in its factories and to staff its public and social services. In France the influx of Algerians (Algeria was considered part of metropolitan France) had begun before the First World War, but became a mass phenomenon following the conclusion of the Algerian war of independence (1954–61). In Britain the age of mass immigration is considered to have begun with the landing of nearly 500 Jamaicans on the SS Empire Windrush at Tilbury on 22 June 1948, followed by large numbers from the Indian subcontinent. The migration of large numbers of Turkish Gastarbeiter (guest workers) into Germany may be considered a case of intra-European movement if one considers Turkey part of Europe.

While the populations of most West European states have become more heterogeneous since the war, those in the East repudiated centuries of mixed populations during and after the Second World War. The Jewish population was destroyed as a conscious act of policy by Nazi Germany and its local supporters; and from 1945 the German populations were summarily expelled from East Prussia, Silesia, the Sudetenland and elsewhere. At a stroke 800 years of German civilization and settlement came to an end. By 1948 some 10.7 million had been expelled or had fled from Eastern Europe, most of whom went to West Germany; the country by 1950 had become home to 8 million 'out-settlers' (Aussiedler), who remain a significant political force there. The legacy of the expulsions continues to haunt relations between Germany and its Eastern neighbours. Poland alone lost some three million Jews and five million Germans, and became one of the most ethnically homogeneous countries in Europe, with 98 per cent of the population claiming to be ethnic Poles before the fall of the Wall. The states of the former Soviet Union remain heterogeneous, with Russia alone hosting at least 142 different peoples. Renewed ethnic cleansing in the Balkans after the end of the Cold War displaced some two million from Bosnia, and led to the deaths of about a quarter of a million. The wars in former Yugoslavia forced Europe once again to face its demons as the 'dark continent'. The issue, starkly put, was either the Europeanization of the Balkans, or the Balkanization of Europe (Mestrovic, 1994).

As Europe entered the second decade of the twenty-first century some of the optimism that followed the end of the Cold War in 1989–91 had dissipated. Instead of a new era of peace and prosperity, new divisions came to the fore. The West European economic zone had moved to the East with enlargement, but the economic crsisi from 2008 saw some devastating falls in economic activity. Democracy was far from consolidated in much of the post-communist world, in particular the area (with the exception of the three Baltic republics) that had once comprised the Soviet Union. The war in Kosovo in 1999 revealed the underlying tensions between Russia and Europe, while the second Chechen war beginning in September of that year demonstrated once again (as in the Bosnian war of 1991–95) the inability of pan-European institutions to avert or to mediate conflicts. The emergence of a number of 'de facto states' in Europe (Kosovo, Transnistria, Abkhazia, South Ossetia, Nagorno-Karabakh) and the threat of international terrorism appeared to marginalize traditional institutions. At the same time, tensions remained in relations with the East, notably with Russia. It appeared that a new 'post-ideological' Cold War was latent between Russia and the West. Contrary to the view of Francis Fukuyama, history certainly did not end in 1989. The features of Europe's twentieth century and the challenges facing the continent in the twenty-first will be the subject of the following chapters.

The three Europes

If the slogan of the anti-communist insurgency in 1989 was 'return to Europe', we need to examine which Europe the demonstrators in those stirring events had in mind. The EU is only one vision of Europe, and itself is divisive in that it is unlikely in the near future to encompass countries like Russia and Ukraine, while Turkey's accession will at best be a long drawn-out affair. The EU is only one form of European integration, although by far the most important. The principles on which the EU will be built are still not entirely clear, and the failure to adopt a formal constitution only deepened debate over its identity. Fundamental questions about the role of federalism and political accountability remain unresolved: is official Europe embarking on a state-building enterprise on the American *Federalist Papers* tradition; or is it designed to pursue a more complex but innovative renewal of the Grotian tradition of multi-level governance and genuinely dispersed state sovereignty? The fact that federalism can take two such fundamentally contrasting forms is the reason why federalism in Britain is seen as centralizing, which it was in America where it acted as the cornerstone for the state-building endeavour, whereas in continental Europe the version based on the ideas of Hugo Grotius stresses decentralization and subsidiarity. And what about the outsider countries? Are they to remain eternal supplicants grateful for whatever crumbs might fall from the European table? This is not a recipe for European solidarity and prevents a broader European identity from developing.

There remain fundamental tensions between the dynamics of official European integration, processes of pan-European unity that bring together the whole of the continent, and forms of cultural coherence that reflect the distinctive features of a separate continent-wide European civilization. Three concepts of European solidarity, if not unity, can be identified.

Institutional Europe

Various forms of official integration are central to 'institutional Europe'. Chapters 2, 3 and 4 describe the beginnings and current form of the most powerful manifestation of this trend, the development of the EU. The 15-member EU of the late 1990s by 2007 became a union of 27 states, making it one of the most successful supra-national institutions in world history. The extent of its eastward enlargement remains problematic (see Chapter 3). Ukraine, for example, was left out of official definitions of what constitutes 'Europe' until the 'orange' revolution in late 2004. Turkey could not be left out in the cold indefinitely, and in late 2004 a timetable for negotiations was adopted that makes membership possible. While Russia sought to make the CIS an official counter-Europe, most of its members sought to distance themselves from the idea, which they viewed as a way of projecting Russian hegemony over the former Soviet space. The enlargement of NATO and the EU threatened to isolate Russia, although both organizations tried to sweeten the pill. For institutional Europe, the definition of 'European-ness' is based on the Copenhagen criteria (see Chapter 3): democracy, the rule of law, human rights, full citizenship rights for national minorities, and a functioning market economy.

The programmes for EU and NATO enlargement were powerful catalysts of change in Eastern Europe, and in turn fed back and forced an agenda of reform and adaptation on the enlarging institutions themselves. EU enlargement challenged the whole continent to rethink what it meant to be 'European'. Deepening (that is, intensification of the pace of institutional integration within the existing membership) took precedence over widening (the incorporation of new members), a priority that many have argued to have been wrong (e.g. Garton Ash, 1999), leaving the East Europeans in the lurch. According to Garton Ash (1996), 'EU-rope' caught the wrong bus in the 1990s; as he put it elsewhere, 'Instead of seizing the opportunities, and preparing to confront the dangers, that would arise from the end of communism in half of Europe, they set about perfecting the internal arrangements of an already well-functioning, peaceful and prosperous community of states in western Europe' (*Prospect*, July 1999, p. 24). In the event official Europe both deepened and widened, although digesting its new members will take years and reduce the appetite for further enlargement. There will be further enlargement in the Balkans, but the focus in future will be on making the EU work better.

Pan-Europe

The idea of the establishment of a European federation had long been part of the European intellectual agenda, and was most eloquently advocated by Count Coudenhove-Kalergi in 1923 in his book *Pan-Europa*. Mikhail Gorbachev's espousal of the 'common European home' from the Atlantic to the Pacific (the trans-Urals region is European in all but name) appeared to signal a new reconciliation of all parts of the continent, not opposed to North America but separate from it, in a deepening process of pan-European integration. Mitterrand in early 1990 floated the idea of a European confederation, and the idea was later taken up by

other French leaders and President Václav Havel of the Czech Republic, but the Gorbachevian ideal of pan-European unity and of a 'common European home' has been eclipsed in the post-Cold War era. Instead, while some pan-European institutions continue to develop, the ideal itself has been marginalized.

The institutions of pan-Europe are intergovernmental rather than supra-national. They include the Council of Europe, established on 5 May 1949 by the Treaty of London (see Box 1.4) in partial fulfilment of Churchill's aspirations voiced in his Zurich speech, but as early as 1943 he had spoken about a Council of Europe in a broadcast to the nation. Its key bodies include an independent European Commission on Human Rights and the European Court of Human Rights (ECtHR), both responsible for the enforcement of the European Convention on Human Rights (ECHR) of 1950. Supported by the Council of Europe's European Social Charter, the pan-European space is now a uniquely intense arena of human rights development. The Parliamentary Assembly of the Council of Europe (PACE) brings together deputies from all 47 member states, with a population of some 800 million people. With the fall of communism the Council gradually extended its reach to the East as countries deemed to have fulfilled certain conditions of democracy and human and civil rights, including the abolition of the death penalty, were integrated. The vigorous human rights agenda raised sharp questions about the balance to be drawn between national and supra-national rights.

The 56-member Organization for Security and Co-operation in Europe (OSCE) (see Chapters 3 and 10) is another of the founding blocs of pan-Europe and remains the world's largest regional security organization. Established as part of the enduring legacy of the Helsinki Final Act of 1 August 1975, the Conference on Security and Cooperation in Europe (as the organization was known until December 1994) was a forum for political negotiation and decision-making in the areas of early warning, conflict prevention, crisis management and post-conflict rehabilitation. The OSCE played a crucial part in the final days of communism, above all at its Vienna follow-up meeting from November 1986. By 1989, Gorbachev had accepted the whole agenda of human rights

BOX 1.4
The Council of Europe

The Council of Europe (which should not be confused with the European Council, the meeting of Heads of State and Government of the member states of the EU; see Chapter 4) was established on 5 May 1949, by ten Western European states (Belgium, Denmark, France, Ireland, Italy, Luxembourg, the Netherlands, Norway, Sweden and the UK); 13 more West European states joined before 1990 (Austria, Cyprus, Finland, West Germany, Greece, Iceland, Liechtenstein, Malta, Portugal, San Marino, Spain, Switzerland and Turkey). After 1990 former East Germany was incorporated as a result of German unification, and since then 17 Central and East European states have joined (Albania, Bulgaria, Croatia, the Czech Republic, Estonia, Hungary, Latvia, Lithuania, Macedonia, Moldova, Montenegro, Poland, Romania, Russia, Slovakia, Slovenia and Ukraine), along with Andorra and, later, the South Caucasian republics of Armenia, Azerbaijan and Georgia, to bring member-

ship up to 47. The Council is based in Strasbourg, France.

The Council of Europe consists of four principal bodies: the Committee of Ministers, which meets twice annually; the Parliamentary Assembly (PACE), which meets four times a year; the Congress of Local and Regional Authorities of Europe; and the Secretariat. The Council issues reports and consultative documents, and draws up conventions, which are binding only on those member states that ratify them, and become operative when a minimum number of member states have done so. The most important of these is the European Convention on Human Rights (4 November 1950), which established the European Court of Human Rights (not to be confused with the European Court of Justice, an EU body), and its Five Protocols (20 March 1952, two on 6 May 1963, 16 September 1963 and 20 January 1966).

and civil society formulated by the concluding document of the Vienna conference. He assumed that this ethical individualism could be grafted on to the communist system to create a more humane form of socialism. Perhaps in different circumstances this might have been possible, but by this time the repressive legacy of communism and its systematic denigration of representative democracy meant that few were willing to give this new experiment the benefit of the doubt. In the early 1990s the OSCE developed a stronger institutional identity, but wars in the Balkans starkly revealed its inadequacies, even in its new form (see Box 10.2). Above all, the tension between the core OSCE principles of national self-determination and the inviolability of borders has still to be reconciled. Russia's aspirations to make the OSCE the main security body in Europe to replace NATO were not fulfilled (Chapter 10). Instead, NATO became the dominant security body, and in the sphere of integration the EU began the long process of enlargement (Chapter 3).

Civilizational Europe

While Europe has been divided politically, and new sources of division remain, there can be no doubt that Russia, for example, is part of a broader European civilization. Its literature and arts have embellished European culture, its music and philosophy are part of the currency of European thinking, and its people are firmly part of the European tradition. This cultural unity transcends political divisions and geographical barriers.

Of the three Europes, the civilizational one in formal terms is the weakest. Economic globalization and the Western-centred process of European integration cannot conceal an underlying unease about the loss of national and regional identities. In spite of the end of overt organized ideological conflict, above all between capitalism and socialism, and despite rhetorical support for the view that there were no winners or losers at the end of the Cold War, Europe has remained divided, but in new ways. Ideological conflict gave way to amorphous 'culture wars' where issues of identity and separateness came to the fore. In a landmark article, Samuel Huntington (1993, and see also 1996) suggested indeed that the new era would be characterized by 'the clash of civilizations'. In Europe he identified an Orthodox civilization and a Western European one. While this division might be questionable, the fact of tensions between the various parts of Europe, in particular in the Balkans and in the former Soviet Union, confirms the view that just as one block of conflicts came to an end, a new set emerges. Although Huntington failed to address those elements that unite Europe culturally, he raised important issues. Above all, the end of the Cold War division of the continent allowed its peoples to argue that 'we are all Europeans now'; but the history of the post-Cold War years brought home that there was no unanimity over who *we* were, quite apart from the question of what was distinctively *European* about Europe.

Thus, three conceptions of Europe are in tension. One, the institutional Europe represented by European integration in the form of the EU and its predecessors, has traditionally served to fulfil French strategic aims, the German search for rehabilitation after the war, and Italian hopes for good governance and participation in Europe, while for the Benelux countries it has provided them with markets and a political stature quite incommensurate with their size. Only Britain has not perceived any vital national interest in membership, other than fear of exclusion from the most dynamic market in Europe, and thus has traditionally been Europe's 'awkward partner' (George, 1998). Western Europe, and above all the EU, has become the 'ideal' to which the rest of the continent aspires. Enlargement after the fall of communism, however, has been a concession granted, as it were, by sufferance rather than conceded as a right, and thus represents a very different political dynamic. This is 'official' Europe at its starkest, contrasted with the more amorphous universalistic concept embedded in the pan-European ideal. The second conception, associated with pan-Europe, is based on inclusivity and the principle of the universal applicability of human rights and democratic aspirations. Although the Council of Europe had been established in Western Europe, it became a genuinely pan-European body after the fall of communism and was not dominated by any single state or alliance of states. The origins of the OSCE were even more genuinely pan-European, it having originally been sought by the Soviet Union and its allies to enshrine by treaty what it had achieved at the end of the Second World War by force; but then it went on to become one of the main instruments to overcome the Cold War. By contrast with official Europe, pan-Europe was inclusive and consensual. The third Europe is that of peoples and cultures, where gradually the outline of a single cultural space, not only at the elite but also at the mass level, is beginning to emerge. Mass tourism, electronic communications, student exchanges, cheaper air flights and much else are gradually creating a single European people. Whether this can take an effective political form will be explored further in this volume.

SUMMARY

- The meaning of 'Europe' is contested, but a peculiar pattern of historical evolution has given the continent a distinctive identity, although this common identity is divided between a Western and an Eastern part. At the base of Europe's civilizational identity is the notion of modernity, whereby a society is turned to the future in the belief that societies progress towards constant improvements.

- Europe differs from other civilizations in its dynamism, which is in part derived from its 'fission' (i.e. explosive) pattern of development, based not on stability and continuity but on change and division. A number of key divisions can be identified, but cumulatively they allowed a distinctive relationship between the individual and the community to emerge, generally understood by the term 'liberalism'.

- The challenge to liberalism in the form of communism proved unviable in Eastern Europe. Socialism, however, took two main forms, and while the revolutionary socialism developed by Marx and Lenin ultimately was unable, literally, to deliver the goods, evolutionary socialism (otherwise known as social democracy) left a permanent mark in creating the modern welfare states of Europe. Both evolutionary and revolutionary socialism are themselves now being transcended by 'third-way' agendas.

- The geography and settlement pattern of Western Europe encouraged territorial fragmentation and the creation of numerous statelets fighting against each other, and this in turn encouraged the creation of the modern administrative state, concentrating fiscal, economic and military resources in its hands. The attempt to maintain multinational empires failed and today the nation-state is the dominant political form in Europe. The disintegration of the USSR, Czechoslovakia and Yugoslavia can be seen as only the latest stage in the development of nation-states.

- The emergence of the EU, however, is a way of re-creating a multinational community on wholly new principles. The EU is moving away from being simply a trading bloc and is beginning to take on some of the attributes of a state in its own right. The question of enlargement to the east for most of the 1990s was subordinated to the aim of intensifying integration within the organization itself, a set of priorities that has been questioned by many. The enlargements of 2002 and 2007 pose new challenges of governance within the EU itself.

- The end of the Cold War in 1989 inaugurated not an era of peace but, notably in the former Yugoslavia, allowed regional wars to be fought in Europe for the first time since 1945. In response, NATO has rethought its role and has enlarged to the east. This in turn threatens Europe with a new division, between those who are members of the Western European alliance system and those who are not.

- New patterns of inclusion and exclusion are emerging, reflecting the ambiguities over Europe's own borders. The question of where Europe, as a geographical and political entity, ends and begins is one of the most important facing the continent today.

QUESTIONS FOR DISCUSSION

- What was so distinctive about European modernity?

- What were the main divisions that fuelled European development?

- What have been the main consequences of the end of the Cold War?

- Are the three Europes compatible with each other?

- What are the natural limits to Europe?

FURTHER READING

Davies, Norman (1996) *Europe: A History* (Oxford: Oxford University Press). A magisterial survey of the history of Europe from the very beginning until the present.

Dussen, Jan van der and Kevin Wilson (eds) (1995) *The History of the Idea of Europe* (London: Routledge). A very useful introduction to the main intellectual currents underlying European development.

Hayward, Jack and Edward C. Page (eds) (1995) *Governing the New Europe* (Cambridge: Polity Press). An essential collection of essays on politics in contemporary Europe.

Judt, Tony (2005) *Postwar: A History of Europe since 1945* (London, Penguin). A critical and compendious study of the world born of the Second World War.

Lane, Jan-Erik and Svante O. Ersson (1996) *European Politics: An Introduction* (London: Sage). An accessible introduction to the main political processes in Europe today.

Urwin, Derek W. (1997) *A Political History of Western Europe since 1945*, 5th edn (Harlow: Longman). A concise history of Europe since the Second World War.

There is more detailed discussion and fuller references on many of the issues discussed in this chapter in subsequent chapters.

CHAPTER 2

Historical Background

ROBERT LADRECH

> The contribution which an organised and living Europe can bring to civilisation is indispensable to the maintenance of peaceful relations.
>
> Robert Schuman, *The Schuman Declaration* (1950)

Europe in the second decade of the twenty-first century is the product of several world-historical dynamics and the unpredictability of human choice. In the period of about two-thirds of a century since the end of the Second World War in 1945, the colonial empires of Britain, Belgium, France, Portugal and the Netherlands have disappeared – in many cases as a result of armed independence movements; the establishment of the USA and USSR as superpowers with Europe at the centre of their rivalry turned the continent into the most heavily armed territory on earth; rival ideological systems each produced political–socioeconomic systems vastly different from each other – the democratic welfare state in the west, and the communist command economy in the east; in the last decade of the twentieth century, concerted efforts by people, elites as well as ordinary citizens, have undermined institutions and systems of thought and practice held to be nearly immutable – the nation-state in the West, and Soviet rule in the east; and finally, as Europe entered the second decade of the new century, the upheavals of the end of the Cold War period are giving way to new patterns of politics and issues such as immigration and environmental sustainability.

Europe between the wars

The Europe that entered the twentieth century (see Map 2.1) was a continent characterized by extremes – in the gap between rich and poor; between industrializing and growing consumerist cultures on the one hand, and agrarian, peasant societies on the other; autocratic forms of government as well as parliamentary party government; and modernism and positivism in the arts, philosophy and sciences coexisting with traditional religious social control and patron–client relations. Europe was, in other words, a mix, volatile in some areas, of the promises of material and cultural progress and the ageless traditions and authority of Church and King. By the end of the First World War, these juxtapositions had begun to change, and the certainties that imbued these different dimensions of European society were tested. Europe had entered what E.H. Carr (1939) termed its 'twenty years' crisis'.

By 1919 four European empires ceased to exist – the German, Russian, Austro-Hungarian and Ottoman (see Map 2.2). Defeat and social and economic collapse brought about by the course of the war were the immediate causes, and ill-adapted forms of governance and administration help to explain why conditions were ripe for the overthrow of these governments. In their wake, successor governments, many of them

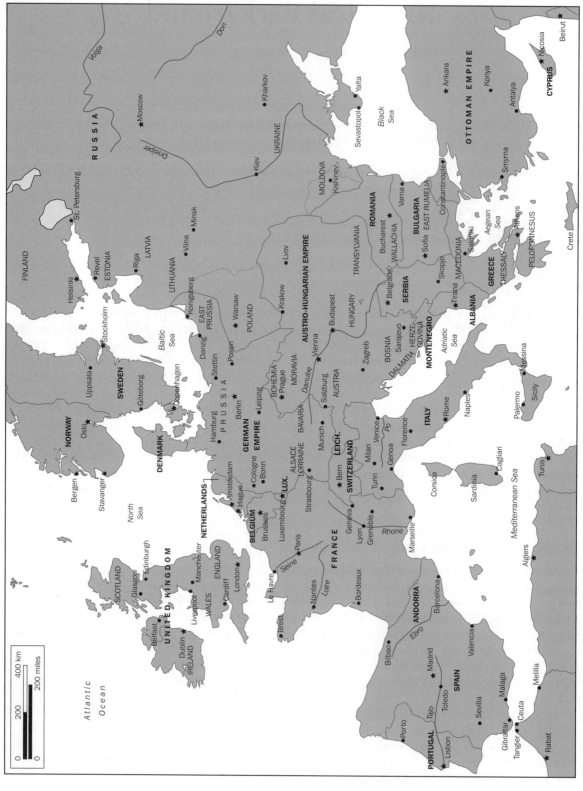

Map 2.1 Europe prior to the First World War

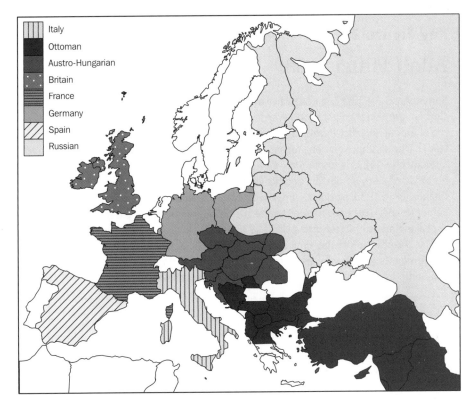

Map 2.2 Balance of power of the empires, 1871

Legend:
- Italy
- Ottoman
- Austro-Hungarian
- Britain
- France
- Germany
- Spain
- Russian

constituting newly independent countries, especially in the case of the **Austro-Hungarian Empire**, were established in a variety of political forms, ranging from parliamentary to authoritarian. In many cases, initial acceptance of parliamentary and constitutional government was soon supplanted with authoritarian rule, whether in its traditional form as in Poland, Hungary and Yugoslavia, or in the new one-party state of the communist-ruled Union of Soviet Socialist Republics (USSR).

In addition to the patchwork of liberal democracies and authoritarian states, the political landscape began to polarize even within the democracies. The success of the Bolsheviks (in 1918 named communists) in Russia inspired other left-wing groups to organize on a similar basis.

Consequently, often as a result of a split within a social democratic or labour party, communist parties appeared in many European countries, most often in the industrializing states of Northern and Western Europe. In some, attempts, ultimately unsuccessful, were made to seize power, as in the case of Germany in 1918 and Hungary in 1919. In others, the Communist Party became a small but sometimes decisive factor in parliamentary coalition government, as in the French Third Republic. On the other side of the political spectrum, discontent with parliamentary rule, fuelled by resentment with the terms of the peace treaty ending the war, led to the development of right-wing extremist movements, some constituting themselves as political parties. In the two most famous cases, Italy and Germany, **fascism** took the form of resistance to the liberal democratic state. Together with communists, the anti-democratic bloc in many countries sometimes nearly approached a majority, as in the

---

● **Austro-Hungarian Empire**: A multinational empire which comprised, among other political units, Austria proper, the Kingdom of Hungary, Bohemia and northern Italian provinces such as Lombardy. The people who inhabited the Empire differed in language, customs and historical background, and included Germans, Czechs, Slovaks, Poles, Magyars, Croats, Serbs and Slovenes, among others. The Empire fell at the end of the First World War.

● **Fascism**: An ideology characterized by a belief in anti-rationalism, struggle, charismatic leadership, elitism and extreme nationalism; associated historically with the Mussolini regime in Italy.

Key Figure 2.1

Adolf Hitler (1889–1945)

Born in Austria, Hitler began a rather unsuccessful career as an artist. He served in the German army in the First World War, in which he was wounded and gassed. He joined the National Socialist (Nazi) Party in Munich after the war, and rapidly rose to be its leader. During imprisonment for his part in an attempted political takeover (*putsch*) in Munich in 1923 he wrote *Mein Kampf* (*My Struggle*), expressing his racial theories, his sense of German destiny and his virulent anti-Jewish views. Elected into office as Chancellor in 1933, he quickly imposed a totalitarian one-party state with himself as Führer (leader). His aims for German territorial aggrandizement led to the annexation of Austria and of the German-speaking areas of Czechoslovakia in 1938 and the invasion of Poland in 1939, which prompted the outbreak of war. The Nazi pursuit of the 'final solution' and of 'racial purity' led to the Holocaust – the mass murder of millions of Jews, along with gypsies, homosexuals, communists and resisters, in the death camps. He committed suicide in Berlin as the Allied forces were about to occupy the city.

1932 German legislative elections, which led to Adolf Hitler (see Key Figure 2.1) being named Chancellor. In Italy, the Fascist Party led by Mussolini simply took power in 1922 from the constitutional monarchy and replaced it with a fascist 'corporate' state. Other countries, from Sweden to France to Austria, also experienced political polarization, which manifested itself both in parliamentary competition as well as in paramilitary clashes. Democracy was indeed sorely tested during this period.

If parliamentary democracy in Western and Northern Europe came under pressure during the inter-war period, the economies of most countries were severely affected by the Great **Depression**, whether they were industrial or agrarian. Added to this was the burden of war reparations paid by Germany, whose economy was part of a wider central European investment and development area. Widespread unemployment contributed to the instability of the political environment. Many of the poorer agrarian countries in the south and the east experienced high levels of emigration, especially to North and South America. Even in coun-

tries not experiencing the intensity of political polarization by fascist and/or communist parties and movements, organized labour in the form of trade unions mounted concerted challenges to the prevailing political-economic order, as in the General Strike of 1926 in Britain.

By 1939, communist or fascist regimes had consolidated themselves in Portugal, Spain, Italy, Germany and Russia. Parliamentary democracy, under strain from powerful nearby dictatorships and their domestic sympathizers, clung on to the hope of ameliorating the conditions, giving rise to extremist movements through the creation of the welfare state in some Scandinavian countries and the Popular Front reforms in France. Economically, a rise in industrial output linked to rearmament in Germany helped to attenuate the worst aspects of the Depression. Forced industrialization in the USSR, though terrible in its toll on human life, led many to believe a rise in living standards had occurred. Free-market capitalism had therefore given way, in many cases, either to the new Soviet centrally planned economy, or to state-led industrialization in fascist countries, or to state interventionist policies in the remaining democracies. In many countries of Eastern Europe, stretching from Lithuania in the north to Yugoslavia in the south, economic modernization had failed to be sustained, and they coexisted with the rest of

---

● **Depression**: An economic contraction resulting in high unemployment. The Great Depression was triggered by the stock-market crash on Wall Street in New York in October 1929 and lasted throughout the 1930s.

Europe as generally subsistence-type peasant societies combined with traditional dictatorships.

As we shall see below, life for most Europeans in the period after the Second World War differed markedly from the turmoil of the years between 1914 and 1945. For the generation born in the years soon after the turn of the century, their experience of the dislocations of war, economic deprivation and political extremism translated into strong support for leaders and regimes promising stability and security. Europe after 1945, although divided for the next 45 years owing to the bitter rivalry of two competing ideological systems, represented a peaceful and stable environment compared to the pre-war period.

Post-war Europe: Cold War and bipolar division

At the end of the war in 1945, with the defeat of fascism, one might have expected a return to the European state system which had arisen in the previous two centuries, that is, a system of independent states engaged in various levels of competition and accommodation – militarily by way of alliances and occasional wars outside or else at the periphery of Europe, and economically through trade and investment among themselves and their colonial possessions. Yet this system was already being undermined by the events and trends of the inter-war period from 1918 to the outbreak of war in 1939 – the Russian Revolution and rise of the Soviet Union on a course of development isolated from the rest of Europe; the collapse of tentative attempts at liberal democracy in Italy and Germany and in the process the rise of fascist states and movements; the increasingly lethal nature of armaments and the breaching of the prohibition against targeting civilian populations, i.e. total war; and the growing challenges to Europe's empires by independence movements in the colonies, for example in India.

Instead, the 'new order' that emerged from the ashes of the Second World War was largely determined by the new superpowers, the USA and USSR. Within a few years from the ending of the war in May 1945, the USA and USSR became more intimately involved in the affairs of Europe than at

any previous time. During the inter-war period, both of these countries had been marginal to the events and dynamics convulsing Europe. In general, the USA and USSR were preoccupied with domestic priorities. In the case of the USA, its isolationist foreign policy and economic problems following the stock market crash of 1929 kept it out of European affairs and the League of Nations (a forerunner of the UN) for most of the 1920s and 1930s. The newly established Soviet state took until the early 1920s to consolidate itself, and then crash industrialization and collectivization under its new leader, Josef Stalin see Key Figure 2.2), rendered the country effectively isolated from the rest of Europe during the 1930s, a situation well expressed by Stalin's phrase regarding 'socialism in one country'. Yet at the war's end, both countries were effectively the dominant country in their respective areas of Europe. How this came about depended to a large degree on the condition of the other formerly 'great' powers.

Within several years of the end of the war, it had become clear that the two former wartime allies were now securing their respective spheres of influence in Europe, and the bipolar division of Europe ensued, not to be overcome for another 45 years. This period of armed confrontation came to be known as the Cold War, and although two mighty military alliances faced each other across the political–ideological divide in Europe – most notably in the divided Germany – actual fighting between the two camps – the American-led North Atlantic Treaty Organization (NATO – see Box 1.2) and the Soviet-led Warsaw Pact (see Box 1.1) – never occurred. The very possibility of nuclear war taking place in the heart of Europe was in itself a deterrent to using warfare as simply a 'continuation of politics by other means', as Clausewitz put it. This Cold War environment permitted, perhaps paradoxically, a period of stability never before seen in Europe in modern times, which allowed economic development to reach unprecedented heights and spread its affluence throughout societies, both east and west. Before we turn to the details of this 'golden age' and its later trends, let us recall the state of affairs in Europe at the end of the Second World War. This is important in order to understand just how much the political and military stability and economic development of the

Key Figure 2.2

Josef Vissarionovich Djugashvili-Stalin (1879–1953)

As Secretary-General of the Communist Party of the Soviet Union (CPSU) from 1922, Stalin came to power following Lenin's death in 1924. He was born in Georgia and had been active in Marxist revolutionary politics, joining the Bolshevik Party in 1903. From the late 1920s onwards Stalin ruled the Soviet Union through a **totalitarian** dictatorship underpinned by terror. His political approach, which came to be known as Stalinism, involved a cult of his personality, the rewriting of history, the pursuit of a policy of massive industrialization based on heavy industry and organized by the state through five-year plans and the collectivization of agriculture. This caused famine and great loss of life in the early 1930s. In the 1930s show trials and purges directed against the Communist Party itself, the army, intellectuals and many others consolidated his personal domination. Anxious to defend the Soviet Union against the rising power of Nazi Germany, Stalin made a pact with Hitler in 1939 and then annexed eastern Poland, Estonia, Latvia, Lithuania and parts of Romania; he also attacked Finland. However, in June 1941 Hitler invaded the Soviet Union. Stalin organized the Soviet Union's heroic resistance, and joined the Western powers as a valued ally (see Box 2.1). After the war he imposed the Stalinist system on the Soviet Union's satellites in Eastern and Central Europe (except for Yugoslavia; see Key Figure 2.3). His repressive system based on terror continued until his death in 1953. Stalin was denounced by his successor Khrushchev (see Key Figure 2.4) in 1956.

period after the Second World War meant to the generation born soon after the turn of the century, and how it came to represent the core of political competition and issues up to our present day.

Political and economic conditions in 1945–49

The war ended in Europe with the defeat and occupation of Nazi Germany by the allied armies in May 1945. Bitter fighting to the end rendered Germany a devastated country, and its formal occupation by the USA, USSR, Britain and France presaged the eventual division of Germany into two states, each allied with one or the other superpower. At the same time, all of the principal combatants save the USA had suffered enormous damage due to bombardment and heavy fighting. The USSR emerged essentially as a military superpower, its industrial base converted to produce arms. Britain, although not occupied by Germany, sustained damage to its industry from German bomb and rocket attacks, and its financial reserves

were dangerously depleted by the war effort. France also sustained physical damage, together with deep social and political divisions created by the years of collaboration with the Nazis. Italy and southeastern Europe also were physically traumatized by the war, an added factor being the unleashing of ethnic and political vendettas by groups in the Balkans against those having allied themselves with the occupying Germans. France and Italy also had

● **Totalitarianism**: The term was first used by Benito Mussolini in the 1920s in Italy to signify the consolidation of power in a one-party state. In the late 1930s Western social scientists began to apply the term to describe the phenomenon of the massively expanded powers of the state in Germany and the USSR. It was developed into a political philosophy by Franz Borkenau, and Hannah Arendt argued that a new social form had emerged in Germany under Hitler and in the Soviet Union that was not synonymous with traditional forms of tyranny, dictatorship or authoritarianism. The classic definition of totalitarianism provided by Carl Friedrich and Zbigniew Brzezinski (1966, p. 22) identified six key elements: an official ideology; a single mass party typically led by one man; monopolistic control of the military by the party; a similar monopoly of the means of effective communication; a system of terroristic police control; and central direction and control of the entire economy.

BOX 2.1
Yalta, Potsdam and the division of Europe

The leaders of the Second World War Allies (the USA, the Soviet Union and the UK) met in Teheran in November 1943, in Yalta in February 1945 and, after the end of the war, in Potsdam in July and August 1945, to discuss their plans for a post-war world. In October 1944 Stalin, the leader of the Soviet Union, and the British Prime Minister Churchill had come to a 'percentages' agreement in which Eastern and South-Eastern Europe was carved up into respective 'zones of influence' for either side. The USSR would have 90 per cent control over Romania and 75 per cent control over Bulgaria, but there would be 90 per cent control over Greece by the West, and Hungary and Yugoslavia were to be controlled equally. At the conference at Yalta, boundaries were settled between Poland, the Soviet Union and Germany, with the Soviet Union gaining the borders it sought in the East, with the Polish westward frontier on the Oder–Neisse line. These arrangements were said to be temporary. In addition the organization of the United Nations was agreed upon and the issue of German reparations was raised. At Potsdam they agreed that Germany was to be demilitarized, de-Nazified, decentralized and democratized. The decisions of these conferences resulted in the division of Germany into four zones of occupation – French, British and American in the West, Soviet in the East – and a similar division of Berlin, which lay within the Soviet zone. In the event, the frontiers persisted and the dividing lines came to mark the great division between the West and the communist bloc until 1989.

---

large, and as a result of participation in the resistance, well-developed, communist parties. In all, the political and economic situation at the end of the war represented a vacuum into which the USA and USSR stepped.

Mutual suspicion and miscomprehension of the others' intentions and motivations contributed in large part to the developing hostility between the USA and USSR. Stalin had what he considered to be good reasons to assume that Soviet occupation of Eastern Europe – accomplished during the drive towards Berlin – would be accepted by the West as de facto political control, a buffer zone between the USSR and a possibly resurgent Germany. First, there was the simple fact that the Red Army was in place from Bulgaria through to the eastern half of Germany and all points in between (except Albania and Yugoslavia, where communist partisans consolidated their positions on their own). Second, the fact that the Western Allies chose to invade Germany not from the Balkans but instead from the west, across France, seemed to leave the area to the east open to Soviet strategies. The third factor was an understanding Stalin thought he had from the Western Allies through his 'deal' with British leader Winston Churchill, in which Eastern and South-Eastern Europe were carved up into respective 'zones of influence' for either side.

The Americans had expected free elections to take place in all of the liberated countries; instead, governments sympathetic to the USSR were set up, many of them dominated outright by communist parties. The question of what to do with Germany, however, represented the focus of debate. Should Germany be neutralized as much as possible to prevent it ever rising again as a threat to peace in Europe? What sort of reparations would be required? Many of these questions were first addressed in a series of wartime and post-war conferences, including Yalta and Potsdam. For instance, in February 1945 the Yalta Conference produced a Declaration on Liberated Europe, which called, among other things, for governments responsive to the will of their people throughout Europe, and more specifically, disarmament of Germany by the Allies as they saw fit 'for future peace and security'. In the end, the occupation zones of the Allies in Germany crystallized into two, a fused western half and an eastern, Soviet-dominated half. Between 1946 and 1949, a number

BOX 2.2
Bretton Woods

Even before the end of the war a meeting in Bretton Woods in New Hampshire, USA in September 1944 established the foundations of the post-war economic system that lasted until the early 1970s and whose institutions remain to this day, establishing a monetary system based in Washington, DC, where the World Bank and the International Monetary Fund (IMF) have their headquarters. At the conference the 44 delegates agreed to create common institutions to avoid a return to the protectionism of the inter-war years that had turned the economic slump of 1929 into the Great Depression. In order to achieve this, the IMF and International Bank for Reconstruction and Development (known as the World Bank) were created, together with a system of fixed exchange rates based on the gold–dollar standard. The IMF had the task of holding the currency or gold deposits of its 29 original members and using them to regulate the international exchange-rate mechanism. The World Bank was to act in parallel with the IMF as a development bank providing long-term loans on a profit-making basis to projects which could not find funding from private sources. The IMF and the World Bank were intended to oversee the creation of a single world market based on fixed exchange rates and the use of the dollar and the pound sterling as reserve currencies. Many of the principles espoused by John Maynard Keynes, including demand-led management of economies, were accepted. The formal Bretton Woods system of fixed exchange rates collapsed in the early 1970s under the double impact of the oil crisis and stagflation (a combination of stagnation and inflation that was not foreseen in the Keynesian scheme of things), but in the post-communist era the IMF reshaped itself as the main Western agency policing the economic transitions in Eastern Europe.

---

of events and crises took place in which American and Soviet stances hardened towards each other and laid the foundations – politically and militarily – for the next 40 years of 'Cold War'. These included the articulation of what came to be known as the Truman Doctrine (February 1947), the offer of **Marshall Plan** economic aid to Europe and Stalin's rejection of it (July 1947), the expulsion of communists in coalition governments in Italy, France and Belgium (May 1947), a coup d'état in Czechoslovakia (February 1948), the Berlin Blockade (June 1948–May 1949), and in 1949 the establishment of a West and an East German state, and the new military alliance, NATO. In many of these cases, each side inter-preted as aggressive what the other considered defensive. The Truman Doctrine, in particular, gave an ideological hue to diplomatic manoeu-vrings, and together with the political–military concept of **containment**, the rivalry between the USA and USSR permeated many aspects of European and American society.

Foundations of divided Europe

By the mid-1950s, the division of Europe seemed set to continue for the foreseeable future. Each superpower, in a de facto manner, recognized the other's sphere of influence, and despite American rhetoric of 'rolling back' Soviet military dominance over Eastern Europe, when apparent opportunities arose to give support to domestic moves towards removing such control, as in the Hungarian

---

● **Marshall Plan**: Officially named the European Recovery Program, this US initiative involved massive financial aid and loans to European countries (totalling some $14 billion in contemporary prices) in order to hasten their economic recovery following the Second World War, and thereby, hopefully, strengthen their political stability. Although offered to East European countries as well, most recipients were Western European.

● **Containment**: The US-inspired doctrine of the Cold War aimed at stopping the spread of communist influence, through the use of military alliances, subversion and diplomatic and economic isolation.

Uprising of 1956, none was forthcoming. As the Soviet Union sought to extend its type of economic model – the command economy – to its new 'satellite' states, the Western countries began rebuilding their economies with American Marshall Plan aid, and in the process formed part of what became known as Bretton Woods (see Box 2.2), essentially a global, capitalist, US-dominated trade regime. With the formation of the Soviet-led Warsaw Pact, in 1955, the bipolar division of Europe seemed fixed, with Soviet-supported communist governments and command economies in the east, and American-supported liberal democracies and market economies in the west.

In Western Europe, economic recovery during the 1950s was complemented by moves towards formal economic integration (see Chapter 4). Some of the lessons learned from the mistakes of the inter-war period, especially economic nationalism, practised in 'beggar-thy-neighbour' policies, translated into a belief among many elites that cooperation rather than cut-throat competition would hasten economic reconstruction. Promoted by influential individuals such as Jean Monnet (see Key Figure 4.2), an initial attempt to pool resources and planning in the areas of coal and steel – vital for the rebuilding of industry – was launched in 1950, known as the European Coal and Steel Community (ECSC). Building upon its success, the countries involved – France, Germany, Italy, Belgium, the Netherlands and Luxembourg – created a much more ambitious effort in economic integration, the European Economic Community (EEC), established by the Treaties of Rome in 1957 (which also included cooperation in atomic energy – Euratom). More than simply a **free-trade** area – this option was pursued by Britain, Austria, Denmark, Norway, Portugal, Sweden and Switzerland beginning in 1959 as the European Free Trade Association (EFTA) – but less than a federal United States of Europe, the EEC began as a free-trade area with a common tariff but above all with a set of supra-national institutions. By the end of the 1960s, common policies in atomic energy and agriculture were in

place, and some of the supra-national institutions, especially the European Commission, had become significant institutional players on the political and diplomatic front.

Economic recovery was rapid and unprecedented, so much so that the years of high growth in the 1950s and 1960s are known variously as the economic miracle, the **_trente glorieuses_** in France, the **_Wirtschaftswunder_** in Germany, and so on (although Britain actually experienced a relative economic decline during this period). Relations between organized labour and business, never harmonious in the inter-war period, became in many countries much less confrontational and in fact more cooperative, especially in Scandinavian countries, the Low Countries, Germany and Austria. In most of these cases, the state, along with business and labour, became part of a system of economic management known as _neocorporatism_, whereby under the auspices of the state, business and labour elites worked out accommodations among themselves. This relationship was very significant in the development of the welfare state. In southern European countries (apart from Portugal and Spain, which carried over into the post-war period dictatorships that had established themselves in the 1920s and 1930s, respectively) business and labour relations continued to be characterized in confrontational and ideological terms, especially as major industrial labour confederations were allied to communist parties, most notably in France and Italy.

At the same time, the proceeds of this economic growth and expansion were directed by governments into income-redistribution and social-welfare policies. This macro-economic management was influenced very much by the writings of the British economist John Maynard

---

● **_Trente glorieuses_**: Literally the 'thirty glorious years' of economic expansion in France, this phase of post-Second World War economic growth ended in the mid-1970s, and was characterized by rising personal incomes, affluence and low unemployment.

● **_Wirtschaftswunder_**: Literally the 'economic miracle' of West German post-war economic expansion, characterized by rising incomes and affluence. This unprecedented economic performance helped to legitimize the new West German state in the first few decades after the end of the Second World War. The 'miracle' ended in the mid-1970s.

● **Free trade**: The notion that the pursuit of barrier-free trade will benefit all those involved, regardless of relative economic strength.

Keynes, who argued for explicit government manipulation of expenditure and taxation as a means of promoting demand for goods and services, thus helping to keep employment levels high. Thus in complementing rising wages and salaries, the state actively set about to build and strengthen the social infrastructure – in health, education, unemployment insurance, pensions, and so on – to create, in other words, the welfare state. The prosperity accruing from economic reconstruction in the late 1950s and 1960s spread to just about all levels of society, a state of affairs never before witnessed in Europe (see Chapter 8).

The 'stability' of the Cold War, cooperation between labour and business, rising affluence among the working class and an expansion of the salaried middle class – all of this was in stark contrast to the conditions of the inter-war period, and this was reflected in politics as well. The political polarization of the inter-war period, between communist and other left-wing parties on the one hand, and fascist groups and parties on the other, gave way by the late 1950s and early 1960s to a much more stable and accommodating environment. First, parties which had actively supported Nazi and other fascist governments were de-legitimized by this experience in the post-war period. Second, although many communist parties joined the anti-fascist struggle after 1941 (Hitler's invasion of the USSR) and emerged from this experience as national heroes, it was primarily only the French and Italian parties that profited in electoral terms. With a taste of government responsibility in the immediate post-war coalitions, these parties moderated their programmatic identities as they strove to be accepted as 'governmental' rather than revolutionary actors. Third, the Social Democratic and Labour parties, many of which lost members to newly formed communist parties in the 1920s, began to focus their policies and attraction to the electoral centre, and in the process began to emphasize a multi-class appeal rather than being seen as strictly working-class parties. And finally, centre-right parties, both conservative and confessional, came to accept many of the basic foundations of the welfare state, thus reducing the hostility with centre-left parties. By 1960, then, a political scientist observing the political landscape in Western Europe could posit the creation of an ideological consensus between the major parties of the centre left and centre right, consisting of a general anti-communist perspective, economic managerialism, and a commitment to further improve the lot of all citizens. One commentator went so far as to dub this situation 'the end of ideology' (Bell, 1960).

This picture of political stability and economic growth must be supplemented by another consideration, specific to certain countries and having implications up to the present day, and this was the process of **decolonization**. By 1960, the major colonial powers (minus Portugal), had granted independence to most of their former overseas possessions (see Map 2.3). The most significant exception was France and its relationship with Algeria. In many cases, independence was won only after bitter and protracted fighting between national liberation forces and the colonial power, for example France and its war in Indochina. In some cases, for instance Britain and Jamaica, the process was relatively smooth. One significant result of decolonization was large-scale migration of indigenous peoples from the newly independent countries to their European 'mother' country, so much so that the ethnic and racial balances were noticeably altered. This was the case concerning Belgium and the Congo, France and North Africa, Britain and the Caribbean and South Asia, and the Netherlands and Indonesia. In the expanding economies of the day, many found work in the new factories, while others became part of a marginalized underclass, either unemployed or underemployed.

In Eastern Europe, economic reconstruction was from the start undertaken on very different bases than in the West. In the first place, as a result of the devastation suffered during the war and its victor status immediately afterwards, much of the remaining industrial matériel in the East was shipped to the Soviet Union for use in its rebuilding efforts. Second, the Soviet Union was intent on maintaining political control of its territorial gains, and this translated into structuring the economies of Eastern Europe along a Soviet model. The Soviet-type economy, sometimes referred to as

---

● **Decolonization**: The retreat of European powers from their colonies in the mid-twentieth century.

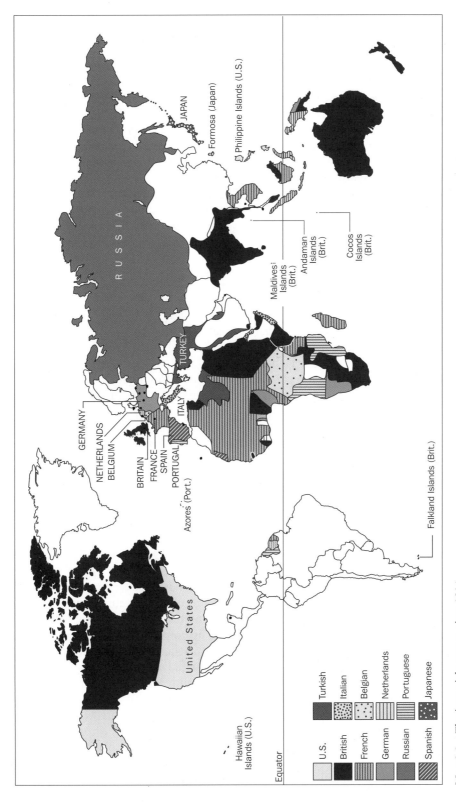

Map 2.3 The imperial powers, circa 1914

Key Figure 2.3

Nikita Khrushchev (1894–1971)

Born in southern Russia, close to the Ukrainian border, Nikita Khrushchev worked as a fitter in the mines. He joined the Communist Party in 1918. He rose in the Party, moving to Moscow in 1929, and after serving as a political officer with the Red Army in the Second World War he became head of the government and Party leader in the Ukraine. He returned to Moscow in 1949 and became first Secretary of the Communist Party after Stalin's death in 1953. In 1958 he became head of both Party and government. In 1956 his speech to the Twentieth Party Congress denouncing Stalin began the process of 'de-Stalinization'. He attempted reforms of agriculture, with a marked lack of success, and encouraged technological advance. His deployment of missiles to Cuba led to the 1962 confrontation with the USA known as the Cuban missile crisis. He was forced out of office in 1964 and lived effectively under house arrest until his death in 1971.

intensive in its developmental orientation, emphasized rapid industrialization, especially of heavy industry, according to a series of Five-Year Plans. The collectivization of agriculture was also part of the model, whereby the displacement of peasants from their land supplied labour for the new factories. In the case of the Eastern European countries, some, such as Czechoslovakia and to a certain extent Poland, had already developed industrial economies during the inter-war period, while others, for example Bulgaria and Hungary, were basically agrarian. Nevertheless, forced industrialization promoted rapid economic growth, but at the price of enormous problems.

Another dimension of the Soviet model was its levelling of social classes. In order to accomplish this, massive social upheaval was introduced via the abandonment of private property, the nationalization of industry, and the development of social measures, rudimentary in the beginning, such as education and health care for all citizens. After Stalin's death in 1953, his successor, Nikita Khrushchev (see Key Figure 2.3), attempted to moderate several aspects of the Stalinist economic model. He sought to introduce greater specialization into the Soviet economy by regionalizing production, a form of economic decentralization. In the end, his method of redirecting Soviet production upset too many Communist Party officials, and his reform was ended, as was his position at the head of the Party in October 1964.

In many respects, the political situation between the Soviet Union and Eastern European states mirrored the economic reality. If Stalin sought a monolithic communist order in Europe, resistance to this view was soon apparent. By 1949, communist parties loyal to Stalin had succeeded in consolidating power (Yugoslavia was the exception, when in 1948 its leader Josip Broz Tito (see Key Figure 2.4) broke with Stalin in favour of a 'national path' to socialism).

As mentioned above, the Soviet economic model was imposed, but the harshness of forced industrialization and agricultural collectivization soon generated protests outside government – as in Berlin, and the Czechoslovak demonstrations in 1953 – and within ruling communist parties, between nationalists and those loyal to Stalinist methods and plans. The assumption of power by Khrushchev, and his denunciation of Stalin in his 'Secret Speech' at the Twentieth Party Congress on 25 February 1956, led to a slightly wider latitude for some communist governments, particularly in Poland, where collectivization of agriculture was abandoned.

By the mid-1950s, Khrushchev maintained Soviet political control over some Eastern European states by accommodating more nationalist leaders who took full advantage of the relaxed

Key Figure 2.4

Josip Broz Tito (1892–1980)

Yugoslav statesman. As leader of the partisans fighting the Germans during the Second World War, Tito was in place to assume leadership of post-war Yugoslavia. In 1948 he broke with Stalin and pioneered a 'national path' to socialism based on self-managing enterprises. Himself a Croat, he maintained a decentralized and federal territorial organization of the country, which was made up of six republics and two autonomous provinces. In the early 1950s, along with Nasser of Egypt and Nehru of India, he was instrumental in setting up the movement of non-aligned countries, an attempt to remain independent from the two superpowers (and to exploit this position).

economic trends. However, these leaders had acquired their positions as a result of political crises between their countries and the Soviet Union, for example after such calamitous events as the Hungarian Uprising of November 1956, in which pitched battles between Hungarians and Soviet Red Army troops took place in Budapest. In other countries, for instance Bulgaria and Romania, Communist Party bosses playing the 'nationalist hand' came to power in the late 1950s and early 1960s and virtually ruled these countries in an autocratic manner for the next 30 years until their overthrow with the downfall of communism generally. In August 1961 the Berlin Wall was built, enclosing the eastern part of the city and insulating the German Democratic Republic (GDR) from the West. During the years of its existence some five thousand people tried to escape over the wall, and between 100 and 200 were killed. The wall became a stark symbol of the division of Europe.

The overall effect upon East European societies of the changes in Soviet economic planning, the political crises of the early and mid-1950s, and the imposition of a communist model of society, was that by the 1960s many of these countries began to exhibit a pattern of authoritarian political rule and modest economic growth, an attempt to balance the requirements of heavy industrialization with attention to consumer needs. With the end of Khrushchev's economic experimentations came a relatively peaceful and orderly period of growth in the Soviet economy throughout the 1960s, from

which East European countries benefited (with the exception of Albania, which pursued an autarchic policy). Although far behind the material gains of West European economies, which were then experiencing their economic 'miracles', most East Europeans and Soviets compared their situation in the 1960s with the pre-war period, much as adults in the West also did. Of all the social changes introduced into Eastern Europe, apart from the elimination of the aristocracy, probably the most dramatic was the expansion of education, especially higher education. Thus a high percentage of professionals, including academics, judges, industrial managers, and so on, came from working-class backgrounds, a far higher proportion than in Western European countries such as France, Britain or West Germany.

By the late 1960s, Soviet-style modernization had transformed many of the countries of Eastern Europe. Although imbalances between countries remained, usually owing to pre-war levels of development, in general the distinction between industrial and agrarian societies disappeared, especially as collectivization of agriculture destroyed the peasant basis of rural economies. Although Communist Party rule did not allow for opposition parties, and a secret police stifled attempts at coordinating opposition among individuals, the countries also varied in the intensity of communist rule. One could say that by the late 1960s a communist European society had been created, but unlike the liberal democracies in the West, official conformity to the Soviet Union in terms of political, economic, and even cultural directions necessitated the authoritarian nature of these regimes. The apparent stability of both East and West Europe, however, was soon to unravel, as underlying political and economic dynamics came to the fore, beginning in the pivotal year 1968.

Diversity within blocs and economic slowdown

The year 1968 was a watershed in that the events associated with it represented a puncturing of the mindset that 'business as usual' in political, social and even economic and military affairs could go on undisturbed. Although there were of course antecedents to the events of 1968, the challenge to both Western and Eastern European orthodox views of society laid the foundation for trends in the latter 1970s and 1980s which eventually changed the very complexion of European politics.

1968 and the challenge to authority

The two most singular events that occurred in 1968 took place in France and Czechoslovakia. In each country, the political status quo was directly challenged by mass demonstrations involving students, workers and professionals. In France, student resentment of the de Gaulle (see Key Figure 2.5) government's educational policies sparked a widespread strike at universities, which was then joined by trade unions. For a moment in May, it almost seemed as if the very legitimacy of the Fifth French Republic, and its president, was about to fall. In Czechoslovakia, a reformist communist, Alexander Dubček, became head of the Party, and set about instituting reforms opening up the political process, such as freedom of assembly and organization, and other measures which were clearly out of step with prevailing communist orthodoxy in the communist world. The 'Prague Spring' was, in fact, seen as a threat by other communist leaders, who saw the Czechoslovak changes as possibly spreading into their countries and thereby challenging their grip on power. In late August, a Warsaw Pact force led by the Soviet Union ousted Dubček's government and crushed the experiment in 'socialism with a human face'.

These two episodes shared a common theme, that is, a desire to challenge centralized, bureaucratic, authoritarian structures. Although the 'May events' in France and the 'Prague Spring' in Czechoslovakia were the most spectacular of the challenges to political orthodoxy, other dynamics were also at play in the late 1960s. The bipolar division of Europe had, by the late 1960s, begun to become much more diverse in terms of intra-bloc relations. Ironically, in the west, it was President de Gaulle's foreign policy that challenged American leadership, particularly over military and political relations between east and west and within NATO. NATO strategy was itself an issue during this period, as the USA sought to substitute its strategic doctrine of the 1950s – massive retaliation – with a 'war-fighting' strategy known as 'flexible response'. Although presented as a more credible deterrent, the thought of positioning battlefield nuclear weapons on European soil caused much consternation in Allied capitals.

Similarly, in economic matters, de Gaulle threatened to unravel part of the US-dominated global monetary system, Bretton Woods (see Box 2.2), by 'cashing in' dollars for gold held in Fort Knox, USA. The US promise of backing the dollar by gold was one of the foundations of the international trading regime. For a country to actually test this promise was a direct challenge to American top-currency status and its management of the system, especially its use of running deficits. German support for the US position caused some friction between France and Germany, which highlighted the great difference in these two countries' relations with the USA. France emphasized autonomy in foreign policy, and Germany saw its interests as congruent with those of the USA regarding east–west relations. In the end, although de Gaulle's action did not alter US behaviour, it was part of a series of events that eventually led to the demise of the Bretton Woods system in 1971.

In the east, although Yugoslavia went its own way in 1948 in escaping Stalin's control, it was under Khrushchev that the seeds of relative diversity in the communist world were planted. By the 1960s Romania had joined Yugoslavia in pursuing a more independent foreign policy, while remaining an ultra-orthodox communist country. Politically, although communist regimes were not overtly

Key Figure 2.5

Charles de Gaulle (1890–1970)

Pivotal French general and statesman. In the years from the outbreak of the Second World War until his death, de Gaulle was France's most influential and controversial leader. During the war he organized France's resistance to German occupation and briefly headed its first post-war government. Resigning in protest at what he called a return to 'politics as usual', he retired from active politics but capitalized on his authority to argue for a new and modern force in French politics. Thus began the first of many political parties that were dubbed 'Gaullist'. Recalled to power by the French parliament during the Algerian crisis in 1958, de Gaulle put an end to the French Fourth Republic's unstable governance by inaugurating the Fifth Republic, built upon the premise that France needed a strong executive. Elected as the first president of the new Republic, de Gaulle put an end to the Algerian issue by granting independence to it and other African colonies, asserted French sovereignty vis-à-vis the USA by emphasizing an independent foreign policy along with the development of a nuclear deterrent, and continued with a programme of economic modernization begun under the Fourth Republic.

threatened again by domestic change after the Prague Spring, each country evolved its own system of internal relations, ranging from Poland, where the Catholic Church enjoyed a degree of autonomy not found elsewhere in the communist world, to Albania, which practised an autarchic policy, maintaining relations generally only with the People's Republic of China and Romania. As for communist economics, the variation was greater. Poland had turned from collectivization in the 1950s, Hungary pursued a somewhat market-oriented socialist economy, while in the main, others followed the Soviet model. Deviation from the Soviet model was tolerated by Moscow as long as the political and military status quo was unchallenged. The suppression of the Czechoslovak political reforms was a demonstration of the Soviet Union's resolve in this matter.

By the early 1970s, then, although the bipolar division of Europe was still in place, a loosening of internal bloc relations had occurred. Beginning in 1969, under the newly elected Social Democratic chancellor, Willy Brandt, West Germany pursued a foreign policy which aimed to normalize relations with Eastern European countries, including East Germany. This policy, tolerated by a new American administration, was known as *ostpolitik*. In an improved international environment between the USA and USSR, known as

détente, contacts, especially economic and financial relations, began to multiply between the two sides. By 1975, under the auspices of the Helsinki Accords, an agreement on mutual recognition of both sides' boundaries, although with commitments to respect human rights and in fact monitor infractions against them, was signed. Thus stability in political and military matters on the continent appeared at hand in the early to mid-1970s. Such was not to be the case in economic matters.

Economic downturn in the west; failure of reform in the east

Clouds on the economic horizon had begun to gather in the west in the 1960s, and de Gaulle's challenge to US global economic leadership was in a way a complaint about the 'mismanagement' of the system. In 1971, the US unilaterally declared an end to gold–dollar convertibility, and in 1973 the fixed-exchange-rate system, upon which international trade had grown during the 1950s and 1960s, was ended. In 1973, another

● **Détente**: Literally this means 'loosening', but it is used to describe the relaxation of tension between previously antagonistic states, notably between the USA and USSR in the latter stages of the Cold War.

Key Figure 2.6

François Mitterrand (1916–96)

A French politician and statesman who served for two full seven-year terms as President of the French Republic. As a student in pre-war Paris his closest links were with right-wing political organizations. He was mobilized in 1939, captured, and after escaping, worked as an official of the Vichy government before going into hiding as a resistance activist. He was elected to Parliament in 1946 as a centre-left independent, and occupied ministerial posts throughout most of the Fourth Republic period. He opposed de Gaulle's return to power in 1958. It was not the least of the paradoxes of this complex man that, having opposed the Fifth Republic's constitution, he later presided over a period where the role of that constitution in the working of the presidency and in political life was accentuated. In 1971 he joined the Socialist Party and two days later became its leader. He renewed the structures and alliances of the party and in 1981, at his third attempt, was elected President. The early years of his presidency were marked by economic and social reform, including the nationalization of key industries. Economic difficulties forced an about-turn in 1983. Between 1986 and 1988 and again from 1993 to 1995 he shared power, in what was known as 'cohabitation', with a right-wing government. He was a partisan of the 'construction of Europe', though doubtful about German reunification. He was a subtle and clever politician, even if astuteness grew, during his second term of office, to look more like deviousness, and cleverness seemed mere machination. He was also a noted author of political books, and the instigator of a number of major architectural projects in Paris including the renewal of the museum of the Louvre.

dramatic event hit Western industrial economies, and this was the leap in the price charged for oil by the cartel OPEC (Organization of the Petroleum Exporting Countries) – in effect, a price shock. The politics of OPEC's move was also bound up in the vagaries of Middle Eastern politics, in particular the Arab–Israeli conflict. To a certain extent, the manner in which Europe and the USA responded to this event added another division in intra-west foreign-policy cohesion. The West European countries were heavily dependent on oil imports to supply their industries (except countries such as Norway that had off-shore oil supplies), whereas the USA had large domestic reserves, especially with the opening of a pipeline from the Alaskan oilfields in the 1970s. The combination of now floating, or competitive, exchange rates and their impact on trade, together with the oil-price shock, precipitated the worst recession in Europe since the Great Depression of the 1930s. As the 1970s wore on, very sluggish growth (or none at all), together with continued high levels of inflation, resulted in a condition

called '**stagflation**'. Whereas most economists assumed a trade-off between employment and inflation, persistent high inflation and not enough economic growth to generate employment confounded government economic policy-makers. The Keynesian consensus began to unravel (see Chapter 8).

Every country's situation varied, of course, and some national economies were more at risk from global economic trends than others. The French economy, very much influenced by state intervention in investment and a large public sector, witnessed double-digit unemployment and inflation rates by 1980. The British economy was also in a parlous state, having in 1976 to approach the IMF (International Monetary Fund) for a loan to meet government expenditures. Although some of the smaller economies, such as Sweden and Austria, weathered this period relatively unscathed, most

---

● **Stagflation**: A combination of stagnating output and inflationary pressures which typified the depression of the late 1970s and early 1980s.

Key Figure 2.7

Margaret Thatcher (1925–)

Margaret Thatcher, who was British Prime Minister from 1979 to 1990, took a degree in chemistry and was called to the Bar before her election as Conservative MP for Finchley, London in 1959. Having served in the Heath government of 1970–74 as Secretary of State for Education and Science, she became leader of the Conservative Party in 1975. A politician of conviction and determination, her approach, which came to be known as 'Thatcherism', espoused robust values of monetarism, competition and self-help. She declared herself an advocate of rolling back the frontiers of the state. She attempted to reduce public expenditure, introduced legislation to curb the privileges and powers of the trade unions, undertook substantial bureaucratic reforms in the interests of efficiency and good management, capped the spending of local government, and abolished the Greater London Council. Privatization was a major theme of her programme after the re-election of the Conservative government in 1983, to which her performance as leader during the Falklands War in 1982 certainly contributed. She supported the deregulation and free-trade elements of European Community policy as embodied in the single-market programme, but stoutly opposed closer economic and political union, an opposition which became even more prominent after her resignation, which was caused by her party's increasing distrust of her domineering style, her strident anti-Europeanism, and the unpopularity of her introduction of the system of local taxation known as the 'poll tax'.

governments by the end of the 1970s began to impose economic austerity policies, seeking to reduce expenditure rather than generate revenue by raising already high levels of taxation. The election in 1981 of the French Socialist Party, the first time the Left had come to power in the French Fifth Republic, saw probably the last effort to buck the international trend of cutting back on state expenditures, and instead attempted a massive Keynesian-style reflation of the economy. Within two years, the French government under President Mitterrand (see Key Figure 2.6) reversed policy direction, and essentially followed the course of its neighbours.

It was during the 1980s that an alternative economic orientation, dubbed 'neo-liberalism', and associated with the British prime minister elected in 1979, Margaret Thatcher (see Key Figure 2.7), came to the political fore. Arguing that business was hampered by high taxation and over-regulation, and that this was a primary cause of under-investment by business and thus the absence of growth in the economy, the neo-liberal cause sought to reduce the presence of the state in the economy by privatizing

public companies such as national airlines and public utilities; reducing taxes; and limiting the influence of trade unions. Although never adopted elsewhere as rigorously as in Britain, elements of this economic recipe were implemented by many governments in the 1980s. Complementing these national strategies, after languishing for most of the 1970s and early 1980s, was the resumption of broader, more coordinated attempts to revive the West European economy, namely European economic integration (see Chapter 4).

Restarting the European integration process

By the mid-1980s, West European economies generally had not been able to discover any magic formula allowing a return to the 'golden age' of high growth, expanding employment, and more extensive public services. In fact, compared with the US and Japanese economies, Europe appeared to be 'falling behind'. The failure of the French Socialist government in applying a neo-Keynesian strategy, and the fears of some European companies that advances in computer technology and their broad application by American and Japanese firms would eliminate domestic European rivals, led to a re-examination of the benefits of coordinated action at the European level. The European Commission obliged with a White Paper that proposed an accel-erated drive to dismantle the barriers to trade within the EC by 1992. Thus the Single Market programme was initiated as a means to revive European economies and, by virtue of the new economies of scale that were to be created, compete globally with the USA and Japan. Essentially neo-liberal in character because it focused on eliminat-ing barriers to trade – negative integration – it also had a few provisions for social concerns and the enhancement of European institutions' decision-making power – positive integration. Adopted by all 12 member states of the EC as the Single European Act in 1986, it created a renewed dynamism in the integration process that led, by the early 1990s, to an agreement to create a single European currency (see Chapter 8).

The failure of reform and modernization in the East

'Détente' between the USA and USSR in the 1970s allowed many Eastern European governments to involve themselves in the wider capitalist system, though usually on very elementary levels. In a drive to satisfy consumer needs, many governments went deeply into debt to import consumer goods from the West. In the Soviet Union itself, under Brezhnev in the 1970s and 1980s, similar small openings to the West occurred, especially the exchange of certain goods and grain for energy exports, gas in particular. Eastern European governments were permitted to experiment in economic reform, espe-cially after their growth rates of the 1960s had begun to slow in the 1970s. Where reformers tried to introduce some measure of market dynamics into their economies, however, their efforts were frustrated by a coalition of vested interests, ranging from mid-level government bureaucrats, plant managers (especially in the big heavy industry and defence sectors), workers fearing for their job secu-

rity, and finally, by the limits of what the Soviet leadership would tolerate. Thus in many cases, reform programmes were never fully implemented, and sometimes partial reform policies actually made the situation worse than no reform at all. By the mid-1980s, then, many Eastern European coun-tries found themselves heavily in debt to western funding agencies, countries and banks, and a lack of capital meant that their industrial plant was woefully outdated. Growth rates for countries as varied as Hungary and Romania declined all through the 1980s, while the rest generally stag-nated including the Soviet economy. With political and bureaucratic barriers to innovation, the entire region sank into an economic malaise.

Challenging the Cold War political order

By the late 1970s, new social movements and politi-cal dynamics began to appear in both East and West European states. In the West, many new issues appeared on political and social agendas, and by the end of the decade, some had been transformed into political parties. Issues ignored by or outside the usual policy programmes of major political parties included opposition to nuclear energy, ecological and women's issues, human rights, etc. Extra-parliamentary movements pushed these causes in new and often dramatic ways. In the East, as a result of the 1975 Helsinki Accords, human-rights watch groups were set up to monitor govern-ment compliance with human rights obligations. Under the threat of harassment and even imprison-ment, many of these groups criticized the perform-ance of their governments. Recognition from western governments of these groups and promi-nent individuals associated with them, and pressure on eastern governments in the form of witholding economic aid, became part of the wider political environment. By the end of the 1980s, this unoffi-cial opposition in eastern countries often came from those spearheading the efforts to push communist governments out. In the West, the issue agenda was changed such that the new issues became part of everyday politics, and new parties associated with them affected the party systems of many countries.

New social and political movements in Western democracies

In challenging the political order of the day, many of the former student activists from 1968 became advocates of more freedom in lifestyles and opponents of top-down bureaucratic practices and policies. The environmental movement varied according to specific issues in different countries – from opposition to nuclear energy in France to the promotion of sustainable economic development in West Germany. The women's movement sought to change legislation in the areas of divorce and abortion, as well as calling for equality in the workplace in terms of wages, and similar demands. Continuing the critique of bureaucratic structures from the late 1960s, many of these movements resolved to reject hierarchical forms of organization, and their tactics – including peaceful protests and demonstrations, encouraging boycotts, even theatrical and dramatic events to focus media attention – represented a call for a 'new politics'. In the late 1970s, a new issue was taken up by many in these movements, opposition to NATO's deployment of Cruise and Pershing II nuclear-armed medium-range missiles in Germany, Italy and elsewhere in response to the Soviet Union's deployment of a new generation of nuclear-armed missiles (SS-20s) with ranges that included most of Western Europe. The massive protests, particularly in Germany, were a trying period for participating governments, and the anti-American critique of the demonstrators signalled a generational difference with their parents regarding US Cold War strategy.

Although in the end the missiles were deployed, the momentum from the protests was a factor in the decision to transform many of the loosely organized movements into political parties, in order to attempt to change public policy directly 'from within'. In many countries, these parties adopted the name 'Greens', as in Die Grüne in West Germany, or else a label suggesting their placement on the left of the political spectrum, but sufficiently different in order to distance themselves from traditional labour and social democratic parties, for instance the Danish Socialist People's Party. The German Greens, winning their first parliamentary seats in 1983, have gone the furthest of these 'new politics' parties in terms of electoral support, aver-

aging close to 10 per cent in national elections and participating in German state (*Land*) coalition governments, and finally becoming junior coalition partners in an SPD-led government after the September 1998 German elections. In the competition between these parties and the traditional social democratic and labour parties for members and voters, one of the most widespread results was the broadening of the new-issues' appeal into the political mainstream, so that by the 1990s even Conservative and Christian Democratic parties had 'greened' many of their policies.

The rise of Solidarity, crises of legitimation and the impact of Gorbachev

Emerging from a series of workers' protests in 1976, a self-government movement calling itself Self-organization of Polish Society represented a sort of anti-government focal point in Poland in the late 1970s. With the election of Polish archbishop Cardinal Karol Wojtyla as Pope in 1978 and his subsequent visit to huge crowds around the country in 1979, coupled with widespread resentment at the decline in economic well being, momentum was generated to more forcefully oppose the discredited government. A workers' organization emerged from the movement, calling itself Solidarity, led by Lech Wałęsa, and quickly attracted mass support, securing the unprecedented right in a communist country to strike and organize independent unions in 1980. The following year witnessed more concessions by the government until Solidarity appeared to as counter-government itself. In December 1981, martial law was declared and Solidarity was banned, its leaders arrested and imprisoned. Although pushed underground, Solidarity survived and, with international support, was eventually recognized by the government, leading to round-table talks on the opening up of the political system. In August 1989, a Solidarity-led coalition became the first non-communist-led government in the Eastern bloc.

The dynamics helping to propel Solidarity into power were apparent in other eastern states, namely economic stagnation and the consequent decline of living standards. Apart from the ideology of Marxism–Leninism, the other foundation that communist parties could suggest to legitimize their rule was an improvement in the standard of living. Between 1960 and 1980 this appeared to be the case, although increasing contacts with the west revealed the comparative backwardness of social and economic achievements. Poland was but the tip of the iceberg when it came to the lack of popular support for ruling communist parties. Indeed, by 1989 popular support for the communist regimes had largely evaporated. Much of communist officialdom itself realized that the old regimes were exhausted, and prepared for the transition to something new.

Mikhail Gorbachev (see Key Figure 1.2) was elected as General Secretary of the Communist Party of the Soviet Union in March 1985. Within two years he had begun to encourage reform with the aim of winning popular support (see Chapter 1). Emboldened by the change in Soviet expectations as well as by the experience of Poland, some parties, such as in Hungary, began a concerted effort at political as well as economic reform. Others, for instance in East Germany or Romania, simply kept the 'lid' on even harder, refusing to acknowledge the depth of resentment.

The end of the Cold War era

Between 1989 and 1991, events of a historic nature unfolded, and all were quite unexpected. On 9 November 1989, the Berlin Wall was breached, and hundreds, then thousands of East Germans entered West Berlin. The political dynamics within the East German government quickly slipped out of the control of the ruling Communist Party, and within a year (October 1990) the unification of the two Germanies was officially sealed. The speed with which events transpired – the East German currency disappeared in July 1990 and the West German mark took over, and all-German parliamentary elections took place in December – left not only Germans stunned, but their surrounding neighbours as well. The French president and British prime minister, while not opposed outright to the unification of East and West Germany, urged prudence in the steps towards unification, if not a 'go-slow' policy. With the support of the USA, the German chancellor, Helmut Kohl, nevertheless proceeded with a rapid approach to unification and

to settling international agreements regarding Germany dating back to the end of the war. However, perhaps as a way of demonstrating that the new Germany was still a 'good European', the German government joined the French in launching a move towards an even greater degree of European integration, monetary unification, of which the outcome was the Maastricht Treaty (see Chapter 4).

Events in the east accelerated from this point onwards. Although Solidarity had managed in mid-1989 to establish itself at the head of a coalition government, within two years communist parties in other Eastern European countries had either been forced from government – as in Czechoslovakia – or else changed their character such that open and free elections were held which they then lost, for example in Hungary. Most of these changes would no doubt not have happened, or else would have been much more complicated, were it not for the 'critical distance' Gorbachev in the Soviet Union put between himself and those communist leaders opposed to reform. On the other hand, Gorbachev had given himself a gigantic task, that is, to reform the Soviet Union. Through policies such as openness – *glasnost* – in society, the introduction of some competitiveness in the economy with a view towards its restructuring – *perestroika* – and 'new political thinking' (NPT) in foreign policy, Gorbachev hoped to turn around the dire state of the Soviet economy in order to remain a superpower. Consequently, Gorbachev made it plain that East European communist governments would have to depend upon the support of their citizens in order to stay in power, not Soviet tanks.

Gorbachev set into motion forces over which he eventually lost control. The limited democratization he introduced led the Russian Republic, and its elected leader Boris Yeltsin, to form its own power base independent of Union and Party control. After

---

● **Glasnost:** Literally, this means 'openness', but was used to describe the relaxation of censorship and cultural repression during Gorbachev's time in power in the USSR, 1985–91.

● **Perestroika:** This literally means 'restructuring' but was used by Gorbachev to describe his attempts to reform the Soviet Union between 1985 and 1991, suggesting plans to liberalize the Soviet system within a communist framework.

Map 2.4   Member states of the CIS

a failed coup in August 1991, events rapidly unfolded and by the end of the year, Gorbachev resigned as the last leader of the USSR. This followed just weeks after the announcement by Yeltsin and the leaders of Ukraine and Belarus of the formal establishment of the Commonwealth of Independent States, or CIS, of 11 of the 15 successor states from the former Soviet Union, leaving out Georgia (which joined in 1993 and left in 2008) and the Baltic states (see Map 2.4).

Ukraine's overwhelming vote for independence on 1 December 1991 precipitated the break-up of the USSR, since without Ukraine there was not much point to the continuation of the Union, or so it appeared at the time. Many of the successor states began a search for formulas with which to continue on the road to economic and political reform. Many of these new states suffered violence internally – Russia and the Chechen wars, Georgia and breakaway Abkhazia and South Ossetia – or else disputes with neighbours – Armenia and

Azerbaijan over Nagorno Karabakh. By the end of the 1990s, many of the former communist states of Eastern Europe, such as Poland, Hungary and the Czech Republic (on 1 January 1993 Czechoslovakia divided itself into the Czech Republic and Slovakia), had sought stability and assistance by turning westward, and had applied to join the European Union (EU) (see Chapters 3 and 4).

Although the 'velvet divorce' between the Czech Republic and Slovakia was fairly smooth, the disintegration of Yugoslavia in 1990–91 was less peaceful, accompanied by genocidal wars provoked by President Slobodan Milošević's dream of a 'greater Serbia' to encompass Serbian populations in Croatia and Bosnia. In 1991, four out of Yugoslavia's six republics effectively left to become independent countries (Bosnia, Croatia, Macedonia – sometimes known as the Former Yugoslav Republic of Macedonia, FYROM – and Slovenia), leaving a rump Federal Republic of Yugoslavia (FRY) comprising Montenegro and Serbia. Serbia

Map 2.5   Post-1945 Yugoslavia

itself potentially contained two other republics, Vojvodina and Kosovo, which according to the 1974 Yugoslav constitution enjoyed autonomous status that in effect made them equal voting members of the collective presidency (see Map 2.5). In 1989 Milošević stripped the two provinces of their autonomy, ultimately provoking a war in Kosovo from 1998 that was potentially yet another war of state formation. Kosovo had only been conquered by Serbia in 1912 but was considered the spiritual homeland of Serbian Orthodoxy and was the site of Serbia's great defeat by the advancing Turks in 1389 at Kosovo Pole. In 1999 nearly the whole Albanian population was driven out in an operation reminiscent of the Second World War. Unlike in the Bosnian war of 1992–95, this time the 'international community' forced a settlement on Miloševi , allowing the refugees to return. In October 2000 Milošević was removed from office in the first of what were to become 'colour revolutions', popular mobilizations against attempts by incumbent leaders to steal elections. Shortly afterwards he was sent to the International Criminal Tribunal for the former Yugoslavia in The Hague to stand trial for genocide. His departure from office came about as a result of elections won by pro-

democracy forces, which have since been able to set Serbia on a democratizing path, with hopes of joining the EU at some point in the not too distant future. As for Kosovo, it eventually proclaimed its independence on 17 February 2008, though Serbia and a large part of the international community has yet to recognize it as a sovereign state.

The post-Cold War order

Over two decades after the fall of the Berlin Wall and the setting into motion of events and pressures which demolished the Cold War order, it would still be prudent to talk of an *emergent* European order, as there is still much that remains in flux. In the West, although the plans for monetary union have proceeded apace, above all with the introduction of the Euro in 1999, the success of steps towards further convergence of the participating economies is uncertain. Some member states have chosen to stay outside 'Euroland', at least initially. They are Britain, Sweden and Denmark. The EU, now expanded to 27 countries after the enlargements of 2004 and 2007, suffered several setbacks in attempts to reform and modernize its institutions. First, referendum failures in the ratification process for a Constitutional Treaty in the Netherlands and France in 2005 effectively ended hopes for a 'constitution'; then its successor, the Lisbon Treaty, was defeated in an Irish referendum in 2008. A second Irish referendum on the Lisbon Treaty finally led to its ratification, and on 1 December 2009 it came into force, presenting the world with two new offices and personalities, a permanent president of the Council – Herman von Rompuy – and a foreign minister presiding over an expanded foreign service, Baroness Ashton (see Chapter 4). Apart from the EU institution-building process, the financial crisis and recession across Europe (sparked by the collapse of portions of the investment banking system in the USA and its associated global debt), shook the foundation of accepted wisdom about the relationship between international finance and national economic well-being, nowhere more so than in Britain (see Chapter 8). Greece became the first eurozone country from 2010 to teeter on the brink of financial insolvency, eventually leading other eurozone states, in particular Germany, to agree tighter monitoring of national accounts, though not without massive strikes and demonstrations in Athens protesting against the austerity measures agreed. The recession triggered by the financial crisis was felt differently in countries depending on their exposure to the type of debt that became 'toxic'. The newly elected coalition government in Britain, the Conservatives and the Liberal Democrats, promised a 25 per cent reduction in government expenditure over the life of the government, threatening a still fragile recovery. Though not as massive as Greece's debt levels as a percentage of gross domestic product (GDP), other southern European economies, such as Spain, Portugal and Italy, embarked on massive budget-cutting exercises in order to avoid financial market speculation undermining their already precarious positions. The result of this drastic cutback of state spending has had repercussions on the nature of the public sector in general.

In the east, political and economic reform has not been uniform. Some countries, such as Poland, the Czech Republic and Hungary, have progressed far in both spheres, while others, such as Slovakia and Romania, continue to struggle with the legacies of their recent past, in some cases with personnel from the communist system still wielding power.

Elsewhere, tragic events have forestalled political and economic development, for instance the wars in the former Yugoslavia. In the CIS countries, democratization has similarly been patchy, with autocratic rule prevalent in Belarus and Central Asia. Ukraine and Georgia witnessed large-scale popular mobilizations that overturned rigged elections. These so-called 'colour' revolutions – Rose in Georgia in 2003, Orange in Ukraine in 2004, and Tulip in Kyrgyzstan in 2005 – gave hope to those who sought to set their countries on a democratic and western path. In the event the colour revolutions did not live up to expectations – for Georgia bitter internal divisions and a failed war with Russia in 2008, and in Kyrgyzstan a second revolution in April 2010 that overthrow the government that came to power in the first. The election in Ukraine in 2010 of a less virulently pro-western president in Ukraine (Victor Yanukovich) opened the way for the resolution of numerous conflicts with Russia, including the long-term resolution of the status of the Russian Black Sea Fleet in Sevastopol in the Crimea and put NATO membership on indefinite hold. Democratization, it was clear, could not simply be equated with membership in western organizations. As for Russia, compared with its communist past, great progress has been made in opening up both the political and the economic system. Still, the immensity of the country, and the legacy of 70 years of communism, has meant that reform of the economy has proceeded in fits and starts. Politically, one party (United Russia) dominates parliamentary and presidential elections, though other smaller parties continue to contest these. Political violence also continues to afflict Russia in the North Caucasus, a legacy in part of the two Chechen wars of the 1990s and early 2000s. The original national liberation movement in Chechnya has given way to a jihadist Islamic insurgency across the region.

If a pattern can be discerned in the events of the past handful of years, it is that the optimism of the immediate post-Cold War period – an 'end of history' as one commentator put it (Fukuyama, 1992) – has been replaced by a mixture of cautious optimism regarding international relations in Europe, in particular, between the EU and Russia, and fundamental changes in domestic politics that are challenging the basis of post-Second World War political patterns. Although the western Balkans remains a tinderbox as regards flare-ups of violence, especially in places such as Kosovo and Bosnia, the intervention of NATO and the EU has established some tentative hope for continuing democratization and economic development. More widely, EU and NATO relations with Russia, under the leadership of presidents Medvedev and Putin, has settled into a more businesslike relationship, with concerns over energy policy becoming a central issue of mutual concern for both sides. It is the domestic politics of European states, especially in the west, that have witnessed emerging, and in some respects, disturbing patterns. First, the financial crisis and subsequent recession has forced (or been an opportunity for some) political parties of both centre-left and centre-right to revisit some of the core policies of the western European welfare state, in particular that of old-age pensions, for which the retirement age is being set at a later age (for both cost-saving purposes as well as arguments concerning the effects of increased longevity). Second, the issue of immigration has firmly established itself in the popular mind, and therefore in electoral politics, as the rise and increasing success of right-wing populist parties has demonstrated across Western as well as Eastern European party systems. Some of these parties are a curious mix of anti-immigration and postmodern concerns, such as the Dutch Party of Freedom (PVV), or else anti-immigrant and extreme right-wing ideology harkening back to the inter-war period, such as the Hungarian Jobbik Party. The effect of the success of these parties, especially in the Western European states, is to put pressure on the centre-left and centre-right parties, both of which appear increasingly identified with the policies and reality of the pre-1989 period. Thus a crisis of social democracy and Christian Democracy – from the Netherlands to Austria, as well as in some Scandinavian states, signals a potential remaking of the patterns of party politics that were first established in the early decades of the twentieth century.

Establishing a new European order will mean confronting at least two challenges. First, firmly to ground democratic norms and procedures across all of Europe in order to forestall a new segregation of the post-communist states, evidence of which suggests that progress is indeed being made. Second, to respond creatively to globalization and European integration, in the sense that these processes can complicate the relationship between state and nation. In this context, the great recession from 2008 may have 'speeded up' the response in ways that may have lasting effects on democratic politics. Meeting both of these challenges may result in new notions of European citizenship as well as signal the beginning of a post-Cold War period.

SUMMARY

- Europe emerged from the Second World War physically devastated and exhausted.

- The remaking of Europe included two new powers, the USA and USSR, each with predominant influence in their half of Europe.

- This chapter traces the division of Europe into two, the political and economic events and trends in each half, and then describes the eventual demise of the Cold War and the division of Europe.

QUESTIONS FOR DISCUSSION

- In what ways were the Cold War and political and economic stability related?

- In what ways was the year 1968 a turning-point in bipolar politics?

- Why was the USA considered the leader of the Western nations?

- What were some of the components of Soviet-style modernization?

- What role did Gorbachev play in ending the Cold War?

- What are the key challenges facing post-cold war Europe?

FURTHER READING

Dinan, D. (2010) *Ever Closer Union: An Introduction to European Union*, 2nd edn (London: Palgrave Macmillan). A useful introduction to the history of the European integration process, as well as an accessible presentation of the workings of its institutions.

Gaddis, J.L. (1998) *We Now Know: Rethinking Cold War History* (Oxford: Oxford University Press). A stimulating, comprehensive comparative history of the conflict from its origins to its most dangerous moment, the Cuban missile crisis.

Glenny, M. (1996) *The Fall of Yugoslavia: The Third Balkan War* (London: Penguin). A fascinating exploration of the tragedy and wars unleashed by the break-up of Yugoslavia in the first half of the 1990s.

Unwin, T. (1998) *A European Geography* (Harlow, Essex: Longman). A competent introduction to various dimensions of European society, especially in the post-Second World War period, covering cultural issues and politics, including European integration, economic issues and social agendas.

Wegs, J.R. and Ladrech, R. (2006) *Europe since 1945: A Concise History*, 5th edn (Basingstoke: Palgrave Macmillan). A good and accessible coverage of political events and social and economic trends in both Eastern and Western Europe.

Towards one Europe?

JACKIE GOWER

Thanks to the yearning for freedom of the peoples of Central and Eastern Europe the unnatural division of Europe is now consigned to the past. European unification shows that we have learnt the painful lessons of a history marked by bloody conflict. Today we live together as was never possible before.

Declaration on the occasion of the fiftieth anniversary of the signature of the Treaties of Rome, 25 March 2007

The dramatic fall of the communist systems in Eastern Europe and end of the Cold War led to a widespread expectation that the post-war division of Europe into separate, and antagonistic, ideological, economic and security systems would be ended. The hope was that in future there would be 'one Europe', but it was clear from the beginning that the convergence between the Western and Eastern systems would be asymmetrical: the movement would be in one direction only as the Central and East European states adopted the Western post-war system that was accepted as the 'European' model. The conflation of 'Europe' and the Western model was demonstrated by the almost immediate pledge by the new leaders in Central and Eastern Europe to 'return' their country to 'Europe'. In much of the academic literature the transformation of the political and economic systems of the former communist states is described as the 'Europeanization' of the region (e.g., Ágh, 1998, Ch. 2).

What did they understand 'Europe' to mean?

1. Liberal democratic constitutional government and adherence to democratic political norms and values: free elections; protection of human rights and civil liberties; respect for the rights of minorities; the rule of law; media freedom; a thriving civil society.
2. Capitalist market economies: private ownership; liberalized prices; integration into European and global markets; sharing in the economic prosperity and consumer society enjoyed by most Western Europeans.
3. Membership of what had hitherto been seen as the 'Western' European institutions: the Council of Europe; the North Atlantic Treaty Organization (NATO); the European Union (EU).

There is a clear link between the three facets of Europeanization: membership of the main European institutions is dependent on the former communist states making the successful transition to the political and economic systems characteristic of Western European states. Their determination to secure membership of those institutions was in turn a powerful external lever or anchor, both setting the domestic reform agenda and mobilizing support for its achievement. To meet the accession conditions, candidate states had to adopt norms, policies and institutional models which transformed their national polities, making them much more similar to those found in Western Europe (Grabbe, 2006, p. 6). Once they had attained membership, the influence of the institutions would continue to make their mark through the same processes of socialization, norm transfer and policy convergence as observed among the 'old' members and in the literature on European integration, also characterized as 'Europeanisation' (Ladrech, 2004).

The hope was that after a period of necessary 'transition', there would be 'one Europe' based on common norms and values, with its people and goods moving freely across the continent in an environment of shared security. The realization of that goal took far longer than many people had expected back in the heady days after the fall of the Berlin Wall, and even now significant areas of the continent remain outside. This chapter will chart the progress of the political and economic transition in Central and Eastern Europe and the enlargement of the membership of European organizations. It will consider the impact of enlargement on those European states not yet members of the EU and NATO and ask whether new dividing lines have been drawn across Europe. The potential of the European Neighbourhood Policy to mitigate, if not completely overcome, the new division will be assessed. Finally, the position of two of the largest and most geo-strategically important states – Turkey and Russia – will be considered in this new European order and the question asked: is it inevitable that they will be 'outsiders', or does their future too lie within the 'one Europe' that is slowly taking shape?

Political transition: the democratization of the east

For over forty years Europe had been divided into two quite separate and distinctive political spaces: in the west (with the exception of Spain and Portugal until the mid-1970s and Greece, 1967–74) they were liberal democratic parliamentary systems, whereas in the east there were the so-called 'peoples' democracies' dominated by the ruling communist parties. Superficially, the constitutions of the states in the two halves of Europe did not seem all that different, with elected parliaments, presidents and prime ministers and constitutional guarantees of political rights and freedoms. However, in reality the political systems in Eastern Europe operated completely differently from those in the west. The key to this essential difference could be found in a single article included in all their constitutions which guaranteed the 'leading role' of the Communist Party and thereby ensured that all other institutions were subordinated to it. Although elections were held at regular intervals and indeed the turnout was very much higher than in the west, there was no meaningful choice between competing parties or even in most cases of individual candidates. Even in those countries where other political parties continued to exist after the late 1940s, such as Poland and the GDR, there was no competition for power: the number of seats each party would win was determined *before* the election and the Communist Party was assured of an overwhelming majority. Parliaments in Eastern Europe met infrequently and generally only served as a theatre for set-piece debates and the rubber-stamping of decisions that had already been made by the government. The real locus of power was the Politburo of the ruling Communist Party and the most important political figure was the General or First Secretary of the party. All appointments to any positions of authority or influence in the state administration, the economy, the judiciary, police, armed forces, education, the media and trade unions had to be approved by the party through the **nomenklatura** system. Political freedoms and civil liberties were severely constrained by censorship and the operations of the secret police and although throughout the communist period there were political dissidents and varying degrees of

---

● **Nomenklatura**: Literally, the list of jobs that could only be held by people approved by the Communist Party. This political vetting of appointments applied not just to posts in the government but also to senior positions in the army, police force, judiciary, education, media, culture, trade unions, industry, agriculture, transport, and so on. It became a shorthand term to refer to the ruling elite which not only dominated all walks of life but also enjoyed privileged access to scarce resources such as consumer goods and good quality housing and health services.

opposition in the states in the region, their activities were illegal and the personal costs very high.

When the communist systems collapsed in 1989, all the new governments proclaimed their commitment to creating new democracies conforming to the norms and values that were seen as characteristic of 'Europe', as epitomized by the states in the west. Although this was presented as 'returning to Europe', in fact for most of them it meant developing a totally new political system and political culture virtually from scratch. With the exception of Czechoslovakia, which had maintained a successful parliamentary system throughout the inter-war period, they had at best only very limited experience of constitutional democracy in their pre-communist history. Their **democratic transition** and **democratic consolidation** were therefore inevitably going to be at least as difficult as it had been for Spain and Portugal in the late 1970s. Furthermore, at the same time they all had to undertake the equally challenging economic transition discussed below, and for many of them also the problem of nation-state building as they established their independence in the wake of the break-up of the multinational states of the USSR, Yugoslavia and Czechoslovakia.

Not surprisingly, progress in achieving what Claus Offe (1991) called the 'triple transition' (political, economic and social) has been very varied across the region and three distinct groups of states can be identified. First, there are the Central

---

● **Democratic transition**: The shift from authoritarian to democratic systems. According to Huntington (1991), democratization has come in waves: the first from the 1820s to the 1920s; the second from 1945 to the 1960s; and we are currently in the third, beginning with the Portuguese revolution in April 1974, extending to encompass other countries in Southern Europe (Greece and Spain), before moving to Latin America, and then returning to Eastern Europe in 1989. The post-communist transitions are sometimes classed as part of a fourth wave, since for them the shift was from totalitarian systems, however decayed, rather than from authoritarian ones. The fourth-wave transitions are 'total' in the sense that everything has to be created and changed: market systems, civil societies, political orders, international orientations, and in many cases even the post-communist states themselves are new.

● **Democratic consolidation**: The point at which a democratic transition becomes effectively irreversible. The idea of a 'two turnover test' was introduced by Huntington (1991) to suggest that when a government has changed democratically twice, a certain point of consolidation has been reached.

European (including Slovenia) and Baltic states which joined the EU in 2004 and can now be considered stable liberal democracies. Second, there are the South-East European states where the transition was delayed, especially by the wars in the region in the 1990s, but also by domestic factors that proved particularly difficult to surmount. Bulgaria and Romania did achieve EU membership in 2007 but are widely thought to still lag behind other EU member states in terms of the quality of at least some aspects of their political and economic systems. All of the other states in the region now appear to be on the path towards democracy, even if they still have some way to go, Third, there are the Eastern European states (Belarus, Moldova, Ukraine, Russia, Armenia, Azerbaijan and Georgia) where the transition to formal democratic institutions was generally accomplished by the mid-1990s but the actual workings of the system continue to fall short of international standards of liberal democracy, and indeed in the case of Russia, Belarus and Georgia, the movement has in recent years seemed to be backwards.

Central European and Baltic states

The vital first stage of the political transition is the holding of free elections, which facilitate and legitimize the transfer of political power from the old party elite to representatives of the reform movement. The first semi-free election to be held anywhere in the region for over forty years took place in Poland in June 1989 and the opposition movement Solidarity won all but one of the parliamentary seats they were permitted to contest (Millard, 2003, p. 25). This led to the formation of a coalition government led by Solidarity ministers and the election the following year of its leader Lech Wałęsa as the new President (see Key Figure 3.1). Free elections were also held in Hungary, Czechoslovakia, Slovenia, Estonia, Latvia and Lithuania in 1990 and new governments assumed power with a mandate to create constitutional democracies and market economies. Elections have subsequently been held at regular intervals according to each state's electoral laws and monitoring observers from international organizations such as the EU, Organization for Security and Cooperation in Europe (OSCE) and the Council of Europe have

Key Figure 3.1

Lech Wałęsa (1943–)

An electrician in the Lenin Shipyard in Gdańsk who in 1980 founded Solidarity, the independent trade union which was to spearhead the reform movement in Poland. He was imprisoned when martial law was declared in 1981 and became an international symbol of resistance to the communist regime, winning the Nobel Peace Prize in 1983. He led the strikes in 1988 which resulted in the collapse of the communist system the following year. He was elected President of the Republic of Poland in 1990, but failed to establish a firm political base and lost the 1995 election to Aleksander Kwaśniewski, leader of the post-Communist Social Democratic Party (SLD).

confirmed that they have been free and fair. Equally important has been the fact that in all countries there has been more than one occasion when the incumbent government has suffered defeat and power has been peacefully handed over to the opposition party/parties, providing an orderly succession (Millard, 2004, p. 275). According to Huntington (1991), it is this 'two-turn-over test' which is the real mark of a successful democratic consolidation because it demonstrates that all the main actors in the political process accept the 'rules of the game' and are prepared to accept the verdict of the electorate. This has been particularly sensitive when it has been the former Communist Party, albeit completely reformed (see below), that has returned to power via the ballot box as for example happened in Poland when Alexander Kwaśniewski defeated Lech Wałęsa in the 1995 presidential election and in Hungary in 1994 with the landslide victory of the Hungarian Socialist Party. However, the regular alternation of governments from the right and left of the political spectrum should be seen as evidence that 'normal' politics is at work in the new democracies. It has been a feature of elections in all the Central and Eastern European states where electoral volatility has been unusually high and the incumbent government rarely re-elected for a second term.

The revival or reform of old political parties and the development of new ones through which electoral choice can be exercised and political power mediated has been crucial to the successful transition. Initially the opposition contested elections under the banner of broad umbrella movements that were very loose coalitions of reformist individuals and groups with no permanent organization or membership. Typical of such 'movement parties' were the Solidarity Citizens' Committee in Poland in 1989 and Civic Forum and Public Against Violence in what was still Czechoslovakia in 1990. In many respects these early 'parties' resembled more closely the new social movements in the west such as environmentalism and feminism than the traditional political parties that are part of the institutional fabric of modern parliamentary democracies. However, in most cases they split up into a number of more ideologically coherent organizations and today resemble more closely the main political parties found in Western European states, despite their often rather esoteric names. They still tend to be rather centralized and elite-dominated organizations with only very patchy grass-roots structures and with the exception of the reformed communist parties, cannot really be considered mass parties. Membership levels remain very low, which in part reflects the communist legacy of a general distaste for political parties, but is also in line with the trend in the west for party membership to decline quite steeply in recent years (see Chapter 6).

Today it is possible broadly to identify the same ideological or party families in Central Europe as in the west: ex-communist, social democrat, liberal, Christian democrat, nationalist-conservative, ethnic/regional and, more recently, the radical populist/extreme right. On the left social democratic parties dominate, in most cases the product of a remarkably successful modernization and rebranding of the old ruling communist parties. The change of name, however, is far more than cosmetic and reflects a total break from the policies of their communist past. International recognition of their commitment to democratic norms and values and the market economy enables them to work comfortably alongside western social democratic parties in international fora such as the EU or Council of Europe. The consolidation of stable and coherent centre-right parties has proved more problematic, although the Civil Democratic Party (ODS) in the Czech Republic and Fidesz in Hungary have been notable exceptions. (Szczerbiak and Hanley, 2005). In most cases the centre-right parties are *sui generis* not easily equated with either the Christian democratic or conservative parties of Western Europe, although most have now identified themselves with one of the established party groups in the European Parliament. Unusually in contemporary Europe, where the rural–urban cleavage has become much less salient, there are also significant agrarian parties in Poland, Latvia, Lithuania and Estonia where there are large agricultural work forces. For many years the Greens had a low profile in Central Europe compared with most Western European states, almost certainly attributable to the lower incidence of post-materialist values found in less affluent societies. In recent years Green parties have made modest electoral breakthroughs in Hungary, the Czech Republic and Estonia, but there were only two member of the European Parliament (MEPs) (out of a total of 53) from new member states in the Green Group of the European Parliament after the 2009 election. A less welcome sign of the Europeanization of electoral politics in central Europe in recent years has been the rise in support in several countries for populist radical right parties claiming to champion 'the man in the street' against capitalism, modernization, the political establishment and the EU and also extreme right parties with openly racist and homophobic agendas (Jasiewicz, 2003, p. 187; Pankowski, 2010).

Although there are still some distinctive features of party politics in Central Europe, it is clearly not that dissimilar to that of Western Europe. It is significant that almost all MEPs from the region have identified themselves with one of the established party groups, and equally importantly, been accepted by them. The successful integration of the MEPs from the new member states into the work of the European Parliament party groups has played a major part in overcoming the political divisions of the past.

The other key institutions of liberal democracy are also now secure in the Central European and Baltic states. New constitutions were adopted in the 1990s which established European-style parliamentary democracies, although Poland is more akin to the French premier-presidential system than the Westminster model. The constitutions guarantee the full range of political and civil rights and establish constitutional courts to uphold the rule of law and provide domestic recourse for violations of rights. The states also subscribed to the European Convention on Human Rights (ECHR) on admission to the Council of Europe (see below) and accepted the jurisdiction of its European Court of Human Rights (ECtHR) based in Strasbourg. At the level of the state, therefore, European norms and values are respected. However, at the level of society attitudes are often much less liberal, particularly towards minorities, whether in terms of ethnic, national, religious or sexual orientation, although the same is true in many western countries. The treatment of national minorities is an especially big challenge for most of the states as there are very large numbers of Russians living in Estonia and Latvia, a sizeable Hungarian minority in Slovakia and Romania and the Roma are despised and discriminated against throughout the region. During the accession negotiations, the EU used the lever of political conditionality to help secure fairer citizenship and language laws for national minorities (Rose, 1997; Pridham, 2002). But once they had attained membership the EU lost a lot of its leverage and the rights of the Russian-speaking minorities in Estonia and Latvia continue to be a cause for concern. It has become one of the most sensitive issues between Russia and the EU, with the former accusing the Union of operating double standards with respect to minority rights and not respecting its own supposedly strict conditions.

The accession of these eight countries to the EU

in May 2004 reflected the progress they had made in establishing stable democracies. Now, as members of the EU, they are experiencing a greater intensity of interaction with their western counterparts at all levels, and it is expected there will be a significant socialization impact on politicians, officials, judges and lobbyists as they participate in the institutions. The process of Europeanization will be a continuing process for the new members just as it has been for the older member states (Featherstone and Radaelli, 2003).

South-East European states

Democratization has proved to be much more difficult in South-Eastern Europe, and during the 1990s it seemed that the region was actually moving in the opposite direction from the rest of the continent. Although multi-party elections were held in Bulgaria, Romania and Yugoslavia in 1990 and in Albania in 1991, the new governments were unwilling or unable to embark upon the sort of radical political and economic reforms taking place in Central Europe at that time. Ágh (1998, p. 186) argues that in the early 1990s all the Balkan countries were still in the pre-transition stage, 'stuck half-way between the old and the new systems', with façade rather than real democracies. Often the old elite managed to hang on to power under the guise of pseudo-new parties and the state apparatus was largely unreformed. The concentration of power in the hands of the right-wing nationalist Franjo Tudjman in Croatia and the former communist-turned-nationalist Slobodan Milošević in Serbia meant that until their demise there was no prospect of genuine moves to democratic political systems or lasting peace in the region. They abused their powers of patronage to pack the public administration, judiciary, police and the media with their supporters and connived to the widespread corruption in the financial and business sectors. Corruption was systemic throughout the region, with state assets plundered by 'well-connected insiders' (Gallagher, 2003, p. 78). The rule of law was nowhere respected and the opposition was denied equal access to the media. In Bulgaria and to a lesser extent in Romania the position was marginally better than in the former Yugoslav republics, but they still lagged behind

their Central European neighbours throughout the 1990s.

There are a number of factors that help to account for this lack of progress in political reform in the region. The Balkans had been under the domination of the Ottoman Empire until the First World War and had had virtually no experience of democracy during the twentieth century. Furthermore, during the communist era there were long periods of autocratic rule: Josip Tito in Yugoslavia from 1944 to 1980, Enver Hoxha in Albania from 1945 to 1985, Todor Zhivkov in Bulgaria from 1954 to 1989 and Nicolae Ceauşescu from 1965 to 1989. The political tradition in the area was therefore authoritarian and deferential. There had also been much weaker reform movements among the intelligentsia and other sections of civil society than in Central Europe, where alternative elites were already evident prior to 1989. The legacy of history was therefore not conducive to the development of democratic political cultures which would support a smooth transition to liberal democratic government and it was not surprising that formal constitutional changes failed to effect genuine political change. Instead, the collapse of communism allowed political entrepreneurs to exploit ethnic nationalism and plunged Yugoslavia into a series of internal wars that further delayed democratization for at least a decade.

Yugoslavia had always been a multinational federation with extensive intermingling of the ethnic communities throughout its constituent republics. When in 1992 it finally split up into independent states, the former internal administrative borders of the federation were recognized as the new international borders, leaving large numbers of people living in the 'wrong' state. The solution to this perceived problem was seen to be a policy of 'ethnic cleansing', whereby millions of people were forced to leave their homes, often where their families had lived for generations, and move to a neighbouring state where they would be part of the majority community. Obviously, movement of people on such a scale was inconceivable without the widespread use of violence, which in turn led to direct confrontations between the states in the region as they attempted to protect their compatriots and extend their own territory in the ensuing chaos. The result was a huge number of casualties and evidence of atrocities that evoked memories of some of the darkest hours of European history. Mass graves of massacred civilians, the systematic rape of thousands of women, concentration camps, the desecration of churches and mosques and the shelling of ancient cities shattered the illusion that the 'new Europe' after the end of the Cold War was going to be united by liberal norms and values. The televised images of the siege of Sarajevo, the shelling of Dubrovnik, the evidence of the massacre of 7000 Bosnian men at Srebrenica and then, in 1999, the mass exodus of refugees from Kosovo had a profound impact not only on the people of the Balkans but on the whole of Europe, where there was almost disbelief that such things could be happening so close to home. Under pressure from public opinion, international intervention was organized first in Bosnia in 1995 and then in Serbia in 1999 during the Kosovo crisis, and a fragile peace was restored to the region (see Chapter 10).

Domestic developments in both Croatia and Serbia at the turn of the millennium also created optimism that at last political reforms would get under way in two of the pivotal states. In Croatia, Franjo Tudjman died in December 1999 and the opposition parties won the election early the following year. They immediately embarked on a programme of radical reforms to try to catch up with their neighbour, Slovenia, a frontrunner for EU membership. In October 2000 Milošević was forced from office and was eventually handed over to the International Criminal Tribunal for the Former Yugoslavia in The Hague to face charges of war crimes and genocide, where he died in March 2006. The fragility of democracy in Serbia was dramatically demonstrated with the assassination of the first democratically elected non-communist Prime Minister, Zoran Djindjic, in broad daylight in Belgrade in March 2003, but it remained broadly on track. In the judgment of Freedom House (2004), which monitors the observance of political rights and civil liberties worldwide, both countries had made enormous progress since 2000 and were classified as 'free', although concerns persisted about other aspects of their political and judicial systems. Montenegro, which declared its independence from Serbia in 2006, has also been considered 'free' since 2010. Other states in the region continue

to fall short of international standards with Albania, Bosnia-Herzegovina, Macedonia and Kosovo still only considered 'partly free' (Freedom House, 2010), with particular concerns about the treatment of minorities.

The wars of the 1990s have inevitably left deep scars on the societies of the states in the region and there has been a reluctance to come to terms with the atrocities committed by all sides and actively promote reconciliation between former enemies. The international community, especially the EU, has exerted enormous pressure on the governments to hand over those indicted for war crimes to the International Criminal Tribunal for the Former Yugoslavia, but it is a deeply divisive issue, with many people regarding those concerned as national heroes, not war criminals. Formal compliance with European norms and values is now accepted by all the governments in the region as the condition for integration into the EU and NATO, but civil society remains extremely weak and ethno-nationalist prejudices and intolerance are endemic. The authority and stability of the states are also undermined by the prevalence of corruption, thriving black economies and the activities of organized crime syndicates. The weakness of many of the states continues to be one of the major obstacles to both their own successful political transition and the long-term stability of the region. Potentially the most damaging is Bosnia-Herzegovina, which as a result of the Dayton Peace Agreement in 1995 was divided into two separate 'entities': the Muslim-Croat Federation of Bosnia and Herzegovina and the Bosnian-Serb Republika-Srpska, each with its own government, parliament, police, judicial services and schools. For over ten years it has essentially been run as an international protectorate and cannot be considered a functioning state. Furthermore, in the light of Kosovo's apparently successful unilateral declaration of independence in 2008, there have been calls in Republika-Srpska for their independence from the rest of Bosnia, which could reopen the issue of the boundaries of neighbouring states as well. While the future of Bosnia-Herzegovina and the final status of Kosovo remain unresolved, the political transition in the western Balkans cannot be considered complete.

The Eastern European states

Democratization was always going to be most diffi-cult in the successor states of the Soviet Union, where centuries of tsarist autocracy had been followed by 70 years of Communist Party rule. Economic transition and nation-state-building were also more difficult as the highly integrated Soviet economy had to be separated out into individual national economies and the borders and identities of the new national communities established. The largely unreconstructed communist parties have continued to attract significant levels of support from those who are nostalgic for the socioeconomic security of the old system, while extremists on the right have exploited the rebirth of nationalism. There has consequently been much more debate than in Central Europe and the Baltic states about whether they want to adopt the Western European model or instead develop their own variant based on their very different historical and cultural tradi-tions. It is significant that the EU has exerted much less influence on the domestic evolution of these states as they have either not aspired to membership or been denied the status of even 'potential candi-dates' by the Commission. The EU hopes that with the adoption of its European Neighbourhood Policy (ENP) and the launch of the Eastern Partnership (see below) this may change, but without the 'golden carrot' of accession, the EU's leverage seems likely to remain rather weak.

In the early 1990s, relatively free multi-party elections were held and new constitutions adopted which established the institutional framework for the democratic transition. All the states in the region opted for presidential or presidential-parlia-mentary systems (although Moldova changed to become a more purely parliamentary system) and have experienced long periods of personalized and authoritarian leadership: Leonid Kuchma in Ukraine from 1994 to 2004; Boris Yeltsin from 1991 to 1999 in Russia, followed by Vladimir Putin as President from 2000 to 2008, and then continuing to wield enormous influence as Prime Minister until he returned as President in 2012; Alexander Lukashenka since 1994 in Belarus; Eduard Shevardnadze in Georgia from 1992 to 2003 and then Mikheil Saakashvili since 2004. In some respects, therefore, there has been more political stability than in many of the other post-communist states, but the negative consequences have been the concentration of power in the hands of the presi-dent and his supporters and the use of the state apparatus to weaken the opposition and obstruct its efforts to play its proper role in a democratic system. Of particular concern has been the erosion of the independence of the media and their subor-dination to the interests of the presidential faction. Corruption has also become endemic in all spheres of public life and the rule of law is very weakly established.

The 'colour' revolutions in Georgia in 2003 (Rose) and Ukraine in 2004 (Orange) seemed to mark a decisive break, with tens of thousands of people taking to the streets to protest against flawed elections and demand a radical change of govern-ment. The hope was not only that effective liberal democracies might at last be established in those states, but also that similar popular movements might instigate a new wave of democratization in the region. Within months, however, it was appar-ent that the leaders of the revolutions were failing to deliver the radical changes they had promised and the leaders of the other states in the region were successfully consolidating their positions, clamping down on the opposition and taking measures to restrict the activities of western NGOs, which they accused of having orchestrated the colour revolutions.

In the case of Ukraine, tensions and rivalry between Viktor Yushchenko and Yulia Tymoshenko, the charismatic leaders of the Orange revolution, resulted in five years of chronic government insta-bility and failure to deliver on the radical reform agenda that had brought them to power. However, according to the Freedom House monitors, since 2005 Ukraine has been the only Eastern European state to be classified as 'free' in terms of political rights and civil liberties. This important develop-ment was graphically confirmed in 2010 when Viktor Yanukovich, who had been forced to stand down by the Orange revolution amid claims of electoral fraud, was elected President in an election judged by the International Election Observation Mission to have met most OSCE and Council of Europe commitments (OSCE, 2010). His defeated opponent, Yulia Tymoshenko, initially challenged the result but when she subsequently accepted it,

Ukraine's position as a functional democracy was confirmed, albeit still with a lot of deficiencies.

Georgia was hailed by George W. Bush when he visited Tbilisi in May 2005 as 'a beacon of liberty for this region and the world' (Booth, 2005). However, President Saakashvili's government became increasingly illiberal and autocratic, centralizing executive power, weakening the legislature and compromising media freedom. After the violent crackdown of peaceful protesters in November 2007 and seriously flawed presidential and parliamentary elections in early 2008, Freedom House (2009) concluded that Georgia had actually gone backwards in terms of both political rights and civil liberties. Moldova is also considered only 'partially free', while Belarus has acquired pariah status in the new Europe, having the dubious distinction of being the only state still not a member of the Council of Europe.

Democracy in Russia, too, is judged to have become weaker since the mid-2000s, dropping from 'partially free' to 'not free' in 2005. Under President Putin state power was centralized, elections flawed, restrictions placed on non-governmental organizations (NGOs), media freedom curtailed, the opposition intimidated and the rule of law compromised. Although when President Medvedev was elected in 2008, it was hoped that a more liberal regime might develop, so far there are few signs of real change. What is significant, though, for the theme of 'one Europe' is that while Putin has repeatedly stressed his commitment to democracy, he has insisted that Russia 'would do it in its own way' (Sakwa, 2008, p. 311). In recent years, the Russian political elite has rejected the west's claim to pronounce on what constitutes 'proper' democracy and how it should be attained and instead asserted its right as a 'sovereign democracy' to pursue its own path in keeping with its own historical and cultural traditions, and encourage other post-communist states in its neighbourhood to follow its example.

Economic transition: the marketization of the east

One of the most characteristic features of the communist states was their centrally planned economies, which meant that what was produced, how much was produced, what it was produced from and at what price it was sold for were determined by central planning agencies rather then the market forces of supply and demand. The result was not only highly inefficient in terms of the use of national resources but also deeply unsatisfactory for consumers. The contrast between the shopping malls of Western Europe and the depressing scene in most of the east, with queues for basic commodities like food and chronic shortages of even poor-quality and old-fashioned consumer goods, was a major cause of the popular discontent that eventually brought down the regimes. There was, therefore, a consensus that **marketization** was the only way forward, although the strategies adopted and the pace of the reforms varied.

'Shock therapy', or gradualism

Most of the states adopted the Anglo-American neo-liberal model of capitalism espoused by Margaret Thatcher and Ronald Reagan rather than the gentler social-market model that had developed in most Western European countries in the post-war period. In large part this was due to the role played by the international financial institutions such as the International Monetary Fund (IMF), the World Bank and the European Bank for Reconstruction and Development (EBRD), which provided financial support for the economic reforms and hence exercised great influence over the measures adopted. Poland in the early 1990s became the role model for the 'Washington consensus' that what was needed was 'shock therapy' to throw off the shackles of the old system and move rapidly to a free-market economy. Finance Minister Leszek Balcerowicz launched his plan on 1 January 1990 for immediate price liberalization and currency convertibility backed by stiff wage control and a tight fiscal squeeze (Blazyca, 2003, pp. 224–5). The effects of the 'shock' were extremely harsh, with a sharp recession, rising unemployment, high infla-

---

● **Marketization**: The move from central planning to a market economy in which the economic forces of supply and demand would determine what was produced and the price at which it would be sold. The key reforms required are price liberalization, privatization, restructuring and the adoption of an effective competition policy.

tion and a big drop in real income. Most other states shied away from following such an extreme strategy and opted instead for varying degrees of gradualism. But everywhere the social costs of the economic reforms were high and there were many 'losers': pensioners; older workers, especially those in traditional industries; state employees whose salaries did not keep up with inflation and others without the skills to adapt to the new economic environment. This was the climate in which the post-communist parties managed to make an electoral comeback, as discussed in the previous section.

Privatization

Privatization was regarded as the key to the transition to a market economy so that profit would govern economic choices and entrepreneurs replace state planners. As virtually all economic entities had been state owned under communism, the scale of the privatization exercise was enormous and the strategy for achieving it contentious. The main choices were between direct sales of shares to institutions or individuals able to afford them, including foreigners; the indirect disposal of assets by the distribution of vouchers to the population at large, who could then in turn sell them; and management–employee buy-out schemes. Most states adopted a mixed strategy, but the direct sale of shares was the primary method in Poland, Hungary, Slovakia, Bulgaria, Latvia and Estonia, while voucher schemes were preferred in Russia, the Czech Republic and Lithuania. Other states such as Ukraine, Croatia and Romania opted for management–employee buy-outs (World Bank, 2002, p. 75). The result was that within a decade the majority of economic activity had been transferred to private ownership and one of the most obvious differences between the economies of Western and Eastern Europe had disappeared. However, the results were not entirely positive, with the voucher schemes in particular open to widespread corruption and the accumulation of former state assets in the hands of powerful oligarchs.

Progress in transition

There is a close correlation between the level of political democratization achieved in the post-communist states and the success of their economic transitions to functioning market economies (World Bank, 2002, p. 103). Thus the central European states have been the most radical and successful economic reformers while countries like Ukraine and Russia are some way behind, particularly with regard to the quality of the business environment, where issues such as the reform of financial institutions, competition policy, the rule of law and corruption still have to be addressed. The Central European and Baltic states had to adopt the laws of the single market before their accession to the EU, and so from a legal perspective their economies are very similar to those of the west. This makes them a much more attractive destination for foreign direct investment than the economies further east or south, and may lead to a growing gap between their economies and those of their neighbours. But even in the most advanced reform economies it is clear that it will take several decades before the living standards of their citizens match those in the west. Figure 3.1 shows the large gap in per capita income between the old and new EU member states, even when allowance has been made for the differences in prices (the purchasing power standard). So although the shopping centres across Europe now all look very similar, consumers in Central and Eastern Europe are finding that just because the goods they want are now in plentiful supply, it does not necessarily mean that they can buy them.

The enlargement of European institutions

The Conference on Security and Cooperation in Europe (CSCE) was the only pan-European international organization during the Cold War. It was transformed into the Organization for Security and Cooperation in Europe in 1994 and now includes all European states as well as the USA, Canada and the non-European post-Soviet states. The other main European organizations – the Council of Europe, the EU and NATO – have always only been open to democracies and so during the Cold War their membership was exclusively western. The progress achieved in enlarging their membership has therefore been a key indicator of the extent to which the

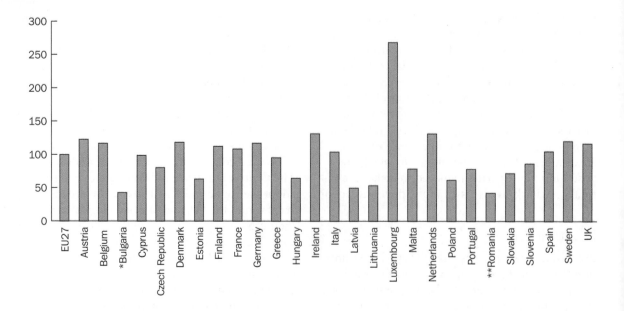

Note: PPS: purchasing power standards eliminate the differences in price levels in different states and therefore make comparisons of living standards more accurate.

Figure 3.1   Comparative gross national product (GDP) per capita in PPS* of EU member states, 2009

Source: Data from Eurostat 2010.

goal of 'one Europe' based on shared norms and values has become a reality (see Table 3.1; NATO enlargement is considered in Chapter 10).

Widening membership of the Council of Europe

The Council of Europe was founded in 1949 and has been the most important institution setting the standards on human rights in Europe (see Chapter 1). Its Convention for the Protection of Human Rights and Fundamental Freedoms adopted in Rome in 1950 has become the 'gold standard' throughout the continent for the norms and values seen to define a European democracy. Membership of the Council of Europe therefore is seen as the badge of international recognition of a state's democratic status and was an early goal for all the post-communist states. As an intergovernmental organization with only quite limited policy responsibilities, the obligations of membership were

much easier to take on than those of NATO and the EU, provided of course that human rights are indeed properly respected and protected in the candidate state. As is shown in Table 3.1, almost all the former communist states had gained membership of the Council of Europe by 2003, and many of them have been members since the mid-1990s. The one exception is Belarus, which is not deemed to share the key values of human rights and democracy and continues to use the death penalty (Council of Europe Directorate of Communication, 2010).

In principle Europe is now united on the basis of shared norms and values and it is important that all governments except Belarus have legally committed themselves to ensuring respect for a very wide range of political rights and civil liberties, including respect for religious and ethnic minorities. They have also accepted the jurisdiction of the ECtHR, based in Strasbourg, and therefore the legitimate international scrutiny of their record in upholding the principles of the

Table 3.1 The enlargement of European institutions, 1990–2009

Council of Europe	NATO	European Union
Hungary (1990)	Czech Republic (1999)	Austria (1995)
Poland (1991)	Hungary (1999)	Finland (1995)
Bulgaria (1992)	Poland (1999)	Sweden (1995)
Czech Republic (1993)	Bulgaria (2004)	Czech Republic (2004)
Estonia (1993)	Estonia (2004)	Cyprus (2004)
Lithuania (1993)	Latvia (2004)	Estonia (2004)
Romania (1993)	Lithuania (2004)	Hungary (2004)
Slovakia (1993)	Romania (2004)	Latvia (2004)
Slovenia (1993)	Slovakia (2004)	Lithuania (2004)
Latvia (1995)	Slovenia (2004)	Malta (2004)
Albania (1995)	Albania (2009)	Poland (2004)
Moldova (1995)	Croatia (2009)	Slovakia (2004)
Macedonia (1995)		Slovenia (2004)
Ukraine (1995)		Bulgaria (2007)
Croatia (1996)		Romania (2007)
Russian Federation (1996)		
Georgia (1999)		
Armenia (2001)		
Azerbaijan (2001)		
Bosnia and Herzegovina (2002)		
Serbia and Montenegro (2003)		
Montenegro (2007)		

Charter. The admission of some states, notably Russia, has been controversial as critics have argued that their record on human rights, particularly in Chechnya, has been inadequate, but the hope is that more influence can be exerted from inside the organization than on a state excluded from its membership. There are a very large number of cases pending against the Russian government and there have certainly been strong objections in the Duma and the media at what is seen as unwarranted interference in Russia's domestic affairs and politically biased judgements. However, it is important that so far at least the Russian government and courts have accepted the jurisdiction of the ECtHR and in February 2010 the duma finally ratified Protocol 14 to the Convention, which means that the long-awaited reform of the Court can begin.

The enlargement of the European Union

With the ending of the Cold War, four of Europe's traditionally neutral states (Austria, Finland, Norway and Sweden) which were members of the **European Free Trade Association (EFTA)** decided they were now free to apply for EU membership. All except Norway, where membership was rejected in a referendum, acceded to the EU on 1 January 1995. The Central and East European (CEE) states announced their intention to seek membership of

● **EFTA (European Free Trade Area)**: EFTA was set up in 1960 by seven states (including the UK) that were interested in establishing a free-trade area but did not want to commit to the more ambitious objectives of the EEC. Most of them subsequently did decide to become EU members, leaving just Iceland, Norway, Switzerland and Lichtenstein.

the EU almost immediately after their democratic revolutions, but it took until 1 May 2004 for them to achieve their ambition. Bulgaria and Romania also joined three years later, Croatia is expected to join in 2013 and a number of other states in the western Balkans are hoping to begin accession negotiations in the coming years. Turkey and Iceland are also candidates, so the EU enlargement agenda extends from the far north to the far south of the continent, but the eastern border is still unclear, with the EU unwilling to make any commitment to either Ukraine or Georgia.

The main reason why EU enlargement is generally such a slow process is because it entails the candidate states undertaking a phenomenally complex process of reform to enable them to take on the obligations of membership. The only exception is when the candidate states are members of the **European Economic Area (EEA)** and therefore have already accepted a large part of the *acquis communautaire* governing the single market into their own legal systems. Austria, Finland and Sweden therefore concluded their negotiations in 13 months and Iceland too is expected to make rapid progress, although fishing quotas may prove a tough negotiating challenge. Enlargement also requires the EU itself to adapt many of its institutional and policy arrangements in order to be able to accommodate new members, and the unprecedented scale of the prospective enlargement to the countries of Central and Eastern Europe both in terms of numbers and the impact on the budget also accounts for the frustratingly long time it took to achieve.

The initial response of the EU to the dramatic changes that took place in 1989–90 was cautious,

and there was reluctance to make any firm commitment about the future membership prospects of states just embarking on the difficult tasks of democratization and radical economic reform. Part of the unfortunate legacy of the Cold War bifurcation of Europe was that there had been little or no formal contact between the EC, as it then was, and the states in Eastern Europe until the late 1980s, and therefore the relationship had to be built almost from scratch. The Commission was invited by the EU member states to draw up association agreements (known as **Europe Agreements**) which would provide the framework for closer economic and political relations without making any formal commitment to eventual membership. The economic provisions of the Europe Agreements proved especially useful in that they enabled the economies of the states to be progressively integrated into the single market even before accession. Considerable levels of financial and technical support were also provided for their reforms through the **PHARE Programme**.

However, the EU member states were under strong pressure to give a clear commitment on the future membership of the CEE states so as to strengthen the hands of the domestic reformers and give them a clear framework within which to work. At the Copenhagen European Council in June 1993 the member states made a historic decision: 'The associated countries in central and eastern Europe that so desire shall become members of the European Union. Accession shall take place as soon as an associated country is able to assume the obligations of membership by satisfying the economic and political conditions required' (Council of the European Communities, 1993).

● **EEA (European Economic Area)**: The agreement between the EU and Norway, Iceland and Lichtenstein came into force 1 January 1994. It allows the three EFTA countries to participate in the internal market, including the free movement of people, on the basis of their application of the relevant *acquis*. Switzerland is not part of the EEA, although on the basis of bilateral agreements with the EU now enjoys comparable rights and obligations. The significance of the arrangements is very plain at the UK border, where EU and EEA citizens are directed through the same channel.

● *Acquis communautaire*: A French term which roughly translates as 'what the European Community has achieved'. It consists of all the legislation (decisions, directives and regulations) passed by the EC/EU since its creation and the judgements of the court which together make up EU law.

● **Europe Agreements**: The legal framework for relations between the EU and the accession countries of Central and Eastern Europe. Each was tailored to the specific needs of the individual country while establishing a common framework for political, economic and social relations. They created a framework for the accession process.

● **PHARE**: An EU aid programme introduced in 1989 to support the reforms taking place in Poland and Hungary (the acronym stands for 'Poland and Hungary: Aid for the Reconstructing of Economies'). It was later extended to cover the Czech and Slovak Republics, Bulgaria, Romania and the three Baltic states. Similar aid programmes were introduced for the CIS states (TACIS) and the Balkan states (CARDS).

BOX 3.1

The Copenhagen criteria (1993)

Membership requires that the candidate country has achieved

- stability of institutions guaranteeing democracy, the rule of law, human rights and respect for and protection of minorities;
- the existence of a functioning market economy as well as the capacity to cope with competitive pressure and market forces within the Union;
- the ability to take on the obligations of membership including adherence to the aims of political, economic and monetary union.

The statement then spelt out what those conditions would be, clarifying for the first time the basis on which a state's eligibility for membership would be judged (see Box 3.1). Significantly, the member states also stressed that 'the Union's capacity to absorb new members, while maintaining the momentum of European integration, is also an important consideration in the general interest of both the Union and the candidate countries'. The EU itself therefore also had to undergo reform before enlargement on the scale envisaged (see Chapter 4) and the potential tension between the goals of 'deepening' and 'widening' integration was hotly debated among the member states.

The accession negotiations

The starting point for the accession process is the decision on whether an applicant state has made sufficient progress in meeting the Copenhagen conditions, for it is reasonably assumed that by the conclusion of the negotiations, the conditions will be fully met. The position taken by the Commission and the member states is that the political criteria are prioritized over the other conditions in reaching the decision to invite a state to commence negotiations, and it is then hoped that during the accession process conditionality will provide a powerful incentive for the domestic reform agenda to be continued. On this basis, negotiations were opened in 1998 with the five CEE states considered to be most advanced in terms of meeting the Copenhagen criteria: Hungary, Poland, Estonia, the Czech Republic and Slovenia. Cyprus was also included in this group on the basis of what was to prove the over-optimistic assumption that its divided status would be resolved by the time of its eventual accession.

The five CEE states that were excluded from the initial negotiations were assured that they were all part of the same accession process and their position was described as 'pre-in' rather than 'out'. The strategy of differentiating between the candidates provided a strong incentive for the 'laggards' to renew their efforts at reform and in the Commission's annual reports in October 1999 all five were deemed to have made substantial progress. In the case of Slovakia, this was a result of the defeat of the illiberal Prime Minister Vladimir Mečiar and the election of a new government that was committed to ensuring that the country met the Copenhagen political criteria. In the case of the other four, there were more optimistic signs in relation to their economic reforms. At the Helsinki European Council in December 2000 it was decided to extend the accession negotiations to all the other five CEE countries, together with Malta, which had revived its membership application. The inclusion of Bulgaria and Romania in the group probably owed more to the member states' concern to reward them for supporting the bombing of Serbia during the Kosovo crisis than to a realistic assessment of their prospects of being able to fulfil the requirements for membership in the near future (Grabbe, 2006, p. 18). The only applicant state still not invited to begin negotiations was Turkey, although it was awarded official 'candidate' status (see below).

In some respects 'negotiations' is not a very accurate way of describing the process of preparing the way for new states to join the Union. Like any successful club, those that want to join it basically have to accept its rules. In the case of the Union this is the *acquis communautaire*, which is divided into chapters such as free movement of goods, capital, services and people; the environment; agriculture; competition policy, and so on. The candidate state has to demonstrate that it has not only incorporated all the relevant EU law into its domestic legislation but also that it has brought its administrative and judicial systems up to EU standards to ensure that it is implemented and enforced satisfactorily.

The final negotiations at the Copenhagen Council in December 2002 were extremely tense, as the EU member states were determined to keep the costs of enlargement within the agreed budget limits while the candidates were anxious not to be treated as second-class members. In the end, the clearly asymmetric power relationship of the negotiations resulted in the candidates being forced to accept the phasing-in of agricultural subsidies to their farmers and restrictions for up to seven years on their citizens' right to work in another member state, with the notable exception of the UK and Ireland. However, there seems to have been a strong sense of history in the making, and agreement was finally reached with ten states (all except Bulgaria and Romania) making it a 'big-bang' enlargement rather than the series of smaller 'waves' that had been predicted earlier.

credibility of the EU's conditionality policy but also created a serious obstacle to progress in Turkey's own future accession negotiations (see below).

In the case of Bulgaria and Romania's accession in 2007, there have also been criticisms that political considerations trumped the strict adherence to the EU's conditions for membership. In the Commission's Monitoring Report (2006) it was quite explicit that although considerable progress had been made towards meeting the Copenhagen criteria, serious concerns remained with respect to the judiciary, public administration and the fight against corruption. Nevertheless, the decision was taken to go ahead with accession and to rely on the unprecedented continuation of regular monitoring of a member state by the Commission to improve the situation. However, not surprisingly, the leverage on a state once it has attained its goal of membership has proved much weaker than when it is still knocking on the door, and serious concerns remain about aspects of governance in both states. As already noted, doubts have also been raised about the position of minority rights in Latvia and Estonia, despite assurances given prior to their accession. The lasting impact on the EU's enlargement policy has been a determination to ensure that in future a state must completely satisfy all the criteria prior to accession. This re- tightening of conditionality is already having an impact on the negotiations with Croatia, and future candidates are almost certainly going to feel that the bar has been raised for accession to the EU.

The weakening – and retightening – of conditionality

The decision to include Cyprus without waiting until a peace settlement had been approved was a concession to Greece, which otherwise threatened to block the whole enlargement package. When the Greek Cypriots overwhelmingly rejected a UN-brokered peace plan just one week before the planned enlargement on 1 May 2004, it was deemed politically impossible to halt the accession of Cyprus without jeopardizing the accession of the other nine states. However, allowing Cyprus to become an EU member without first resolving all disputes with its neighbours not only weakened the

The impact of European Union enlargement

The impact of enlargement on a scale totally unprecedented in its history on the EU's institutions and internal dynamics is considered in Chapter 4. Here the impact will be assessed primarily on its relations with neighbouring states and on its external policy towards them.

One of the main reasons so many states want to join the EU is because of the perceived costs of being outside it. As a result of its recent enlargements the Union has a new external border (see Map 3.1) and the implications for those living on the other side of it are significant. For the ordinary

Map 3.1 The 27-member EU after the 2007 enlargement

citizen, the most important consequence was that in most cases it became much more difficult to travel to neighbouring states, whether for family reasons, tourism or business. On accession, the new member states had to apply the EU's visa, immigration and asylum regimes, which in many cases involved imposing new restrictions on the movement of people across their borders. In December 2007 all except Bulgaria, Romania and Cyprus became part of the **Schengen area**, which led to a further tightening of controls on borders with those outside it. The contrast between the free movement enjoyed by citizens within the Schengen area, where not even passports need to be shown,

and the bureaucratic delays and expense of those living the other side of the border in obtaining a Schengen visa has resulted in a deep sense of resentment and exclusion among the EU's new neighbours (see Map 3.2).

The most sensitive case was undoubtedly that of Kaliningrad, a Russian region which became an enclave inside the Union when Lithuania and Poland became members. Since the break-up of the Soviet Union its citizens had been accustomed to enjoying visa-free travel to and from the 'motherland', and bitterly resented the prospect of having to spend time and money obtaining a visa once its neighbours became EU members. A compromise was eventually found whereby a 'facilitated transport document' rather than a full visa would be accepted, but it is still a source of friction between the EU and Russia. The same problem affects the movement of people across the borders between Poland, Slovakia or Romania and Ukraine; between Poland, Latvia or Lithuania and Belarus; and between Latvia or Estonia and Russia. When Bulgaria and Romania became EU members in

● **Schengen area**: The Schengen Agreement (1985) and the Schengen Convention (1990) provide for the removal of border controls to allow the free movement of people between the territories of the signatories without the need to show passports at the frontiers. Since December 2007 it covers all EU members except the UK and Ireland (which have chosen to retain national control over their borders) and Bulgaria, Romania and Cyprus (nor yet judged to meet the criteria). In addition, three non-EU states are members: Iceland, Norway and Switzerland.

Map 3.2   The Schengen area

2007, visas were introduced for travel from Macedonia, Serbia and Moldova, although from 1 December 2009 visa-free travel was restored. This imposition of a 'paper curtain' of visa requirements across Europe is widely seen as a retrograde step after the celebrations over the removal of the iron curtain in 1989 (Smith and Jenkins, 2003), and it has seriously disrupted often very long-standing patterns of cross-border interaction.

The other main consequence of the new border is that it delineates the reach of the single market. Within its borders, there is free movement of goods, services, capital and labour based on a common legal framework of standards and regulations. A common external tariff and other trade regimes such as quotas apply to all imports from outside the Union. Inevitably, therefore, businesses inside the Union enjoy a privileged position in comparison with those operating outside it. Even before enlargement, the trade flows of the Central European and Baltic states had shifted dramatically away from their former eastern (CMEA) neighbours towards western markets. The fear of those outside the

Union was that enlargement would further encourage that trend. Their citizens also do not have the right enjoyed by EU citizens to seek better employment opportunities in the more advanced economies of the EU and their students are required to pay the much higher 'international' tuition fees if they want to study at EU universities. The social and economic consequences of enlargement may therefore exacerbate the already large income differentials between members and non-members and create a 'welfare curtain' alongside the paper curtain already discussed (Dannreuther, 2004, p. 210). The psychological consequences are also serious, with a widespread perception of exclusion from the mainstream of European life and relegation to second-class citizenship of the 'new Europe.'

The European Neighbourhood Policy (ENP)

To try to minimize some of the negative consequences of enlargement, the EU launched a new initiative in 2003 specifically to reach out to its neighbours to the south and the east and 'draw closer to the 385 million inhabitants of the countries who will find themselves on the external land and sea border' (Commission of the European Communities, 2003). It was based on the concept of a 'wider Europe' that extends beyond the limits of the current EU enlargement perspective, not only to include the Eastern European states but also the southern and eastern Mediterranean countries of North Africa and the Middle East, which had enjoyed a special relationship with the EU since 1995 through the **Barcelona Process**. The central assumption is interdependence: the security, stability, prosperity and sustainable development of the Union are interlinked with that of its neighbours and vice versa. The aim therefore is to create a 'zone of prosperity and a friendly neighbourhood' or, in the words of former European Commission President Romano Prodi (2002), 'a ring of friends surrounding the Union'. The EU has two 'overarching objectives':

1. To work with the partners to reduce poverty, and create an area of shared prosperity and values based on deeper economic integration, intensified political and cultural relations, enhanced cross-border cooperation and shared responsibility for conflict prevention between the EU and its neighbours.
2. To anchor the EU's offer of concrete benefits and preferential relations within a differentiated framework which responds to progress made by the partner countries in political and economic reform (Commission of the European Communities, 2003, p. 9).

The 'offer' is that, in return for progress on specific political and economic reforms as agreed with each partner state in Action Plans covering periods of three to five years, the EU will be willing to grant progressive access to its single market and the four freedoms of movement of goods, capital, services

and people. An essential part of this process would be the adoption by the partner state of the relevant EU *acquis* in much the same way that a candidate state is required to do before attaining accession. The eventual outcome is potentially a similar sort of privileged and close relationship currently enjoyed by the members of the EEA. The key principle of the strategy is that of differentiation: how far each partner moves towards effectively being integrated into the EU single market will depend on their progress in the reforms and their willingness to embrace EU norms and values in general, as well as those expressly embodied in the *acquis*. If progress could be achieved in the Middle East peace process, Israel would be well placed to take full advantage of the ENP offer and Morocco and Ukraine are already negotiating significant upgrades in their relationship with the EU (Sasse, 2010; Bicchi, 2010). Other states like Syria, Egypt or Armenia are clearly a very long way behind Other states are clearly a very long way behind, but if the momentum of the political revolutions in Tunisia, Egypt and Libya in spring 2011 is maintained, they (and possibly also other states in the region if they follow a similar path) may be in a position to take advantage of the ENP offer.

The European Neighbourhood Policy (ENP) (see Map 3.3 for the area covered) has been widely criticized by some of the states towards which it is directed for failing to meet their aspirations and by academics for its ambiguity and ineffectiveness (e.g. Dannreuther, 2006; Edwards, 2008). The title of the policy is actually rather misleading because it is not designed for all those states that are now neighbours of the enlarged EU, but only those which are not envisaged becoming part of the EU family, at least for the foreseeable future. So therefore it is important to note that it excludes all the states in the western Balkans which are covered by the EU's Stabilization and Association Process and who are explicitly recognized as candidate or potential candidate members. It also excludes Turkey on the basis that it is also officially a candidate state. Russia, which although initially envisaged by the Commission as part of the ENP, rejected being treated within the same policy frame as states like Lebanon, Egypt and Moldova and insisted on developing a privileged partnership with the EU (Turkey and Russia are considered in more detail in the final section).

● **Barcelona Process**: The name commonly given to the strategy of promoting intensive interaction between the EU and the states on the southern and eastern shores of the Mediterranean. It was launched in 1995 and involves the development of both bilateral Euro-Mediterranean Association Agreements and numerous multilateral fora for regional dialogue and cooperation on a wide range of social, economic and cultural issues.

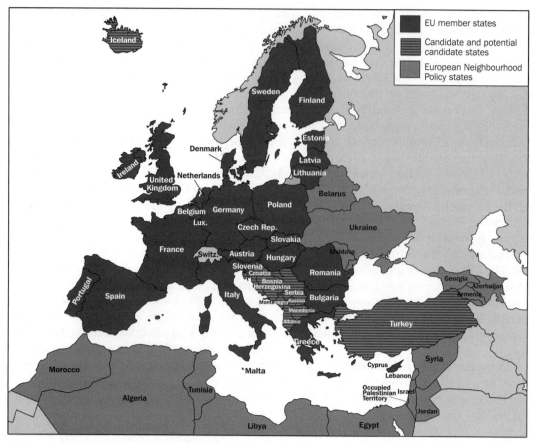

Map 3.3   The area of the European Neighbourhood Policy (ENP)

The ENP is therefore an alternative to the pre-accession strategy which was applied so successfully to the countries of CEE Europe, and it is hoped will also achieve the transformation of the western Balkans. For the southern and eastern Mediterranean littoral states, that is perfectly acceptable and the policy initiative has been broadly welcomed. However, for Eastern European countries such as Ukraine, Moldova and Georgia, the ENP has been a bitter blow to their aspirations to achieve full EU membership on a par with Poland, Slovakia and Lithuania. There is also considerable doubt as to whether a policy that deliberately excludes what has been regarded as the 'golden carrot' of accession can expect to achieve the same 'transformative agenda' (Dannreuther, 2006, p. 185). The ENP strategy is based explicitly on positive conditionality, but it is not clear whether the incentives offered will be enough to encourage states to show greater respect for human rights or take on the very considerable costs of harmo-

nizing their laws with the EU single market *acquis,* if membership is not available. While freer access to the single market for manufactured goods may be possible, the EU has a poor record on trade liberalization in agricultural produce and other goods like textiles which could undercut EU producers. Above all, in the current climate of rising support across Europe for extreme right-wing and radical populist parties exploiting fears about levels of immigration, it is inconceivable that there will be any significant concessions on the free movement of people, which would be so highly prized by the populations of the ENP states.

The Eastern Partnership and the Union for the Mediterranean

It is clear the inclusion of the Mediterranean and Eastern European states within the same policy framework owed more to the political dynamics of the EU itself than an objective assessment of the respective needs and interests of the target countries. Spain, Italy and France were determined to 'balance' the move to strengthen the EU's eastern policy that countries like Germany and Poland were pressing for in the context of the 2004 enlargement. The ENP was thus the product of the need to build a consensus within the European Council. A similar 'balancing' policy perspective partly accounts for the launch of the Union for the Mediterranean (see Map 3.4 for the area covered), sponsored by President Nicolas Sarkozy in 2008 and the Swedish–Polish sponsored Eastern Partnership launched in Prague in May 2009 (Commission of the European Communities, 2008a, 2008b). However, both initiatives were intended to try to reinvigorate the EU's relationships with the ENP partner states and to promote greater multilateral cooperation at the regional level in tackling common problems.

President Sarkozy's original proposal envisaged the Union for the Mediterranean only including those EU states with Mediterranean shorelines together with the Barcelona Process partners. However, other EU member states, led by German Chancellor Angela Merkel, refused to endorse such a scheme and insisted that it should include all 27 EU members. The eventual Union therefore runs to an unwieldy total of 43 states, including Croatia, Bosnia and Herzegovina, Montenegro and Monaco (see Map 3.4). The Heads of Government are scheduled to hold biannual summits, a greater sense of shared ownership is to be created by establishing a co-presidency involving one of the Mediterranean partners and a number of multilateral regional policy initiatives are planned covering energy, the environment, civil protection and transport.

The Eastern Partnership (EaP; see Map 3.5) includes the six Eastern European states except Russia. From their perspective, its most important innovation is the provision for the conclusion of Association Agreements to upgrade the Partnership and Cooperation Agreements that have provided the legal basis for their contractual relations with the EU since the 1990s. In most respects they are very similar to the Europe Agreements which paved the way for the CEE states to achieve EU membership, but there is still no commitment to even a long-term perspective for accession. Ukraine and Georgia in particular were therefore bitterly disappointed and the return to power of the more pro-Russian President Viktor Yanukovich in February 2010 is at least partly attributable to disillusionment with the EU. However, the Eastern Partnership does offer the prospect of a deep and comprehensive free-trade area and gradual visa liberalization to enable easier travel to the EU for those states that meet the EU's conditions for 'well-managed and secure mobility' to curb the dangers of illegal immigration (Commission of the European Communities, 2008b, p. 7). It also provides for the first time a multilateral framework bringing together the six east European states and the EU in regular high-level meetings of ministers and senior officials to encourage cooperation on democracy and good governance, economic integration and convergence with EU sectoral policies, energy security and contacts between people. Although provision is made for the participation of third states 'on a case-by-case basis', the prospect of not necessarily participating in these meetings involving its immediate neighbours contributes to Russia's sense of exclusion, to be discussed below.

The outsiders: Turkey and Russia

In principle, neither Turkey nor Russia are outsiders as they both have very well-established and institutionalized relationships with both the EU and NATO. Turkey has been a member of NATO since 1952 and its geo-strategic position makes it an important and valued member of the alliance. It has had a contractual relationship with the EU since 1963 when it signed an association agreement which was understood at the time as marking the first step towards eventual accession. A customs union with the EU was established in 1995 and negotiations for full membership opened in 2005. Russia also has a highly institutionalized relationship with both NATO and the EU, although obviously much more recent than that of Turkey. The NATO–Russia Council was created in 2002 to provide a forum for high-level and regular consultation and there are regular meetings at political, parliamentary and official levels with the EU in a relationship described by both parties as a 'strategic partnership'.

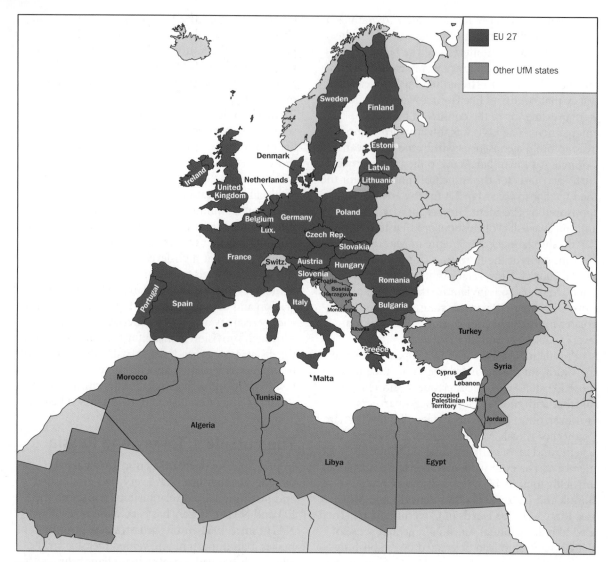

Map 3.4 The Union for the Mediterranean

Yet both states in many important respects seem to perceive themselves to be 'outsiders' and seem unlikely to be fully integrated into the emerging EU-centred European order. Part of the explanation can undoubtedly be found in doubts about their European identity both in policy circles and in public opinion in many European states (see Chapter 1). It is also significant that within both Turkey and Russia themselves there are debates as to whether they are 'really' or 'wholly' European or whether by virtue of geography, history and culture (with religion an important factor) their identities are more Eurasian. But it is also undoubtedly the case that both have a sense of rejection and grievance at not having been afforded the respect and consideration rightfully owed to them on the basis of their importance as major regional powers. Recently there have been signs that this frustration, together with a reappraisal of their strategic interests, has encouraged the strengthening of their bilateral relationship amid fears of an emerging 'axis of the excluded' (Hill and Taspinar, 2006).

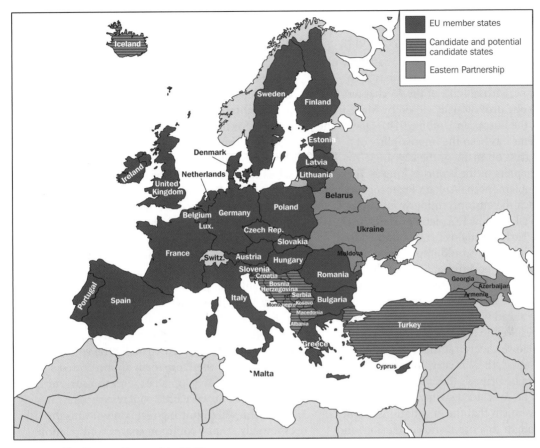

Map 3.5   The Eastern Partnership (EaP)

Turkey

Turkey applied for EU membership in 1987, several years before any of the new Central European members were able even to dream of such a possibility, and it has bitterly resented being overtaken by them in the accession process. The reason for this long delay in even opening negotiations with Turkey was officially its poor record on democracy and human rights, especially in relation to its Kurdish minority. But as time went on, it became clear that some people have more fundamental doubts about Turkey's eligibility for EU membership, questioning its European identity on both geographic and cultural/religious grounds. There are also fears about the implications of such a very large and very poor state becoming an EU member, such as its voting strength, its likely receipts from the budget and the number of migrant workers

who might exercise their right to free movement. However, the EU had made numerous clear commitments over the years that as soon as Turkey met the Copenhagen criteria, negotiations could begin. The 'golden carrot' of EU membership proved sufficiently attractive for the new government elected in 2002 to undertake some very fundamental reforms, described by the European Commission as constituting 'substantial legislative and institutional convergence in Turkey towards European standards' (Commission of the European Communities, 2004, p. 3). It therefore concluded that 'Turkey sufficiently fulfils the political criteria' and recommended opening negotiations (ibid., p. 9). However, in a move that may herald the end of the goal of 'one Europe', the Commission raised the possibility that a 'permanent safeguard clause' might be considered 'to protect serious disturbances of the EU labour market', in other words, excluding Turkey from one of the key freedoms of the single market (ibid., p. 5).

In December 2004 the European Council took the historic decision to open the negotiations with Turkey in October 2005 but progress has been extremely slow, with only 12 of the 35 chapters opened and one provisionally closed by May 2010 (Council of the European Union, 2010). One of the main problems has been the impossibility of making progress on many of the key single-market and trade chapters of the *acquis* as long as Turkey refuses to implement the Ankara Protocol agreed in 2005 by which the customs union would be extended to all the new EU member states, including Cyprus. Turkey remains firmly opposed to taking any action that would imply recognition of the Greek–Cypriot government and so the EU–Turkey relationship is at an *impasse*. As mentioned earlier, this is one unfortunate consequence of having gone ahead with the accession of Cyprus in May 2004 despite the rejection of the UN peace settlement. However, even if the Cyprus problem could be resolved, there is very little confidence in either Ankara or Brussels that the accession negotiations would be concluded swiftly. Indeed there is a growing pessimism that the negotiations might never be brought to a successful conclusion, and that even if they did, the necessary Accession Treaty would never be approved by all the EU member states. While the UK government remains committed to Turkey's accession, Germany and France are seen as particularly hostile to Turkey's EU aspirations and both Chancellor Merkel and President Sarkozy have advocated offering it a privileged partnership rather than full membership. The potential offer of what is seen as second-class membership increases the risk of Turkey taking on the role of an 'outsider', although a realist calculation of its national interests, particularly with regard to trade and tourism, is likely to prevent a major reorientation of its foreign policy perspective.

Russia

The problem with Russia is somewhat different, as it has never seriously expressed any interest in becoming an EU member. In its Medium-Term Strategy for Relations with the EU, the Russian government ruled out membership on the grounds

that 'as a world power situated on two continents it should retain its freedom to determine its own domestic and foreign policies'. It was greeted with considerable relief in Brussels and the hope is that it does not change its mind. Instead, Russia and the EU officially share the goal of creating a 'strategic partnership'. Precisely what this might mean was unclear for the first decade after the end of the Cold War, but at the St Petersburg Summit in 2003 the leaders of Russia and the EU committed themselves to work towards the creation of four common European spaces: economic, with a free-trade area as the goal; freedom, security and justice, involving cooperation between police and border authorities; external security, including counter-terrorism, non-proliferation and crisis management; and research, culture and education. Potentially this ambitious and comprehensive policy agenda would integrate Russia into all areas of European public life in much the same way as the ENP is intended to do so for the partner states. If it were to be achieved virtually the whole of Europe would therefore form an integrated social and economic area, on a par with the current EEA. However, so far very little concrete progress has been achieved in putting real content into the still essentially empty 'common spaces' and relations between the EU and Russia in recent years have been very strained.

There are a number of reasons for this situation. EU and particularly NATO enlargement up to the borders of Russia has generally increased its sense of encirclement and the prospects of further enlargement deeper into the post-Soviet space is an ongoing source of suspicion and resentment. Russia also believes that the new member states have at best complicated and at worst poisoned its relations with the EU, forming an anti-Russia bloc in the Council and European Parliament. It is undoubtedly true that almost all the new member states have inevitably brought a great deal of negative historical baggage to Brussels, especially Poland and the Baltic States, and have tried to upload their bilateral disputes with Russia on to the common EU–Russia agenda. In 2010 there were some optimistic signs of a rapprochement between Poland and Russia, especially arising from the publicly shared grief at the tragic plane crash which killed the President of Poland and much of the country's military and political elite while on their way to commemorate the Katyn massacre, one of the most sensitive legacies of the Second World War. However, it would probably be premature to assume that there will not be recurring problems involving the new member states and Russia.

Two areas where the new member states have been particularly active in trying to shape the post-enlargement agenda with Russia are human rights and good governance issues, both in Russia itself and in the 'colour revolutions' in Ukraine and Georgia, and generally pushing for a stronger and more supportive eastern policy for the eastern neighbours. Whereas some of the 'older' EU member states, notably Germany, France and Italy, have preferred to prioritize relations with Russia over support for the reformers in Ukraine or Georgia, the governments of Poland, Lithuania and other new member states have been their champions in EU policy-making fora. The new member states have also generally been among the most outspoken critics of political trends in Russia itself that were discussed earlier, and have resisted proposals that the EU should abandon its normative agenda towards Russia and pursue a more pragmatic approach.

Nowhere is Russia's fear of being cast as an 'outsider' greater than in the post-Soviet space along its western and southern borders. It has deep suspicions about the EU's motives with regard to what it calls its 'neighbourhood' and what Russia believes is its legitimate area of privileged interest. Russia therefore regards the ENP with great suspicion, believing that the EU is deliberately seeking to extend its civilizational reach into countries that it believes are by virtue of history, culture and economic interests its natural allies. Competition for influence over these 'in-between' countries are a challenge to the idea of 'one Europe' united on the basis of EU norms and values, with Russia hoping to offer an alternative model. Increasingly, Russia is challenging the claim that the EU equals Europe (EU-rope) and is trying to establish itself as a counterpoint.

However, despite these creative tensions, there is unlikely to be a rupture between Russia and Europe. Russian foreign policy is largely driven by realist calculations of national interest and there are signs also that EU policy-makers are prepared to adopt a more pragmatic and instrumental approach to Russia, accepting that it cannot expect to exert anything approaching the degree of leverage over a state like Russia that it has been used to with regards to small candidate states. There is a high degree of interdependence between Russia and the EU in terms of trade, energy supply and hard and soft security which makes the stakes too high to risk it becoming an 'outsider', and the more probable scenario is the continuation of a complex and challenging but nevertheless workable relationship.

Conclusion

As the quotation at the beginning of the chapter suggests, Europe today is very different from the Cold War period, when it was artificially divided into 'the West' and 'the East', and also from previous centuries, when 'bloody conflict' among its peoples seemed endemic. In many important respects, we do now 'live together as was never possible before', with a widespread consensus on core liberal democratic values and the expectation that conflicts will be resolved through negotiation rather than war. For the 500 million citizens of the EU, the goal of 'one Europe' has probably been largely achieved, although there is still very strong support for preserving and celebrating national and, indeed, regional differences within the Union. However, it is important to remember that there are a significant number of countries that remain outside the EU, either from choice or for other reasons considered in this chapter. For the citizens of these countries, the perception (and indeed the reality) is often that they belong to 'another' Europe, or in some cases they even feel they are outside Europe altogether. So although considerable progress has undoubtedly been made towards the achievement of 'one Europe', some significant obstacles still need to be overcome.

SUMMARY

- It was widely expected that the post-war division of Europe would be rapidly overcome once the communist systems had collapsed in Central and Eastern Europe. But the creation of 'one Europe' has taken longer and proven more difficult than many people had expected in 1990.

- Most of the former communist states set themselves the goal of 'returning to Europe', by which they meant embracing the liberal democratic political systems and market economies characteristic of the Western European states and joining the Council of Europe, NATO and the European Union.

- The rate of progress on political and economic transition has varied: the Central European and Baltic states were the most advanced and had achieved accession to both NATO and the EU by 2004. Bulgaria and Romania lagged behind but attained membership in 2007.

- The EU has committed itself to the eventual accession of all the states in the western Balkans once they meet its accession criteria. Negotiations with Turkey were opened in 2005, but it is by no means certain that it will ever become a full member. It has not yet been decided how far east the final borders of the EU should reach.

- The European Neighbourhood Policy is intended to reduce the danger of creating permanent 'outsiders' by developing a much closer relationship with the countries on its eastern and southern borders.

- Two states – Turkey and Russia – are potentially 'outsiders' while the position of others like Ukraine and Georgia has yet to be resolved.

QUESTIONS FOR DISCUSSION

- Why have some of the former communist states been more successful than others in making the transition to stable liberal democracies and market economies?

- Why do so many states want to join the EU? Are there any states that do not, and if so, why do they take that position?

- How has the EU used enlargement as a foreign policy instrument?

- Can the ENP mitigate the danger of drawing new dividing lines across Europe?

- Why is Turkey's application for EU membership so controversial?

- What place should Russia have in the new Europe?

- To what extent is there now 'one Europe'?

FURTHER READING

Ágh, Attila (1998) *The Politics of Central Europe* (London: Sage). A good analysis of political developments in the region, effectively combining discussion of conceptual and theoretical issues with much useful empirical information.

Cameron, Fraser (ed.) (2004) *The Future of Europe: Integration and Enlargement* (London: Routledge). An interesting collection of essays on some of the key issues arising from the 2004 EU enlargement.

DeBardeleben, Joan (2008) *The Boundaries of EU Enlargement: Finding a Place for Neighbours* (Basingstoke, Palgrave Macmillan).

Grabbe, Heather (2006) *The EU's Transformative Power: Europeanization through Conditionality in Central and Eastern Europe* (Basingstoke: Palgrave Macmillan). A detailed analysis of the leverage exercised by the EU over those states seeking membership by a former adviser to the European Commissioner for Enlargement.

Henderson, Karen (ed.) (1999) *Back to Europe: Central and Eastern Europe and the European Union* (London: UCL Press). A good introduction to enlargement issues from the perspective of both the candidate states and the EU.

Sasse, Gwendolyn (2008) 'The European Neighbourhood Policy: Conditionality Revisited for the EU's Eastern Neighbours', *Europe-Asia Studies* 60(2): 295–316.

Schimmelfennig, Frank, Stefan Engert amd Heiko Knobel (2006) *International Socialization in Europe:* *European Organizations, Political Conditionality and Democratic Change* (Basingstoke: Palgrave Macmillan).

Toje, Asle (2010) *The European Union as a Small Power: After the Cold War* (Basingstoke: Palgrave Macmillan).

Whitman, Richard G. and Wolff, Stefan (eds) (2010) *The European Neighbourhood Policy in Perspective: Context, Implementation and Impact* (Basingstoke: Palgrave Macmillan). Provides a very useful assessment of the overall strategy, as well as more detailed examination of key theoretical and conceptual themes and chapters on the empirical application of the policy in Eastern Europe, the Southern Caucasus, North Africa and the Middle East.

Zielonka, Jan (2007) *Europe as Empire: The Nature of the Enlarged European Union* (Oxford: Oxford University Press).

Also very useful are the EU official websites, where the key documents can be found, together with a great deal of other information:

For enlargement see http://ec.europa.eu/enlargement/

For the European Neighbourhood Policy see http://ec.europa.eu/world/enp/index_en.htm

For relations with Russia see http://ec.europa.eu/external_relations/russia/index_en.htm

The website of the Council of Europe is also helpful: http://www.coe.int/

CHAPTER 4

The European Union: the Challenge of Success

ANNE STEVENS

The founders of Europe envisaged a Europe that decided it would no longer make war on itself, no longer destroy itself, no longer massacre its young people in the ghastly mud of the trenches: a Europe that had learnt the lessons of a tragic history . . . The founders of Europe envisaged a Europe . . . which made, and won, a crazy bet that after the two most destructive wars of history, working together would cause peoples who hated each other to understand each other better, to respect each other more and perhaps even to like each other . . .

We need to rediscover this spirit for Europe . . .

We need to stop talking of Europe as something outside ourselves. Europe is not 'them'; Europe is us. If we do not make the effort to achieve change, it will not change all by itself.

Nicolas Sarkozy, speech in Nîmes, May 2009 (translated by the author)

Over the second half of the twentieth century and the first decade of the twenty-first the states, nations and societies of much of Europe came to work together and cooperate in very many ways (see also Chapters 2 and 3). This has created a new dimension to many of their activities that can be called the 'European dimension'. The links between states in Europe are closer and more dense than those between states in other regions of the world, and, with the ending of the sharp division of Europe, new patterns of relationship have emerged, with the disappearance of the networks that held the Soviet bloc together and the expansion and deepening of what were previously somewhat limited West European networks. The process through which this geometry has developed, known as European integration, cannot simply be regarded as involving a steady expansion of the European Union (EU), since its architecture and impact are neither simple nor uniform. The EU, even in its enlarged form and taking into account candidate countries, does not cover the whole of the continent of Europe (see Box 4.1), nor is it the only integrating body amongst the countries of the European continent.

Nevertheless the EU is the principal focus of the 'European dimension'. Taken as a whole, it is large: were it a single political entity it would, in its 2011 configuration of 27 member states, be the third largest in the world in population and the seventh in surface area (CIA, 2010; Eurostat, 2010). But (see below) the resilience of the member states, the architecture of the Union after the entry into force of the Lisbon Treaty and the existence of economic and monetary union, amongst other factors, point to complex and varied patterns of relationships within a political entity that is not a single political unit nor comparable to a nation state. This is not least because '[i]t unites states, but not on the basis of their traditional functions – defence, public order, justice, relations with foreign countries, budget – but on the basis of an element that is potentially external to the state, namely the market.' (Cassese, 2009, p. 1).This chapter sets out some of the major aspects of the current geometry and impact of the networks that constitute the (non-military) European dimension as well as the current state of the European Union which principally embodies it.

Integration: how and why?

As late as the end of the 1970s it could still be argued that it was precisely its 'cold war' division which ensured peace within Europe, and hence Western European prosperity (De Porte, 1979). However, the

BOX 4.1
The states of Europe

The exact dimensions of Europe are much disputed (see Chapter 1). For example, some would place Cyprus geographically wholly in Asia. The list opposite, utilizing a combination of geographical and political criteria, comprises 49 states, including four very small states which are nevertheless members of the Council of Europe and the United Nations (UN): Andorra, Liechtenstein, Monaco, San Marino and one, Vatican City, which is not. Belarus is a member of the UN but not of the Council of Europe. Of the 44 major states only nine (marked *) are not members, candidates or potential candidates for EU membership. This list does not include a number of European entities diplomatically recognized by some other countries but not generally recognized nor members of the UN. Of these the most notable is Kosovo, which the EU will accept as a potential candidate once it has achieved UN membership.

Albania	Denmark	Luxembourg	Slovakia
Andorra	Estonia	Macedonia	Slovenia
Armenia*	Finland	Malta	Spain
Austria	France	Moldova*	Sweden
Azerbaijan*	Georgia*	Monaco	Switzerland*
Belarus*	Germany	Montenegro	Turkey
Belgium	Greece	Netherlands	Ukraine*
Bosnia and	Hungary	Norway*	UK
Herzegovina	Iceland	Poland	Vatican City
Bulgaria	Ireland	Portugal	
Croatia	Italy	Romania	
Cyprus	Latvia	Russia*	
Czech	Liechtenstein	San Marino	
Republic	Lithuania	Serbia	

disappearance of the formal divisions that had shaped Europe and relationships between the European states since the late 1940s altered the balances and made the old patterns of alliance and enmity obsolete (see the speech by President Nicolas Sarkozy (Key Figure 4.1) quoted at the head of this chapter). 'Neutrality' ceased to have quite the same connotations, and it became more straightforward for states which, by choice or necessity, had jealously guarded their neutral position between east and west, such as Austria, Finland and Sweden, to participate in an unequivocally 'western' process of integration, while still remaining outside military alliances.

Equally, for many of the Central and Eastern European countries, admission to the organizations which had begun as mechanisms to link only Western European countries quickly became an important goal and the enlargements of 2004 and 2007 brought eight of them, alongside Cyprus and Malta, into the EU (see Table 3.1). In early 2011 five countries altogether (three from the Balkans – Croatia, Montenegro and the Republic of

Macedonia – as well as Iceland and Turkey) had the status of candidate countries and a further three (all from the Balkans – Albania, Bosnia and Serbia) had indicated their desire to join and were classed as potential candidates. In addition, the EU will accept Kosovo as a potential candidate once it has achieved UN membership.

In the case of the Mediterranean enlargement of the EU in the 1980s (when Spain, Portugal and Greece joined what was then the European Community) the states involved had all fairly recently emerged from a period of non-democratic government. Membership of the EU provided a confirmation of their status as fully-fledged democracies, and an external constraint on any tendency to revert to **autocracy**. Thus their engagement in the process of integration constituted an affirmation of their identity as autonomous nation-states. Much the same logic applies to the states of the former Soviet bloc and of former Yugoslavia, which joined

● **Autocracy**: Government by a single person having unlimited power.

Key Figure 4.1

Nicolas Sarkozy (1955–)

Nicolas Sarkozy is the son of a Hungarian immigrant to France and a French mother of Greek-Jewish extraction. He was raised as a Roman Catholic. He practised professionally as a lawyer, specializing in business law, and began his political trajectory quite young, at the age of 23, as a member of the Rassemblement pour la République (RPR), the centre-right party led by Jacques Chirac, as a municipal councillor in the wealthy Paris suburb of Neuilly-sur-Seine. In 1983, aged 28, he became its mayor. He was elected to the National Assembly in 1988. He became Minister for the Budget between 1993 and 1995 and in 1999, briefly leader of the RPR. The centre right was in opposition between 1997 and 2002 , but when Jacques Chirac was successful in the 2002 presidential election Sarkozy was appointed Minister of the Interior, despite having backed a centre-right rival of Chirac in the 1995 election. He became Minister of Finance in 2004, but briefly left the government between autumn 2004 and summer 2005, as he took over as leader of the Union pour un Mouvement Populaire (UMP), the party that Chirac had founded from the RPR and its allies to support his presidential bid in 1992. Sarkozy was elected President of France in 2007.

Sarkozy is a dynamic politician and orator, frequently controversial, and careful of his image. Press comment veers between according him status as a celebrity (he has divorced and remarried since his election to the presidency) or as a statesman. His response to the 2008 financial crisis has been broadly protectionist, calling for stronger regulation of financial markets. When France held the presidency of the EU in 2008 he took action to intervene diplomatically in the conflict between Russia and Georgia. He is publicly strongly opposed to Turkish accession to the EU. Faced with large numbers of refugees from North Africa transiting Italy to France in the spring of 2011 he took steps to close French borders, and called for the revision of the Schengen convention which allows free movement. As unemployment in France worsened in 2010 and changes to retirement ages and pension provisions were pushed through his popularity ratings plunged.

in 2004 or are candidates, for whom membership of the EU, as of NATO and other organizations, symbolizes autonomy and a move 'back to Europe' (Henderson, 1999). The EU has attempted to ensure that acceptance of the rules of the organization provides external constraints as extra guarantees of the consolidation of democracy, even if this 'conditionality' has proved to be more limited and constrained than many may have hoped.

The Cold War division of Europe had produced frameworks for cooperation in both Eastern and Western Europe, but very few which spanned the divide, one of the exceptions being the UN Economic Committee for Europe, concerned with monitoring and forecasting economic developments. Some of the bodies which took the place of the Soviet-dominated institutions in Eastern Europe, such as the Central European Free Trade

Association, were generally perceived as interim provisions pending EU membership. Some less ephemeral new bodies were created to encompass countries across the old divisions. For example, in the north, the 12-member Council of the Baltic Sea States (http://www.cbss.st), established in 1992, brought together the European Commission, all the Scandinavian countries, Germany, Poland, the Baltic Republics and Russia. Iceland joined in 1995. The CBSS is concerned with a wide range of matters including co-operation on public health, intra-regional trade, maritime safety and pollution, and police cooperation.

In addition to the creation of new bodies, the European dimension is also embodied in enlarged versions of longstanding bodies which had previously comprised only western countries. The Council of Europe (http://www.coe.int), founded in

1949, had brought together all the Western European states to work together through a framework of intergovernmental conventions, which are binding only upon those states which actually ratify them, and come into force only when a quorum of states have done so. The Council of Europe was one of the first West European organizations that the East European countries sought to join as they emerged from the shadow of the Soviet Union, and the Council was particularly active in promoting democratization. Its 47 members in 2010 include all those states west of the Urals which are members of the UN except Belarus (http://www.coe.int). It remains an important forum for wider patterns of cooperation. It has concluded (by the end of 2009) 207 conventions, of which 32 have not come into force. Most deal 'with low-key issues that facilitate public policy-making' (Laffan, 1992, p. 47), covering areas such as educational and cultural exchanges and developments and the conservation of the environment. The transnational nature of many increasingly serious issues, such as cybercrime (Convention on Cybercrime, CETS 185, which came into force in July 2004) or human trafficking (Council of Europe Convention on Action against Trafficking in Human Beings of May 2005, CETS 197, which came into force in February 2008), have made such arrangements particularly important. The Council of Europe cooperates with the EU and in 1989 the European Community (EC) was for the first time a signatory to a Council of Europe convention (on the elaboration of a European Pharmacopoeia) (Laffan, 1992, p. 47).

By far the most important of these conventions is the European Convention on Human Rights. An enforcement mechanism, with a European Court of Human Rights, which is binding on those states that have accepted it, considers complaints which allege that the Convention has been breached. Moreover the EU's European Court of Justice (based in Luxembourg, overseeing the enforcement of EU law and, it is important to note, quite separate from the Strasbourg-based European Court of Human Rights) accepts that the European Convention on Human Rights sets out the general principles of human rights, which ought to obtain in the cases that it tries. The EU Charter of Fundamental Rights, first endorsed by the EU

Heads of Government at Nice in 2000, and now included (with opt-outs and reservations in the case of the Czech Republic, Poland and the UK) in the Lisbon Treaty, incorporates the principles of the Convention.

The Organization for Economic Co-operation and Development (OECD – http://www.oecd.org) is the successor to the body that was set up on the demand of the USA to oversee the distribution of the 'Marshall aid' reconstruction funds that the USA made available in the 1940s to the West European states (Spain was excluded, and under Soviet influence the Central and East European states turned the offer down). Its membership, 30 in 2010, now includes countries from both East and West Europe and seven countries quite outside the continent, so it can be seen as having transformed itself into a body for the developed world as a whole.

The European dimension is also expressed through a number of more specialized agencies that promote cross-border cooperation. To take an example from the area of transport, the European Civil Aviation Conference, which until the early 1990s comprised only West European states, now has an expanded membership, which means that for the purposes of technical discussions on civilian air-transport matters Europe now extends from Reykjavik to Vladivostok. The grouping of countries (originally 29 in 1999) that have agreed to carry forward what is known as the Bologna Process for the creation of a European Higher Education Area now numbers 46: it includes the Vatican and extends as far east as Azerbaijan and Georgia (http://www.ond.vlaanderen.be/hogeronderwijs/bologna/about/).

The most comprehensive body embodying the European dimension is, however, the EU (see below). It was initially a West European product of the Cold War context. The first of the founding treaties of what is now the EU was the European Coal and Steel Community Treaty of 1951, between six states (Belgium, France, Germany, Italy, Luxembourg and the Netherlands). This was followed in 1957 by the Treaties, between the same six states, which created, from 1 January 1958, a European Economic Community (EEC) and a European Atomic Energy Community (Euratom) (see Box 4.2). Out of those beginnings the 27-member EU of the early twenty-first century has

BOX 4.2

Key points of the 1957 Treaty of Rome

- The free movement of goods, persons, services, and capital.
- A customs union and common external tariffs.
- Various Community policies (e.g. the Common Agricultural Policy, transport).
- Supervision by common institutions: the Council of Ministers, Commission, and Assembly (the future European Parliament).

evolved, to incorporate not only these initial areas of interest, but an extensive range of internal policies (including a monetary union of 16 of the states with a common currency (http://ec.europa.eu/economy_finance/euro/ – see below) and diplomatic, defence and security policies.

In the 1990s relationships within Europe, compared with those of the Cold War period, became more fragmented, more problematic, more uncertain. Despite the rhetoric of democratization, the role of the market and a **New World Order**, any easy euphoria about the changes was quite promptly dispelled (see Chapters 3 and 10). Problems of ethnic and territorial conflict, suppressed so often in Eastern Europe by the ideological and political straitjacket of Marxism–Leninism, came very rapidly onto the scene after 1990, in particular in the Balkans. The process of democratization and **marketization** in the former Soviet bloc turned out

---

● **New World Order**: A term used by President H. George Bush at the end of the Cold War which called for a world governed by international law, the respect of human rights and the renewed authority of the United Nations.

● **Marketization**: The move from central planning to a market economy in which the economic forces of supply and demand would determine what was produced and the price at which it would be sold. The key reforms required are price liberalization, privatization, restructuring and the adoption of an effective competition policy.

---

to be frequently accompanied by opportunism, profiteering and corruption and by organized crime that pays little attention to national frontiers. The rationale for integration now became one of managing the new relationships.

Further acute challenges to cohesion and the integration process arose during the first decade of the twenty-first century: these included the wars in Iraq and Afghanistan, the economic crisis (See Chapter 8) and the long process of negotiation and ratification of what became the Lisbon Treaty, which revealed different approaches to the 'European project', including outright hostility. In the changing context it rapidly became clear that the institutions that had been developed by the 1990s to provide a framework of cooperation among Western European states in the context of the Cold War, including the EU, now provide a basis on which to manage the new links and networks.

The resilience of the nation-state

The European dimension is thus a patchwork of relationships, embodied in a range of organizations of varying scope and influence, some highly political and others largely technical. In many cases participation in these organizations springs from clear technical incentives and they function by consensus. The EU is different: from the start it was not just a functional project, but embodied a fundamentally political design, expressed institutionally through its voting procedures and through the new legal order it created, giving its decisions binding force (Grabbe and Sedelmeier, 2009, p. 376). Partly as a consequence, many member states, however, continue to have a paradoxical relationship with the EU, and the rationale of membership of the Union as contributing to the protection, indeed advancement, of vital national, as opposed to collective, interests remains a powerful one. 'European integration', one of its foremost scholars concludes, 'has not been a preordained movement towards federal union but a series of pragmatic bargains among national governments based on concrete national interests, relative power, and carefully calculated transfers of sovereignty'(Moravcsik, 1998, p. 427).

Member states, while they have from the first

been willing to pool their own sovereignty in areas where this offers clear advantage, or where issues obviously cross boundaries, have thus been notably unwilling to do so where the issues are nationally – and hence electorally – highly sensitive. The Treaties that they have accepted ensure that the EU can only act through its legislative powers in those areas where powers are specifically conferred upon it. Resistance to pooling takes a number of forms. There has been a simple refusal to allow the extension of the EU system to cover certain areas: most aspects of taxation policy, national social security, educational provision and health care are simply excluded from the competence of the EU. Many countries have such 'red-line areas', and the maintenance of them has been a major area of bargaining and contention in treaty negotiations since the late 1990s. Equally resistance may be partial, involving the insistence that legislation and decisions in certain areas will always require unanimity. In the interests of effective decision-making in a much enlarged Union attempts have been made to reduce the number of areas to which unanimity applies, but Poland along with a number of smaller member states, ensured that the Treaty of Lisbon contained some ongoing limitations on the likelihood that smaller states will be outvoted. Another form of resistance is the achievement by any particular country of an opt-out from Treaty provisions which it cannot accept (see below).

All the major powers have sought to shape the Union in ways that will enhance their national interests. For several decades France consistently assumed, in both policy-making structures and in approach, that the EC and now the EU provides a mechanism 'constructed on the idea that a larger economic entity would be more capable of defending itself against external economic aggression' (Picq, 1995, p. 145) for the expression of French ideas and the protection of French interests on a wider stage – that is, that it is traditional French **protectionism** writ large. In contrast, for the UK governments in the 1980s and 1990s the essence of EU membership was the extension to a wider

sphere of the deregulation being implemented in the UK, with concomitant opportunities for competitive goods and services.

The discrepancies between the varied popular perceptions of the nature and purpose of the EU to be found within the different member states, and between those perceptions and the collective logic of the institutions, underlie some of the recent debates and conflicts around this element of the European dimension. In the first place, as such discrepancies have emerged, disaffection with the integration process has developed. In France, for example, through the 1990s, 'the feeling came up that too much integration ran counter to more immediate French interests' (Balme and Cornelia, 2005, p. 104). This manifested itself notably in the referendum of 1992 which approved the Treaty of Maastricht by only a tiny majority, and again in 2005 with the rejection of the proposed Constitutional Treaty by a slightly larger referendum majority. The confidence which a significant proportion of the French electorate had placed in the European dimension as providing a 'European social model' that would produce solutions to economic difficulties and unemployment had dissipated (Ivaldi, 2006, p. 34). In the Netherlands, where the Constitutional Treaty was similarly rejected at the same time, '[t]he strongest impact on voting "no" came from a perceived threat from the EU to Dutch culture' (Lubbers, 2008, p. 59). The rejection of the Constitutional Treaty resulted in the production of a new Treaty, signed at Lisbon in 2007, but its entry into force was delayed until 1 December 2009 as a consequence of an initial rejection in an Irish referendum, overturned by a further referendum in October 2009, and by resistance from the president of the Czech Republic.

If France and the UK offer the most prominent examples of EU members who have sought to shape the EU to their own liking, recent years have also seen a marked shift in attitude of the German government. From the beginning of the integration process and until after the turn of the century German leaders insisted that German and European unity '"were two sides of the same coin" . . . only by reassuring Germany's neighbours that Germany had changed and was utterly devoted to integrating itself into Europe could the Germans hope to achieve their national goal: the reunifica-

---

● **Protectionism**: The use of trade barriers such as tariffs, taxes, technical rules and invisible barriers in order to protect a state's economy from imports.

tion of Germany in peace and freedom. It worked' (Timothy Garton Ash, *Economist*, 3–9 April 2010). But the price was the highly unpopular abandonment of the Deutschmark for the euro, which nevertheless failed to catalyse the closer political integration across the whole EU which many assumed would be the consequence. And Germany has, as demonstrated, for example, by its bilateral deal with Russia to secure its energy needs, and by its response to the debt crisis in Greece in early 2010, become just like other member states, determined to secure its own interests, with its public opinion 'not prepared to make any more sacrifices for the sake of "Europe"' (Garton Ash, 2010).

Reactions such as these serve to underline the continuing tensions within the processes of European integration. On the one hand national populations are firmly attached to aspects of their national political and social culture, and to the notion that their destinies are in the hands of their national leaders. On the other hand are the dynamics of the single market, of monetary union, of EU regulation – which seeks to set a single framework for much economic and social activity in the interests of competitiveness and of the political norms which apply not only to applicants but also (as in the case of Austria in 2000 when the other 14 members of the EU attempted to impose diplomatic isolation in reaction to the entry into government of an extreme right party) to existing members (Bulmer and Radaelli, 2005, pp. 339–40).

Institutional architecture and decision-making in the institutions of the EU

The institutions of the EU have evolved to handle the tensions described above, and the increase both in the number of member states and in the scope and range of EU concerns. The institutions of the EU have remained broadly constant in shape since the start: in formal terms the architecture of the current organization is markedly similar to that of the 1952 Coal and Steel Community, differing, however in the existence of some new bodies (including, for example, the Committee of the Regions, the Court of Auditors, the Community Agencies, the Ombudsman) and in some differences

in the manner of designation (a directly elected, not nominated, Parliament, Commissioners approved by Parliament). In terms of their dynamics – functions, powers, and role within the decision-making process – they have, however, changed and evolved. The result is a somewhat bewildering complexity, which tends to hinder efforts at transparency and democracy. This is not assisted by the impenetrable nature of some of the key documents. When an attempt was made, in the so called Constitutional Treaty, to bring together and codify the legal basis for the EU, the result was a complex document of well over 300 pages, which may well have contributed to its referendum defeats. Its successor, the Treaty of Lisbon, consists of provisions which amend and extend previous treaties, rendering it peculiarly obscure, although the EU has published a consolidated version of the major treaties.

The EU institutions

The EU is now a single body with a single legal personality: the 'pillared' structure which existed between 1992 and 2009 has gone. The senior body of the EU, the European Council, which consists of the heads of government (in the case of France the President, who is head of state) of the member states has now been clearly established as a formal institution meeting four times a year, and given its own chairman, the President of the Council of Ministers, with a two-and-a-half-year term of office. The first holder of this post is the Belgian Herman van Rompuy. The European Council's main role is to guide the development of the EU and its policies, to set priorities and strategic aims, and to resolve, at the highest level, disputes which cannot be settled elsewhere. It does not have legislative or executive powers. The role of the other institutions is to formulate policy, to express it in decisions or in legislation, and to oversee the implementation of policy and legislation and the identification, and where necessary punishment, of breaches of the law. The Council of the European Union, usually known as the Council of Ministers, is a body which, although legally a single institution, takes a large variety of different forms, since it usually meets as a specialized group of ministers from each of the member states dealing with any specific policy area. It shares in the legislative process with the European Parliament, making decisions primarily by voting through a system of weighted votes (qualified majority voting – QMV: as a consequence of the Lisbon Treaty new weightings will apply from 2014 (Council of the European Union, 2009)). The meetings are normally chaired by a minister from the country whose turn, on a six-monthly rota basis, it is to preside, so that each member state will hold office once between 2007 and 2020 (Council Decision 2007/5/EC). Since 2006 the Council's procedural rules have, in the interests of continuity, required that three successive presidency countries draw up an 18-month work programme: the first such trio was Germany, Portugal and Slovenia for 2007–8, and the first under the Lisbon Treaty arrangements was Spain, Belgium and Hungary. However, the Foreign Affairs Council is chaired by the person holding the appointment of High Representative of the European Union for Foreign Affairs and Security Policy who is simultaneously an officer of the Council and a Commissioner. The first holder of this combined post is Baroness Catherine Ashton.

The other central institutions are the European Commission (see below), the European Parliament, the European Court of Justice (ECJ), the European Court of Auditors and the European Central Bank. The term 'the European Commission' refers both to the College (board) of (currently 27) Commissioners and to the administrative staff who support them. The Commission elaborates policy, proposes the necessary legislation, has important powers of secondary legislation and implementation in some fields, such as agriculture and coal and steel, and has quasi-judicial functions in some regulatory areas, such as the control of large-scale trans-European company takeovers and mergers. The Parliament debates, considers and advises, and exercises quite extensive powers of decision and veto (see below). The ECJ can deal directly with cases involving the Union's institutions, but its main role is in providing authoritative guidance on the interpretation of Union law to the national courts who have the duty of seeing that it is applied. Through its interpretation and application of legislation, the ECJ has at times played a major role in the development of the EC's scope and powers and the balance of its institutions. In the first three decades of the Communities the ECJ did reinforce the authority and supranational character of the EU, and the priority to be given to the achievement of integration, through a number of forceful interpretations of Community Law and it has continued to play a crucial role.

The other institutions are the Court of Auditors, which has an essentially supervisory role, and the independent European Central Bank, which manages the euro and runs the monetary policy for the common currency. There are two advisory bodies, the Economic and Social Committee and the Committee of the Regions.

The dynamics of European Union processes: decision-making and democracy

The EU now has a range of functions and of methods for achieving them. However, the production of law is the key means to achieving its aims, and remains central to its activities. Law can either be so-called 'hard law' – legally binding regulations, directives or decisions – or 'soft law' – such as reports, recommendations or opinions. The mode of production of this law has long given rise to the claim that there is inadequate democratic control. In response to this there has been considerable change in the recent past. In the early years of the EU the fact that the actual drafting of many proposals was undertaken by an unelected Commission, whilst the determination of the final details took place essentially in secret negotiations between the member states within the framework of the Council of Ministers, helped to support this notion. That the national ministers involved were each in fact potentially accountable to their own national parliaments, at least to the extent that their national arrangements provided for accountability, was little remarked, and governments may have preferred to hide behind the smokescreen of 'Europe' to justify unpopular measures that they nevertheless favoured. Moreover, the European Parliament, in most instances, had, until the 1990s, a purely consultative role.

There have been important changes, most notably since the Amsterdam Treaty in 1997 and the Lisbon Treaty in 2009. The so-called 'co-decision' procedure, which gives the Parliament and the

Council of Ministers an equal say in legislation, has now been extended to almost all legislative proposals. Effectively this means that the two bodies must negotiate the details of legislation: so the European Parliament can propose amendments which it must then persuade the Council to adopt, and can – though it rarely does – veto bills if they are unacceptable. The procedures are undeniably complex, and often act essentially as a threat or an inducement. The knowledge that the powers are there and could be used is sufficient to produce compromise. The negotiations within the Council of Ministers remain largely confidential: governments seeking to arrive at mutually acceptable accommodations do not often want to display their hands to their partners, let alone their national political opponents and potentially hostile domestic media. The Lisbon Treaty provides for the meetings at which laws are finally adopted to be public via direct television, but by the time that the proposals have reached this stage the proceedings are almost entirely formal. It remains the case that, partly because of the complexity of the procedures, the very real potential powers of Members of the European Parliament – arguably greater than those of any national MP within a well-disciplined party system – are frequently underestimated, and national ministers are very seldom held seriously to account for what they do in Brussels.

Within the context of resilient national states described above, of dissatisfaction with perceived lack of democracy, and of a sense that legislative powers were leaching away from national Parliaments, measures were taken by a protocol attached to the Treaty of Lisbon to enhance the role of national Parliaments within the system, by ensuring that proposals from various EU institutions are sent to them directly and giving them eight weeks to indicate if they think that the proposal infringes the '**subsidiarity**' principle – that action should be taken by the EU only on the bases both that it cannot be done by member states acting alone, and

that it can be better done by the EU. This rather vague notion has been incorporated in the Treaties since Maastricht, and is politically crucial in persuading citizens that what is occurring is a pooling, not a surrender, of sovereignty. If a third of the national parliaments do object then the proposal must be reviewed and reasons supplied if it is not withdrawn. If these new powers are to operate effectively national parliaments will need to be well organized and they do not allow national parliaments to alter specific details, which is what their electorate may expect. Moreover, like the ultimate powers of the European Parliament, these procedures are likely to have an effect more by inducing proponents of proposals to be careful in their propositions than by actually being utilized.

A further gesture to counterbalance the view that the EU is remote and undemocratic is the introduction of 'citizens' initiatives' – petitions which will require the Commission to introduce legislative proposals if requested to do so by a million citizens coming from across at least one-third of the member states. 'But these are not binding, EU-wide referendums or, failing that, Californian-style popular initiatives that could lead to binding referendums, . . . [They] can only place an idea on the agenda, not actually oblige the commission to do anything' (Charlemagne, *Economist*, 31 March 2010). For its proponents 'the citizens' initiative carries risks of populism . . . but it is worth having if it "helps with the birth of true European political networks"' (ibid.). However, the procedures for producing such a petition in due legal form seem likely to be burdensome, and it is not clear that pan-European movements will emerge rapidly in a highly differentiated and fragmented EU. Decision-making and democratic processes within the EU have changed and developed, with ongoing attempts to make them more patently democratic. However, the various balances that have to be struck between operational effectiveness and transparency, between the interests of member states and the desire for cooperation, between the various institutions of the EU, between governments and their citizens, all add up to a complex system, which, because it is different from anything else, is often poorly understood. This is equally the case in relation to the modes of policy-making which are considered in the next section.

● **Subsidiarity**: The principle, developed from Roman Catholic social thought, that public policy decisions should be made, and action taken, at as low a level and as close to the citizen as possible. It is enshrined in the Treaty of European Union, which requires that the Community act only if, and in so far as, the desired objectives cannot be sufficiently achieved by the member states. Some argue that the principle also requires devolution from central to local government.

Key Figure 4.2

Jean Monnet (1888–1979)

French economist, statesman and 'father of Europe'. In the First World War he coordinated Franco-British war supplies, and was later appointed Deputy Secretary-General of the League of Nations. During the Second World War he acted as a senior official in the British Supply Council for war purchases in the USA and in 1943 he helped to form the French Committee of National Liberation. In 1946, backed by de Gaulle, Monnet launched a five-year investment and modernization plan to rebuild the French economy. In 1950, together with French Foreign Minister Robert Schuman, he produced the Schuman Plan, from which the European Coal and Steel Community (ECSC) and the European Economic Community (EEC) were subsequently developed. Monnet was president of the ECSC High Authority from 1952 to 1955, whereupon he set up the Action Committee for the United States of Europe (ACUSE), intended to bring together leaders of political parties and labour unions in the cause of European unification.

The dynamics of European Union processes: the Community method and the role of the Commission

As Helen Wallace has pointed out (Wallace, 2005, pp. 74ff.), the processes of the EU now operate in several different modes, depending upon the political and institutional context. The classic model was the so-called 'Community method'. This allots a central role to the European Commission. In very many areas it alone has the right to lay before the Council of Ministers the text that, if agreed, would become European Community law. Ideas and proposals for such laws come from many sources, including the European Council, the Council of Ministers and the European Parliament, and not just from within the Commission. Indeed less than 20 per cent of Community legislation derives from new proposals from the Commission (Bomberg, Cram and Martin, 2003, p. 49) but legislative measures are worked up by the services of the Commission, and the Commission controls their priority and progress. So it can be described as an 'agenda-setter'. The Commission has also been described as a 'broker of interests' and as a 'purposeful opportunist' (Cram, 1999, p. 48), its purpose frequently being to extend its scope for action and increase the range of matters dealt with through the processes of integration.

The Commission can trace its antecedents back to the High Authority of the European Coal and Steel Community, the body that was given executive responsibility by the Treaty of Paris to propose and implement policy for the coal and steel sector. Given the restricted and relatively technical policy area in which the High Authority operated it was feasible for it to be designed as a body of selected experts (Radaelli, 1999, p. 4), who would be able to discern the 'best' policy. As Jean Monnet (see Key Figure 4.2), who designed the system, perceived it (Peterson and Bomberg, 1999, p. 232), they would gradually draw the affected groups in society into involvement in making the 'right' decisions. Once this system was seen to be working well in one sector there would be pressure for it to be applied also to other areas, and in this way integration would gradually spread outwards, through the processes known as *engrenage* (enmeshing) and spillover. In such a system political visions and choices become almost irrelevant, and the Council of Ministers something of an afterthought.

Until the late 1990s the Commission, especially under the charismatic leadership of Jacques Delors between 1985 and 1994, retained a very prominent role as the 'engine' of the process of integration. One consequence of the increased range of affairs with which the EU deals, of the increased size of the College, and of the legacy of past Commission Presidents, especially Jacques Delors, has been a growing role for the President of the College, as a leader and figurehead (Kurpas, Grøn, and Kaczy ski, 2008). However the overall position of the Commission has since altered in several ways.

- Public perception of its legitimacy and competence have been damaged by the mismanagement which led to the resignation of the whole Commission in 1999, and by a persistent trickle of allegations of scandal and fraud.
- Enlargement of the Union has increased the size of the Commission which has, in any case, partly in response to the 1999 events, been reinventing itself. Its administration has undergone substantial internal reform, while the College of Commissioners is 'younger, more flexible and more "presidential"' even if its role 'has not been fundamentally altered by enlargement': rather this has 'reinforced the impact of other secular changes' (Best, Christiansen, and Settembri, 2009, p. 114)).
- Since much of the major work on completing the single market has been done, and with the post-enlargement renewal of the Commission, there has been an emphasis on less (if better) regulation (ibid.). This focus leaves somewhat less scope for Commission activism: whilst the legislative activity of the Barroso Commission in its first few years was roughly comparable with that of its predecessor, only a quarter of its proposals were for entirely new measures rather than amendments to existing laws, compared with well over a third of the proposals made in the comparable period of its predecessor (Kurpas et al. 2008).
- Some apparently technical measures such as the registration, evaluation, authorization and restriction of chemicals (REACH) regulation, which came into force in 2007, proved highly controversial: despite considerable efforts at consultation by the Commission it was eventually members of the European Parliament who succeeded in brokering a compromise (Watson and Shackleton, 2008, p. 106). As a consequence of this and of the need to adapt to a much larger College of Commissioners since 2004 the Commission has tended to eschew controversy, produced more reports and recommendations and fewer legislative proposals and shown 'an apparent reluctance to present proposals on sensitive matters' (Kurpas et al., 2008, p. 48).
- The focus of movement towards integration has shifted towards security, defence, external relations and reactions to globalization, all areas in which, since they came formally within the purview of the EU after 1992, decision-making methods in which the Commission is not central (see below) have predominated.
- The major problems confronting the EU at the end of the first decade of the twenty-first century, such as the scope of enlargement and the economic crisis after 2008, have seemed to demand fundamentally political responses: it is the role of the European Council to provide these. For example, in the discussions in the spring of 2010 about measures to be taken to avert major crises arising from the Greek deficit, the president of the European Commission, José-Manuel Barroso, found himself 'away from the heart of the action' and 'sidelined' (*European Voice*, 1 April 2010).

Whilst a 'college' with one or (in the case of the large member states until 2004) two members of each nationality may have worked well with six member states, this formation has become increasingly problematic with successive enlargements: the second Barroso Commission (2010 to 2014) consists of 27 members. Since, despite the requirement that all commissioners should be independent of national influence, all member states have perceived it to be of value to have 'their' commissioner(s) in the college, proposals to reduce numbers have proved hard to swallow. The Lisbon Treaty provides, from 2014, for a college of two-thirds as many members as there are member states, with each country to be equally represented on a rota basis. However, largely to appease the Irish, for whom this was a crucial issue in their two ratification referendums, the European Council has decided, as the Treaty entitles them to if they act unanimously, not to implement this.

The administration is divided into departments, known as Directorates-General, each looking after a specific policy area, plus a number of specialized services, such as the interpreting and conference service and the statistical service. Each Commissioner has responsibility for one or more of these areas and is supported in his or her tasks by an extended private office (*cabinet*).

The President of the Commission and the High Representative are nominated by the European Council and then elected by the European Parliament. The remaining member states then nominate their Commissioner in consultation with the President-elect. All the nominees are then called to hearings before the Parliament. Even when there are misgivings about an individual, the Parliament can only ratify or reject the team as a whole. However, in both 2004 and 2009 the President-elect was obliged to negotiate changes in the team with the nominating governments in order to avoid the whole team being voted down. While some 80 per cent of the members of the post-1967 European Commissioners have been career politicians before their appointment to the College (Hix, 1999, pp. 35–6), they have come from a broad spectrum of the mainstream political parties from Left to Right. The College thus does not come into office on the basis of any defined or agreed political programme, and is not necessarily a very coherent team. Although the Commission is responsible for proposing policy developments and detailed policy measures, sometimes at the behest of either the European Council or the Council of Ministers, it is not like a national government, even a coalition government, in terms of programme or ideology.

Nor, despite the requirement for initial ratification by Parliament, is it like a national government in terms of accountability. The Parliament has the power to force the collective dismissal of the whole college, though on the only occasion when the Commission as a whole has resigned (the Santer Commission in 1999) it was in response to a highly critical report from a committee of independent experts set up by the Parliament, rather than a vote of no-confidence. The Members of the European Parliament (MEPs) can ask Commissioners questions. But the College of Commissioners never has to face the electorate, its priorities and programmes are not the outcome of a popular mandate, and it can seem remote from democratic processes and public opinion. The impression of a democratic

deficit in the classic 'Community method' was, moreover, enhanced until the 1990s by the process for determining the final details of legislation described above.

Other modes of policy-making

From the late 1980s onwards the dynamics of policy-making have shifted and other modes of policy production have emerged to complement the Community method. One is policy coordination, and specifically the 'open method of coordination' developed since the late 1990s to encourage member states to compare their performance and policies in areas such as economic, employment and social policy (Wallace, 2005, p. 85). This method involves a framework for political cooperation with common objectives, agreement on indicators for the success of those objectives and a degree of monitoring of member states' progress in achieving them. Thus in the area of social welfare the Commission states that it aims to encourage member states, amongst other goals, to combat poverty and social exclusion and to tackle the problems likely to be posed by ageing societies, and to report regularly upon their activities (European Commission: Employment, 2010). The intention is to identify successful policies and encourage processes of policy-learning between member states. This has the effect of intensifying networks between experts, national officials, and Commission officials as experts and monitors. The outcome of this method is not law, but non-binding recommendations and targets.

A third mode of policy dynamic alongside the Community method and the coordination method is what has been called 'intensive transgovernmentalism' (Wallace, 2005, p. 87). This terminology indicates that this mode (as compared with looser intergovernmentalism found in other bodies such as the Council of Europe; see above) involves a relatively close, intense and structured level of cooperation. It involves coordination and agreement (which usually has to be unanimous) between the member states, using the mechanisms of the Council of Ministers, but involving the Commission only marginally and the Parliament not at all. This was the mode chosen in the early

1990s for foreign and security policy and also for justice and home affairs. Although the Lisbon Treaty has brought almost all of the latter area under the Community method (with an opt-out for the UK, Denmark and Ireland), common foreign and security policy remains within the transgovernmental mode.

Towards a 'Europeanized' Europe?

Although other regions of the world are developing networks of connections in both the military and civilian (especially trading) areas, Europe is distinguished by the extent of the cooperation which has developed. With the ending of the Cold War the dual structures of the previous 40 years have been superseded by more all-embracing networks, modelled on the West European patterns. Of the states west of the Urals only Belarus is not a party to the European Convention on Human Rights and a member of the Council of Europe and as Table 6.1 shows, only six (excluding the micro-states), the most notable being Georgia, Russia and Ukraine, remain uncommitted to either the EU, or NATO or both. The extent and density of these relationships have led some commentators to speak of Europeanization. The concept is used in different ways but essentially seeks to capture the notion that these relationships have consequences: ways of ordering society and implementing policy develop which reflect 'European' norms, expectations and best practices. The process may be seen as benign, pulling all countries up to the level of the best. It can equally be seen as malign, threatening to subsume individuality, identity and national culture into a homogenous and undifferentiated mass. It may be seen as simply one aspect of a much wider globalization which is affecting trade, manufacturing, consumption (both material and cultural) and identity worldwide, or alternatively as a specifically European defence against such tendencies and a protection as new world powers – China, perhaps India – arise alongside the USA. What is undisputed is that membership of these networks imposes new rights, obligations and responsibilities upon the countries involved. The fact of being enmeshed in a network of European institutions has inevitably affected the behaviour and reactions of the national governments involved. The dense pattern of contacts and interactions ranges from those in which decision-making is fairly informal, such as regular bilateral meetings between heads of government, through the more formalized arenas of the intergovernmental organizations, to the EU, with its complex structures and procedures that can make laws which apply directly to every citizen.

The processes of negotiation, coordination and often compromise which are involved in such policy-making have had a number of effects to which governments have had to adapt. As noted above, one governmental reaction has been to attempt to use the scope offered by the European level to seek to extend national policies into a wider field. A second effect has been to force politicians to confront and agree to actions and decisions that they might not otherwise have taken. At both its creation in the late 1950s and its relaunch in the 1980s governments looked to the European Community to have a galvanizing effect upon industry and commerce and to induce necessary modernization. An example of this is the changes introduced to Italian budgetary and financial policy in the 1990s so that Italy could fulfil the conditions for participation in the single currency. In a country where achieving sufficient agreement between a multiplicity of political parties and factions to achieve radical reform is often well-nigh impossible, civil servants and experts could appeal to rationality and necessity, since the overall aim of maintaining Italy's position in 'Europe' was accepted by all (Radaelli, 1999, pp. 2–3).

However, the processes of Europeanization are not in fact uniform and certainly do not proceed at the same speed everywhere. Various factors affect the pace of Europeanization, including the operation of opt-outs and conversely of enhanced cooperation, and equally the operation of conditionality and conversely problems of implementation, including corruption. These are discussed in the next sections of this chapter

Opt-outs and enhanced cooperation

A key aspect of the initial European Community approach to closer integration and one of the main features of its nature and originality from the beginning was that it should be not merely an

international institution but **supranational**. Policy should be expressed in legislation binding on all the member states, even if they had voted against it in the Council of Ministers. However, since the early 1990s and the creation of the EU, pragmatic but complex political responses have emerged to the challenges presented by some of the broader variations in the political and economic circumstances of member states stretching from north of the Arctic Circle to the Mediterranean and constituting a EU of ever-increasing scope. First, as we have seen above, new modes of policy-making have emerged. Secondly, during the negotiation of the Maastricht Treaty the other member states, tacitly acknowledging irreconcilable ideological differences (which disappeared after the Labour victory in the UK election of 1997, so that the opt-out was abandoned), deserted the supranational principle by permitting the UK to exclude itself from the operation of the social policy chapter attached to the TEU. Equally, it was explicitly recognized during the Maastricht negotiations that the Economic and Monetary Union (EMU), despite being seen as a key stage in the achievement of integration, would not involve all the member states. 'Not every country would be economically able, and no country would be politically forced, to join the currency union at the outset' (Dinan, 1994, p. 177; see Box 4.3). Thus, when the EMU came into existence on 1 January 1999 Denmark, Sweden and the UK had chosen not to participate, a choice they have so far maintained.

In general, however, the member states have, however, been unwilling to envisage the 'pick-and-mix' approach of using opt-outs, which, indeed, have only been applied to existing member states and only in circumstances when they have seemed

to be the unavoidable price of the overall forward movement involved in a new Treaty. Thus the Lisbon Treaty allows for the continuation of Danish opt-outs in the area of justice and home affairs, and allows for the UK and Ireland to opt out of common policies on asylum, visas and immigration. Similarly a protocol to the Treaty applicable only to the UK and Poland (and to be extended to the Czech Republic) states clearly that the Charter of Fundamental Rights, which is given legal status by the Treaty, does not independently create any rights in those countries that are not provided for by national law. However, whilst some flexibility on membership terms has been seen as essential for the ongoing development of the EU, it has not been recognized for non-member states that wish to join. The Copenhagen criteria for the accession of new member states made it clear that a willingness to adhere to all the Union policies was required and the adoption of all the currently existing EU legislation (the *acquis communautaire*). This is no light matter: at the end of the 2000s some 35 chapters are required to cover the key topics for enlargement negotiations (*Hansard*, 16 January 2007, written answer 113827), and in 2009 the Commission suggested that reducing it by nearly ten per cent would involve the repeal of 1300 measures (Commission Press release MEMO/09/31, 28 January 2009).

Thus, for example, the compromises made available to the UK, Denmark and Sweden on membership of the EMU were not on offer to new member states joining in 2004 and 2007, and they were obliged to undertake to work towards joining the Common currency, even if they could not actually do so, until they fulfil the economic criteria. Since 1999 five states have joined – one pre-2004 member (Greece – which was assumed to have met the criteria by 2001, even if it has subsequently been suggested that complex financial mechanisms were used to conceal the size of its deficit (*Observer*, 28 February 2010)) and four new members: Cyprus, Malta, Slovakia and Slovenia.

● **International intergovernmental institutions**: organizations set up by agreement among a number of countries for specific purposes, serviced by a secretariat and capable of taking decisions on behalf of their members. However, these decisions are only binding on the member states if they agree to and accept them.

● **Supranational institutions**: bodies which resemble international intergovernmental institutions but differ from them in that their members have agreed, in specified cases, to be bound by their decisions when these have been legally arrived at – for example by some form of majority voting – even if the member does not agree or voted against the proposal.

● *Acquis communautaire*: A French term which roughly translates as 'what the European Community has achieved'. It consists of all the legislation (decisions, directives and regulations) passed by the EC/EU since its creation and the judgements of the court which together make up EU law.

BOX 4.3

The 'Maastricht criteria' for membership of the common European currency

- An average inflation rate not exceeding by more than 1.5 percentage points that of the three member states with the lowest inflation rates.
- A budget deficit of less than 3 per cent of GDP.
- A public debt ratio of not more than 60 per cent of GDP.
- Participation in the European Exchange Rate Mechanism (ERM) for at least two years 'without severe tensions'.
- An average long-term nominal interest rate not exceeding by more than 2 percentage points that of

the three member states with the lowest inflation rates.

See http://europa.eu/legislation_summaries/other/l25014_en.htm.

These criteria were mitigated by a number of qualifications – for example, government debt could exceed 60 per cent of GDP if it were diminishing steadily and fast enough. The final decision on eligibility was both a political and an economic one.

Similar arrangements have operated for border controls and visa policies. Agreement on this took the form, in 1985 and 1990, of international conventions between five countries named after the town where they were signed, Schengen in Luxembourg, to which other countries subsequently signed up. Since all the initial five were members of the EU, in 1997 the Amsterdam Treaty incorporated these conventions into the EU and took the administration, previously a separate international secretariat, into EU hands. The Treaty of Lisbon reshapes the provisions under the general heading 'Area of Freedom, Security and Justice'. All subsequent new members of the EU, once they meet certain conditions, have been brought into these arrangements, now regarded as part of the *acquis*, which allow, amongst other things, for movement of individuals between participating states without border controls. They have also been adopted by Iceland, Norway and Switzerland. Bulgaria, Cyprus and Romania had not, in 2010, met the conditions while the UK and Ireland, which were not parties to the original conventions, have remained outside these arrangements, a position confirmed by Protocol 19 of the Treaty of Lisbon.

Opt-outs are one side of the coin of flexibility: the other side is arrangements for enhanced coop-

eration. Both have the effect of decreasing the uniformity of supranational arrangements. Enhanced cooperation involves utilizing the Union's structures and methods to achieve policy objectives but not involving all the member states. They relate only to future developments, so will not allow member states to 'pick and mix' within existing policy provisions, and 'it will be very difficult for flexibility to be practised in the EU's core policy areas' (Nugent, 1999, p. 89). These provisions have existed since 1997 but been very little utilized, possibly because of caution about the image of a 'two-speed Europe' that would result. The first proposal to be put forward formally by the Commission, as the EU methods require, at the request of a reduced number of member states, was published in March 2010. It would introduce, in the ten states requesting this enhanced cooperation, a common procedure for handling international divorce cases (European Commission Press Release IP/10/347, 24 March 2010).

Conditionality and implementation

For long-standing members of the EU the development of the *acquis* has been an incremental process. The process has contributed to

Europeanization in all member states. Individuals have acquired new rights and new obligations as a result of aspects of this involvement, including the applicability of European law directly within the member states. For example, the European Convention on Human Rights allows individuals to require their governments to recognize certain rights, while equal rights between working men and working women have been much enhanced in a number of countries as a result of the development of EU law. Equally, however, citizens of the Union find themselves under an obligation not to hunt and shoot migratory birds, an obligation much resented by those, for example in the south of France, who see it as disturbing traditional habits and lifestyles. This has resulted in political protest and the rise of social movements. So the European dimension also affects groups, associations and political parties. And at the highest levels it constrains the behaviour of national governments, However, whilst one result has been a gradual application of common standards throughout the EU, except where opt-outs have operated, there has been substantial national variation in the detail and impact of EU policy (Falkner and Treib, 2008, pp. 296–8).

Where regulation seems burdensome popular comment and the press may be quick to ascribe it to faceless Brussels bureaucrats lacking all common sense. Indeed the prevalence and tenacity of 'Euromyths' in the British media have resulted in the creation by the EU of a rebuttal website. The allegation is often extended to suggest that some countries (and especially the UK) are unduly rigorous in their transposition, and 'gold-plate' the legislation. For example, the EU requires the national authorities to set 'standards on good agricultural and environmental conditions and as part of that the UK has decided to adopt a prohibition on using such machinery on waterlogged soil or saturated ground' (http://ec.europa.eu/unitedkingdom/press/euromyths/index_en.htm), resulting in protests about prohibitions on the use of combine harvesters in wet weather (*Yorkshire Post*, 23 October 2008). In part the issue is one of differing national legal cultures: some are content with rather broad-brush provisions which are filled in by local discretion on the part of state officials. Others, as a government witness explained to a House of Lords select committee, demand clarity:

> EC law . . . tends to be drafted in a very broad brush manner, there is a lack of detail . . . [J]ust as much as [Industry] are saying please do not gold plate . . . they . . . ask us, above all, for clarity. Clarity is not a predominant feature of a lot of European law, so we do our best to make the law as clear as possible for business. Sometimes people feel that this is gold plating. (House of Lords Session 2006–7 European Union –Twenty-Second Report, 19 June 2007, para. 197, http://www.publications.parliament.uk/pa/ld200607/ldselect/ldeucom/120/12002.htm)

For the most recent EU members and candidates the process of Europeanization is more fraught and rapid, as a consequence of what is known as conditionality. Membership of the EU attracted countries which had formerly been excluded from Europe's most prosperous and far-reaching organization, both because of the material benefits it offered and because membership would mark a symbolic move to legitimization as a European state with a history, culture and current values located within the European mainstream. This was important in the beginning for Italy and especially Germany in rehabilitating themselves after the Second World War, and later for Greece, Spain and Portugal, all emerging from totalitarian regimes. After 1989 the prospect of a much wider demand for membership prompted a more rigorous policy towards potential applicants than had previously been the case, not least because what was required of them was both an economic and a political transformation. The

> formula of a membership promise plus tough conditions helped post-communist central and eastern Europe . . . to achieve a massive transformation. In the countries that were emerging from central planning and authoritarian rule, the EU's conditions for 15 years provided both an anchor and a catalyst. The anchor of EU-focused reforms gave a sense of stability and direction to the public administration even when governments changed every year, while

the promise of accession was a catalyst that made reforms go faster because the rewards of membership were only a few years away. (Grabbe, 2010)

This policy, however, has proved a demanding one. As Heather Grabbe points out, it requires consistency, coherence and credibility from the EU in continuing to ask for reforms. Member states need to set aside any special relationship with an applicant country so that a single message is being delivered, and at the same time to remain committed to accepting the applicant country if the conditions are indeed met. For the applicant states, the transformation at which conditionality is aiming is most readily achieved when there is a strong and competent administration, a substantial consensus on the desirability of EU membership, and external investment to ease the economic pain of restructuring (Grabbe, 2010). In the case of the 2004 enlargement the policy appears to have been rather successful, especially in relation to the transposition of EU legislation into national law and compliance with it (Grabbe, 2010; Wallace, 2007, p. 20), even if there is still a considerable gap between the formal processes and substantive implementation (Falkner and Treib, 2008, p. 308). Concern about progress in, for example, tackling organized crime and corruption, in protecting minority (especially Roma) rights and in judicial reform in the 2007 enlargement countries (Vachudova, 2009) has led some to conclude that the absence of reform inducements (other than monitoring; see European Commission, 2010) after accession requires that future enlargement should involve a tighter attention to substantive change (Rehn, 2008).

Opportunities and constraints

The European dimension has thus resulted in a complex pattern of rights, opportunities, responsibilities and constraints for all the countries involved. In most cases these have been the consequence of deliberate choices, whether or not the advantages and disadvantages, gains and losses, were fully apparent at the point of decision. Arguments around costs and benefits continue, especially between proponents of integration and

eurosceptics in relation to membership of the EU. Some of the issues are illustrated by the question of economic and monetary union.

For its initial proponents, as far back as the late 1960s, but equally when the idea revived in the 1980s, economic and monetary union was, at a practical level, an obvious way to create a genuinely single market by eliminating the transaction costs of changing money when purchasing goods across the whole area and by enabling price comparisons without the complication of fluctuating exchange rates. For other people, notably for example German Chancellor Kohl in the 1990s, it was a profoundly political project. The cost of giving up the Deutschmark, so important to Germany as a symbol of revival, stability and good government, was outweighed by the benefit of a Europe which would be so bound together within the world financial and economic system that it could never again be torn asunder.

Symbolic arguments – the 'loss' of the pound equating to an abandonment of identity for an important proportion of the British public, for example – weighed in the considerations of those countries that opted out of the EMU, as did practical considerations, such as the fact that, compared to many other EU countries, changes in central bank interest rates tend to impinge rather immediately on a large proportion of the electorate in the UK. From the beginning it was recognized that the euro would be adopted by countries with very varied economies and very varied capacities for adapting to the loss of at least two of the major tools that countries habitually use for keeping their economies stable and competitive – the setting of interest rates and the manipulation of the exchange rate. In an attempt to ensure that low inflation was not compromised by the actions of any member state, a stability and growth pact was introduced in the run-up to the introduction of the common currency in 1997 with penalties for running an

● **Euroscepticism:** A point of view critical of, or opposed to, the processes of European integration, especially any trend towards an overarching federal body. 'Eurosceptics' are in particular critical of the policies or existence of the EU; 'hard' eurosceptics are opposed on principle to their country's membership of the EU; 'soft' eurosceptics are critical of specific aspects and policies of the EU without necessarily opposing all moves towards European integration (Szczerbiak and Taggart, 2008).

Key Figure 4.3

Angela Merkel (1954–)

Angela Merkel was brought up in the German Democratic Republic (East Germany), the daughter of a Protestant pastor. She has a doctorate in physical chemistry from the University of Leipzig and worked as a scientific researcher. Following the collapse of the communist regime and the unification of Germany she was elected to the German parliament in 1990. She became a member of the Christian Democratic Union (CDU) when her new East German centre-right party, founded after the collapse of the regime, merged with the CDU following unification. She rapidly gained ministerial office, becoming minister for women and youth in 1991 and then minister for the environment from 1994 until the CDU defeat in the general election of 1998. In 2005 she became the leader of the CDU. In 2005 she became the CDU's choice as candidate for the post of Chancellor (Prime Minister) in the 2005 general election. That election resulted in a 'grand coalition' of the Christian Democrats and the Social Democrats, with Merkel as Chancellor. She retained the position following the general election of 2009, with the CDU going into coalition with the smaller Free Democratic Party (FDP).

Merkel is a pragmatic, hardworking and effective politician, neither showy nor image-conscious, who has been able to hold together difficult coalitions, and operate convincingly and robustly within the EU, benefiting not only from her style and capabilities but also from Germany's relatively strong economic position as it has weathered the recession, combining reforms her government has implemented with an economy that has seen some growth and falling unemployment. The rather tough terms imposed upon the financial bail-outs for the struggling euro-zone economies reflect her determination to ensure that her vision of Germany's and Europe's interests prevailed. She has for several years been rated by Forbes magazine as the most powerful woman in the world.

excessive deficit (see also Box 4.3). The pact proved effectively unenforceable, since even core members of the euro (France, Germany) infringed its terms, and a softer version was embodied in Council of Ministers' regulations in 2005. These did not, however, make any provision for the management of crises (Quaglia, Holmes, and Eastwood, 2009, p. 73).

The first major crisis to hit the euro was the banking crisis of 2008. EU gross national product fell by 6 per cent in the last quarter of 2008, and the International Monetary Fund (IMF) estimated that over August, September and October 2008 world trade declined by 42 per cent (Quaglia et al., 2009, p. 64). The heads of state or government of the eurozone countries and then the European Council were able to agree an action plan in October 2008. Importantly, it seemed that the political institutions of the eurozone were sufficiently robust and their analysis of the crisis sufficiently shared, despite different and even conflicting national interests

(Quaglia et al., 2009, p. 84), for clear policy to merge in the face of a crisis that had originated elsewhere.

Subsequent, and interlinked, crises, however, seemed to threaten the euro even more directly and emerged from within the system. In the spring of 2010 it became apparent that the national deficit of Greece was so high, and its credit rating so poor, that it was at risk of defaulting on its debt. But the politics were complicated: loans were clearly required, but should these be provided only by fellow eurozone countries or should the IMF also participate? If the deficit was the consequence of a failure by Greece to control levels of public spending, for example on wages, pensions and benefits for public employees, could more frugal members of the eurozone, and in particular Germany, under Chancellor Merkel (see Key Portrait 4.3), which would take a major share, be expected to subsidize profligacy? Could the necessary cuts be imposed without serious social unrest? A 'bail-out' loan involving both the EU and the IMF was agreed and in May 2010 the EU created a European Financial Stability Facility (EFSF) – a fund to pay for loans to member states in serious risk of bankruptcy. In November 2010 this fund and the IMF jointly provided a substantial loan facility (€85 billion) to Ireland, which was undergoing a prolonged banking crisis. Such crises have political consequences: in Ireland the governing party was ejected from power in a general election in February 2011, with the incoming government promising to renegotiate the terms of the loan. In Portugal in March 2011 the Prime Minister resigned, prompting a general election in June, when the Parliament declined to accept an austerity package designed to avert the need to have recourse to the EFSF. The responsibilities and constraints, as well as the rights and opportunities offered by the integration of countries which have marked differences, as well as shared values and aspirations, were sharply pointed up by these crises.

Europeanization and political behaviour

At the level of relationships between states the European dimension thus enmeshes them in a plethora of networks and institutions, with the EU as a particularly dynamic and dominant part of the pattern. There is also a 'European dimension' to the way in which parties, groups within civil society, and individuals behave in contemporary Europe.

As a consequence of the policy implications of engagement within the network of European institutions political parties have also been affected by increasing integration. Many, for example the Christian Democratic parties of much of Western Europe, have consistently favoured closer union. Others have been more hostile – the extreme Left and the extreme Right have generally opposed increased integration – or, as is the case of the Gaullists in France and both the British Labour and Conservative Parties, have shifted in their attitudes. This has resulted, from time to time, in considerable tensions within some parties, and even in the emergence of breakaway groups distinguished primarily by their attitude to the process of integration. Thus in France in 1999 former Interior Minister Charles Pasqua broke away from the Gaullists to form the 'Eurosceptic' Rassemblement pour la France, while in the UK the United Kingdom Independence Party (UKIP) contains defectors from the Conservative Party. But even those parties which oppose integration fight the elections for the European Parliament, and a number of Eurosceptic parties such as UKIP are represented there. The Europe of Freedom and Democracy group in the European Parliament comprised, in 2010, the twelve UKIP MEPS, nine members from the Italian Lega Nord, and ten other members from seven other countries. However, political parties have in general primarily been concerned with their own country's relationship with the EU and the domestic impact of specific EU policies. Although they do form cross-national groups within the European Parliament, some of them rather uneasy alliances, the parties have in general engaged in rather little transnational cooperation and organization. Traditional concepts of 'government' and 'opposition' translate awkwardly into the context of the European Parliament, and national parties have found it difficult to project into the national political debate a sense of the growing role of the Parliament in co-decision and scrutiny. The campaigns for election to the European Parliament are invariably rather nationally based. One consequence has been the institutional provisions for an enhanced role for national parliaments described above.

For groups within civil society the growing weight of the EU as a regulator in economic, commercial and industrial matters, and its role as a provider of grants and funds for various purposes, has resulted in an increased awareness, especially among businesses and interest groups, of the European dimension of their activities and interests. And reciprocally the European bodies, especially the European Commission, have sought to incorporate the representatives of 'organized civil society' – interest groups and especially the 'social partners', that is, employers and employees – into consultations on policy, with the aim of rendering it more legitimate and widely accepted (Eising, 2007, p. 209). Article 11 of the Treaty of Lisbon states: 'The institutions shall maintain an open, transparent and regular dialogue with representative associations and civil society.'

One consequence has been the growth of EU-wide interest groups, of which the European Commission lists some 700 (Eising, 2007). Most of the groups active in Brussels federate national associations or other bodies. There has also been a mushrooming of lobbyists, and of local offices for public and private bodies, groups and enterprises in Brussels (Eising, 2003, p. 198). Some estimates suggest that there are over two and a half thousand such offices (http://www.euractiv.com/en/pa/brussels-lobbyists-come-tighter-scrutiny/article-136454 15 May 2007), but the size of the Brussels lobbying community 'is the subject of many guesses but no agreement' (*European Voice*, 3 September 2009). Anxious to improve the transparency of the process, in 2008 the European Commission set up a voluntary register of lobbyists, which after a year registered over 1800 lobbyists, but was known not to include, for example, many of the large law firms (ibid.). Groups representing business and employer interests constitute the majority of such groups, but it is a measure of the extent to which Europeanization is increasingly affecting all aspects of public life that the representation of 'religious, social, human rights and consumer interests' (Eising, 2007) has increased, sometimes, as, for example, in the case of the European Women's Lobby (http://www.women-lobby.org), with substantial financial help from the European Commission.

Ministers, officials, politicians, business people and the leaders of interest and pressure groups have adapted their behaviour and policies to the existence of a European dimension. The governing elites in Europe are by and large supportive of the process of integration. 'National elites had shared interests in promoting European integration yet preventing the erosion of national interests that provided their own legitimacy . . . The result was the so-called "permissive consensus", whereby Europe's publics were content to delegate responsibility to their leaders to tackle the European integration project' (Hix, 1999, p. 164). However, in both the longer standing and the new members of the EU, governments and politicians have equally been inclined, from time to time, to use 'Europe' as an umbrella, to deflect blame or criticism when things seem not to be going well, or policies turn out to be unpopular.

Popular support for membership of the EU across all member states fluctuates, varying over the period between 2001 and 2009 from a minimum of just below to a maximum of just above half of the total population who think that their country's membership of the EU is 'a good thing'. But these averages conceal wide differences between countries, which in the spring of 2010 ranged from low figures in Latvia (26 per cent) and the UK (29 per cent) to 69 per cent in the Netherlands (see Figure 4.1).

In Eastern Europe there was, after 1989, a high level of support for a 'return to Europe', in the sense of a desire to escape from the communist model (Mayhew, 1998, p. 10; Hyde-Pryce, 1998, pp. 264–5), to be incorporated within the network of international organizations which link West European countries, and above all to symbolize a return to Europe by joining an EU (and in some cases NATO – see Chapters 3 and 10) which, at the beginning of the 1990s, seemed to be achieving its targets – prosperity, growth and the completion of the single market – and moving forward. By the time that accession actually occurred in 2004 for the first eight Central and East European countries, support had waned.

During the 1990s and 2000s a series of referendums in various countries opened up the issues surrounding integration to widespread debates in an unprecedented way and revealed the extent of dissent around the integration project. As noted above, the process of ratification of the Maastricht Treaty produced referendums in Ireland; in France, where ratification was approved by a tiny majority; and in Denmark, where an initial referendum was lost. In 1994 referendums on membership in Austria, Sweden, Finland and Norway revealed far from universal support, although only Norway (again) rejected membership. Similarly, 9 out of 12 applicant countries for the 2004 and 2007 enlargements had their accession approved by national referendum, although in some instances with rather low turnouts and not very large margins. The early years of the next century saw the rejection by referendum of the proposal that Sweden should adopt the common currency, and in 2005 the Constitutional Treaty was put to referendum in four countries. When the Netherlands and France voted against it, other countries which had planned

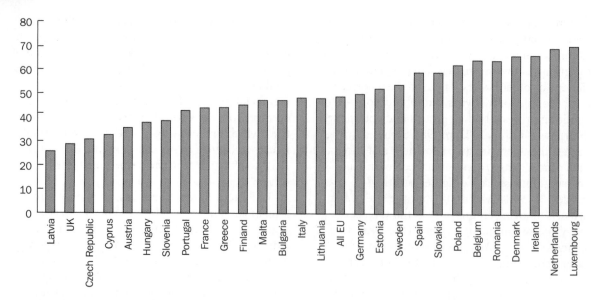

Figure 4.1   Is membership of the EU a 'good thing'? (respondents answering 'yes', May 2010, %)

Source: compiled from data in http://ec.europa.eu/public_opinion/archives/eb/eb73/eb73_vol1_fr.pdf p. 143.

referendums cancelled them. The subsequent Treaty of Lisbon was subject to referendum only in Ireland, where the Irish constitution required that one be held. Defeated at the first referendum in 2008, the Treaty was accepted at a second referendum in 2009 after a number of assurances had been given to the Irish. The divisions revealed by the debates around these referendums exist between political parties, with both the far right and the far left in general opposed to the integration process, but also within them, for example in the Green parties (Church, 2009). Moreover, the opportunity provided by referendums to express opposition to the integration process galvanizes other groups, such as a movement created by an Irish millionaire calling itself 'Libertas' which 'claimed to be pro-Europe but opposed to the Lisbon Treaty and the anti-democratic elite responsible for it' (Church, 2009).

The divisions in the support for the process of integration, and over what sort of outcome should emerge from it, are related to a wide variety of cultural, political and economic factors, including a decline since the mid-1980s in the willingness of people to support integration simply because they believe that a united Europe would be 'a good

thing'. The perception of being a 'winner' or a 'loser' as a consequence of the policies of the EU seems to be more crucial as a determinant of support for integration. The divisions which result from these complex factors cut across traditional party divides, have a considerable impact on the internal politics of the countries of Western Europe and result in complex and fragmented political competition (Hix, 1999, pp. 133–65). As is apparent, for example, from the case of the Irish referendums, any self-evident rationale for integration can no longer be taken for granted, but instead the case has to be made and fought for.

Conclusion

The various institutional expressions of the European dimension, including NATO, the Council of Europe, and the EU, work separately and together so that the result is an ever more complex, interconnected, overlapping system of rights, obligations and relationships. Within the EU the changing policy dynamics, the political issues posed by major crises, and the increased emphasis now placed upon flexibility and subsidiarity, and the arrangements made for post-accession transition periods for the new member states, all support this view. Despite vociferous protests, whether generally against perceived losses of national sovereignty or against particular policy outcomes, the undoing of the multiple functional cooperations that have grown up is not a credible scenario. There will be a need for long-term management of relationships between the Union and its member states, and those states – some of them large and potentially, if, not actually, powerful, such as Russia, Ukraine, even Turkey (see Chapter 3) – where membership is either not likely at all, or likely to be substantially delayed. The challenges and pressures are considerable, but must be viewed in the context of the 50 years since the last pan-European civil war and the two decades since the end of the division of Europe. The web of cooperation and integration that constitutes the European dimension has withstood substantial pressures. It will certainly evolve and change: much of Europe's prosperity and peace depends upon its survival.

SUMMARY

The institutions that had been developed by the 1990s to provide a framework of cooperation among Western European states in the context of the Cold War, including the EU, now provide a basis on which to manage the new links and networks which incorporate Central and Eastern European states. The EU is the most prominent of these bodies. There is continuing tension between the dynamics of integration and the persistent individualism of nation-states. Decision-making and democratic processes within the EU have changed and developed, but the system remains complex, and, because it is different from anything else, often poorly understood. Responses to these problems have evolved within a complex framework with varying levels of flexibility. Recent responses to the financial crises within the eurozone exemplify some of these features. Europeanization is, however, pervasive and persistent.

QUESTIONS FOR DISCUSSION

- Can, and should, the process of European integration be halted or reversed?

- Is the eurozone sustainable?

- Why are EU processes so complex? Could they be simplified?

- How democratic is the European Parliament?

- Does the 'European dimension' imply a convergence of national policies and/or cultures?

FURTHER READING

The Palgrave Macmillan European Union series contains a growing number of detailed studies of aspects of the EU: John McCormick, *Understanding the European Union*, 5th edn (Basingstoke: Palgrave Macmillan, 2011) is a very useful concise introduction.

Neill Nugent, *The Government and Politics of the European Union*, 7th edn (Basingstoke: Palgrave Macmillan, 2010) is the authoritative and comprehensive guide to the institutions of the Union. Simon Hix and Bjørn Høyland, *The Political System of the European Union*, 3rd edn (Basingstoke: Palgrave Macmillan, 2011) analyses the EU from a political science perspective.

The processes of the EU are well covered by Elizabeth Bomberg and Alexander Stubb (eds), *The European Union: How Does It Work?*, 2nd edn (Oxford: Oxford University Press, 2008) and Michelle Cini and Nieves Perez-Solorzano Borragan (eds), *European Union Politics*, 3rd edn (Oxford: Oxford University Press, 2009), which also includes introductions to a number of policy areas.

John Peterson and Elizabeth Bomberg, *Decision-Making in the European Union* (London: Macmillan, 1999) provides extensive insight into the dynamics of policy-making, as does Helen Wallace, Mark Pollack and Alasdair Young, *Policy-Making in the European Union*, 6th edn (Oxford: Oxford University Press, 2010).

An insider's view of one nation-state's relationship to the EU is given by Stephen Wall, *A Stranger in Europe: Britain and the EU from Thatcher to Blair* (Oxford: Oxford University Press, 2008).

For a chronological approach see Martin J. Dedman, *The Origins & Development of the European Union 1945–2008: A History of European Integration*, 2nd edn (London: Routledge, 2009). Desmond Dinan (ed.), *Origins and Evolution of the European Union* (Oxford: Oxford University Press, 2004) also provides a historical overview, as does Richard McAllister, *European Union: An Historical and Political Survey* (London: Routledge, 2009).

CHAPTER 5

Government and Politics

THOMAS SAALFELD

In framing a government to be administered by men over men, the great difficulty lies in this: you must first enable the government to control the governed; and in the next place oblige it to control itself.

James Madison, *Federalist Papers* (1788), p. 51

Our perceptions of the state and political institutions are changing. Phenomena such as globalization or European integration ('Europeanization'; see Chapter 4) have had a number of beneficial effects for people, but many observers claim that they have also undermined the power of national governments to make policy autonomously. Governing has become more complex and – especially in the economic and fiscal sphere – more constrained. In addition to such challenges emanating from the supra-national level (from 'above'), the national governments and institutions of Europe have also been confronted by the growing demands of actors at the sub-national level such as regions (see Chapter 9) or particular linguistic, ethnic or faith communities (from 'below').

New social movements have questioned the monopoly of 'institutionalized' politics and politicians (see Chapter 6). The internet and social media have turned local protests into global events. New methods of delivering public services through, for example, the 'new public management', 'private–public partnerships' and the 'enabling state' have further contributed to a situation where national governments have become one actor amongst many in a number of interlocking networks made up of representatives of interest groups, voluntary associations, non-governmental organizations and executive agencies. Some observers argue that transnational developments such as Europeanization have strengthened the role of national governments at the expense of national or regional institutions, because intergovernmental decision-making in the European and global arenas is less constrained by domestic accountability mechanisms.

Government and politics in a changing world

The global financial crisis that began to affect Europe in 2007 showed that the governments of the larger national economies were the most important actors to step in and restore confidence in the national and global banking systems. More generally, the national governments of Europe continue to dominate policy-making at the domestic level and have remained important actors on the international stage. Not only does their legislation continue to shape policy at the national level, but they also participate in the shaping of the rules of international politics. Their preferences are reflected in decisions of supra-national bodies such as the European Union (EU) or intergovernmental bodies such as the G8, the G20 or the United Nations (UN). They still have tremendous powers to raise revenue and redistribute resources. Figures 5.1 and 5.2

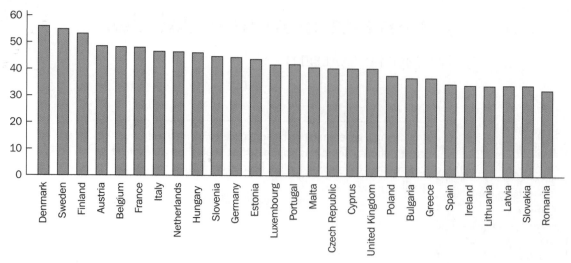

Figure 5.1   Total general government revenue in the 27 EU member states, 2009 (in % of GDP)

Source: Eurostat (Table tec00021).

illustrate the share of **gross domestic product (GDP)** the national governments of the 27 EU member states raised (mainly through taxation) and spent in 2009. Figure 5.1 shows that these governments raised revenues worth between 55.9 (Denmark) and 32.1 per cent (Romania) of the respective country's GDP with a median just above 40 per cent. Figure 5.2 tells a similar story with regard to public expenditure, which ranged from 58.7 (Denmark) to 40.4 per cent (Romania) of GDP in the same sample of countries, with a median of over 48 per cent (European Commission, 2010).

Although such data suggest that national governments continue profoundly to influence their citizens' lives, and although there have been fierce academic and political debates about the actual effects of globalization and Europeanization, national political institutions have clearly been affected by developments such as those mentioned above. The nature of governing has changed unquestionably. It has become more complex and less hierarchical. Governments are less able to impose policies 'from above' than in the 1950s. They have 'become more coordinating bodies, seeking to ensure that their country's firms and people (or most of

them) can prosper in an era of global competition' (Hague, Harrop and Breslin, 1998, p. 39).

Voters and their elected representatives find it increasingly difficult to understand and influence, let alone control, the complex bargaining processes between governments, bureaucracies, regulatory agencies and interest groups at the national, sub-national and supra-national levels ('multi-level governing'). This raises the serious question of whether, and how, citizens can learn what they need to know in order to participate meaningfully in democratic politics in an increasingly complex political environment (Lupia and McCubbins, 1998). To whom are government agencies politically accountable? How can a degree of democratic 'control', accountability and responsiveness be maintained under such circumstances? How can Madison's 'dilemma', the tension between strong and simultaneously accountable government expressed in the epigraph at the beginning of this chapter, be 'solved' under such conditions?

In many ways this raises a fundamental political question that was posed by Max Weber a century ago. He observed the growing importance of experts, technocrats and bureaucrats in the modern world and considered this a challenge for democracy. He recognized the tension between the efficiency and necessity of bureaucratic rule on the one hand, and popular political participation on the other. Modern democracies cannot be run effi-

---

● **Gross domestic product (GDP)**: a common indicator of the level of a country's economic activity. It represents the total value of the goods and services produced by a country's economy during a specified period of time excluding the income of the country's residents from investment abroad.

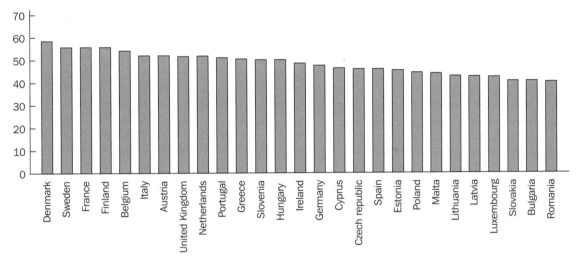

Figure 5.2   Total general government expenditure in the 27 EU member states, 2009 (in % of GDP)

ciently without delegating powers to experts in political and bureaucratic organizations. Bureaucratic organizations in his sense include not only public administration and executive agencies, but also major interest groups and political parties. Weber predicted a growing tendency for politics to be dominated by officials in such organizations rather than by publicly accountable politicians. There have been many valid criticisms of aspects of Weber's work on bureaucracy, and some of it may be outdated. Nevertheless, the fundamental problem remains a perennial one for students of government and politics and has recently been severely compounded by developments such as the ones sketched above.

How serious are these challenges to modern European democracies? What institutional arrangements do different political systems use to cope with these problems – and to what effect? The aim of this chapter is to compare and analyse the main features of European governments from this important perspective: to what extent do different political systems offer solutions to Madison's problem of **accountability** and Weber's related

problem of bureaucratic rule? To what extent are they responsive to popular preferences? What scope is there for democratic political leadership (rather than bureaucratic or '**technocratic**' rule), and how effectively are political leaders held to account? What are the costs and benefits of different forms of political delegation and accountability?

Most European states are **representative democracies** where citizens delegate (varying degrees of) political authority to representatives, whose task it is to act on behalf and in the best interest of 'their' peoples. They are systems of government in which – at least ideally – 'the popular majority, through its elected representatives in the legislative branch, effectively controls public policy' (Strøm, 1995, p. 53). In most European states they elect parliamentary assemblies which then choose a head of government. Heads of government delegate the authority to formulate and enforce detailed policies to individual cabinet ministers who are in charge of specialized departments of state. Together with the Members of

● **Accountability**: the requirement for agents (or representatives) to answer to the principals (or represented) on the exercise of their powers and duties. Political systems typically employ certain institutional arrangements (e.g. parliamentary investigations, public inquiries, ministerial responsibility, collective responsibility, etc.) to ensure at least a degree of accountability.

● **Technocratic rule**: a tendency in complex, modern states to delegate more and more powers to bureaucratic experts rather than elected politicians, who cannot match the former's expertise.

● **Representative government**: a form of government where a legislature with significant decision-making power is freely elected. Political decisions are made by elected representatives on behalf of the represented.

Parliament (MPs) and the heads of governments, these ministers take political decisions. Yet they usually transfer the authority to draft and carry out these decisions to appointed officials: civil servants, executive agencies or, in some cases, private firms or voluntary organizations.

In most political systems the processes of delegation do not end with a transfer of authority. Those who delegate power and authority want to make sure that it is used competently and in their best interest. They want to hold those on whom they confer authority accountable – including the possibility of checking, controlling and, if necessary, removing from power those agents who abuse their delegated authority, or use it incompetently. With the decline of generalized trust in politicians in many advanced industrial democracies in recent years (see, for example, Pharr and Putnam, 2000), there has been more and more emphasis on the accountability of elected politicians through parliaments, courts, ombudsmen, regulatory watchdogs and the like. Yet, accountability is very difficult to achieve at an acceptable cost. Certainly, voters can choose not to re-elect an MP who is perceived not to have represented their local interests faithfully ('retrospective voting', i.e. basing voting decisions on perceptions of past performance). But *how* do voters know whether or not their representative has done a good job? Many of them do not have enough time and expertise, and most do not have access to sufficiently detailed information about their representative's performance. If they did have the resources they might not wish to concentrate them on monitoring their elected representatives. The same type of informational problem occurs at all other levels of the political process: MPs delegating authority to a prime minister and a cabinet do not have the expertise and resources to obtain sufficiently accurate information on their behaviour. Ministers will find it almost impossible to monitor the behaviour of civil servants and executive agencies in charge of carrying out their policies. In fact they depend on civil servants to formulate their policies in the first place. In this chapter we follow through the whole 'chain' of democratic delegation and accountability (Strøm, Müller, and Bergman, 2003) and consider the nature of delegation and its implications for democratic accountability at each stage.

How citizens express their political preferences: direct versus representative democracy

Democracy, as one textbook author (Heywood, 1997, p. 66) notes, 'links government to the people' and adds that 'this link can be forged in a number of ways: government of, by and for the people'. It is clear that most modern democracies in Western Europe are not governed directly *by* the people themselves. There are obvious practical reasons for this: many citizens do not have the time, expertise, experience and political judgement to make political decisions on complex issues themselves. In politics as in all other organizations, delegation of powers to specialists (e.g. elected politicians or civil servants) can be highly beneficial for the citizens. Although there is considerable variation between individual democracies, only a handful of European constitutions allow 'the people' to participate directly and continuously in decisions over public policy, usually in the form of referendums (see below). All European democracies are representative democracies where elected officials usually act as 'agents' who 'represent' the interests of a 'principal', namely the citizens.

Direct participation through referendums

Nevertheless, many European democracies do allow some elements of direct popular participation in issues of public policy. The extent to which this is the case varies considerably. In Switzerland and, to a lesser extent, Italy referendums are now used regularly to decide on policy issues. In countries such as Germany or the UK, they are never or only rarely used. In many European countries, popular pressure for stronger citizen involvement in policy making through referendums has increased since the 1970s. Most countries of Central and Eastern Europe, which have gone through democratic transitions since 1989–90, have introduced the (often restricted) possibility of direct popular participation. However, because of the limitations of referendums and popular initiatives (see Box 5.1) they usually *complement* representative forms of government in exceptional circumstances rather than replacing them.

BOX 5.1
Referendums and popular initiatives

Referendums and *popular initiatives* are the most important mechanisms by which voters may participate directly in public policy-making and make choices between alternative policy proposals.

In a *referendum* the initiative to put a question to the voters does not rest with the voters themselves. A referendum may be:

- initiated by the government or the parliamentary majority (as in the UK);
- initiated by a constitutionally specified parliamentary minority; or
- mandatory on certain specified issues such as constitutional amendments or major international treaties (as in Denmark).

In the case of *popular initiatives*, the right to initiate a popular vote on a matter of public policy rests with a specified number of *voters*. An issue will be put before the electorate if a specified number or percentage of signatures can be obtained from voters in a specified time period.

Referendums and popular initiatives can be called 'decisive' if the result of the vote binds the government. They are 'consultative' if it is up to the government or the parliamentary majority to decide whether or not it will accept the expressed will of the people (Möckli, 1998, p. 91).

Referendums have a number of advantages:

- They allow citizens to decide a policy issue directly.
- They may ensure that elected politicians do not lose touch with voters' preferences.
- They may enhance democratic accountability: campaigns conducted in the context of referendums can be an important device for informing citizens about major issues of public policy.

- Some forms of referendum can be an important institutional check on the power of elected governments and can increase the government's political accountability to the people. On the other hand, referendums as instruments of **direct democracy** also have a number of disadvantages:
  - If the electorate decides an issue, this is usually at the expense of other constitutional bodies such as parliaments. Parliamentary minorities may use the referendum to overturn a legitimate decision taken by the parliamentary majority or destabilize the government. It is often said that in the first German republic, the 'Weimar Republic', extremist parties used referendums to destabilize democracy, for example.
  - Frequently referendums acquire the character of a general popular vote of confidence or no-confidence in the government rather than the expression of a political preference on a specific policy issue.
  - The parliamentary majority only has an incentive to use a referendum if it expects political benefits from it. If it is in political difficulties, a successful referendum may give it renewed popular legitimacy and respect at home and abroad. It will then find it difficult to resist the temptation to 'secure the desired result of referendums by controlling their timing and wording' (Hague et al., 1998, p. 108).
  - Where it is easy for minorities to request a referendum, or the support required to initiate a popular initiative is low, governing may become a very difficult and time-consuming process. It may be difficult to make vital but unpopular decisions at all, and governments may find it difficult to pursue coherent policies.

● **Direct democracy**: a form of government where those entitled to decide do so directly in sovereign assemblies or referendums.

Electoral systems

In representative democracies, competitive, free and fair elections are the most important way for voters to express their political preferences and delegate their right to make public policy to elected politicians for a specified period of time. Elections are the most important mechanisms for citizens to choose politicians as their agents and to hold them to account. The citizens' opportunities to influence the selection and election of persons who represent them are constrained by the nature of the electoral system, that is, the way in which votes for a candidate or party are counted and 'translated' into parliamentary seats. Such rules can be problematic: For example, the US system of voter registration and the use of an electoral college in presidential elections almost certainly contributed to George W. Bush's victory over Al Gore in 2000; in order to avoid wasting their vote under the **first-past-the-post system**, British voters may have strong incentives to vote tactically for a less preferred party rather than supporting 'sincerely' a party they really feel politically close to; or, if electoral systems are insufficiently robust, elections can be rigged and some people's votes do not get counted at all, perhaps encouraging citizens to express their views through protest (e.g. Kuntz and Thompson, 2009).

There are a number of basic requirements for a democratic electoral process: for elections to be competitive, citizens must have a choice between several parties or candidates, and their vote must potentially have an influence on the composition of the parliamentary assembly. For elections to be free, certain civil liberties must be guaranteed: freedom of speech, freedom of association, freedom to register as a voter, party or candidate, freedom from coercion, freedom of access to the polls, confidentiality of the vote, and the freedom to complain. For elections to be fair they must be administered in a non-partisan fashion. There must be universal suffrage. The counting of the vote must be open and transparent, and parties must be treated equitably both by the government and by other public authorities. Fraud and vote-rigging are not permissible (Hague and Harrop, 2004, p. 130; Taagepera and Shugart, 1989, pp. 11–18). In Western Europe, the freedom and fairness of elections has been guaranteed since 1945. In so far as the successor states of the Soviet Union and its former satellites have experienced a transition to liberal democracy, the electoral process has also been democratized dramatically in the rest of Europe since 1989/90 (see Chapter 3).

Even if elections are free and fair, as they now are in most European countries, there may be considerable differences in the specific way electoral rules translate votes into seats or positions of political power, in particular the proportionality between the share of votes cast by the democratic principals in the electorate and the share of seats allocated to candidates and political parties in the respective representative assemblies (parliaments). Rules governing this process have a strong influence on how many parties are elected to parliament, which ones are not represented at all, which party or parties govern and which ones are in opposition. What electoral systems structure the delegation process between voters and politicians in Europe?

We can distinguish between (a) **plurality** and majority systems, on the one hand, and (b) systems of **proportional representation (PR)** on the other. There are three main types of plurality and majority systems: the simple plurality vote (also known as the first-past-the-post-system), the **second ballot** and the **alternative vote (AV)**. The main types of proportional representation are: **party-list** systems (closed and open lists), the **single transfer-**

● **First-past-the-post**: a way of describing simple-plurality electoral systems. They are commonly used to allocate seats in single-member districts. In order to win a seat, a candidate is required to get more votes than each of the others (plurality). The candidate is not required to have the vote of a majority of those voting in the constituency. In Europe, the simple-plurality system is used only in the UK. Its main advantage is its simplicity; its main disadvantage is that it is likely to produce disproportionate outcomes.

● **Plurality (or majority) systems**: electoral systems which emphasize the powers of political candidates or parties backed by an absolute or relative majority (plurality) of the voters. The winner in elections 'takes all' in such systems.

● **Proportional representation (PR)**: an electoral system with multi-member districts, in which parties are represented in an assembly in proportion to their overall electoral strength. Most continental West European electoral systems (except France and Italy) are more or less pure systems of proportional representation.

able vote (STV) and **additional and compensatory member systems (AMS)** (see Box 5.2).

Three key characteristics determine the proportionality of seat allocation:

1. The *district magnitude*, that is, the number of seats allocated in a district. Some systems use single-member districts where each district elects one MP. Others use multi-member districts where several MPs are elected for each district. In extreme cases (like the Netherlands and the Russian Federation), the whole country is treated as one large multi-member district. In general, it is possible to say that the larger the districts, the more proportional the electoral system tends to be.

2. The *allocation formula*, that is, the specific mathematical procedure by which votes are translated into seats. In single-member districts such as those traditionally used in British general elections, no complex formula is required. The candidate with the largest number of votes is awarded the seat. In multi-member districts, certain mathematical formulas are used (for a description, see Lijphart, 1994).

3. There may be *thresholds* specifying a minimum share of the vote a party must gain in order to be represented in the parliamentary assembly. Such rules may reduce proportionality, as they may exclude smaller parties whose share of the vote is below the threshold. Thresholds serve to avoid a strong fragmentation of the party system in parliament by barring small splinter parties and regional parties from parliamentary representation. They are used in a large number of European countries such as Albania, Bulgaria, Croatia, the Czech Republic, Denmark, Estonia, Germany, Greece, Hungary, Italy (for the lower house), Latvia, Lithuania, Moldova, the Netherlands, Norway, Poland, Romania, Russia, Slovakia, Spain and Sweden. In Europe they vary from 0.67 per cent in the

---

● **Second-ballot system**: a form of plurality or majority electoral system requiring a winning candidate to get a majority of the votes cast (50 per cent of the vote in a constituency plus 1) in a first round. If no candidate gains a majority of the votes in the first round, a second ballot is held for the strongest of the first-round candidates. This system is used in France. The candidate with the plurality of votes wins this second ballot.

● **Alternative vote (AV)**: an electoral system where voters rank the candidates in single-member districts according to their preferences. In a first step, all first preferences are counted, and any candidate with more than half of the votes is elected. If no candidate achieves half of the vote, the candidate with fewest first preferences is eliminated and the second preferences on their ballot papers are redistributed. This is repeated with third, fourth, etc., preferences as often as required until a candidate wins more than half of the valid votes. AV is used in elections to the Australian parliament. The system was also under discussion to replace the UK system for elections to the House of Commons but failed to obtain sufficient popular support in a referendum in in 2011.

● **Party-list system**: a proportional electoral system which distributes the seats on a national (such as in Russia and the Netherlands) or regional basis (for example, in Germany or Italy). This order is often determined by party bodies. Once the parties' share of the vote is established, the parliamentary seats are filled using the party lists. Seats are allocated to candidates, starting from the top of the lists. Such lists can be 'open' (that is, the voters may change the ranking on the lists by indicating preferences for certain candidates) or 'closed' (the voters can only accept or reject the list as drawn up by the parties, as in the 1999 European Parliament elections in Britain). Party list systems are used in most countries of continental Western Europe, with varying degrees of party control over the ranking of candidates and openness to changes through the voters.

● **Single transferable vote (STV)**: a system of proportional representation for multi-member districts. It is used in the Irish Republic and Malta. Each voter lists a number of candidates in order of preference. In a first step, first preferences are counted. Those candidates who have achieved at least a certain quota of votes (usually the 'Droop quota', named after a Belgian mathematician, of the number of total votes divided by the number of available seats plus 1) are elected. Their 'surplus votes', i.e. the number of votes by which they exceed the quota, are transferred to the next candidate on those voters' ballot papers. When no further candidates can be elected by this route, the candidate with the fewest first preferences is eliminated and their second preferences are transferred. The process continues until all seats in a district are filled.

● **Additional and compensatory member system (AMS)**: an electoral system with at least two tiers of electoral districts, used, for example, in Germany as well as in the elections for the Scottish Parliament and the Welsh Assembly. AMS involve a lower-level local constituency, with which a representative can maintain personal contact, and a higher-level regional or even national district in which minority interests can be proportionately represented. Voters have two votes, one for each tier. The party vote at the upper level (e.g. the national level) is used to calculate the percentage of parliamentary seats a party will receive. In many cases the mandates won in the lower-level constituency contests are then deducted from this total. Thus, parties winning a less-than-proportional share of seats at the lower level are compensated with a higher number of seats from the party lists at the higher level.

Netherlands and Norway to 7 per cent in Russia and 10 per cent in Turkey.

There has been a long debate about the advantages and disadvantages of different electoral systems for the quality of a democracy, especially in countries where electoral reform has been an important issue (such as in France, Italy and Britain) and in the new democracies of Central and Eastern Europe. Shugart (2001) has suggested distinguishing between an inter-party and an intra-party dimension in evaluating electoral systems. As for *the inter-party dimension*, Shugart considers electoral systems as 'efficient' if they 'offer voters a choice from two parties or blocs of parties, one of which will be likely to attain full control of the government' (Shugart, 2001, p. 174). Plurality (or majority) systems (see Box 5.2) are believed to perform well in this respect as they favour the development two-party systems with one-party majorities in parliament, even if the parliamentary majority party does not have an overall majority of the votes. The potential of electoral accountability can be said to be higher in such two-party or two-bloc systems than in party systems where governments are based on coalitions formed after an election: Coalition governments, which often form in proportional systems (see Box 5.2) of representation, are more likely to be based on a majority of the electorate, but the cabinets that form are usually not easily 'identifiable' for voters in the election campaigns that precede their formation. Shugart (2001, p. 180) establishes that the pre-election 'identifiability' of government choices (and the chances for 'prospective voting', e.g. voters deciding what government will do in near future by choosing a political party on the basis of an election manifesto) is particularly high in the UK and particularly low in multi-party democracies such as Belgium and Finland. Shugart's *intra-party dimension* of electoral 'efficiency' refers to the simultaneous accountability of legislators to constituents and to their party. Meaningful inter-party competition and electoral accountability are only possible when party labels convey credible information about the candidates' policy goals. However, the electoral system is only 'efficient' if it avoids both 'hyper-personalised' and 'hyper-

centralised' (Shugart) candidacies. In the former, the competition between, and accountability of, national parties is believed to be undermined by 'personalistic' candidate strategies: the activities of candidates and elected MPs are strongly influenced by an effort to deliver particularistic benefits to their respective geographic, ethnic, socioeconomic or other constituencies. In the latter the influence of party headquarters on candidate nomination is so high and over-centralized that responsiveness to local constituencies is too low. For example, Shugart (2001, p. 1984) considers the open-list systems of proportional representation in Greece and Italy as extremely candidate-centred, whereas the closed list systems of Portugal and Spain are highly centralized.

Parliamentary democracy, presidential democracy, hybrids and other forms

The link between voters and elected deputies is only the start of a whole chain of further delegation processes. In the following sections, we shall follow these processes through and analyse the institutional arrangements structuring them. Before we do that, it is useful to look briefly at a number of fundamental ways of organizing representative government: parliamentary government, presidential government and several hybrid forms. The key differences between these systems lie in the different relationships between voters, head of state and head of government on the one hand, and the head of state's and head of government's relationship with the parliamentary assembly on the other.

Pure **presidential systems of government** (as found in the USA; see Key Figure 5.1) are found only in one European country (Cyprus; see Table 5.1), and have the following main characteristics:

- The head of government – usually called a president – is popularly elected, that is, the voters

---

● **Presidential system of government**: the head of this type of government is a president whose office is constitutionally separate from the legislature and whose survival in office is not dependent on the confidence of a parliamentary majority.

Table 5.1 Classification of executive–legislative relations in 38 European countries, 2004

Pure presidential	President-parliamentary	Premier-presidential	Parliamentary with a popularly elected president	Pure parliamentary	Assembly-independent
Cyprus	Belarus	France	Austria	Albania	Switzerland
	Russia	Poland	Bulgaria	Belgium	
	Ukraine		Croatia	Czech Republic	
			Finland	Denmark	
			Iceland	Estonia	
			Ireland	Germany	
			Lithuania	Greece	
			Macedonia	Hungary	
			Portugal	Italy	
			Romania	Latvia	
			Slovakia	Luxembourg	
			Slovenia	Malta	
				Moldova	
				Netherlands	
				Norway	
				Spain	
				Sweden	
				Turkey	
				UK	

Sources: M.S. Shugart and J.M. Carey, *Presidents and Assemblies: Constitutional Design and Electoral Dynamics* (Cambridge: Cambridge University Press 1992), p. 41; A. Siaroff, 'Comparative presidencies: The inadequacy of the presidential, semi-presidential and parliamentary distinction', *European Journal of Political Research* 42 (2003): 287–312.

determine in practice directly who leads the government (although an electoral college may be used, as in the USA).

- The president 'is always constitutionally the head of government, *regardless of the party composition of the legislature*' (Budge et al., 1997, p. 239; emphasis added). He or she names and directs the composition of the government and has some constitutionally granted law-making authority (e.g. the right to introduce legislation, or a legislative veto, that is, to block the assembly's legislative proposals).
- Both the president and the legislature are elected independently of each other for a fixed, constitutionally prescribed term.

The key characteristics of a pure **parliamentary system of government**, like the British political system, are that:

- 'The head of the government – for whom there are various different official titles such as prime minister, premier, chancellor, minister-president, and taoiseach – and his or her cabinet are dependent on the confidence of the legislature and can be dismissed from office by a legislative vote of no confidence or censure' (Lijphart, 1992, p. 2).
- There is 'no popularly elected president with real political powers' (Budge et al., 1997, p. 238). In some European democracies, the monarch still serves as a ceremonial head of state; in

● **Parliamentary system of government**: in a general sense any system of government which operates through a popularly elected parliament. In a more specific sense, 'parliamentary systems of government' are systems in which the heads of government are selected by the assembly, govern through a majority in the assembly and can be dismissed by the assembly through a vote of no confidence.

Key Figure 5.1

Barack Obama (1961–)

Barack Hussein Obama, the 44th (and first African American) president of the USA, was born, as the release of his full birth certificate has now confirmed, in Hawaii, the son of a white American mother and a black Kenyan father. As a child he lived for some years in Indonesia. He worked as a community organizer in Chicago, and after graduation from Harvard Law School worked as a civil rights attorney and a lecturer at Chicago Law School. He was elected to the Illinois senate in 1996 and the US Senate in 2004, becoming one of only six African Americans ever to have served in the US Senate. He defeated Hillary Rodham Clinton in the Democratic Party primaries in 2008 and was elected President of the USA, taking office in January 2010.

Obama's intelligence, energy, commitment and charisma first came to wide public attention when he became the first black person to be appointed editor of the *Harvard Law Review*. In his political career he has focused on social issues, such as the reform of health care, while also tackling the great economic difficulties arising from the financial crisis and the recession of 2008/09. He committed his government to a timetable for the withdrawal of US troops from Afghanistan. The result of the mid-term elections in 2010, which returned a Republican majority to House of Representatives, was probably a consequence of the ongoing economic difficulties, but posed problems for the ability of the President to push through his policies. The death of the al-Qaeda leader Osama bin Laden in May 2011 in a raid by US troops on the house in which he was living in Pakistan contributed to a substantial rise in Barack Obama's rating in public opinion, but controversies continue over social issues, public spending and continued economic problems. Obama announced his intention to run for the presidency again in 2012.

others this function is exercised by a president who is elected by parliament or some other form of electoral college.

- The heads of government are selected by the legislature. The political scientist Arend Lijphart (1992, p. 3) uses the term 'selected' rather than 'elected' because 'the process of selection can range widely from formal election to the informal emergence from inter-party bargaining in the legislature followed by an official appointment by the head of state'.

The diagrams in Figure 5.3 summarize the above and characterize the primary links of delegation and accountability between different actors in 'pure' presidential and parliamentary systems of government (although most systems are not 'pure' in the sense of these 'ideal-typical' definitions). Table 5.1 is an attempt to classify European parliaments according to the above criteria. Out of 38 states listed in the table, only 19 fit the model of a (more or less) pure parliamentary system, and only

one the model of a pure presidential system of government. The remaining 18 regimes are not well represented by the traditional classification of parliamentary versus presidential systems of government. Many of them are mixed or 'hybrid' types with a popularly elected president (with varying degrees of constitutional power) *and* a confidence relationship between a head of government (whose office is constitutionally separate from the office of head of state) and parliament (which, as we saw above, is untypical of presidential systems of government). The two most important versions of such systems are depicted in Figure 5.4. The political system of Switzerland, with its rotating presidency and the lack of a confidence relationship between parliament and government, escapes convenient classification altogether.

Duverger (1980) has termed such hybrid systems 'semi-presidential'. Because the constitutions of the countries covered by Duverger's definition vary considerably, some authors have distinguished different types of 'semi-presidential' systems, the

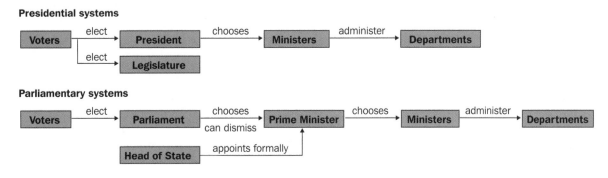

Figure 5.3 The logic of delegation and accountability in presidential and parliamentary systems of government

most prominent being a distinction between 'premier-presidential' and 'president-parliamentary' systems (for a recent summary, see Siaroff, 2003). The French system of the Fifth Republic (since 1958) could be classified as 'premier-presidential' system. The president has significant authority (especially in foreign affairs) and – when the president's party controls a parliamentary majority – his power to appoint the prime minister may be more than a mere formality. However, the prime minister and cabinet still depend for their political survival on the support of a parliamentary majority, and the president cannot unilaterally dismiss a cabinet that enjoys the confidence of a parliamentary majority. If the French president's party controls a majority in parliament, the French system has, in practice, many similarities with a presidential system. In all other cases, the prime minister is in a stronger position, as long as he or she is supported by a parliamentary majority. Under such circumstances, the

French system resembles more a parliamentary system of government. The Russian president, by contrast, has the power to dismiss a government even when it is supported by a parliamentary majority. Therefore, the Russian system can be classified as 'president-parliamentary', a system with stronger presidential power over the composition of the government than in 'premier-presidential' systems. A number of European states have elected presidents, whose powers are so constrained to the role of a ceremonial figurehead that they are in practice parliamentary systems of government (e.g. Austria, Bulgaria, Finland, Ireland or Portugal). A final category in Table 5.1 (with no presidential control over the cabinet and maximum separation of assembly and cabinet survival) can be termed 'assembly-independent' systems of government (Shugart and Carey, 1992). The only European system of government that fits this description is that of Switzerland, which does not have an elected

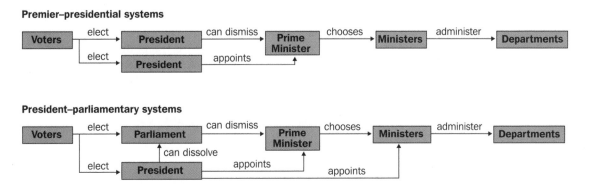

Figure 5.4 The logic of delegation and accountability in hybrid systems of government

BOX 5.2

The advantages and disadvantages of presidential and parliamentary government

In comparison to parliamentary systems of government, the main advantages of presidential systems are said to be:

- They are believed to guarantee executive stability, because the president's term of office is fixed, whereas executive stability in parliamentary systems of government may be threatened by the cabinet's loss of majority support in the assembly.
- They can be said to command a higher degree of democratic legitimacy, as the chief executive (usually called the president) is directly elected. This contrasts with the indirect election or selection of the executive by parliament in parliamentary systems of government.
- They are often believed to have a more effective system of checks and balances, because executive and legislative powers are clearly separated. In parliamentary systems of government, by contrast, executive and legislative powers are 'fused' as long as the cabinet enjoys parliamentary majority support, because the government usually controls the majority in the legislature. Presidential systems are taken to be characterized by more limited government.

In comparison to parliamentary systems of government, the main disadvantages of presidential systems are often considered to be:

- The separation of powers between the president and the executive on the one hand and the legislature on the other may turn into 'deadlock' when disagreement between the two bodies occurs. Unlike in parliamentary systems, with party disci-

pline and the possibility of a vote of no confidence, presidential systems of government often do not have any effective mechanisms for resolving such disagreements.

- Presidential systems are often said to suffer from 'temporal rigidity'. The president's fixed term in office 'breaks the political process into discontinuous, rigidly demarcated periods, leaving no room for the continuous readjustments that events may demand' (Linz, 1992, p. 120). Under parliamentary systems of government, by contrast, 'myriad actors' may at any time between elections adopt basic changes, cause realignments, and above all, make or break prime ministers' (Linz, 1992, p. 124). The possibility for parliament to remove a head of government in the middle of a legislative term or for the head of government to dissolve parliament prematurely, if he or she loses parliamentary confidence, gives parliamentary systems of government more flexibility to respond to political change.
- Presidential government is said to operate on a 'winner-take-all' basis. 'In a presidential election, only one candidate and one party can win; everybody else loses. Moreover, the concentration of power in the president's hands gives him or her very little incentive to form coalitions or other power-sharing arrangements. Especially in an already divided and polarized nation, winner-take-all is highly likely to create even more division and polarization' (Lijphart, 1992, pp. 18–19). This criticism has often been levelled against the presidential systems of Latin America, but could also be applied to the ethnically and/or socially divided new democracies of Central and Eastern Europe.

president as head of state and where the (collegial) government is chosen by the assembly, but cannot be removed by it.

There has been a long-standing and contentious debate in politics and political science about the merits of presidential, parliamentary and hybrid systems of government (see Box 5.2). It is characteristic of this debate that the advantages of presidential systems are simultaneously seen as the disadvantages of the parliamentary system, and vice versa (Lijphart, 1992). The increase in the number of hybrid systems in Europe since 1989 can be seen as an attempt by constitutional 'designers' to combine the advantages and avoid the disadvantages of both 'pure' systems. It could be argued that hybrid forms combine 'the advantages of direct democratic election and stable tenure associated with a presidential executive and the flexibility of a parliamentary cabinet and prime minister' (Lijphart, 1992, p. 20). In hybrid systems deadlock can be avoided and the president can potentially function as an arbitrator between the executive and legislative branches of government. They can, however, also compound legislative instability, as the experience of the 'Weimar Republic' in inter-war Germany shows. In recent years, many Central and Eastern European countries that started as premier-presidential systems directly after their transition to democracy, have – through constitutional reforms or changes in political practice – reduced the role of elected presidents and moved more closely towards the model of parliamentary systems of government (see Ismayr, 2004).

Prime ministers and cabinets

Most voters and MPs expect the government of the day to have a coherent policy and to be able to implement it. If a minimum of coherence were not achieved and ministers had no control over their departments, the idea of democratic accountability to the voters would be in question. Coherence is important, because accountability depends on our being able to identify and attribute political responsibility. If political decisions 'emerge' as a result of a chaotic interplay of various forces, democratic accountability through retrospective voting would be meaningless. Coherence is also a prerequisite of effective and efficient policy-making as decisions in

different policy areas may interact with one another. Decisions in one ministry may affect a policy area for which another ministry is responsible. For example, decisions in a ministry of economic affairs may have serious implications for the ministry of social security or the ministry of labour.

Coherence and 'identifiability' of political responsibility are, however, highly problematic in modern politics. Despite the constitutional powers and political resources many heads of governments enjoy, departmental ministers and their government departments are, on the whole, quite independent. Even where a head of government is relatively dominant, he or she will have to rely on the expertise of the departments, especially the civil servants in the departments. They cooperate intensively and regularly with experts in interest groups and in the scientific community. Such '**policy communities**' around ministries are crucial for the preparation and implementation of policies and tend to resist centralized coordination.

Conflicts between ministries are often avoided rather than resolved through a coherent, common policy. There is a tendency for ministers to be reluctant to interfere in their ministerial colleagues' portfolios as they expect, in turn, their ministerial colleagues to respect their control over their 'own' ministries. This may lead to what is often referred to as '**negative coordination**', which operates solely to ensure that any new policy initiative will not interfere with established patterns of policy and organization. Negative coordination may help to control conflicts between ministries and establish a degree of unity, but has the disadvantage of a reduction in the scope for policy innovation: it is a conflict-avoidance rather than a problem-solving strategy (Scharpf, 1993, pp. 143–4).

There are various institutional mechanisms by which unity of purpose and '**positive coordination**' can be facilitated. It is possible to distinguish

● **Policy communities**: networks of government ministries, executive agencies, interest groups and other non-government actors in a particular policy area. These networks cut across the formal divide between governmental and non-governmental actors and are 'communities' in so far as they share expertise and a common definition of the problems in a particular area. A great deal of public policy, especially uncontroversial and routine legislation, is typically made in such 'communities'.

between *hierarchical* and *collective mechanisms* (Andeweg, 1997).

Hierarchical mechanisms include:

- *Prime ministerial government*, where the head of government enjoys a privileged role vis-à-vis individual ministers, and powers to appoint and dismiss ministers, or the right to formulate general policy guidelines for the government as a whole which are binding on individual ministries. Some prime ministers, such as the German Federal Chancellor, have a full-blown department (Chancellor's Office), with specialized sections monitoring the activities of each department of government. Some have a capacity for centralized policy development (for example the Policy Unit working for the Prime Minister of the UK). The effectiveness of such resources depends on the political circumstances: departmental ministers with a strong position in the prime minister's party, or ministries controlled by a coalition party, are difficult for a head of government to control. Other hierarchical mechanisms are, therefore, frequently used.
- *Inner cabinets* usually include the political 'heavyweights' in a cabinet. Inner cabinets consist of the head of government and a number of important key ministers. They usually meet regularly and attempt to coordinate the government's overall policies. Inner cabinets are smaller, more flexible decision-making bodies than the cabinet. The political weight of the ministers involved (e.g. in their parties) may help to establish a degree of coherence and resist departmental particularism.

● **Coordination, positive and negative**: 'Positive coordination is an attempt to maximize the overall effectiveness and efficiency of government policy by exploring and utilising the joint strategy options of several ministerial portfolios. ... Negative coordination, by contrast, is associated with more limited aspirations. Its goal is to assure that any new policy initiative designed by a specialized subunit within the ministerial organization will not interfere with the established policies and the interests of other ministerial units. ... Procedurally, positive coordination is associated with multilateral negotiations in intra- or interministerial task forces. ... By contrast, negative coordination is more likely to take the form of bilateral "clearance" negotiations between the initiating department and other units whose portfolios might be affected – but whose own policy options are not actively considered' (Scharpf, 1993, pp. 143–4).

- Inner cabinets have one drawback if the government is a coalition cabinet (as it has frequently been in Germany, and was in the UK from May 2010): although they may contain some party-political 'heavyweights', they do not comprehensively involve the wider parliamentary and extra-parliamentary leaderships of government parties. Consent of all parties inside and outside parliament is more problematic in coalition governments than in single-party governments as ministers from different parties may have fundamentally different policy preferences. Therefore, coalition governments often use *coalition committees* and *party summits*, which frequently include non-governmental party leaders. These bodies may prepare decisions, which are then carried out by cabinet and parliamentary majority.

Collective mechanisms are based more strongly on the equal status of ministers and include:

- *Cabinet government*: if the cabinet meets frequently and makes significant collective decisions, it can limit the extent of 'departmentalism', that is, a lack of coordination between the individual government departments. In most contemporary European countries, however, the cabinet's role as a policy coordinator has never been very strong, or is diminishing. The growth of government responsibilities means that cabinets are no longer able to coordinate and prepare all major government decisions. The initiative has shifted 'downwards' to the individual departments and inter-ministerial negotiations and 'upwards' to the head of government. Cabinets are often left with the task of ratifying decisions that were made elsewhere.
- *Overlapping jurisdictions* between ministries can improve interdepartmental coordination and overall coherence. Ministries of Finance such as the British Treasury often have overall responsibility for government spending and may have the statutory right, indeed duty, to interfere in the autonomy of so-called 'spending departments'. Another example is the German Ministry of Justice, which screens government bills from all departments in order to ensure their compatibility with the constitution and

other laws. Bilateral or multilateral inter-ministerial coordination involving a large number of expert civil servants has replaced the cabinet as the dominant collective mechanism to ensure coherence.

- *Cabinet committees* are another, related, collective mechanism that aids cooperation and coordination between different ministries. They may be permanent or ad hoc and usually comprise a number of cabinet ministers (often represented by high-ranking civil servants, or shadowed by parallel committees consisting of civil servants) in a policy area wider than the remit of individual ministries (e.g. foreign and defence policy, home and social affairs). To the extent that the head of government controls the composition and chairmanship of such committees, they can be an important power resource of the head of government.

Most governments employ a mixture of these and other coordination mechanisms to ensure coherence and to control the coordination problems caused by 'departmentalism' and coalition government. However, an equally important relationship is that between elected politicians, government ministers in particular, and civil servants, those officials who advise government ministers and are in charge of policy implementation. This crucial link in the democratic chain of delegation and accountability will be dealt with in the following section.

Ministers and civil servants

The traditional institutional device to ensure the compliance of unelected civil servants with the decisions of elected politicians has been the hierarchical organization of government departments. Government departments can be compared to a pyramid where formal power is concentrated in the hands of very few politicians at the top. Ministers are at the apex of a government department and can give orders to civil servants.

This constitutional position is common to all modern democracies. In reality, however, ministers depend very much on the advice of their civil servants. Insisting on a distinction between ministerial policy-making on the one hand and administration and implementation of this policy by civil servants on the other is unrealistic. Civil servants often have more specialized knowledge of the policy area in question than the supposedly superior minister. Ministers rely on them for advice on policy development. As a result, the formal constitutional position of a minister as an elected – and therefore democratically legitimate and accountable – head of a department who controls the civil servants further down the hierarchy is often a fiction. Even if ministers are determined to stamp their political authority on their department, they depend on the advice of highly knowledgeable experts from the civil service. Some governments have attempted to gain more independence from bureaucratic expertise by making use of outside specialist advisers, expert commissions, public consultation exercises and think-tanks. Nevertheless, the problem remains a significant one.

Another problem for the coherence of government policy is the tendency for ministers to 'go native', that is, they gradually begin to identify with predominant, often long-established norms and 'views' held by the majority of senior civil servants in their departments rather than imposing their own political preferences as electorally accountable politicians. They may acquire what could be called the norms of a departmental 'culture'. The extent to which elected politicians are absorbed into a department's 'culture' depends to some extent on the individual minister's personal convictions and strength. There are, however, *institutional safeguards* that help to tackle the problem:

- In some governments, *frequent ministerial reshuffles* are partly aimed at preventing ministers from 'going native'. The disadvantage of this approach is that departmental ministers spend relatively short periods of time in a department and are never able to acquire at least some expertise in the policy matter concerned. The dependence on civil servants for information and expertise remains considerable.
- In some countries such as Belgium, France or Sweden, ministers have their own *ministerial cabinets*. Members of such *cabinets* are often either policy experts from outside the civil service or expert civil servants politically loyal to the minister. They advise the minister on key decisions.

- In some other countries such as Germany, ministers have powers to appoint a certain number of loyal supporters to key civil service positions (*political appointees*). The minister will still be dependent on civil service advice, but high-ranking civil servants are chosen because they share his or her political views.

Some Western European countries have witnessed a massive privatization and restructuring of their central bureaucracies since the 1980s. In Britain, for example, the Thatcher and Major governments (1979–97) reduced the size of the public sector and increased the financial accountability of the remainder. Many nationalized industries, such as steel, coal, oil, water, electricity, gas, and rail transport, were partly or completely privatized. Government agencies were carved out of the Whitehall ministries to run specific services. Such agencies had an almost contractual relationship with their sponsor department, specifying the extent of public funding and the expected level of services. Wherever possible, public agencies were encouraged to compete with each other for the supply of services. This process was intensified by the coalition government in Britain from 2010.

Some of the reforms of the public sector introduced in Britain were later emulated in a number of countries such as the Netherlands, Sweden and, more recently, Germany. The British experience shows that the devolution of public services to the private sector may lead to a reduction of public expenditure and a more efficient provision of certain services, although the success of the British programmes of the 1980s and 1990s has been variable. The incoming 1997 Labour government, for example, clearly realized that the **internal market** in the National Health Service and local govern-

---

- **Internal market**: A concept from the field of New Public Management (NPM), which has come to dominate debates about the reform of the public sector in the USA, the UK, New Zealand and Sweden in the 1980s. Traditional state functions are increasingly 'contracted out' to external providers competing for a contract from government as a service 'purchaser'. Even within the public sector, funders are systematically separated from providers of services. For example, public health authorities contract with providers – such as hospitals – to supply health care on agreed terms. Public providers compete with other outside providers for the award of a contract.

ment had been problematic both in the generation of unnecessary bureaucracy and in the quality of provision. The privatizations and creation of 'internal markets' in Britain have created *new problems of oversight and accountability* as new techniques such as contracting and franchising were introduced into the management of public services. One of the main problems is that 'Public servants are becoming more responsive downwards, to their users, and less accountable upwards, to their political masters' (Hague and Harrop, 2004, p. 303).

Legislative–executive relations

To what extent are elected MPs able to hold government ministers and civil servants accountable? According to a popular view, parliaments have declined in the past century. It is often argued that the growth of government responsibilities over the twentieth century, the growing power of organized interests, the complexity of contractual arrangements in the regulatory state under the 'new public management' (see above), Europeanization and globalization have overpowered traditional parliamentarism, that governments dominate the legislative process via disciplined parliamentary parties, that backbenchers are powerless, and that the main instruments of parliamentary scrutiny, such as Prime Minister's Question Time, are ineffective. Although it is undeniable that governments dominate parliamentary business in most chambers, there are considerable differences between countries, and parliaments do exercise important powers and functions.

At a general level, all parliaments continue to fulfil important linkage functions between voters and government. Not only do MPs articulate their constituents' interests and preferences in parliament, but they also inform their constituents about political events and decisions. MPs are also an important feedback channel for ministers. They are better able than overworked ministers to maintain close contacts with their constituents, and can convey information on the effects and administration of their policies to government ministers, who – as a result of their workload – often suffer from an increasing degree of isolation from voters. MPs, alerted by voters, function almost like a 'fire alarm' that voters may use to inform ministers about the local implementation of policy (McCubbins and Schwartz, 1984). This may help ministers to monitor the effects of their policies and the activity of civil servants.

In this section we shall examine in what specific way parliaments can scrutinize governments and hold them to account, and in what way they contribute to a better exchange of information between voters and government. Members of parliament have two main types of controls vis-à-vis governments: *ex ante* **controls**, which are effective before a government takes office, and ongoing controls (or *ex post* **controls**), which become effective after a government has been appointed. We shall look at some of those controls, concentrating on the elected lower houses of parliament.

Ex ante controls

One of the key characteristics of parliamentary democracies is that members of the government, including the head of government, usually come from the ranks of the parliamentary parties. Although they may have to give up their parliamentary mandates once they assume government office (as in the Netherlands), they usually become government members after having risen through the ranks of their parliamentary parties, gaining the respect of their fellow members of parliament. In systems where cabinet ministers go through a long parliamentary 'apprenticeship' or, alternatively, gradually rise within their parties, fellow party members and members of parliament have the opportunity to gather information on prospective ministers and (as 'selectorate') exert influence on their political careers.

A comparative study of cabinets in 13 West European countries between the end of the Second World War and the end of 1984 demonstrated that, on average, three-quarters of cabinet ministers

● **Ex ante/ex post controls**: When political authority is delegated from a principal (e.g. a government minister) to an agent (e.g. a civil servant), the principal has two fundamental ways of controlling the agent. *Ex ante* controls apply before the delegation takes place. Principals may screen agents for their suitability or set out the agents' duties in contracts. *Ex post* controls apply after the delegation has taken place. Principals may monitor their agents' performance by requiring them to report on their activities or by using independent bodies to audit agent performance.

were members of parliament at the time of their appointment, looking back at an average parliamentary 'apprenticeship' of nearly nine years before they joined the cabinet for the first time (De Winter, 1991). A comparison of current ministerial recruitment in some European parliamentary democracies with the USA demonstrates the importance of parliamentary careers and membership as an *ex ante* selection mechanism. Six out of the 17 members (35.3 per cent) of President Barack Obama's 2008 cabinet (including the President and Vice-President Joe Biden) had served as Members of Congress at the time they were appointed to cabinet positions. On average, the members of the Obama administration with a parliamentary background had spent 8.5 years in Congress, before they were appointed to the cabinet. In parliamentary democracies *ex ante* screening of this type is much more important: for example, 15 out of 16 members of Federal Chancellor Angela Merkel's 2009 cabinet (93.75 per cent) were Members of the German Bundestag at the time of their appointment. On average, these ministers had gone through a parliamentary apprenticeship of just over nine years before they joined the cabinet. In David Cameron's 2010 cabinet, all cabinet ministers were members of parliament and 91.3 per cent were Members of the elected chamber, the House of Commons. The average cabinet member belonging to the Commons had spent over 13 years on its benches, before they were appointed to the cabinet. (This reflects the long time the Conservative Party and Liberal Democrats spent on the Opposition benches.) The values for the French semi-presidential system are closer to the parliamentary systems of Britain and Germany than to the ones for the USA. Eleven out of 16 members (68.8 per cent) of François Fillon's 2007 cabinet had been Members either of the French National Assembly or Senate. On average, they had gone through a parliamentary apprenticeship of just under eight years.

A further *ex ante* control refers to the process by which governments take office. Parliaments may be closely involved in the formal investiture or election of governments. In some countries incoming governments (or heads of government) must win an 'investiture vote' before they can assume power. This is the case in Belgium, Bulgaria,

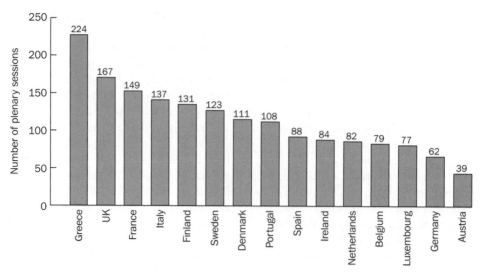

Figure 5.5   Average number of plenary sessions per year (mid-1980s) in the parliaments of 15 European countries

Germany, Hungary, Ireland, Italy, the Former Yugoslav Republic of Macedonia, the Netherlands, Slovenia and Spain. Parliaments in which governments are formally voted in have a stronger say in the delegation process (and stronger *ex ante* control) than parliaments where this is not the case.

Another constraint in executive–legislative relations is what is often referred to as 'recognition rules'. Such rules specify 'who will be asked to form governments, and in what order' (Strøm, 1995, p. 76). In countries with a plurality electoral system and/or countries without coalition government, such as Greece, Spain and the UK, the formation of a government is a relatively straightforward process. The leader of the majority party is firmly in the driving seat. In countries where elections do not produce a single party controlling a majority of seats in parliament, however, the formation process is usually more complex and parliament's role in the process of government formation can be strong, as parliamentary and party leaders negotiate a coalition agreement that may commit the emerging government to a set of policies during the legislative term.

The controls discussed in this section are constraints on the government *before* it assumes office. They do not guarantee, however, parliamentary accountability after a government has been appointed. A parliament's ability to exert scrutiny and influence vis-à-vis the government *after* the latter's formal appointment depends on the strength of ongoing or *ex post* controls. We shall deal with such mechanisms in the following section.

Ongoing (*ex post*) controls

There are a number of ways governments may be required to report on and justify their activities in parliament, thus reducing the informational asymmetry characteristic of the principal–agent relationship described above. Plenary debates in which government ministers have to report their decisions and justify them in the face of criticism by the opposition (rather than the more controlled environment of press conferences and stage-managed media events) are the most important device. Transmitted by the media, such debates are particularly important to inform the ultimate democratic principals, the voters, of the government's record and the political alternatives. As Figure 5.5 shows, parliaments vary greatly in the time they spend on debates. The Greek parliament, with 224 plenary meetings, and the British House of Commons, with 167 per year (in the mid-1980s), are to a large extent 'debating chambers'. The Bundestag, the lower house of the German parliament, where more parliamentary activity takes place in committees than on the floor of the chamber, has often been called a 'committee chamber' where the emphasis of parliamentary activity is on the detailed scrutiny of government legislation rather than providing an arena for public debate.

Usually it is his or her party membership that defines the nature of a member's oversight activities. The government, for example, will generally be more willing to share information with members of the governing parties as long as sensitive information is not disclosed to the public. Some of the processes that are relevant in this context have been labelled the 'intra-party mode' of executive–legislative relations by the political scientist Anthony King in a seminal article on the topic (1976). The monitoring carried out by the parliamentary majority party or parties can be very effective, as the government depends on their votes and other forms of support. Yet these monitoring activities are usually conducted behind closed doors.

A further key dimension of executive–legislative relations is what King (1976, pp. 17–18) calls the 'opposition mode', which is 'characterised by, indeed defined by, conflict' (ibid.). The public confrontation between government and opposition in parliament and the media may not always be popular with the electorate, yet it is crucially important for the information of voters. It prevents the government from monopolizing the political agenda, presents voters with political alternatives to government policy, reveals strengths and weaknesses of government policy, indicates the government's and opposition's competence in answering critical questions, and forces the government to justify decisions in public. Opposition parties usually (except in the case of minority governments) lack the necessary parliamentary votes to block government policy or to unseat the government, but their main aim is to appeal to the public in a permanent election campaign (Crick, 1970). This permanent election campaign is of great importance as a source of information for voters and crucial for public government accountability. A forceful opposition may also influence the government's policy choices indirectly, especially if its criticism is (quietly) shared by members of the majority parties.

Oppositions in parliamentary democracies have a whole 'arsenal' of different tools to extract information from governments and monitor their activities, including parliamentary questions and debates on problems of particular current interest. In all 27 European countries covered here MPs can put oral or written questions to the government. Committees of inquiry and committee hearings are also common instruments of extracting information from the government. Interpellations (i.e. questions to the government followed by a debate and, possibly, a censure motion on the government's answer) and parliamentary ombudsmen are less frequent.

In most parliaments, committees are the single most important monitoring device. Strong committees 'can provide legislators with the information that they need to participate effectively with the executive across a wide range of policy areas' (Mezey, 1998, p. 783). European parliaments vary greatly in the extent to which they allow committees specialization and give them a powerful role in the scrutiny of government policy.

Finally, unlike presidential systems of government, the elected chambers in parliamentary systems of government have the power to dismiss a government for political reasons. In most European democracies, this heaviest weapon in a parliament's armoury is rarely used (for data see Strøm et al., 2003, p. 165); even in cases where it has not been used very often, it is a powerful deterrent that governments have to take into account. A government that does not enjoy the confidence of the elected lower house of parliament has to resign. Yet, resignation rules vary across countries. In Denmark, Sweden, Finland and Ireland a government will usually step down after a defeat on a major bill, even if it is constitutionally not obliged to do so. In other countries (such as Britain), conventions and rules are more restrictive and protect governments more strongly: a government only has to resign after a defeat on an important bill if it has explicitly declared the vote to be a matter of confidence. In Germany, Spain and (more recently) Belgium and Poland, the rules are even more restrictive: only a constructive vote of no-confidence will bring a government down; that is, a government only has to resign if an absolute majority dismisses it by simultaneously electing an alternative government.

Table 5.2 Strength of institutional checks in 18 Western European countries

Country	'Schmidt Index'	'Huber/Ragin/ Stephens index	'Colomer Index'	Strength of institutional checks (summary indicator)
Austria	3	1	3	Medium
Belgium	3	1	3	Medium
Denmark	2	0	2	Low
Finland	1	1		Low
France	1	2	3	Low
Germany	5	4	4	High
Greece	1		0	Low
Iceland	1		2	Low
Ireland	2	0	2	Low
Italy	3	1	4	Medium
Luxembourg	1	1	2	Low
Norway	2	0	1	Low
Portugal	1		2	Low
Spain	2		3	Medium
Sweden	1	0	1	Low
Switzerland	5	6	6	High
UK	1	2	1	Low

- The 'Schmidt Index' expresses the extent of institutional constraints facing the executive branch of government. It ranges from '0' ('no constraints') to '6' ('executive branch severely constrained'). The coding is as follows: (1) executive constrained by EU membership (0 = no; 1 = yes); (2) federal system (0 = no; 1 = yes); (3) high threshold for constitutional amendments (0 = no; 1 = yes); (4) influential second parliamentary chamber (0 = no; 1 = yes); (5) autonomous central bank (0 = no; 1 = yes); (6) frequent use of referendums (0 = no; 1 = yes). The data refer to the period 1960–89 and were updated by the author of the present chapter to include the accession of Austria, Finland and Sweden to the EU (the codings for these countries were increased by 1).
- The 'Huber/Ragin/Stephens Index' ('constitutional structure index') is also an additive index using the following variables: (1) federalism (0 = no, 1 = weak, 2 = strong); (2) parliamentary/presidential government (0 = parliamentary, 1 = presidential or collegial executive); proportional representation/ single-member districts (0 = proportional representation, 1 = modified proportional representation, 2 = single-member, simple plurality systems); bicameralism (0 = no second chamber or second chamber with very weak powers, 1 = weak bicameralism, 2 = strong bicameralism); referendum (0 = none or infrequent, 1 = frequent).
- The 'Colomer Index' of 'institutional pluralism' ranges from 0 to 7. It codes the effective number of parties in parliament, bicameralism, elected president and decentralization (according to intensity from 0 to 2 except for the variable 'elected president').

Sources: Schmidt (1997), p. 252; Huber, Ragin and Stephens (1993), p. 728.

Institutional checks

The parliamentary chain of delegation and accountability in most European democracies creates a number of constraints (limitations and obligations) on governments (for example, the head of government's dependence on a parliamentary majority or the right of parliamentary minorities to request information). Some heads of government such as the prime ministers of Ireland or the UK face very few institutional constraints beyond this core chain. For an example of a head of

Key Figure 5.2

Silvio Berlusconi (1936–)

Silvio Berlusconi was Prime Minister of Italy in 1994, from 2001 to 2006 and again from 2008 to 2011. A very successful businessman in property development and media, he built up a large fortune. His companies now, among other holdings, own three leading television channels, a major advertising and public relations agency and a large publisher, and he is the owner of the AC Milan football team. He launched his own political movement in 1994. It gained sufficient seats in the general election of that year for him to become Prime Minister for the first time between May 1994 and January 1995; he became Prime Minister again from 2001 to 2006 and from 2008 to 2011.

Berlusconi's dynamic and popular image and the application of his undoubted entrepreneurial skills to politics has allowed him to become the longest-serving Italian Prime Minister since the war, based perhaps upon a sense amongst some voters that success in football and in business is likely to guarantee success also in running national life. However, he is also a highly controversial figure. Internationally he has become notorious for diplomatic gaffes and crude jokes. He has had to face multiple trials for allegations of corruption, abuse of office, and recently of sex crimes. In some cases he has been acquitted, in others the trial has expired because of time limits or amnesties on prosecutions, and in others the alleged offence ceased to be a crime under laws passed while he was in office. Some cases are ongoing. Results in elections in May 2011 when his candidate failed to become mayor of his home town of Milan suggested that the controversies might be having an impact on his political success.

Berlusconi's political career can be cited as an exemplar of the increasing role of mass-media exposure and celebrity-like status in politics, of the growing importance of personality rather than ideology in campaigning, of the role of issues of competence, integrity and morality rather than political programmes and of the rise of 'personal parties' (Bobba and Seddone, 2011).

government much embroiled in struggles with institutional (legal and judicial) constraints, see Key Figure 5.2. In many countries, however, heads of government are subject to a large number of external checks on governments outside the core chain (see Table 5.2)

International organizations or supra-national actors may act as powerful checks on national governments. The member states of the EU, in particular, are part of a complex system of multi-level governing, with intergovernmental and supra-national elements shaping the decision-making process. While national governments may have a say in the intergovernmental decision-making processes in the Council of Ministers (depending on the voting method and the country's voting power), the supranational elements (for example, initiatives by the European Commission or rulings by the European Court of Justice) may be difficult to control by national governments. In terms of democratic accountability, European integration is a double-edged sword: not only can it promote efficient policy-making but also government accountability (for example, through the European Court of Justice or benchmarking exercises carried out by the European Commission). However, it can also complicate the accountability of national governments vis-à-vis national parliaments.

Other constraints include neo-corporatist decision-making, especially in Austria, Sweden, Norway, Belgium and Luxembourg, where many policy decisions are frequently resolved through negotiations between key interest groups and the government. In countries such as Austria, Belgium or Switzerland, so-called 'consociational' arrangements provide linguistic, ethnic or faith-based communities with limited veto powers in the policy process.

In federal states such as Germany or Switzerland, regional governments have significant independent policy-making powers constraining the national government. As we have already mentioned, directly elected presidents with veto powers may constrain the government, as well. This is, for instance, possible in France and Poland. Independent central banks at the EU or national level, or constitutional courts (for example, in Germany), may provide additional external checks on the government. Even where powerful constitutional or supreme courts do not exist, the ordinary courts have often become increasingly active in providing citizens with opportunities to challenge government policies (e.g. in the UK).

Finally, in some countries such as Switzerland or Italy, referendums have been used more and more frequently in recent decades to constrain governments and increase their accountability (for a more extensive discussion of such institutional checks see Strøm et al., 2003, pp. 665–95).

The extent to which national governments are constrained by institutional checks in their political 'environment' varies considerably. Table 5.2 constructs standardized index values for each of the most important external constraints mentioned above, ranging from zero (for the country least constrained with regard to the relevant institutional arrangement, compared to all other countries in the table) to one (the country being the most strongly constrained). A summary ranking based on the mean index values of the 17 countries included in the table is designed to measure the relative strength of constitutional 'shackles' national governments are constrained by in (Western) Europe. This index suggests that the governments of Austria, Denmark, Sweden and Germany face the most far-reaching institutional checks in Western Europe. The governments of the UK, Belgium, Luxembourg and Norway are the least constrained by institutions outside the core (electoral) chain of delegation and accountability.

The costs and risks of democratic decision-making

Some national governments operate in a highly constrained institutional 'environment' at the national level. In other countries elected governments are less constrained by formal institutional

checks. From one point of view about what is desirable, the less constrained versions of government are very attractive: democracy is partly defined by majority rule. The party winning the majority (or plurality) of votes in a general election forms a government and ought to have as many political and administrative means as possible at its disposal to implement the promises it made in its election manifesto. Other bodies with lower levels of direct democratic legitimacy ought not to be able to block the execution of the government party's popular mandate. The ultimate judge will be the electorate at the next general election. The British 'Westminster model' has often been seen as an 'ideal type' of political system in which the will of the majority prevails in this way (Lijphart, 1999), although the 'Jacobin' model of the Fifth French Republic follows a similar design. Yet this 'majoritarian' model has also had its critics. In the UK, Lord Hailsham (1976) called it an 'elective dictatorship'. A different point of view about what is desirable therefore sees relatively unbridled majority rule and liberal democracy as being compatible only on two conditions: first, the effective exclusion of the minority from the policy process is mitigated if majorities and minorities regularly alternate in government; secondly, majority rule is less problematic if a country is relatively homogeneous and does not have any significant ethnic, linguistic, religious or other minorities whose demands would be permanently excluded or neglected under unfettered majority rule (Lijphart, 1999). If such minorities exist, a less 'majoritarian' system with more institutional checks on the majority and stronger incentives for the government of the day to seek consensus by consulting minorities is more suitable. One of the main drawbacks is that such a 'consensus model' makes governing more difficult and complex as governments are less able to rely on hierarchical direction than in majoritarian system with few external constraints. Decision-making 'costs' are therefore often high in such systems (see below).

Yet, governing has become more complex in all democracies. The Central and Eastern European states of the former Soviet empire have embarked on far-reaching programmes of democratization, decentralization and privatization. Many of them have joined the EU. The Western European states

Figure 5.6 External risks and decision-making costs

are facing other problems that make governing more complex. Globalization, transnational policy problems such as global warming, international migration or international terrorism, the process of European integration, the growing assertiveness of regions and regional governments, privatization and 'marketization' in the traditional public sector, the continued importance of policy communities and the growing demand on the part of citizens to participate directly in political decisions are but a few examples.

As a result, political decision-making costs have increased in most countries. The political scientist Giovanni Sartori (1987) argues that political decisions always involve a trade-off between two variables: (a) 'decision-making costs' such as the time and other resources, which are required to arrive at a certain decision and (b) 'external risks' such as the risk of incompetent decisions, oppression and similar problems (see Figure 5.6) One of the solutions he offers to the dilemma posed by this trade-off is political representation or, in the language of this chapter, delegation. Delegation reduces the number of decision-makers and hence decision-making costs, as long as agents act in the best interest of, and are accountable to, their principals. Institutional mechanisms ensuring accountability in representative democracies have been one of the main themes of this chapter.

Applying this theory to the figures in Table 5.2 shows that governments in countries with high levels of institutional constraints face high decision-making costs, because they operate in relatively decentralized systems with a relatively large number of other political actors (such as federal-state governments, constitutional courts, independent central banks and the like) with real veto powers. Negotiating compromises amongst such actors may be a cumbersome and time-consuming task. For governments of countries with low levels of institutional constraints it is much easier to reach political decisions without protracted bargaining. However, the involvement of more actors in the decision-making process also diminishes the external risk in countries with highly constrained governments, because representatives of those affected by a decision have more 'access points' to the political process and more opportunities to 'veto', influence or delay decisions, that is, to force the government to think again. The reverse is the case in countries where national governments face only minimal institutional checks.

We might, however, suggest that the processes of globalization, the growing importance of regionalism and the increasing demands citizens make for direct influence on public policy (for example, through the use of referendums) have increased decision-making costs in all European democracies. Governing has become a more time-consuming, multilevel bargaining process in which governments are agenda setters and coordinators, but often do not have the resources and expertise to impose a policy 'from above'. They need the cooperation of other actors both at the national as well as at the sub-national and supra-national level. These difficulties can be seen as undermining the ability of any government to run its country well, but they also open up opportunities. We could argue, from the perspective of Sartori's decision-making model of democracy, that we are witnessing the emergence of political systems with more opportunities for minorities to influence policy. For example, environmental pressure groups which fail to make their voice heard in the national parliament may attempt to pursue a different route and use the level of the EU or the courts to achieve their goals. Nevertheless, the problems are equally evident: if consensus is difficult to reach, the veto and delaying powers of minorities may slow down decision-making, lead to irrational decision-making or prevent necessary decisions altogether. Trade-offs seem to be inevitable in politics.

SUMMARY

- Modern democratic politics in Europe is largely based on representative government where citizens delegate political authority to representatives. Political accountability is usually achieved indirectly, by a chain of further delegation processes from elected parliamentarians via government ministers to civil servants. The nature of these representative institutions shapes the extent to which those who delegate (principals) are able to hold those to whom authority is delegated (agents) accountable.

- The possibility of using referendums, the nature of electoral systems and the degree of transparency of decision-making in political institutions shape the possibilities for citizens to influence policy and the recruitment of political elites (members of parliament, ministers, prime ministers and/or presidents).

- The relationship between members of parliament, heads of government and heads of state is strongly influenced by particular institutional arrangements: there are systematic variations between presidential systems of government, parliamentary systems of government and a number of hybrid systems. In all cases members of parliament find themselves in a very difficult position vis-à-vis the government: the government's level of expertise and information-processing capacity is vastly superior. Parliaments, however, influence the selection of ministers and employ a number of instruments to obtain information and hold the government accountable. Their ability to do so is generally underestimated.

- There is a natural tendency for governments to develop elements of 'departmentalism'. Heads of government employ a number of devices to counter these tendencies and ensure the coherence of government policy. We can distinguish hierarchical mechanisms such as prime ministerial government, inner cabinets or coalition committees, or more horizontal instruments such as cabinet government or cabinet committees.

- Like all other delegation processes, the relationship between departmental ministers and civil servants is characterized by information asymmetry. Ministers can employ a number of institutional devices to reduce the asymmetry (ministerial cabinets, politically appointed civil servants, specialist advisers and outside think-tanks).

- There is considerable variation in the extent to which governments in Europe are subject to external institutional checks such as constitutional courts, federal systems of government, independent central banks or supranational bodies such as the EU.

- The more institutional checks, the higher the decision-making costs. The fewer institutional checks, the higher the external risk faced by actors that are affected by, but not involved in, government decisions.

- The decision-making costs in the process of delegation have increased with phenomena such as globalization and regionalization.

QUESTIONS FOR DISCUSSION

- What are the most important types of referendums? What are the main advantages and disadvantages of referendums?

- What are the most important differences between the various electoral systems used in Europe? What are the implications of each electoral system for the ability of voters to hold elected politicians accountable?

- What are the comparative advantages and disadvantages of parliamentary, presidential and hybrid systems of government?

- How can ministers hold civil servants accountable?

- To what extent are parliaments nowadays reactive and marginal political actors?

- What are the main differences between majoritarian and consensual democracies in terms of the protection of minority interests and decision-making costs?

FURTHER READING

Cheibub, José Antonio (2007) *Presidentialism, Parliamentarism, and Democracy* (Cambridge: Cambridge University Press). This is an advanced book offering the most comprehensive and rigorous empirical analysis to date on the consequences of presidentialism and parliamentarism.

Gallagher, M., Laver, M. and Mair, P. (2006) *Representative Government in Modern Europe*, 4th edn (New York: McGraw-Hill). This text was written mainly for undergraduate students of European comparative government and politics and provides readers with a great deal of important factual information and analytic insights.

Gallagher, M. and Mitchell, P. (eds) (2005) *The Politics of Electoral Systems* (Oxford: Oxford University Press). This edited volume provides a survey of electoral systems and their political implications in 22 countries and a very good introductory overview by the editors.

Lijphart, A. (ed.) (1992) *Parliamentary versus Presidential Government* (Oxford: Oxford University Press). A reader containing excerpts from a number of classic texts on the comparative advantages and disadvantages of presidential and parliamentary systems of government.

Lijphart, A. (1999) *Patterns of Democracy: Government Forms and Performance in Thirty-Six Countries* (New

Haven, CT: Yale University Press). This book contrasts the 'Westminster model' as almost an ideal type of a 'majoritarian' system of government with more consensual forms of democracy. This classic in the study of comparative government and politics provides important insights into some of the basic 'mechanisms' of government and politics in contemporary Europe and beyond.

Page, E.C. (1992) *Political Authority and Bureaucratic Power: A Comparative Analysis*, 2nd edn (Hemel Hempstead: Harvester Wheatsheaf). An accessible comparative study of bureaucracies and questions of political accountability from a Weberian perspective with a focus on Britain, France, Germany and the USA.

Shugart, M.S. and Carey, J.M. (1992) *Presidents and Assemblies: Constitutional Design and Electoral Dynamics* (Cambridge: Cambridge University Press). Although the book's focus is not exclusively on Europe and is slightly more advanced than some of the texts above, it is one of the most important comparisons between parliamentary and presidential systems of government.

Stapenhurst, Rick et al. (eds.) (2008) *Legislative Oversight and Budgeting: A World Perspective* (Washington, DC: World Bank). This survey commissioned by the World Bank provides an excellent overview of parliamentary oversight of the executive branch of government.

Strøm, K., Müller, W.C. and Bergman, T. (eds.) (2003) *Delegation and Accountability in Parliamentary Democracies* (Oxford: Oxford University Press). This collection of essays currently provides the most comprehensive surveys of mechanisms of democratic delegation and accountability in West European countries. It provides theoretical insights, comparative analyses and single-country studies.

Tsebelis, G. (2002) *Veto Players: How Political Institutions Work* (New York: Russell Sage Foundation and Princeton, NJ: Princeton University Press). This advanced text is a standard work on the role of 'veto players' in the working of government and politics. It is based on rational-choice and game theory and suitable for advanced readers.

CHAPTER 6

Political Participation in Europe

DIETER RUCHT

Democracy works towards the self-determination of humankind, and only if the latter materialises does the former become true. Then political participation will be identical to self-determination.

Jürgen Habermas et al., *Student und Politik* (1961), p. 15

This chapter aims to provide an overview of the extent and forms of political participation in Europe, bearing in mind Habermas's injunction that democracy is more than a set of institutional arrangements for government; it is also a form of popular self-management. These terms should be clarified from the outset. First, political participation is understood as a broad category of behaviours that stretch far beyond the conventional and institutionalized forms of citizen activities such as voting (Topf, 1995; Gundelach, 1995; Khan, 1999). Secondly, with the ending of the Cold War, the meaning of Europe as a territorial category has to be broadened. Though in geographical terms Europe always included the territories at least as far east as the Urals, this was less evident before 1989, when Westerners referred to Europe in a political and cultural sense.

We have to take into account that Europe is a highly differentiated conglomerate, with many different states and cultures that each merit individual attention. We lack not only the space for such country-by-country description here, but also information on at least some aspects in some countries. Thus the reader should not expect details on particular countries but rather a rough picture that, at best, highlights some general aspects and trends that would need further elaboration.

This chapter will first discuss the notion of political participation in more general terms, laying out its elementary dimensions and more specific forms of activities. It will then discuss political participation in relation to the organization of power and the **cleavage** structure in contemporary European countries. Based on these more conceptual reflections and discussions, an empirical picture of four major frameworks of political participation will be drawn, namely those of parties, interest groups, social movements, and the mass media. Finally, these frameworks are located in a model of political-interest mediation and some more general conclusions on participation as an asset of democracy are suggested.

Dimensions and forms of political participation

The term 'participation' implies that an actor – an individual, a group, or an organization – takes part in something. Not all activities, however, can be called participation. We do not 'participate' in a meal when we are eating alone, but we may participate in a dinner party. We may be nominal members of a religious congregation, but unless we attend its services at least occasionally, let alone play a more active role, we do not participate in this congregation. Thus, participation means taking part in a *collective* endeavour which usually requires some sort of *activity* from several or all of those involved. When talking about *political* participation, this implies that we are not apathetic citizens but take an active role in political life by following events, articulating our demands and opinions, and trying to influence the processes of decision-making that ultimately have binding consequences for larger groups or even the whole of a society (Keim, 1975; Milbrath, 1965; Verba, Nie and Kim, 1978; Pateman, 1970; Parry, Moyer and Day, 1992; van Deth, 1997).

Acting as one among hundreds of citizens in a neighbourhood, tens of thousands in a city, millions in a nation, and hundreds of millions in a still larger community such as the European Union (EU), usually means that our individual impact tends to be extremely marginal. Nevertheless, people do participate in politics at all these levels, in many forms, and sometimes at considerable cost. Thus, it is likely that reasons and advantages exist that, in the view of participants, outweigh the costs.

Participation can be perceived from very different angles. On the one hand, it means the strategic pursuit of individual goals by influencing political processes that affect the achievement of these goals. In its most reduced form, the mechanism by which this influence can and should be sought is the election of political leaders. In economic theories of democracy which put the cost–benefit calculating individual at the centre, this act of choosing between different groups of elites is what democracy is about (Downs, 1957). According to Joseph Schumpeter (1966 [1942], p. 252), democracy is nothing other than a 'political method'. Whether or not many citizens participate in this process, and whether or not they engage beyond voting, is of secondary importance. Some political scientists (e.g. Morris Jones), who Bachrach (1967) ascribed to the school of 'democratic elitism', even consider intensive participation as an evil in so far as it seems to indicate widespread dissatisfaction among the populace, which distrusts the political elites, or, worse still, it may deter the elites from making necessary and appropriate decisions. These political scientists perceive a 'democratic dilemma' of 'system effectiveness versus citizen

participation' (Dahl, 1994) and therefore want to limit the latter.

On the other hand, some normative theories of democracy consider the range, breadth and intensity of citizen participation as a criterion for a 'good' or, using Benjamin Barber's (1985) term, a 'strong democracy'. Whatever stance one takes in this unresolved debate about what defines and makes democracy work, it should not prevent us from taking a look at political participation as it actually takes place. Such an empirical investigation, however, cannot be undertaken without conceptual tools. A first step in this direction is an identification of four dimensions of political participation.

1. Participation can be institutionalized or non-institutionalized. In the former case, participation is defined by explicit rules which, in their most comprehensive form, define who is entitled to do what by using which channel in targeting which person or institution. Such rules, for example, exist for the election of political bodies, **referenda**, appeals to administrative or constitutional courts, and, to a lesser degree, participation in public hearings and inquiries. In other cases, participation is only defined as a right, with no (or only a minimum of) further specification. For example, most modern constitutions guarantee the right of public assembly and free speech regardless of the place and the particular form. In some countries, gatherings and marches in public places have to be announced in advance to local authorities and then permission is subject to certain requirements (della Porta and Reiter, 1998). Similarly, in some countries professional and relatively continuous lobbying is only allowed by groups that are officially registered. Finally, there are forms of political participation that are completely unregulated simply because formal rules are considered to be unnecessary or because the form of action is illegal anyway and therefore cannot become a matter for rules of

---

● **Cleavages** separate social or political groups that, having a relatively stable and coherent view on fundamental aspects of society, take opposite stances on issues such as religion, individual liberties and state intervention, social justice, and market economy.

● **Referendum**: A ballot which allows voters to make a choice between alternative policies on a particular issue. Referendums (*referenda*) are important instruments of direct democracy.

conduct. An example of unregulated participation is an open letter that a group of citizens addresses to the government; another is a consumer boycott of an enterprise that is trading with an apartheid regime; examples of illegal forms of political participation are a politically motivated wildcat strike or a blockade of car traffic by environmentalists.

Closely related to the aspects of institutional or non-institutional forms of participation is the particular setting or arena in which participation takes place. Some of these arenas, a referendum, for example are highly institutionalized. On the opposite end of the scale are streets and other public places where many forms of participation can take place, ranging from a collection of signatures to a protest rally to violent action. The mass media provide an important forum for political participation (beyond the fact that they report on many relevant activities, including participation in other settings), particularly because they can potentially reach the whole population. In addition to the kind of setting or arena, we can also distinguish them according to their geographical scope, ranging from the local to the international or even to global levels.

2. A second dimension refers to the kind of actor engaged in participation. In some cases, participation is an individual act, either by choice or by institutional definition. This is true for somebody writing a letter to a Member of Parliament. Also, voting is by definition (secret ballot) an individual act, in spite of the fact that millions may vote on the same day. Because the effect of an individual act is unlikely to have a substantial impact, citizens often unite to engage in collective participation. They create informal groups such as citizen initiatives, join a formal organization, such as a professional association, political party, trade union or religious congregation, or they gather on one particular occasion, for example a big demonstration. Participating actors can also be categorized by their socio-demographic and attitudinal characteristics, such as sex, education, political orientation, and so on.

3. A third dimension is the material and non-material 'cost' of participation. Signing a petition for animal rights may take only a few seconds and does not involve any risk. Attending a national demonstration in the distant capital may cost a participant a whole day in addition to travel expenses. Conducting a hunger strike can be a long, awful and dangerous activity which only a few are prepared to undertake, under exceptional circumstances. Other forms of political participation, such as volunteering over many years in a political party, are less spectacular but still require an enormous investment of time and energy.

4. Finally, participation can vary greatly according to its thematic scope and ambition, ranging from moderate attempts to influence very specific political matters to fundamental and radical efforts to change society as a whole. An example of the former is an attempt by a particular social group to prevent an unfavourable new tax regulation. An example of an ambitious and bold activity was the fight of civil society groups against a communist regime in spite of the threat of harsh sanctions.

Numerous empirical variations in these four dimensions can be combined in many different ways. Consequently, political participation is extremely multifaceted. There is a risk of seeing only the trees and missing the wood. Instead of exploring the impressive variety and contingency of countless acts of participation, we should instead look for deeper structures that in many ways underlie and influence the rippling surface of everyday political participation. One way of putting numerous acts of political participation into perspective is by referring to the concept of societal and/or political cleavage structures.

Power, cleavages and political participation

Solidarity, money and power are probably the most important forces that regulate exchanges between individuals, groups and organizations in modern societies. Solidarity is a crucial mechanism in holding together, for example, families, self-help groups, neighbourhoods and ethnic communities. Money is a key mechanism in regulating economic exchanges. Power, according to the famous definition by Max Weber, is the ability to achieve desired ends despite resistance from others.

Modern democratic societies have developed various institutional devices to prevent the concentration and misuse of power in the hands of a few. Most important among these devices are:

(a) the opportunity to replace power-holders via regular elections by the citizens;
(b) the institutionalization of civil liberties;
(c) the horizontal distribution of power between the legislative, executive and judicial branches of the state, together with the latter's capacity to penalize the illegal use of power; and
(d) the vertical distribution of power between the central state and regional and local authorities.

These devices have been suggested and achieved within the framework of nation-states. In more recent times, international governmental bodies have also acquired some formal executive power. However, the means to control these powers democratically still remain underdeveloped, as the example of the EU demonstrates. The European Parliament is still far from having similar competencies in comparison to national parliaments. Moreover, the representatives of the European Commission are not directly elected by the citizens.

Power relations not only characterize the relationship between the citizenry and the state, and exchanges within the state; they also exist between and within groups of citizens, as a closer look at any political party, trade union, religious congregation or even an informal citizen initiative would reveal. Particularly in conflictual situations, we can observe that some individuals or bodies do have the ability to pursue their objectives despite the resistance of others, although the use of power may not be as obvious as in the case of policemen or military forces acting against citizens. For example, discrimination against women, based on more or less subtle mechanisms, continues in many spheres of social and political life in spite of legislation granting equal rights (Orloff, 1996).

Since power is unevenly distributed and tends to privilege some interests at the expense of others, power struggles tend to be ubiquitous in politics; but this does not mean that everybody is in conflict with everybody else. There are two reasons why

power relations and conflict lines within the citizenry tend to crystallize into relatively stable structures. First, some groups acquire considerable power through their large membership, organizational strength, and critical role for the functioning of society in general. In advanced capitalist societies, the most powerful groups besides the state authorities are the representatives of capital, notably the employer organizations, and the representatives of the workers and employees, that is, the trade unions. In some Western European states such as Sweden, Norway, Denmark and Austria, these two blocs, together with the state representatives as the third pillar of power, formed a tripartite system of bargaining and decision-making that, because of its formal parallels to a pre-liberal corporatist society, was called **neocorporatism** (Schmitter and Lehmbruch, 1979; Lehmbruch and Schmitter, 1982; Williamson, 1989). This system of decision-making could only work as long as the elites of each of the three pillars could count on the support (or at least the tacit consent) of the broader groups they claimed to represent. In practice this meant that the rank-and-file was not involved in the neocorporatist game, but had to accept the decisions of their leaders. In other words, political participation was a matter for the very few who acted on behalf of the many who remained passive. Over time, however, and due to processes which will be explained in later sections of this chapter, this relatively clear-cut neocorporatist model was weakened and came closer to the pluralist model.

A second reason why power relations tend to crystallize in relatively consistent and stable patterns has to do with the structuration of society in terms of broader social classes and groups. Many people live in similar situations, adopt common world-views, and have common interests. This is true, for example, of farmers, workers, entrepreneurs and religious people. Because of the commonalities within these groups, and divergent values and interests between them, many concrete conflicts and power struggles are just variants of or

---

● **Neocorporatism** is an arrangement in which the leaders of interest groups, together with representatives of the state, jointly make policies and justify these vis-à-vis their respective members or clientele.

derivations from deeper and more general sources of conflict that are relatively stable over time. These general lines of tension and potential conflicts have been called societal cleavages. Cleavages may lead to conflict, but they are not the manifestations of conflict. The latter indicate the former, but cleavages cannot be directly observed. Referring to Western democratic societies, Lipset and Rokkan (1967) have argued that these societies are marked by deeply rooted cleavages that, at least since the end of the First World War, have been 'frozen' in stable constellations of political parties. From this perspective, divisions and alliances between certain types of political parties are organizational representations of underlying social cleavages. The most important cleavages, according to Stein Rokkan (1997), are those between the rural and urban work forces, the political centre and the periphery, religious and secular groups, and between capital and labour. (In political terms, the two latter cleavages are often conceptualized as the Right/Left cleavage.) More than thirty years after Lipset and Rokkan's analyses of party systems, it has become obvious that the first two cleavages have lost some of their significance, whereas the cleavage between capital and labour is still vital in many countries.

In addition, however, new or renewed cleavages have gained some importance. One is that between Old and New Politics (Hildebrandt and Dalton, 1977) or, in a slightly different formulation, materialism and **postmaterialism** (Inglehart, 1977 and 1981). Old Politics, or materialism, emphasizes the values of economic growth and material security, whereas New Politics, or postmaterialism, focuses on aspects of life quality in terms of democratic rights and the integrity of the social and human environment. In party politics, this cleavage was originally marked by the conflict between the established parties (both rightist and leftist) on the one hand and the New Leftist and Green parties on the other. Leftist and postmaterialist values have influenced each other, so that we cannot really speak of a clear distinction between the Left versus Right and the materialist versus postmaterialist cleavage.

● **Postmaterialism** is a set of values such as freedom of speech and protection of the environment that are supposed to gain relevance after basic material needs (e.g. food and shelter) are satisfied.

Starting in the 1980s, the (re-)emergence of ethnic conflicts seems to indicate a further cleavage. As far as Western Europe is concerned, this became apparent with the increased influx of immigrants and asylum seekers from countries that are culturally distinct from the domestic ethnic majority (see Chapter 3). On the one hand we find a number of parties which, though not *necessarily* nominally liberal parties, pursue a liberal course in dealing with immigrants and asylum seekers; on the other hand we witness the rise of revitalized or newly founded extreme-right parties with nationalistic and xenophobic undertones. It seems that this constellation not only marks one particular area of conflict, but also has implications in addressing labour-market policy, taxation, attitudes towards European integration, and so forth.

Whereas the concept of cleavage structure was essentially conceived to get a better understanding of party constellations and voter alignments, it appears that cleavage structures have much broader implications. Cleavages also determine the constellation of major interest groups and social movements. This will become clearer when political participation is discussed with respect to these three types of interest mediation in European democracies.

Before considering separately the three types of interest mediation, it may be useful to take a brief look at the different levels of membership in voluntary associations in Europe, based on data from the World Values Surveys in 1990 and the European Values Survey in 2000. The underlying question was whether respondents were members and/or currently doing unpaid work for one of more out of a list of 15 voluntary organizations (welfare, religious, youth, sport, trade unions, environment, etc.). Differences between countries are striking regarding overall membership density (measured as the percentage of adults being member or actively involved in at least one voluntary association, with party membership excluded). In 2000, Sweden was at the top with a density of 95 per cent and Lithuania at the bottom with 17 per cent (Weßels, 2003, pp. 4–5). More generally, the northern countries and the Netherlands range high whereas the eastern and south-western countries range low. When comparing changes over time, membership density has increased in a quite a few countries (e.g.

Sweden, the Netherlands, Austria, Ireland, Italy and Spain), decreased in a number of other countries (particularly in Eastern European states) and remained roughly stable in still other countries (e.g., Denmark, Finland and Britain) (Weßels, 2003). Interestingly, based on data from the year 2000, a strong relationship was found between membership density and democracy (measured by two different indices, the Freedom House Index and the corruption index provided by Transparency International). The more democratic and the less corrupt a country, the higher the membership density.

Party politics and voting behaviour

It is hard to imagine modern politics without political parties. Virtually all official decision-makers are members of parties. Moreover, these decision-makers would not have come into office without the support of parties, which, of course, ultimately depend on voters. Political parties are the main conveyor of people's interests and preferences into the polity. Note that the turnout in electoral polls is relatively high in Europe (Borg, 1995) when compared with most other forms of political participation. It is, however, important to note that in some Western European countries, for example Belgium, Luxembourg and Greece, voting is compulsory.

As discussed above, people's interests and preferences are not isolated from each other, but cluster along various cleavages, which are mirrored by the constellation of parties – sometimes called the party system – in a given country. Instead of specializing in one single issue, parties usually represent a broader set of beliefs and aims that are guided by a general perspective on how society and the political order should be. It has been rightly argued that one important function of political parties is to bundle together a great number of particular issues. Although parties directly compete with each other and therefore tend to emphasize differences in their profile, with regard to their own clientele they moderate and balance different demands which, in their original form, would be incompatible. In this perspective, political parties are important mechanisms for pooling, mediating and moderating sets of demands and claims.

By and large, today's parties still mirror the big cleavages that took shape in the last century. Political analysts have identified five major 'party families': the communist, socialist and social-democratic, liberal, conservative, and extreme-right parties. In addition, a separate farmers' party exists in some countries which still have a significant agricultural sector. In most other countries, this constituency has been absorbed by the more encompassing conservative parties, which also tend to represent the conservative-oriented religious groups. Furthermore, some countries also have ethno-regional parties centred around conflicts between centre and periphery and/or cultural cleavages. Finally, from the 1970s, New Left parties and Green parties have been established in most European countries (Richardson and Rootes, 1994; Bomberg, 1998). These additional cleavages have broadened the spectrum of political parties, which had narrowed in the decades after the Second World War.

Whereas Western European countries only gradually tended to broaden the spectrum and increase the number of parties, the fall of the communist regimes in Eastern Europe suddenly triggered a mushrooming of political parties, which represent not only the full spectrum from the far Left to the far Right, but also very particular social groups (Nagle and Mahr, 1999). On average, the number of parties in Eastern Europe is far greater than in the west (Budge et al., 1997, p. 231). It is likely that, after a transition period, some of these parties will simply fade away, whereas others will fuse, so that we can expect a concentration process leading to a party spectrum similar to that in the west.

At least in Western Europe, the lines between the (once ideologically more consistent) party families have blurred, so that, for example, Conservative parties now claim to represent the interests of the working class, whereas Social Democrats are no longer focused solely on the working class. This trend towards 'catch-all parties' (Kirchheimer, 1996) not only facilitated the formation of party coalitions, but also resulted in a dealignment of voters. Voting became less and less determined by status and class (Crewe and Denver, 1985).

In the USA and some other countries parties tend to be loose networks without a regular

Key Figure 6.1

Robert Michels (1876–1936)

A German political sociologist who spent most of his adult life in Italy, Michels was initially a socialist and a proponent of democracy, but in his last years sympathized with Italian fascism. In his main book *Political Parties: A Sociological Study of the Oligarchical Tendencies of Modern Democracy*, originally published in 1911, he studied the reason why a full-blown democracy cannot be established. In his answer, he pointed to the structure of political parties and other large associations, taking the German Social Democratic Party as an exemplary case. According to Michels, the party had transformed itself from a socialist movement to a bureaucratic apparatus that was preoccupied in maintaining and enlarging its own power, neglecting the initial goals. Michels argued that, with continuing existence and growth, informal groups become organized and eventually transform themselves into an oligarchy. The latter is marked by a clear separation between a few leaders and a mainly passive rank and file. The leaders are supported by a bureaucratic apparatus that, with its interest in self-maintenance, loses its zeal for radical change. Though Michels assumed that this trend is inevitable, he still advocated moderating the effects of this 'oligarchical illness' by educating the people. However, he was pessimistic about the chances of broad participation within political organizations, and democratic politics in general.

membership, a consistent programme and a coherent body of sections ranging from the local to the national levels. Political parties in Europe, however, tend to be clear-cut organizations that are ideologically relatively coherent. As a rule, they are based on a strong apparatus of professionals, but also include a significant number of members ready to volunteer. However, as in many other political organizations, numerous activities are concentrated among minorities that are highly motivated, whereas others remain relatively passive and hardly do more than paying their fees and, at best, occasionally attending a meeting. Overall, parties are crucial forums for political participation, offering many possibilities for playing an active role with varying degrees of involvement. Precisely because party politics becomes more and more dominated by the professionals, and in particular by key players in the 'party machinery' (Michels, 1962), the activity of the rank-and-file is important in exercising some control over the leadership, which otherwise may drift towards transforming the party into a fully-fledged oligarchy, as Robert Michels (1962) (see Key Figure 6.1) had predicted early in the twentieth century. More than the average voter who is an outsider to party politics, the rank-and-file member of a political party is able to recognize

the risk of parties degenerating into mere tools for acquiring power against the interests of internal democracy.

In most European countries, parties tend to have a considerable number of members (Katz and Mair, 1992), of whom only a certain proportion actively takes part in the party's life. Today, the biggest parties in Europe, although they have experienced a drastic loss of membership in some countries, still have around three-quarters of a million members. For example, the Social Democratic Party in Germany had about 694,000 members and its allied conservative counterparts, CDU/CSU, a total of 772,000 members by the end of 2002. The Conservative Party in Great Britain claimed 750,000 members in 1994 but was down to roughly 300,000 ten year later. The British Labour Party declined to approximately 250,000 members by the end of 2003, its lowest level for 70 years. Membership rates tend to be particularly high in the two countries which have the most pronounced neocorporatist structure, namely Austria and Sweden. In the 1980s, more than one-fifth of the electorate in these two countries were members of a party, while in West Germany, the UK and the Netherlands, the rate of party membership was relatively low, within a range between 3–4 per cent.

Considering changes over time, we see an over-riding trend towards decreasing party membership when comparing the first elections in the 1960s and last elections in 1980s (Budge et al., 1997, p. 215). More recent data from the European Values Survey suggest that this trend has continued (figures not displayed here). Losses in party members were particularly high in Finland, France and the Eastern European countries for which cross-time data are available. The general trend is also confirmed by data from the European Social Survey in 2002 and 2008. Party membership decreased in most countries, was stable in a few others, but increased only in Denmark and Greece.

Obviously the plethora of new parties that have emerged in Eastern Europe could not numerically compensate for the losses of the old communist or communist-controlled parties. For example, the East German Communist Party, the SED, had 2.2 million members before 1989, whereas its successor, the PDS, had only around 100,000 ten years later. By the end of 2003, the number of members was down to 65,000.

Although party membership is decreasing rather than increasing, and most of those who nominally are party members actually do not play an active role within the organization, we should acknowledge the fact that a sizeable minority of the population continues to be involved in party politics. Many of them devote much time and energy in support of the party and their wider political beliefs. Just consider the tens of thousands of party members who are elected to local and district councils and who work, for the most part, not for their personal interest but for the sake of the party and, more generally, the community of citizens.

Interest-group politics

The term 'interest groups' is used here in a wide sense, covering not only political pressure groups but also the great variety of formal and informal organizations in areas such as welfare, health, sports, education and religion. Many of these organizations are not, or are only occasionally, involved in politics. Since the writings of Alexis de Tocqueville, it has been repeatedly argued that the ensemble of these groups is vital for a working democracy because they express and enhance a sense of community. According to Robert Putnam (1995), these groups embody **social capital** and are crucial in 'making democracy work'. By contrast, societies in which the citizens are not embedded in such associational structures, but rather form a diffuse 'mass', have been perceived as inherently unstable and vulnerable to political alienation, sharp conflict and even dictatorship (Kornhauser, 1959). Other observers have been more sceptical about the flourishing of interest groups – not so much because of the sheer numbers of these groups, but rather because of the asymmetry of interest representation. In contrast to the assumptions of naive versions of pluralist theories, critical observers stress that not every interest in society is represented by a corresponding interest group, nor do the size of the groups and the intensity of their activities reflect the dimension and urgency of the problems that actually exist. Critics point to the fact that it is those interests that can easily be organized and have a great potential for conflict and disruption that dominate the political agenda. They are also likely to be favourably treated in political decision-making. The classic examples of this are the interest groups of employers and workers. In this particular case, because of their inherently conflictual if not antagonistic position, it is unlikely that one side will completely dominate the political game (Marsh, 1983), although studies have shown that the employers tend to be in a stronger position. This is also reflected at the level of EU policy-making (Schmitter and Streeck, 1991).

Another, clearly more problematic, case are the farmers, who, in some countries, have an extremely high organizational membership rate (Sweden nearly 100 per cent, Germany 90 per cent, England and Wales 80 per cent, France 75 per cent; Budge et al., 1997, p. 162), while at the same time lacking a

---

● **Social capital**: Two different meanings prevail. In the understanding of the French sociologist Pierre Bourdieu, social capital consists of an individual's intangible resources based on personal ties with other people – resources that can be used to enhance the individual's social status and career. The US political scientist David Putnam means by 'social capital' the associational life of a society that creates bonds of solidarity and a sense of responsibility for the common good and the functioning of democracy.

direct and strong opponent representing organized citizens. Consumers' organizations are not in a position to provide this opposition. This has led to a situation where farmers' associations in some countries came close to dictating agricultural policy. No wonder that the agricultural sector was heavily subsidized. In the long run, however, this worked to the detriment of small farmers in particular; but, more generally, it was disadvantageous for entire national agricultural sectors. The constant flow of state subsidies prevented this sector from becoming more competitive. It is no coincidence that even today, and in spite of decades of criticism and many attempts to reform, nearly half of the EU budget is devoted to financing agriculture, including the storage and destruction of overproduced goods. In a similar vein, the German coal industry was and still is heavily subsidized owing to the pressure of the mining industry. It produces at costs that are more than double world market prices.

While, as we have seen, some interests are powerfully represented and fiercely protected, others remain virtually invisible. This tends to be the case when the underlying problems are broad and diffuse, thus not fitting the relatively short perspective of electoral periods. An example of such a diffuse interest is the call to 'save the planet' for future generations. Also, the interests of individuals who are structurally isolated from each other tend to be underrepresented, such as those of consumers, women and the unemployed. Finally, the same applies to the interests of those groups which are numerically and/or socially marginal and therefore have difficulties in getting a voice, such as asylum seekers and political prisoners. The situation worsens when the two latter criteria come together, as in the case of poor single mothers. In these situations, there is only hope if other, more central and more articulate, groups act as advocates for those who lack organization and voice.

Broadly speaking, the field of interest groups is structured along the same societal cleavages as are expressed in the political party systems. Thus we find groups situated along the cleavages of the religious versus the secular, centre versus periphery, dominant versus minority ethnic groups, and, most important, Left versus Right. In contrast to the party system, which in most

Western European states includes a very limited number of parties that claim competence in many if not all policy domains, the spectrum of interest groups comprises much more, and more specialized actors. Thus, unlike political parties, interest groups tend to focus on a limited set of related issues. As a result, we find an amazing variety of interest groups, some of them consisting of many millions of people (e.g. automobile clubs), others gathering just a few dozen; some groups having a broad agenda, others being extremely specialized; some being close or even affiliated to an existing party, others carefully trying to remain independent from any party; some acting mainly in closed circles of lobbying, counselling and negotiating, others seeking public visibility and support.

Size of membership is one, but not always the most important, organizational resource to make an impact on public policy. If it were the most important, automobile clubs would have a tremendous say in politics. In practice, other often much smaller groups such as employer associations and trade organizations are likely to be of more importance when it comes to policy impacts. Bowles and Gintis (1986, p. 90), referring to the employers' liberty to invest or not invest, and to hire and fire, stress that the 'presumed sovereignty of the democratic citizenry fails in the presence of a capital strike' by potential investors.

Due to their distinct national traditions and economic and social structures, the relative size and importance of various kinds of interest group varies greatly from country to country – although countries akin to each other such as the Nordic states or Mediterranean states tend to show similar patterns. But we should also note that the aggregate membership in interest groups may vary greatly from country to country, and likewise the comparison of the same kinds of interest groups across countries (see Figure 6.1).

All available data suggest that many more people are engaged in interest groups than in political parties. This probably still holds when we take into account that an individual can be a member of only one political party but have multiple memberships in various interest groups. Table 6.1 shows the percentages of those actively participating in selected types of organizations in European coun-

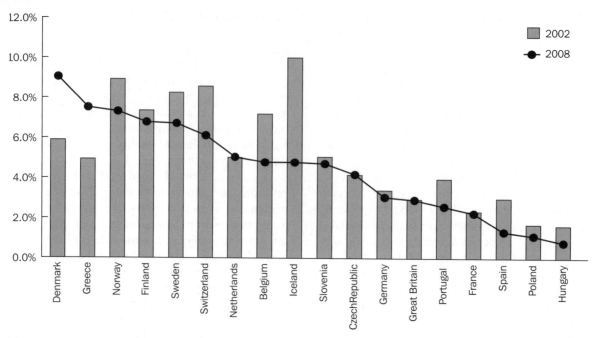

Figure 6.1 Party membership density in 18 European countries, 2002/2008

Source: European Social Survey, Rounds 1 and 4.

tries in 2002. In general, fewer people actively participate in eastern than in western countries. On the whole, activity in organizations concerned with religion, sports/outdoor and culture/hobbies (figures not displayed here) is significantly more frequent than in the organizations listed in Table 6.1. Though not all the groups mentioned in this table are concerned with politics, and some only occasionally so, we can conclude that there exists an extremely rich and multifaceted associational spectrum which creates both needs and opportunities for political participation. For the most part, participation in this context does not mean directly engaging in professional politics, but rather, taking part in societal activities, which, however, may have an indirect impact on policy-making. For example, the many voluntary associations engaged in matters of social welfare and health reduce the load and cost of state activities in these areas; successful strikes for higher wages in industry may increase production costs and thereby reduce the export of goods, which in turn decreases income from certain taxes and thus puts pressure on state finances. Even

seemingly non-political activities are likely to have political consequences. Moreover, the sheer number and size of associations in one policy area may impress politicians so that they tend to take the claims of these associations into account.

Unfortunately, with a few exceptions, we do not yet know the precise international comparative data on trends in associational membership, so the current debate about an alleged decrease of 'social capital', that is, the positive effect of a rich associational life for the overall quality of democracy, cannot be settled. Based on somewhat sketchy and unsystematic data from the USA, the argument has been made that the sense of community and social responsibility, as indicated by participation in associational life, is diminishing (Putnam, 1995). The decrease of party membership in most European countries, as well as the decrease of unionization, suggests this argument may apply outside the USA.

Unionization in the former communist regimes in Eastern Europe was traditionally high, particularly because it tended to be associated with certain privileges. With the fall of communism, union

Table 6.1   Participation of people from 19 European countries in selected organizations (%)

		Business/ Profession/ Farmers Orgs.	Humanitarian Orgs.	Environm./ Peace/Animal Orgs.	Social Clubs	Other Voluntary Orgs.
Austria	3.3	3.0	4.3	5.3	6.2	4.8
Belgium	4.8	4.7	4.4	4.5	15.9	3.7
Germany	3.4	3.0	2.6	3.2	10.0	3.5
Denmark	10.6	5.8	2.7	1.9	9.3	2.5
Spain	1.7	1.7	3.7	2.0	5.3	1.4
Finland	3.5	3.1	2.6	2.1	3.7	3.3
France	2.6	1.8	3.9	2.6	7.7	4.9
Great Britain	2.5	5.3	2.8	3.2	11.5	4.2
Greece	2.3	1.9	0.5	0.7	1.9	0.8
Hungary	2.6	3.1	0.8	1.1	4.6	1.8
Ireland	3.6	5.5	3.5	3.1	7.9	3.2
Italy	5.1	3.2	2.2	2.0	2.2	0.7
Luxembourg	2.6	2.6	2.2	1.9	5.2	1.1
Netherlands	2.2	4.8	1.5	2.1	5.4	4.2
Norway	8.8	4.7	3.3	1.3	13.0	4.3
Poland	1.6	0.9	0.9	0.7	1.6	1.1
Portugal	1.3	1.1	2.2	1.5	2.6	1.9
Sweden	6.9	3.8	4.1	1.7	10.9	5.0
Slovenia	3.0	2.9	1.9	0.5	4.9	2.4

Item: Participation in the last 12 months.

Sources: European Social Survey, Round 1 (2002).

membership in Eastern Europe has drastically decreased. According to data provided by the Organization for Economic Cooperation and Development (OECD), in the average of four countries in Eastern Europe (the Czech Republic, Hungary, Poland, the Slovak Republic), union density dropped from around 47 per cent in 1995 to 20 per cent in 2005 (see Figure 6.2).

In recent decades, union membership has also declined in most parts of Western Europe, including economically strong countries such as Great Britain, France, Italy and the Netherlands (Budge, Newton et al., 1997, p. 172). With the exceptions of Finland, Sweden, Norway and Spain, membership was stable (Denmark) or decreasing across Western Europe between 1985 and 1995. In some countries, such as Italy, France and Great Britain, the considerable decline in union membership had already

begun during the 1970s. In Great Britain, admittedly during the period of aggressive anti-union politics by the Thatcher government, the unions lost 2 million members (16.4 per cent) between 1979 and 1983 (Visser, 1986). When calculating changes of unionization between 1980 and 2005 in Western European countries, we see the biggest losses in Portugal, Ireland and Austria, very small losses in Norway, Sweden and Belgium, but increases in Finland, Spain and, most clearly, in Iceland (see Figure 6.2).

It would be risky, however, to use party and union membership trends to draw more general conclusions about associational life. First, some associational sectors, such as nature conservation and environmentalism, have experienced significant growth since the late 1990s. Secondly, new branches of associations (e.g. consumer groups and

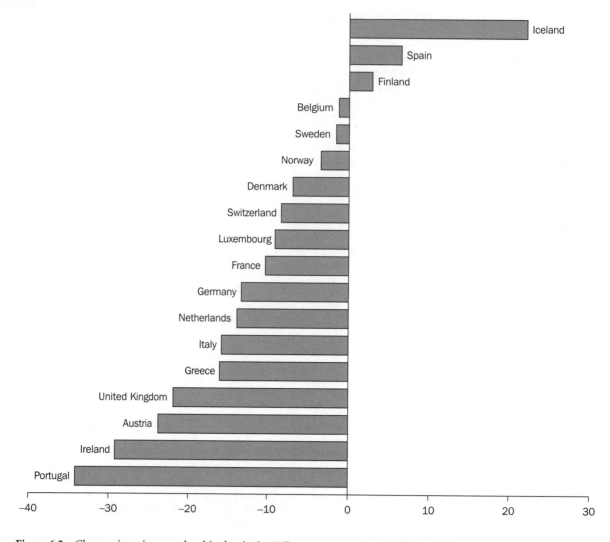

Figure 6.2   Changes in union membership density in 18 European countries, 1980/2005 (%)

Source: OECD Stat Online.

transnational non-governmental organizations) are probably growing to a greater extent than some of the older branches are shrinking. Thirdly, the nature of associational life may be underreported because membership, the category usually asked about in surveys, has a special meaning that does not necessarily fit the more informal adherence to, and type of, association that seems to have become more common in recent decades. These associations, very similar to the social movements to be discussed next, tend to be networks of communica-

tion and action rather than formal interest groups. Let us now take a look at social movements and protest politics.

Social movements and protest politics

In singling out social movements as a particular form of collective behaviour, we should not ignore the fact that they overlap with interest groups and political parties (Rucht, 2010). In contrast to interest groups and parties, however, social movements tend to form loose networks without a clear-cut membership, a definite programme and statutes, and elected bodies. Social movements may incorporate organizations (such as parties and interest groups), but as a whole they do not form an organization.

Major social movements may have a considerable life-span and attract large numbers of people, though these large numbers are typically only mobilized for distinct protest events and do not take part in the other less spectacular activities of such groups. Protest, of course, is not a privilege of social movements. Even well-established interest groups and political parties, sometimes even those in power, may engage occasionally in protest activities. However, in contrast to such established groups who usually have either institutionalized or other ways of access to the polity, social movements typically rely on protest because other channels of influence and pressure are not available, and material resources tend to be scarce. For this reason, social movements also rely heavily on means of electronic communication (email lists, social networking sites, etc.) which are cheap to use and may have a great reach. These tools are not only used by specific movements or for specific campaigns, for example to call for participation in global and continental social forums or so-called counter summits. Moreover, media groups based on electronic tools such as Indymedia have emerged since the late 1990s and quickly spread to many countries. Generally speaking, however, the new media serve to get and distribute information rather than to recruit and mobilize activists. For the latter purpose, face-to-face communication continues to play a central role, especially when it comes to participation in more demanding if not risky forms of activity.

As emphasized earlier in the chapter, the activities of social movements and protest groups (henceforth social movements) constitute an important, though often neglected, part of political participation (Rucht, 2007). Social movements have brought about major changes in history, for example, the abolition of feudalism and slavery, the breakthrough of liberal democracy, the ending of colonial exploitation, the granting of full citizen-ship to women, and the fall of some communist regimes in Eastern Europe. All this became possible only because millions of people stood up and fought for their rights, often taking high risks when acting against the established political forces.

In common with political parties and the more or less established interest groups, social movements are not distinct entities that act in isolation from each other and their wider environment, but rather form clusters along societal cleavages. This, for instance, was true in the 1920s and 1930s when fascist movements challenged the leftist movements in Italy, Germany and Spain. Today, we find similar conflictual constellations, though these tend to be more focused around particular issues, such as the rights of immigrants and asylum seekers, abortion, law and order, and so forth. Besides the opposition between movements and counter-movements, more often we see movements targeting the state, in particular the political elites in power. Given the central role of the state not only for political order but also for many societal conditions, social movements, which by definition want to change society, can hardly avoid trying to influence or challenge the state directly. This is true, for example, in conflicts around regional autonomy, in which social movements quite often act alongside regionalist parties to oppose the central government. Other groupings such as the women's movement also have to target the power-holders if they want to change the public policies which, taken together, have a great influence on women's conditions of life (equal opportunity, equal pay, paternal leave, provision of child-care, abortion, etc.).

How relevant in quantitative terms is participation in social movements when compared with political parties and interest groups? Large-movement organizations, which come close to being regular interest groups, may comprise several hundred thousands of regular supporters and many more sympathizers and/or donors. Greenpeace in Germany, for example, had over half a million regular donors since the late 1980s. The activity of those donors, however, hardly goes beyond signing an annual cheque, so we may question whether this 'credit-card participation' (Richardson, 1995) can be counted as true political participation. At the opposite end of the scale, we find numerous citizens' groups which, taken together over the full

Table 6.2   Changes in unconventional political participation in 17 European countries, 2002–08 (%)

	Signed a petition		Taken part in a lawful demonstration		Boycotted certain products	
	2002	+/- in 2008	2002	+/- in 2008	2002	+/- in 2008
Belgium	33.9	-6.4	8.4	-1.0	12.8	-1.7
Czech Republic	15.1	-0.3	4.3	-0.1	11.0	-3.2
Denmark	28.2	5.7	8.3	1.0	22.9	-1.4
Finland	24.0	8.3	2.0	0.5	26.8	3.4
France	33.8	-0.7	16.9	-2.3	25.8	1.8
Germany	31.3	-0.1	11.4	-3.4	24.6	4.1
Great Britain	39.5	-2.2	4.4	-0.5	26.2	-1.8
Greece	4.6	0.2	4.3	1.5	8.5	6.7
Hungary	4.2	3.0	3.7	-1.5	4.8	1.6
Netherlands	22.8	0.7	2.8	0.5	10.9	-1.3
Norway	37.1	0.6	9.0	-1.8	20.2	2.3
Poland	7.1	0.6	1.4	0.2	3.9	0.9
Portugal	6.8	-1.7	4.2	-0.5	3.2	-0.1
Slovenia	11.8	-3.1	2.7	-1.2	5.1	-0.1
Spain	22.3	-4.6	16.1	-0.2	7.7	0.2
Sweden	40.8	6.4	6.4	0.0	32.5	4.8
Switzerland	40.4	-2.1	7.7	-0.3	33.6	-7.8

Item: 'There are different ways of trying to improve things in [*country*] or help prevent things from going wrong. During the last 12 months, have you …'.

Sources: European Social SurveyH Rounds 1 and 4.

spectrum of political areas, may number as many as tens of thousands in each of the large European countries. A study on 'Left-alternative groups' in West Berlin identified over one thousand groups in 1993, focusing on new social movement issues such as peace, the environment, women, gay and lesbian rights, nuclear power, civil rights, and development in Third World countries (Rucht, Blattert and Rink, 1997).

A second source for identifying the activities of social movements is surveys. The Political Action Study (Barnes, Kaase et al., 1979), its follow-up study (Jennings, van Deth et al., 1990) and analyses based on the World Values Survey (Roller and Weßels, 1996) show that in all countries under investigation: (1) a sizeable minority of the population actually participated in various kinds of unconventional activities and (2) many of the participants tended to combine conventional and unconventional forms, with very few (admitting to) having been involved in illegal activities. It was

found that the proportion of people participating in unconventional activities has increased over the last few decades (Topf, 1995). This trend even continued until relatively recently (see Table 6.2).

When comparing three forms of 'unconventional political participation' as studied in the European Social Survey in 2002 and 2008, we find mostly minor changes only. The percentage of people who have signed a petition during the previous 12 months has decreased in 9 out of the 17 countries under consideration, with the biggest decline in Belgium (–6.4 percent), while the largest increases were in Finland (8.3 percent) and Sweden (6.4 percent). Changes in participation in lawful demonstrations were mostly insignificant. Worth to mention is only the case of Germany (–3.4 per cent). The proportion of people who boycotted products during the previous 12 months was also fairly stable in most countries, with the exceptions of Switzerland (–7.8 per cent), Greece (6.7 per cent) and Sweden (4.8 per cent). In sum: According

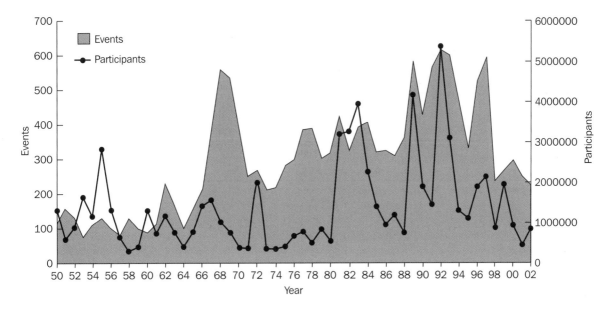

Figure 6.3 Protest events and participants in Germany, 1950–2002

Source: Prodat/Rucht (Wissenschaftszentrum Berlin für Sozialforschung).

to the European Social Survey, unconventional participation underwent no dramatic changes in the early twenty-first century.

Probably the best indicator of the strength and development of various social movements is their actual protest activities as reported in daily newspapers. A comparative study on protest movements in France, Germany, the Netherlands and Switzerland in the period 1975–89 found significant differences in the levels and thematic distribution of protests (Kriesi et al., 1995). The mobilization in 'unconventional' protest (such as collections of signatures, demonstrations, strikes, blockades and violent attacks) per million inhabitants was strongest in Germany (211,000), followed by the Netherlands (198,000), France (178,000) and Switzerland (156,000). When strikes are included, the volume of participation was highest in France, followed by Germany, the Netherlands and Switzerland (Kriesi et al., 1995, p. 22). If the issues of the new social movements are grouped together, they account for 73.2 per cent of all identified protests in West Germany but only 36.1 per cent in France. In contrast to France, the peace movements in Germany and the Netherlands attracted many

protesters. However, the student movement, the area of education, the labour movement and the anti-racist movement had most participants in France. Switzerland takes the lead for the solidarity and regionalist movements, whereas Germany ranks highest in mobilization against nuclear-energy installations.

More detailed data covering the period from 1950 to 2002 for West Germany (including East Germany from 1989) show that the number of protests increased until the mid-1990s, while mobilization in these protests followed a more discontinuous pattern (see Figure 6.3). The peak of participation in the first half of the 1980s was mainly an effect of the peace movement. The peak in 1989 reflects the mass demonstration in East Germany that brought down the communist regime, while the peak in 1992 is mainly a result of several large demonstrations, all taking place in West Germany, against xenophobia. The structure of protest in West Germany has changed considerably over these 45 years. The average size of protest was highest in the 1950s and lowest in the 1960s. Whereas protests in the 1950s were predominantly organized by single, national, interest groups, in

Table 6.3   Types of protest activities in Germany, 1950–2002 (%)

	1950–59	1960–69	1970–79	1980–89	1990–99	2000–02
Moderate	34.7	49.6	42.5	20.3	17.4	11.0
Demonstrative	52.2	35.6	42.1	53.1	51.3	71.1
Confrontational	10.2	10.3	11.1	17.0	13.1	9.0
Violent	2.9	4.5	4.3	9.6	18.2	8.9
Total	100	100	100	100	100	100
N	1138	2556	3005	3788	4668	775

* Including East Germany since 1989.

Source: Prodat/Rucht (Wissenschaftszentrum Berlin für Sozialforschung).

later periods both informal groups and alliances of different kinds of groups moved into the foreground. Overall, issues of democracy and citizen participation, labour and peace were most important, though their relative weight changed over time. While during the 1970s and 1980s most protests centred around new social movement issues, in the 1990s 'bread-and-butter issues' (unemployment, housing, welfare) and – partly related to that – conflicts around right-wing extremism and immigrants became important in East Germany and, to a lesser extent, in West Germany, where new social movement issues continued to be significant. (see Table 6.2).

The distribution of forms of protest activities has also changed over time. Most importantly, the proportion of violent events increased from the 1950s to the 1990s. The extraordinary rise in the 1990s is almost exclusively due to right-wing extremism and xenophobia. We should also note, however, that compared with the other activities, very few people participated in all kinds of violent events and, moreover, mobilization *against* right-wing extremism and xenophobia by far outnumbered the opposite forces.

The growing relevance of movement and protest politics, sometimes perceived as a result of the failure of political parties (Lawson, 1988; Kitschelt, 1990; Richardson, 1995), has raised the question of whether some countries are on their way to becoming 'movement societies' (Neidhardt and Rucht, 1993; Tarrow, 1994; Meyer and Tarrow, 1997). It seems that protest that previously was

more concentrated in particular social strata has spread out to many groups in society, including even relatively privileged groups such as teachers, dentists and airline pilots. Obviously, the threshold for engagement in protest politics has been lowered (Norris, 2002). At the same time, distinct forms of protest are no longer bound to particular issues and social groups. Sit-ins and blockades that used to be the tactics of civil-rights groups are also practised by conservative protesters. Previously unconventional forms of protest have become 'normalised' (Fuchs, 1991) so that the distinction between conventional and unconventional participation is gradually becoming meaningless. Modern means of communication have contributed to diffuse protest within and across national boundaries and some groups, most notably Greenpeace, have become professionals in the staging of protests and, through their sophisticated public-relations work, are widely known. Moreover, these groups tend to be more trusted by the populace than established political forces. Dalton (2004) has shown that citizens in the liberal democracies have become more sceptical about their government. 'Thus, one of the consequences of decreasing political support is a search for new democratic models or reforms that will move the democratic process closer towards its theoretical ideal' (Dalton, 2004, p. 203). Protest politics is an important factor in this process. Overall it seems that protest has become a common practice that complements rather than competes with the more established forms of political participation.

The mass media

Modern politics, including most forms of political participation, is strongly shaped by the mass media (Lichtenberg, 1990). Clearly the mass media are in a different position from parties, interest groups and social movements because they are not primarily created to influence political decisions, let alone to achieve political power. However, most of our information about political issues, players, and activities and decisions comes from, or is transmitted by, the media. Protest, for example, is practically nonexistent for those who are not participants or bystanders unless it is reported in the media. It follows that most political activities are geared to receiving (positive) media coverage.

As many studies have shown, the media do not just mirror but also shape developments. In other words, they select, comment on, evaluate, take part in and are sometimes partisan in political matters. Thus, at least in some instances, the media participate in political matters in very similar ways to, say, interest groups. This is most obvious when the media are directly concerned, for example, when it comes to defending the freedom of the press and access to information. But they also play a political role in many other instances: they may more or less openly favour a political candidate or party during an electoral campaign, as was the case with the UK tabloid newspaper the *Sun*, which bluntly supported the Conservative Margaret Thatcher in the late 1970s, Tony Blair's New Labour in the late 1990s – as long as he did not stray too far from the owner's (Rupert Murdoch) views on Europe – and eventually again a Conservative, namely David Cameron in 2010.

A second reason why the media have implications for political participation is that they can provide a crucial forum for various kinds of political actors. Although the mass media establish a structural asymmetry between the few who are audible and visible and the millions who merely read, listen or watch, the media can choose whether or not to accept advertisements from political groups, and can give a voice to protest groups or individual citizens as well as to key figures, invite letters to the editors, organize debates and political talk-shows, and so on. The new electronic media in particular have the potential for more participatory and interactive ways of communicating political issues and arguments. Thus the media themselves can contribute to strengthening the idea of active citizenship or, alternatively, rely mainly on prefabricated statements issued by the professional public relations units of the established players.

Compared with the early decades of the twentieth century when most mass media were closely bound to, if not directly controlled by, particular political groups, the mass media have become more independent and probably more balanced in their views *in so far as they follow an ethos of professional journalism*. Related to this, it also appears that relevant parts of the mass media put more emphasis on their role in providing a forum for information, debate and deliberation rather than perceiving themselves as educators, tutors, agitators or entertainers of the 'masses'. This complements a perception of citizens as not restricted merely to the role of selecting between competing sets of political elites. By and large it seems that the mass media mirror and shape the trend towards a more active citizenship, though we should not forget the existence of media segments that are deplorable if our ideal is to encourage an informed and active citizenship.

Towards a participatory society

The extent to which political participation is valued depends on how one views what democracy ought to be like (see, for example, the views of Jürgen Habermas quoted at the head of this chapter) (see Key Figure 6.2) On the one hand, proponents of a purely representative model tend to reduce the political activity of the ordinary citizen to the act of voting. In this perspective, the citizen has the right and duty to select the political leadership which, to judge by its professionalism, expertise and relative detachment from any particular social group, is likely to take the best decisions. Hence intensive participation should be reserved for a relatively small elite. On the other hand, proponents of an 'associative' (Hirst, 1994), 'strong' (Barber, 1985) and **participatory democracy** (Pateman, 1970)

● **Participatory democracy** connotes decentralization of power for the direct involvement of amateurs in authoritative decision-making.

perceive high levels of participation as an expression of a healthy democracy. In this perspective, participation is not only a means to reach certain goals but a goal in itself, that is, a desirable form of political life. Although it has been argued that low levels of participation may indicate high levels of satisfaction among the citizenry, this is not substantiated by empirical evidence (Dalton, 1996). In fact low participation seems to indicate disappointment, apathy and political alienation among those who stand aside from the political process. Typically, these are the people who are less privileged, educated and articulate, so their interests are further marginalized by their low voice (Key, 1958; pp. 642–3; see also Lijphart, 1997). Based on his secondary analysis of various surveys, Dalton (1996, p. 79) concluded that 'protest is more common among the better educated'. Hence both high and socially broad levels of participation should be considered as a strength rather than disregarded. An informed citizenry, and especially a citizenry which is also active 'Beyond the Ballot' (Smith, 2005) is an asset for the quality and stability of democracy. It may prevent elites from pursuing essentially their own interests, and it may contribute to a more balanced sharing of responsibility within the community – from the local to the international levels. Currently, we are witnessing both disenchantment especially from professional party politics (Hay, 2007) and a growing interest in new forms of citizen participation (Brannan and Stoker, 2007; Smith, 2009).

Looking back over history, the evolution of modern democracy can be interpreted as a progressive inclusion of groups that were initially perceived as not worthy and/or not capable of taking part in the political process (Dryzek, 1996). Having reached a stage where, with the exception of a few borderline cases, all social groups in the Western world have acquired the right to vote, we should encourage people to broaden and intensify political participation so that we come closer to the meaning of democracy as 'the rule of the people by the people for the people'.

Historically, modern political parties, interest groups and social movements have emerged and developed largely in parallel to each other, so that their development has not been a 'zero-sum game' in which one player can only gain at the expense of the others. We have no reasons to assume that the growth of one type of actor is inherently bound to the stagnation or decline of another. Moreover, many people tend to combine participation in these different structures according to their strategic assessments of their situation and needs. Finally, it appears that the borderlines between these three forms are blurring – thus, parties and interest groups tend to adopt forms of protest politics, whereas protest groups tend to seek close alliances with parties and interest groups. Also, we should not forget that many established parties and interest groups are outgrowths of social movements.

Parties, interest groups, movements and the mass media are located in the public sphere, where they mediate between individual citizens and the political decision-makers. Though these systems of interest may empirically overlap, they have distinct functions and properties and so cannot replace each other. Therefore, from an analytical perspective, they should be conceived as distinct entities. With regard to the politically oriented segments of the mass media, this seems to be relatively clear. They are, for the most part, commercial enterprises whose main function is to report and comment on news. In contrast to the three other systems, the mass media relatively rarely act politically to further their own interests.

We can conceptualize the structural location of parties, interest groups and movements in a model of interest mediation as illustrated in Figure 6.4. At the centre of the model is the public domain, to which, in principle, every actor has access. The non-public environment of this domain is composed of two spheres that form separate worlds and have to be bridged by the four systems of interest mediation. One sphere is that of the private lifeworld of the citizens; the other is composed of the segments of the political–administrative system that are kept apart from the public, in particular the state bureaucracies. Other parts of the state, most notably parliament and the courts, are to a large extent part of the public domain.

The systems of interest mediation which are more or less centred in the public domain have differential reaches in each domain. Parties tend to be less strongly anchored in the social milieux of citizens, but reach far into the realm of the state, including its non-public institutional settings. In

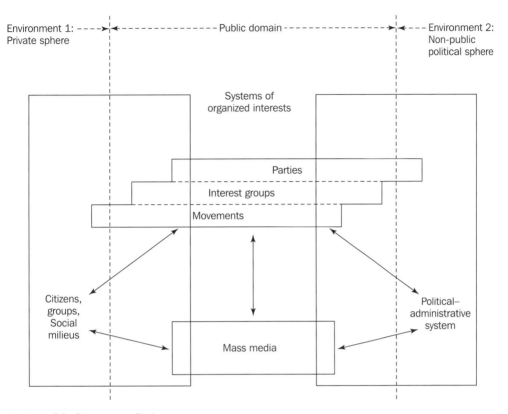

Figure 6.4 A model of interest mediation

Source: Adapted from Dieter Rucht, 'Parties, Associations and Movements as Systems of Political Interest Mediation', in Josef Thesing and Wilhelm Hofmeister (eds), *Political Parties in Democracy* (Sankt Augustin: Konrad Adenauer Stiftung, 1995), p. 108.

some countries, such as Austria and Sweden, there are even fears that parties have achieved a quasi-statist role. Parties are also distinct in that they not only transfer the demands of the citizens into the decision-making systems but, at least as governmental parties, they also try to legitimize political decisions and, quite often, to defend the state's interest vis-à-vis challenging groups. Thus there is a two-way process of interest mediation.

Interest groups tend to be more symmetrically centred in the public domain, having both roots in the social milieux of the citizens and some leverage within the state institutions, though not to the same extent as political parties (for example, associations are not officially represented in parliaments).

Social movements are probably the most strongly embedded in the life-world of the citizens, and claim to be their most authentic voice, but have hardly any access to state institutions.

Finally, the mass media certainly have links to both environments of the public sphere, but do not tend to have significant overlaps with them. Instead, the mass media concentrate on reporting what is going on in the public sphere and therefore attentively watch the other systems of interest mediation, including the public parts of the political–administrative system.

As far as empirical data are available, they suggest that political participation is increasing rather than decreasing in most European countries. Moreover, it seems plausible that political participation is unlikely to recede, even though we have witnessed, more recently, decreasing participation in some groups and some areas. First, according to survey data, interest in politics is stable or even tending to increase. In addition, more and more people are drawn into higher education. We know that there exists a strong correlation between

education, interest in politics, and political participation.

Secondly, the technical means and the facilities
both to follow and to intervene in political matters
are becoming more easily available, cheaper and
more efficient. Given modern techniques of
communication, it is not difficult to organize a
group, to produce a newsletter, and to reach people
by other channels of communication. Not surprisingly, the internet and, more recently, Twitter are
becoming important tools for mobilization among
protest groups. Demonstrations, for example by
UK Uncut, and camps, for example in Madrid's
Puerta del Sol, in early summer 2011 against
government programmes for expenditure reduction, are examples of participation in which a
major part was played by informal electronic
communication and networking rather than organization by pre-existing bodies.

Last, but not least, we have witnessed a diversification of social groups and group-specific needs
and claims which cannot easily be adopted and
promoted at an aggregated level. Today, it is very
difficult to identify the common denominator of a
social class. Though this category is far from being
useless, it is obvious that we also need more specific
concepts such as 'socio-moral milieux' or 'lifestyles'
to adequately cover the diversity of social positions,
interests and behaviours. Similar to the constantly
growing variety of specialized journals covering
virtually every aspect of social life, we also witness a
proliferation of groups, both outside and within
broader associations, which articulate very specific
political demands and critiques. Whereas in the late
nineteenth and early twentieth centuries political
activism was usually closely bound to embeddedness in a distinct ideological camp, which, in turn,
was bound to a particular social class, today's
activism is more situational and contingent on the
specificities of the groups to which we currently
feel close at any given time. As with the growing
volatility of rational voters, other forms of political
participation also become more flexible and more
diverse, allowing for a broad variety of combinations.

Considering these trends, it also becomes apparent that the act of voting every few years for a
particular candidate or party is not an effective way
to feed very specific interests into the political

process. First, we can only vote for parties as a
whole, whereas ideally we would wish to combine
some aspects from one manifesto with other
aspects from other manifestos. Secondly, voting
results at best only vaguely indicate a certain direction in which the majority wants to see things
move – they are certainly not a clear instruction
regarding the whole variety of policy matters at
stake. Because the act of voting closely resembles
signing a blank sheet of paper whose text will only
take shape afterwards, other forms of participation
in concrete policies in particular settings and at
critical points of time become more and more
important.

Even though societal conditions for increased
political participation in Europe may be favourable
today and in the foreseeable future, it is clear that
participation has its limits for several reasons. First,
the time an individual can spend on political
participation is restricted to the extent that people
have to work and fulfil their other daily duties.
Secondly, participation in modern policy-making
requires one to have specific knowledge and skills
in order to be recognized as a serious player and
eventually become influential in specific policy
areas. Thus, even when better equipped than ever,
we may restrict participation to those questions we
are most familiar and/or concerned with, while in
many other areas we tend to rely on some sort of
representatives, not necessarily elected politicians,
who supposedly express and promote our interests
without our explicit instructions. Closely related to
this is the fact that many political matters are influenced by non-local and even international factors
beyond our immediate field of vision and control.
At these higher levels, however, it becomes more
difficult to participate. Although some groups,
particularly international non-governmental actors,
try to follow and adapt to this shift towards higher
levels of decision-making (Greenwood and
Aspinwall, 1998; della Porta, Kriesi and Rucht,
1999), they tend to do so as small circles of political
entrepreneurs acting on behalf of a diffuse audience of supporters who may or may not applaud
but have no real say within the organization, as the
case of environmentalists suggests (Rootes, 1999). A
striking example of this is Greenpeace – a highly
professional organization supported by many
donors but essentially lacking the rank-and-file that

Key Figure 6.2

Jürgen Habermas (1927–)

Born in Germany, a philosopher, sociologist and political commentator in the tradition of leftist critical theory. He is preoccupied with two concerns: first, the analysis and critique of modern capitalist societies; secondly, the study of the normative, legal and empirical foundations of modern democracy. Inspired by the principles underlying an 'ideal speech situation', that is a discourse ruled by nothing else than the 'power of the better argument', Habermas, in political terms, advocates an enlightened citizenry that actively takes part in public life and political decisions, and a procedural rationality of political decision-making that, on crucial issues, is ultimately based on universal values instead of a mere compromise between conflicting interests. In his two-volume book *The Theory of Communicative Action*, originally published in 1981, Habermas argues that societal systems such as the economy (ruled by money) and the state (ruled by power) tend to colonize and undermine the 'life-world', which is geared towards 'communicative' as opposed to instrumental and strategic action. In his more recent work, Habermas acknowledges the role of associational groups at the periphery of the political system as critics and challengers of those groups who are essentially power-oriented.

would represent the organization below the national level. These difficulties in participating as a layperson in national and international politics probably also account for the fact that, in spite of the fashionable talk about globalization, the cross-national cooperation of many political groups is still very moderate and, as the German case demonstrates, protest activity continues to concentrate on sub-national levels. Also EU-related protest has increased to a much smaller degree than one might expect (Tarrow, 1995; Rucht, 2002).

Sceptics such as the German sociologist Niklas Luhmann (1969) have argued that demanding intense participation for everybody in every political decision would mean installing frustration as a principle. Others, such as Jürgen Habermas (1992; see also the epigraph at the beginning of the chapter), without denying the advantages of the division of labour in economy and politics, advocate broad participation at least in those matters which are crucial for an order that deserves to be called democratic.

SUMMARY

- Political participation needs to be defined broadly. Power and political cleavages are significant dimensions and forms of participation.

- There are three major frameworks for political participation: party politics and voting behaviour, interest group politics, and social movement and protest politics.

- Political participation in Europe varies considerably in form and degree, ranging from voting to violent protest, concentrating in some countries mainly on institutionalized participation while in other countries also including substantial elements of protest politics.

- The activities of these frameworks of participation, as well as parliamentary and governmental actions, are presented to a wider public via the mass media. These, though not allowing for much citizen participation, play a crucial role in providing information about the political process and linking the citizens with the state.

- The complex interplay between various political actors can be represented in a model of interest representation that puts the activities in the public sphere at the centre of the political process.

- Extensive use of different forms of participation is an asset rather than a danger to viable democracies.

QUESTIONS FOR DISCUSSION

- What are the characteristics of political parties, interest groups and social movements?

- What are the main political cleavages in modern European democracies?

- In which respects do patterns of political participation in Eastern and Western Europe differ?

- Are political parties sufficient to make democracy work?

- Why are the mass media important for the political process?

- Is broad political participation a danger to democracy?

- What are the implications of the wide extension of mobile telephone and internet communications (social networking and messaging) for political participation and organization?

FURTHER READING

Budge, Ian, Kenneth Newton et al. (1997) *The Politics of the New Europe: Atlantic to Urals* (London and New York: Longman). A solid and encompassing introduction with many empirical data, including aspects of political participation.

Dalton, Russell J. (1996), *Citizen Politics: Public Opinion and Political Parties in Advanced Industrial Democracies*, 2nd edn (Chatham, NJ: Chatham House). A comprehensive discussion of the involvement of citizens in the political process, including the politics of parties and social movements.

Greenwood, Justin and Aspinwall, Mark (eds) (1998) *Collective Action in the European Union* (London and New York: Routledge). An up-to-date collection of essays on various aspects of collective political participation in the EU.

Marsh, Allan, Barnes, Samuel H. and Kaase, Max

(1990), *Political Action in Europe and the USA* (London: Macmillan). A shortened version of the Political Action Study whose first results were published in 1979.

Roller, Edeltraud and Weßels, Bernhard (1996), 'Contexts of Political Protest in Western Democracies: Political Organization and Modernity', in Frederick Weil et al. (eds), *Extremism, Protest, Social Movements, and Democracy: Research on Democracy and Society*, vol. 3 (Greenwich/London: JAI Press), pp. 91–134. A broad cross-national comparison of the extent and underlying factors of political protest.

van Deth, Jan (ed.) (1997) *Private Groups and Public Life: Social Participation and Political Involvement in Representative Democracies* (London: Routledge). A collection of informative articles covering a broad range of aspects of political participation with special emphasis on European countries.

More than other variants of modernity, the European one has been strung between the poles of clear-cut individuality and solidarily-constructed collectivity . . .

Göran Therborn, *European Modernity and Beyond* (1995), p. 15

Sociologists have commonly distinguished between 'social structure' and 'social change' and between social structure and culture. We have, however, learned from theorists such as Norbert Elias (1897–1990) and Anthony Giddens (1938–), among others, that it is more useful to consider social structures as structures-in-transformation and to think of them in terms of their causal effects rather than looking only for their material embodiment. Social structures are not things, like the islands and the subcontinental mass of which Europe is composed, but nor are they just collections of people, like a crowd or the population of a territory. To talk about social structures is to abstract from what is immediately given, as when we talk about the structure of a bridge or the structure of a DNA molecule rather than about just the bridge or the molecule. But social structures are more problematic than structures of the kinds just mentioned, because we rapidly encounter theoretical and even political disagreements about how they should be described. Some social scientists, for example, believe that class structures explain a great deal; others that they do not, or that they do not even exist.

We are most likely to find agreement about some of the spatial and demographic aspects of social structure. We can look up the population figures for towns, regions and states in contemporary Europe with reasonable confidence, making estimates to cover underrecording by censuses and other surveys, and note some interesting differences in age structures, birth rates, and so forth. But this would not get us very far. In discussing population we should perhaps, as Coleman (1996) does, go well beyond this and consider such issues as the values of young adults, as well as their physical living arrangements, or the effects of welfare benefits on families. In other words, structural and cultural processes can be seen to interrelate in all kinds of ways, and any differentiation between the two can only be a matter of temporary convenience. In thinking about social structure we should include not just structural elements in the narrow sense of the term (birth rates and other demographic variables, spatial distribution, classes, strata and other aspects of social stratification), but also, perhaps, cultural traditions and ways of life and cultural transformations such as those in post-war France described by Kristin Ross (1995). We must also pay attention to the constant interactions between real processes and their intellectual representations in the media or in the heads of ordinary members of society. We are concerned, in other words, not just with 'social facts' but also with 'social representations'.

Historical background: Europe in its place

The term 'modernity' is both the broadest and the most helpful way in which to describe the form of society which developed in Europe and its settler colonies from around the eighteenth century onwards (see Chapter 1). This form of society has spread, to a greater or lesser extent, across much of the world; as a result, any serious discussion of European culture or social structure has to be primarily concerned with discriminating it from other regional versions of modernity and from modernity in general. Europe can be usefully seen as a crucible in which social and cultural forms, whether indigenous or imported, are warmed up and (re-)exported to other regions of the globe, where they develop in ways which often eclipse their European variants. This can be shown in relation to capitalism, individualism, the nation-state, and so on. The nation-state, for example, often seen as somewhat passé in Western Europe, remains the dominant political form on the world stage; the European Union (EU) itself, even if it achieves full political union, will arguably only be one (large) state among others. Communism or Marxism–Leninism is another striking example: unsuccessful in the more advanced parts of Europe at the end of the First World War, it gained a foothold on the edge of Europe, in Russia, whence it was imposed on much of the rest of Europe in the aftermath of the Second World War and the substantial Soviet contribution to the defeat of Nazism. Now largely repudiated in Europe, communism remains a significant political force in India and elsewhere. Europe since the middle of the twentieth century, as Maurice Roche (2010, p. 193) notes, has been uncharacteristically free of war and the religious influences which dominated its earlier history and substantially shaped its welfare states.

The numerous critiques of Eurocentrism have reminded us that in studying Europe, even historically, one must constantly keep an eye on the rest of the world. Against this comparative background, however, one can, as Dieter Senghaas (1982) put it, 'learn from Europe' – learn, that is, both from the peculiarities of the European experience and from what certain European states and regions had in common with non-European ones on the eve of modernization. Judgements about Europe often tend to get mixed up with judgements about modernity, industrialism, and so forth – inevitably, because of their original conjunction.

Contemporary Europe

In the contemporary context, globalization (see Chapter 12) makes it harder than ever to decide what is specific to the European version of modernity and to European culture and social structure. One possible way of thinking about this conundrum is indicated by Goran Therborn in the passage quoted at the head of this chapter. What is clear is that in Europe we are still living with the results, both positive and negative, of having 'started first'. Michael Mann (1986, 1993) may well be right to argue that what counted in Europe was the competition between smallish political units under the unifying umbrella of Christendom. This, and the religious diversification of early modern Europe may, as Max Weber argued, have contributed to the rise of capitalism. This in turn, for example, reinforced an existing inclination in much of Europe towards nuclear family structures (Laslett, 1971; Seccombe, 1992). As the Swedish sociologist Göran Therborn (1995, p. 24) puts it, 'West of a line from Trieste to St Petersburg, there . . . existed, already on the threshold to modernity, a distinctive family type, characterized by late marriages, a considerable number of people never married, and nuclear family households.' This, together with capitalist wage-labour and industrialization, made Europeans less religious in many ways than other inhabitants of the world. British and then European capitalism enjoyed an early advantage, before being eclipsed (though still not definitively) by North American and then East Asian variants. Similarly, the European nation-state system spread across the world and helped to pull apart the world's remaining big imperial structures, including of course, in the end, those which European countries had established overseas (or, in the Russian/Soviet case, overland). The European states successively and to an increasing degree supervised and shaped the development of capitalism and industrialism on their territories (Moore, 1966), leaving European capitalism much more

Table 7.1 Structure of employment in seven European countries, 1960, 1997 and 2007

		Agriculture	Industry	Services
France	1960	23.2	38.4	38.5
	1997	4.4	25.3	70.3
	2007	3.2	22.6	74.2
Germany*	1960	14.0	47.0	39.1
	1997	2.9	34.8	62.3
	2007	2.3	30.0	67.7
Hungary	1997	8.1	33.9	58.1
	2007	4.7	32.9	62.4
Poland	1997	20.6	31.9	47.5
	2007	14.7	30.7	54.5
Spain	1960	38.7	30.3	31.0
	1997	8.1	30.1	61.7
	2007	4.6	29.4	66.0
Turkey	1997	41.7	23.7	34.6
	2007	23.5	26.7	49.8
UK	1960	4.7	47.7	47.6
	1997	1.9	26.7	71.4
	2007	1.4	22.4	76.3

*West Germany (FRG) only in 1960.

Sources: Data derived from *OECD in Figures*, 2003, 2009: Labour > Employment.

regulated than in the USA or Asia (Albert, 1991; Crouch and Streeck, 1997). There are, of course, exceptions to this tendency in the far west of Europe (the UK) and to some extent, now, the former communist East.

The socialist countries, whose political and cultural version of modernity was strikingly different in the half-century following 1945, appear in retrospect as in many ways simply carrying through many of the same processes by other, more visibly authoritarian means (cf. Therborn, 1995, pp. 121–2). They took control of capitalism to the extent of replacing it with a centrally planned economic system; they pushed through industrialization policies and got rid of their peasantries; they urbanized in similarly drastic ways, to the point of tragic absurdity in Romania; and incorporated their populations into (centrally managed) political, educational and media systems. In the USSR and Eastern Europe, however, the modernization process gave rise to economic, political and cultural strains which the systems could not control. Unable to innovate successfully in any of these domains, the ruling elites yielded to gentle but compelling external and internal pressures and stepped down into the dustbin of history, where many of them found a lucrative second career recycling the rubbish.

The modernization and industrialization process produced ultimately (though not really until the 1950s for most of Europe, with the partial liquidation of its independent peasantry and other self-employed people) an 'employment society', or *Arbeitsgesellschaft* (Offe, 1985), whose alleged end is still a matter of controversy (see Table 7.1, Figure 7.1 and Tables 8.4, 8.5 and 8.6 and Figure 8.7).

Here again, the socialist countries were simply more radical in abolishing (except in Poland and Yugoslavia) independent peasant agriculture and (again to differing degrees) independent commercial activity. In the capitalist countries of 'Western' Europe, the integration of what Touraine and Ragazzi (1961) called 'workers who started on the land' (*ouvriers d'origine agricole*) and of independent proprietors was followed by the integration of immigrant workers and, increasingly, their families (see Table 7.2).

In the course of the 1970s, which one has to see as a crucial turning-point in the development of Western European social structures and ideologies, these two processes of integration began in part to run backwards. The doubling or, in some countries, much worse than doubling of unemployment rates excluded large parts of the populations from labour markets and other forms of social participation, bearing heavily on women, except in the UK and Ireland (Therborn, 1995, p. 63), the old and the young. At the same time, and relatedly, many natives of Western Europe rejected so-called immigrants (though many were second-generation) who were 'here for good' (Castles et al., 1984). Discrimination against ethnic minorities in the labour market could no longer be explained away by language or other difficulties of integration, but racism became more politically entrenched in many countries (see Chapter 3). The ways in which patterns of disadvantage resulting from gender, ethnicity and class background interrelate remains a topic of active controversy.

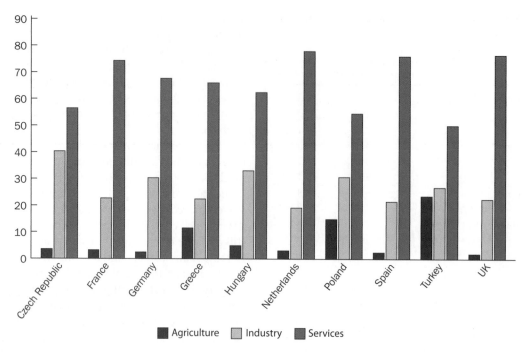

Figure 7.1   Structure of employment in ten European countries, 2007 (% of employed population by sector)

Source: OECD in Figures, 2009.

It is therefore not surprising that what came to be called social exclusion has become a growing preoccupation in sociological reflection and political discussion, particularly in France, where, as H. Silver and F. Wilkinson put it (in Rogers et al., 1995, p. 285), 'In line with the Republican ideology of solidarity, problems like long-term unemployment and rising poverty were construed as manifestations of "social exclusion" or "a rupture of the social bond".' In the UK, which came late to these ideas, the 'New Labour' government which came to power in 1997 briskly inaugurated a 'social exclusion unit'.

The theme of a crisis in the Western European welfare state (Rosanvallon, 1981), and of the work society which underpinned it, is of course a long-standing one. In the German social theorist Jürgen Habermas's (see Key Figure 6.2) early version in 1973, economic crises of capitalism metastasize into the political and cultural sphere, producing irrational state responses or 'crises of crisis-management' (Berger, 1981) and eroding individual motivation. What strikes one in looking compara-

tively at Western Europe is again the diverse political and cultural responses to socioeconomic and social-structural processes which were common to most of the major countries. Despite a generalized commitment to the 'European social model', seen as representing 'an implicit contract between government and citizens, as well as between one citizen and another' (Judt, 2005, p. 793), welfare-state patterns across Europe are remarkably diverse (see Box 7.1).

In Western Europe, it is tempting to offer a state-centred analysis of these differences, rather than the society-centred approaches common to much Marxist and non-Marxist sociology of the 1970s and 1980s (see Theda Skocpol's critique in Evans, Rueschemeyer and Skocpol, 1985). European societies were going through similar trajectories, while their entrenched state responses remained distinct. In communist Eastern Europe, of course, a state-centred approach is inescapable; it was the states which ran most things, and the states which eventually imploded, bringing down the deformed societies they had dominated.

Table 7.2   Non-national residents in selected European countries, 2008

| | Total foreign citizens | | | Citizens of another EU 27 state % total population | Citizens of country outside EU 27 % total population |
| | Number in millions | % total population | | | |
	2008	2000	2008	2008	2008
EU 27	30.80		6.2	2.3	3.9
Austria	0.83	9.50	10.0	3.5	6.6
Denmark	0.30	4.80	5.5	1.7	3.7
France	3.67*	5.80**	5.8*	2.0*	3.8*
Germany	7.25	8.90	8.8	3.1	5.8
Hungary	0.18	1.20	1.8	1.0	0.8
Netherlands	0.69	4.20	4.2	1.6	2.6
Spain	5.26	2.23	11.6	4.7	7.0
UK*	4.02*	4.40***	6.6*	2.6*	3.9*

Notes: *Estimates by Eurostat; ** 1999, Metropolitan France only; *** 2001.

Source: compiled from OECD Trends in International Migration 2002 and Eurostat News Release 184/2009 of 16 December 2009.

In what follows, I shall examine some of these processes in rather more detail. Rather than taking traditional structural concepts (family, class, and so on) as the organizing principle, I have chosen to use more abstract terms to refer to processes and structures of contemporary Europe. Borrowing from Hermann Schwengel's conception of four 'pillars' of European social structuration, I shall focus, as he did, on capitalism, constitutionalism, rationalization and **individualism** (Schwengel, 1999).

Capitalism

Europe was the site where capitalism in its modern form first developed, and as it spread through trade, agriculture and what Marx called 'manufacture' into industrial production it transformed European society in all kinds of ways. Note, however, and this is a point that will recur throughout this chapter, that the spread of capitalism was

extremely uneven and partial. Reading Marx, who of course was writing in what was the most advanced corner of Europe, it is easy to get the impression that almost all men, as well as many women and children, were factory workers, and later historians have often encouraged this misapprehension. Barrington Moore (1978) has shown how small was the proportion of the German population in the industrial proletariat, and how small the units in which they mostly worked, right into the twentieth century. France was also relatively backward in social-structural terms in the early post-war period, still having a large peasantry and independent sector. It transformed itself rapidly thereafter in what the French sociologist Henri Mendras (1988) called 'the second French revolution'. And the industrial and productive core of Western Europe, the banana-shaped region centred roughly on the Rhine and running from south-east England to northern Italy and including bits of southern France, northern Spain and Scandinavia was very different from the peripheries (Mendras, 1988, ch. 10). Fairly soon parts of the banana rotted, with the decline of traditional industries in Wallonia (the French-speaking part of Belgium), the Ruhr, and so forth, and new centres

● **Individualism**: The cluster of doctrines that assert the importance of individual persons and their opinions, rights, welfare, and so on, rather than collective structures such as families, churches and states.

BOX 7.1
The European Social Model: contrasting views

The Trade Unions' View (2005)

The European Social Model is a vision of society that combines sustainable economic growth with ever-improving living and working conditions. This implies full employment, good quality jobs, equal opportunities, social protection for all, social inclusion, and involving citizens in the decisions that affect them. In the European Trade Union Confederation's view, social dialogue, collective bargaining and workers' protection are crucial factors in promoting innovation, productivity and competitiveness. This is what distinguishes Europe, where post-war social progress has matched economic growth, from the US model, where small numbers of individuals have benefited at the expense of the majority. Europe must continue to sustain this social model as an example for other countries around the world.

(ETUC at http://www.etuc.org/a/111, 12 April 2005, accessed 27 July 2010)

A critic's view: interview (2009)

'Herr Scharpf, why do you think trade unions and social democrats are so enthusiastic about the European Social Model, given that so many social rights are now being restricted?'

'They are enthusiastic because they are deluding themselves.'

'Is there actually a European Social Model at all?'

'It may have been possible to talk about a European Social Model when you were comparing the EU 15 with the USA, but even that is not sustainable now the EU has 27 member states. In fact, however, Britain's welfare state and industrial relations are constructed in an entirely different way from Sweden's and both differ from Germany's. Thus even if we just look at the "old" member states and leave on one side the member states with weaker economies, which cannot afford the same levels of social protection, the differences are still so great that it would never have been possible to agree on a single European Social Model either through harmonisation or minimum standards. . . . a political agreement on a single European Social Model is implausible. In fact, it's worse than that: hoping for a Social Europe actually prevents politicians from taking the action that is still possible at national level.' (Scharpf, 2009)

---

and types of production came to replace them. The main political axis of the EC/EU remained, however, Paris–Bonn, the UK having joined only in 1973 and thereafter substantially excluding itself from decision-making by its politically irresponsible half-heartedness. The banana axis remains prominent in the current European distribution both of population and of gross domestic product (GDP) per head (though with outriders in, for example, Northern Spain and southern parts of the Nordic countries).

Soviet-dominated Eastern Europe, despite a standardized Stalinist development strategy which suited the more backward parts of the empire better than it did East Germany or Czechoslovakia, combined this with a quite substantial degree of sectoral specialization by country. Here, the post-communist shake-up and shake-out of the 1990s also shows some states and regions becoming relatively prosperous and others likely to remain disaster areas for decades to come. The EU's eastern enlargements of 2004 and 2007 mark substantial, if temporary, crystallizations of this process of consolidation and division. (On divisions within Europe as a whole, see, for instance, Hudson and Williams, 1999.)

Continental European industrial capitalism developed in tandem with the welfare state, and this continues to give it a different shape from that of other world regions (Albert, 1991; Crouch and Streeck, 1997; Mendras, 1997, ch. 7). Even the UK, where what strategic thinking there is tends to

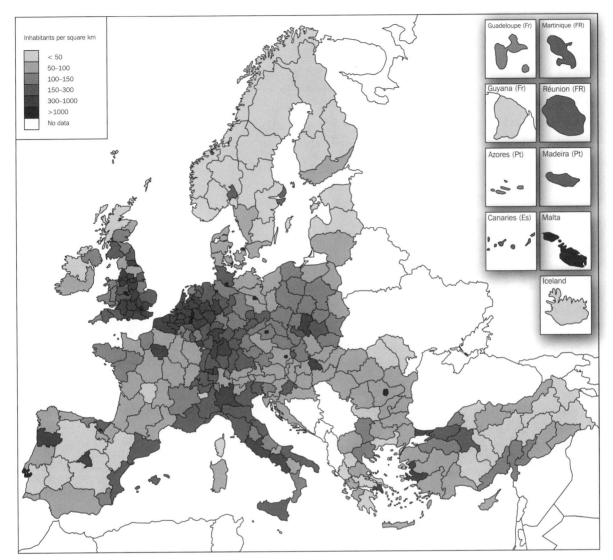

Map 7.1 EU population density by region, 2006

Source: Compiled from Eurostat (2009), p. 224.

follow the USA rather than the rest of Europe, is still recognisably within a European pattern, and further European integration is likely to sustain and even re-enforce this. On the other hand, Europe is not immune from global pressures and its own internal tendencies away from 'organized' and towards 'disorganized' capitalism (Offe, 1985; Lash and Urry, 1987; Crouch, 1993). Like so many of Europe's contemporary predicaments, this is a mixture of the old and the new. Theorists of capitalism have always been pulled between emphasiz-

ing its organized, predictable, calculating character and its unpredictable, chaotic aspect, and as **Fordist** mass production gives way to more flexible post-Fordist methods this dualism returns in new forms. Some jobs, for example, become more specialized,

● **Fordism**: Named after the early twentieth-century US car-maker Henry Ford, refers to standardized and mechanized mass production: the term 'post-Fordism' has been used since the 1980s to denote more specialized and flexible forms of production, often involving the coordination of small-scale producers and catering to small niche markets.

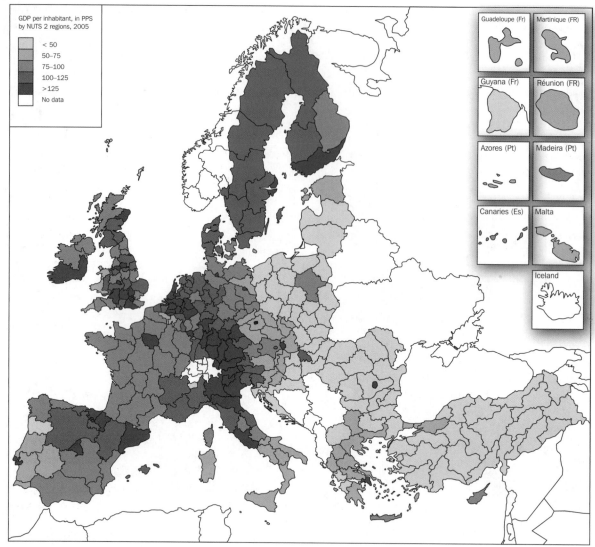

GDP per inhabitant, in PPS
by NUTS 2 regions, 2005

- < 50
- 50–75
- 75–100
- 100–125
- >125
- No data

Guadeloupe (Fr)   Martinique (FR)

Guyana (Fr)   Réunion (FR)

Azores (Pt)   Madeira (Pt)

Canaries (Es)   Malta

Iceland

Map 7.2   EU GDP per inhabitant by region, 2005

Source: Compiled from Eurostat (2009), p. 222.

skilled and professionalized; others are further downgraded, routinized and casualized into 'McJobs'. Once again, Eastern Europe throws up these issues in a particularly stark form.

Some regions of Europe seem better placed to profit from these developments than others, but it is hard to be confident about predicting developments which often seem to result from happy combinations of luck and entrepreneurship yet rapidly become self-sustaining. How far EU policies will follow the imperatives of capitalism itself and encourage regional specialization, or pursue more differentiated redistributive regional strategies (which, however, have largely failed at the level of nation-states), is also an open question.

Capitalism, whatever its virtues (Saunders, 1995), is of course predicated upon inequality and class division, and Europe has been the prime site for anti-capitalist **social movements** based more or less solidly on working-class support. As a general rule, paradoxically, it has been the relatively prosperous north of Europe which had the strongest social-democratic parties, often ruling parties, and trade unions. The south, suffering from greater poverty and more severe strains resulting from industrialization, has been more fertile ground for minority communist parties, these however being mostly excluded from power by one means or another. One way or another, Europe developed a characteristic pattern of association between class and voting which has persisted even when class, like religion, seems to have become merely a variable influencing electoral preferences rather than something directly addressed in political debate. (On class and voting, see Inglehart, 1990; Therborn, 1995, pp. 284–9; also Chapters 5 and 6.)

In East-Central Europe, of course, communist minorities were able to seize power after the Second World War and establish a version of socialism which was probably doomed by the circumstances of its birth, its association with a generally unpopular (even in Germany and Bulgaria) **dominant** power, the USSR, and the means by which it was maintained. Once Stalinized, they could never fully de-Stalinize (see Chapters 2 and 3).

It was in Eastern Europe, once again, that the rise and fall of **social movements** or civil society was most abrupt and striking (see also Chapter 6). The regimes in their final days were mostly confronted by broad coalitions of oppositional forces linked largely by the mere fact of their opposition and an awareness that this was now after all possible. The image of movements of civil society filling the vacuum left by discredited and imploded states was a powerful one on both sides of the falling iron curtain. Almost as soon, however, the movements substantially disaggregated, in a fast-forward version of the life-cycle of many Western European movements, into orthodox parties on the one hand and grumpy outsiders on the other. In East Germany, Disneyfied copies of the main West German parties were rapidly cobbled together by ex-Stalinist stooges and Western carpetbaggers; politics in much of the rest of the former bloc took on a vertiginous back-and-forth between neo-liberals on the one hand, sometimes in alliance with clerical conservatives, and rebadged communist parties on the other, benefiting on the rebound from rapid disillusionment with neo-liberal economic policies. And this was in the relatively more fortunate states; elsewhere, the old *nomenklatura* elites have managed to preserve their position, with, for example, catastrophic results in some of the former Yugoslav republics and, for the moment, stagnation in Belarus (for overviews see Hann, 2002; Outhwaite and Ray, 2004; Sakwa, 1999; Outhwaite, 2010a). This brings us, in a somewhat negative way, to the theme of constitutionalism, which is discussed in the following section.

Constitutionalism

The constitutional and eventually democratic state is another of those European creations better known in its export model – in this case, paradigmatically, the USA. Whatever one thinks about the reality of American democracy, it remains a powerful ideal, deeply entrenched in attitudes and everyday practices, including the defence of free speech in circumstances where even liberal Europeans tend to reach for the penal code. From a North American, and perhaps from an East Asian point of view, Europeans seem somewhat state-centred, waiting for state provision rather than turning to individual or collective self-help. The long-lasting effects of the 1968 protests (see Chapter 2) have, however, sustained a variety of social movements within Europe and increasingly operating on a global scale. Generally, though, we can conclude that twentieth-century Europe produced some of the most decent and attractive states in the world, especially in the north of Europe, but it also provided the two most repellent and destructive ones: Nazi Germany and the Stalinist USSR.

If we take advanced modernity to include not just industrialism and capitalism, urbanism, mass education and so forth, but also certain traditional

---

● **Dominant or hegemonic power**: A state possesses hegemonic power when it is able to create and enforce rules to maintain the international status quo and its own dominance within the existing system.

● **Social movements**: Social movements are loosely coupled networks of groups and organizations that, over a considerable period of time, mobilize to achieve or resist social change and/or change society predominantly by means of collective and public protest.

Euro-American conceptions of citizenship and the public sphere, with roots in the French and American revolutions, then these are not always, at least for the moment, part of the export package when modernity becomes global. There has, for example, been a good deal of debate about whether the state socialism developed in the USSR and imposed on large parts of the rest of Europe should be understood as a variant of modernity, just as it was in previous decades as a variant of industrial society (Aron, 1962), or as in some sense insufficiently, incompletely or unstably modern, in its sociopolitical structures no less than in its automobile industry. On this view, for example, the 1989 revolutions could be seen as a process of catching-up or rectification (Habermas, 1990; cf. Arnason, 1993).

One of the most important recent social and political transformations in Europe has of course been the destruction of these 'socialist' dictatorships. Whether or not one calls these regimes totalitarian in their practice, it is fairly clear that they pursued an essentially totalitarian ideal of centralized control of economic, political and cultural processes, hidden behind a façade of democratic participation. The rapid democratization of most of these states is a dramatic instance of a worldwide trend towards democracy in the later twentieth century (Fischer, 1996; Nagle and Mahr, 1999). In the European case, the more or less realistic prospect of accession to the EU has acted as a powerful external stimulus to further democratization and a brake on possible regression towards authoritarian rule (see Chapter 8). This has of course to be balanced against the economic costs, at least in the short term, of alignment with the EU. Significantly, however, no former communist state has decided against EU membership, as Norway, Switzerland and Greenland did in the west.

With the collapse of the 'people's democracies', and the eclipse of revolutionary socialism, the liberal-democratic state, like capitalism, has no obvious practical alternative. If anything, and despite very important elements of disillusionment or political alienation (Budge et al., 1997; see also Chapter 5), it has acquired stronger roots with the democratization of everyday life: the growing acceptance, exemplified in spheres as diverse as media interviews with politicians, and child-rearing practices, that all our decisions and ways of life are

in principle open to questioning. They become, in Habermas's sense, 'post-conventional'. In the political context, Habermas himself has, for example, popularized the conception of 'constitutional patriotism' (*Verfassungspatriotismus*), based not on membership of a particular ethnic or national community or *Volk* (see Chapter 3) but on a rational and defensible identification with a decent constitutional state, which may of course be the one whose citizenship one holds and/or the one in which one lives.

But if the liberal-democratic nation-state has few internal enemies, it is increasingly seen as inappropriate to the contemporary reality of global processes and challenges as well as to the desire of many citizens for more local autonomy. In Daniel Bell's classic phrase, it is 'too small for the big problems of life, and too big for the small problems of life' (Bell, 1987, p. 14). In this post-national constellation, as Habermas has called it, the progress of European union, combined as it is with attempts to strengthen regional autonomy under the slogan of 'subsidiarity', becomes a crucial external determinant of the internal reconfiguration of many European states, notably the UK. Once again, Europe is pioneering a mode of governance, this time transnational rather than national, which gives some practical embodiment to the current extension of democratic thinking into conceptions of cosmopolitan democracy (Held, 1995). This is as important as the earlier extension of liberal democracy into social democracy; it coexists uneasily, however, with communitarian thinking both in social and political philosophy and in the practice of, for example, Clinton and Blair. And the EU may be an intrinsically cosmopolitan entity (Beck and Grande, 2004), but the image of 'Fortress Europe' conflicts with this, and the Union's hesitant attitude to its eastern enlargements, continuing in relation to Turkey, reveals a much less cosmopolitan face (Outhwaite, 2006; see also Rumford, 2007; Roche, 2010, ch. 9). More broadly, the opposition – described by Tönnies (1955 [1887]) – between the large-scale anonymous and formal structures characteristic of modernity and the survival of localized or now sometimes de-localized communities of co-residents or co-thinkers, remains a feature of contemporary Europe. This brings us to our next theme, that of rationalization.

Rationalization

Max Weber used the term 'rationalization' to refer to processes of systematization in a wide variety of areas of modern societies: the economy, law, bureaucratic organization, religion and everyday conduct. Entrepreneurs, and increasingly their employees, in early modern Europe began to calculate their economic benefits and losses more precisely and to seek a more predictable environment for their activity. This meshed in neatly with a trend to the codification of law, notably in the Code Napoléon, which was imposed in the widespread territories he ruled in Europe and elsewhere. State administrations and other large organizations began to rely more on paid officials in complex hierarchies and with clearly defined tasks and routines: the *fonctionnaire* or *Beamte* in public service and the 'organization man' in the large corporation (Whyte, 1960; Crozier, 1964). Religious belief became more systematic and streamlined, with the partial displacement, especially in Northern Europe, of the saints and intercession rituals of Catholicism by the more austerely monotheistic and formal Protestant versions of Christianity. With industrialization and urban migration, religion became increasingly marginalized. Contemporary Europe appears 'modern' in relation to the USA and many other regions of the world in the extent of its secularization: whatever the difficulties of measurement in this domain, it is clear that religious belief in Europe has mostly ceased to have the kind of importance for social life as a whole which it has retained elsewhere, even in ostensibly secular states like the USA. Scandinavia and East Central Europe have gone furthest in this direction, though France, despite a historically strong Catholic tradition, displays an equally strong secular emphasis in matters of state policy (*laïcité*) and a relatively high level of disbelief in God (Therborn, 1995, p. 275). Since the beginning of the twenty-first century, a number of thinkers have been describing Europe as 'post-secular', pointing to the ways in which religious communities continue to assert their special position even in largely secular states. A number of different trends have come together here. First, European Muslims have pointed out the prevalence of Christian symbols in ostensibly secular states and demanded equal respect for their own symbols and practices. This has been resisted, sometimes on secularist or feminist grounds, as in French bans on the wearing of headscarves in schools, or more traditionalist/xenophobic or aesthetic grounds, as in a controversy in 2009–10 over the building of mosques in Switzerland. In the UK, which is very secular by US standards, the bishops of the established Christian state church are represented in the upper house of Parliament. A secularist position would call for their removal, while a post-secularist argument might be that their presence should be diluted by the addition of some religious leaders of other faiths. Another element is the greater presence of both Christian and Muslim organizations in post-communist Europe, where they had previously been colonized and manipulated by the ruling communist parties. In Poland and elsewhere, for example, Christian social conservatism conflicts with more secular attitudes on issues such as contraception, abortion and homosexuality, and the gender composition of the priesthood itself. The future of both the intellectual and political debates and the development of religion on the ground are of course open. As Olivier Roy (2010) pointed out in a recent interview, 'Europe is deeply divided about its own culture: secularists consider the Enlightenment (with its human rights, freedom, democracy) to be the true birth certificate of Europe, while certain Christian-oriented factions believe that the Enlightenment also led to communism, atheism and even Nazism.'

In another area of the rationalization or calculation of conduct, individuals, too, have increasingly to 'manage' themselves: their time, their careers, their life-choices, and so forth in what Ulrich Beck (1986) has called a 'risk society', which is risky both for societies confronting environmental dangers such as nuclear accidents and for individuals threatened by life-changing personal disasters. In Eastern Europe, again, this has come as something new to citizens who might have had difficulties in acquiring consumer goods but who were largely cushioned by the state from the bigger risks of life: prolonged illness, unemployment, homelessness and so forth. Women suffered particularly from this shake-up and shake-out (Einhorn, 1993).Once again, the processes Weber described at the beginning of the twentieth century, and whose origins he traced back to the seventeenth and eighteenth, continue in new forms in the twenty-first, in management practices of personal appraisal and individual or collective self-management or self-help (Giddens, 1991; Beck, Giddens and Lash, 1994). These are at once liberating, in the way they throw us on to our own resources to define our goals and strategies, and disciplining, in the sense of what Michel Foucault called 'surveillance' (Wagner, 1994). We are constantly under observation, by others and by ourselves. Are you reading this chapter carefully and efficiently? Is it giving you the information and ideas you need? Will it count towards my research output and that of my university? And so on.

Some thinkers have argued that the rationalization processes characteristic of modernity have given place to a more chaotic postmodern world of disorganized capitalism, franchised welfare services and utilities, unstructured belief, chaotic lives made up of juggling a variety of short-term part-time jobs, and so forth. These arguments have perhaps been overstated. What we find instead in what some people have called a second modernity is an accentuation of many of the same processes under conditions where structures have become more complex and virtual, though no less determinant of individual fates. Class structures, thus, remain crucially important determinants of individuals' life-chances, even if they no longer find a direct embodiment in huge working-class occupational communities or mass organizations. The effects of gender, too, have remained pervasive, even as fewer and fewer occupations are explicitly segregated. Metaphors like the 'glass ceiling' reflect this reality. In this newly rationalized world, issues of individual identity return in new but still recognisable forms.

Individualism

Asking what is distinctive about European modernity, Henri Mendras (1997, p. 53) offers a historical answer which emphasizes the long and slow conquest of Europe (by which he means Western Europe) by a particular ideological model. This model consists of ideological innovations: the individualist notion of the person; the distinction between three types of legitimacy conferred respec-

tively by religion, by politics and by economics; the notion of capital; the conjunction of science and technical progress; the power of the majority; the importance of contractual relationships and the mutual trust they involve; the rule of law; property rights as the law understands them. These are, he suggests, the foundations of Western European civilization and they are unique in the history of civilizations.

We have encountered these themes already in the previous section, but the first of these deserves special attention. Modernity is, as the German historical sociologist Norbert Elias described it, essentially a 'society of individuals' (Elias, 1988), and, as Durkheim recognized, individualism has become something of a substitute for religious belief in modern societies. Parents' views on the desirability or otherwise of encouraging independence rather than obedience in their children are, as Therborn notes (1995, p. 292), an interesting marker of differences across Europe. There are striking differences between the value placed on autonomy in the north and central region (Austria, West Germany, the Netherlands and the Nordic countries) and the emphasis on obedience in the south and west (UK, Ireland, France, Italy, Portugal and Spain), and similarly, between some parts of Eastern Europe (Hungary, East Germany and the former Soviet Baltic republics, but also Bulgaria in the south-east) and others (authoritarian Czechoslovakia, Poland, Belarus and Russia). As in the case of work organization, discussed below, it is interesting that the traditional stereotype which contrasts a libertarian or anarchic France with a rigid and authoritarian Germany is contradicted by the evidence.

There can be little doubt about the further advance of individualistic values in the late twentieth century (Inglehart, 1977). However, we must remember that an 'ideal type' of modern individualism should not be taken in an exclusive sense. People, particularly women, continue to be defined and to define themselves in relational terms as someone's child, spouse or parent. **Patronymics** are widely used both as names and as descriptions in many parts of Europe, and families remain very

---

● **Patronymics**: Names derived from a father or other ancestor, for example by suffixes such as -son, -ovich.

important, even in the north. In the South, **clientelism** often persists in quasi-familial forms, and in many countries university professors, for example, surround themselves with a small 'family' of assistants.

The important point, however, is that it is increasingly easy for individuals to define themselves in varied ways, choosing between a repertoire of identities and foregrounding one or another according to context. (The frequent adoption in internet chat groups of a fictitious identity or the opposite gender is one of the most recent examples.) Here again, we see the inseparable interplay of structural and cultural elements in defining identities. Sexual identity is fairly clear-cut, but its salience in social contexts is highly variable. A homosexual identity may be given a central place by its bearer and his or her associates, or it may be kept in the background by both. Some women may change their names to mark their distinctness from their fathers or parents.

Modernity is characterized, then, by a weakening of traditional identities in the anonymity of cities and individual wage-labour. At the same time, we see a desire to categorize and classify, of which Foucault gave the classic examples in his studies of the emergence of the 'mad', 'sick' or 'homosexual' identity. More particularly, the European nation-states became concerned to count and measure their populations, and to impose a common national identity at the expense of regional ones (Eley and Suny, 1996). Boundary changes throughout the nineteenth and twentieth centuries, and migration flows within and into Europe, have increasingly subverted the latter process, but many European states continue to try to preserve a traditional line. France, in particular, has resisted expressions of cultural difference in public institutions, in particular the wearing of Islamic headscarves in schools, and opposed in 1992 a European agreement to support minority languages.

There seems, however, to be an emergent consensus in the multicultural societies of contemporary Europe that it is up to individuals to define their identities, choosing what weight they wish to attach to each, and that 'outing' and 'othering' are unacceptable. Members of ethnic and religious minorities, in particular, have resisted attempts, no doubt well-meaning, to increase their political representation through the incorporation of traditional elites or 'community leaders'. What seems striking (though see Therborn, 1995, p. 242, for a different point of view) is how relatively hard it has been for Europeans to move to a North American pattern where 'Italian-American', 'African-American', and so on are recognisable identities and where it is understood that the bit before the hyphen will have different degrees of salience for different individuals. There are of course significant fundamentalist counter-movements, calling forth, in their turn, responses such as that by Samuel Huntington (1993), which manage to be both hysterical and cynical. More seriously, the fundamentalisms of the 'others' are matched by a 'majority' xenophobic **fundamentalism** which refuses ethnic and cultural difference and for which a black person, say, can never be 'really' British or French, just as a mosque can never really 'fit' in a Swiss town crammed with churches (see Balibar, 2004).

The extent to which a European identity has displaced the traditional primacy of national or regional identities (Scottish, Breton, and so on) is again highly variable between and within states (see Box 7.2).

As noted above, questions of identity are hard to get a hold on, but variations over space and time are worth noting. It is clear that young people and the internationally mobile are more likely to identify with Europe, as are the more educated. One of the more interesting recent studies of young people compared two sites in a number of countries. A strong European identity among those who had *not* had a substantial transnational experience (migration, academic exchange programmes, and so on) was, not surprisingly, roughly twice as common in Central Europe (Austria, Germany and the Czech and Slovak Republics) as on the periphery (Spain and the UK) (Jamieson et al., www.ed.ac.uk/youth/research; see also Checkel and Katzenstein, 2009).

● **Clientelism**: A structure of relations between powerful patrons such as landlords or political leaders and those dependent on them for services, who reward them by political or other forms of support.

● **Fundamentalism**: Religious believers who see literal meanings in their sacred texts are usually referred to as fundamentalists. Often perceived by outsiders as extremists, fundamentalists usually wish to see their religion playing a bigger role in politics and society.

BOX 7.2
Feelings about Europe in the 2000s

A Eurobarometer survey of people in the 15 EU member states in spring 2003 showed that a high proportion of respondents felt very or fairly attached to their country, town or village, and region, but only just over half felt similarly attached to Europe.

In 2002, how attached did people feel to:

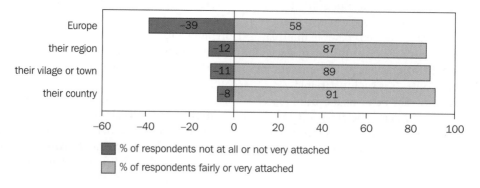

In 2002, how did people characterize themselves (selected countries):

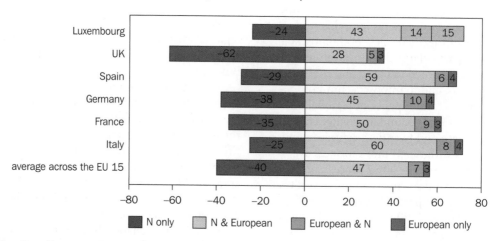

N = Nationality (for example, respondent feels Irish).

Source: Standard Eurobarometer 60 (2002), p. 27.

Attitude to membership of the EU, 2009

Subsequent Eurobarometers have replaced the questions about attachment with more focused (or perhaps more self-serving) ones about perceptions of the EU. Taking the relatively crude question of whether you think your country's membership of the EU is 'a good thing', the most recent results remain disappointing, with a wide spread from a relatively enthusiastic Spain (and even here enthusiasm fell by 7 per cent in 2009) and Netherlands to massively negative Latvia and the UK. Interestingly, no one dares to put the question the other way round: 'Is [your country's] membership *good for the EU?*'

Do you think your country's membership of the EU is a good thing? (% responding yes, selected countries, autumn 2009):

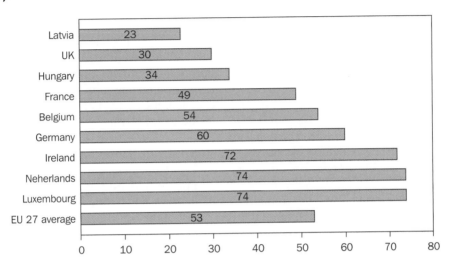

Source: Standard Eurobarometer 72 (2010), p. 146.

Another crucial element is the extent to which Europe represents something like a transnational public sphere (van de Steeg, 2002; Wessler et al., 2008).

Why might the existence or strength of a European identity be important? One answer is that it is essential to sustain civil society at the European level. This in turn is seen as essential to formal European politics and the reduction of the 'democratic deficit' which has been a topic of discussion in the EU for over twenty years (Outhwaite, 2010b). A second answer is in terms of the need to sustain social solidarity at the European level in order to legitimate redistributive and other social policy initiatives. Europeans who feel little or nothing in common with those from other member states are unlikely to be willing to make sacrifices for them. As Joe Weiler (2002 [2001], pp. 569–70) puts it, 'Europe prides itself on a tradition of social solidarity which found political and legal

expression in the post-war welfare state.' Wolfgang Streeck (1999) conceptualizes the EU's developing social model as 'productivist-competitive solidarity'. As we have seen, however, the Europeanization of social policy has barely progressed beyond first base, despite its obvious importance as a policy goal, even from a narrowly economistic perspective focused on the removal of impediments to the free movement of labour. A third answer is cast in terms of cosmopolitan democracy, where Europe is seen as a test bed or springboard for the development of more globalized political structures.

It is perhaps only to be expected that a European identity will be less substantial than state-centred or regional identities, but these are all constructed and reproduced through increasingly mediated and reflexive practices. Some regions, for example in Italy, may have very substantial historical roots and be marked by, for example, highly distinctive dialects; others however will be more a by-product of administrative operations, such as the 'North-East' of England or Humberside. The question then, as noted earlier, becomes whether identities are nested or orthogonal to, and in conflict with, one another. A Welsh or Catalan nationalist may or not affirm a European identity, but is likely to reject a British/Spanish one. A supporter of the unified UK or Spain (a 'unionist' in Northern Ireland) will tend to play down a Scottish or Basque identity, or at least see it as a harmonious component of the state-centred identity.

Among the determinants of strength of these identities one can identify some positive and some negative factors. To begin with the positive, it is clear, as Michael Bruter (2005, pp. 138–9) emphasizes, that a sense of European identity increased almost everywhere in the EU over the last three decades of the twentieth century; the only exceptions are countries like Germany and Luxembourg where it was already strong at the beginning of the period. There is some evidence that a European in the sense of EU identity tends to be strongest in states whose membership of the EC/EU is longest, even if this is distinct from, and not always particularly closely related to support for European integration (Bruter, 2005). As in the case of national identity and nationalism, it is possible to distinguish between broadly cultural and more specific civic versions of European identity.

A broader European identity may be strengthened by cross-border interaction (Grundy and Jamieson, 2005, 2007; Wallace, Datler and Spannring, 2005), which in much of mainland Europe is also a common feature of everyday life. There may also additionally be contribution to at least a European awareness by the presence of major European institutions. In Luxembourg, Strasbourg or Brussels, for example, it is impossible not to be aware of the latter, whereas in London there is only the European Bank for Reconstruction and Development (EBRD) and no EU institution except an obscure pharmaceutical agency. Travel from the UK to the mainland involves substantial planning and expense. A national-state or regional identity may similarly be strengthened either by a central location in the national or regional capital or, conversely, by a frontier location. Regionalist identity may be expected to be stronger the greater the distance from the national capital, though this

can cut both ways: Scottish islanders, for example, may feel too remote from Edinburgh to identify strongly with the government there. A European identity may be negatively affected by hostility to the EU or positively by dissatisfaction with the national state, and both these identities may be strengthened by dislike of the regional language or politics.

What is clear is that there has been a very substantial attempt to inspire and nurture a pan-European identity focused on what we now know as the EU and developed, as Wiener notes, in connection with the ultimately rather half-hearted introduction of a European citizenship.

> a paper on 'European identity' was issued at the 1973 Copenhagen summit. It broadly defined European identity as being based on a 'common heritage' and 'acting together in relation to the rest of the world', while the 'dynamic nature of European unification' was to be respected. This . . . idea of Community development was then approached by a citizenship practice that included the adoption of the two policy objectives of 'special rights' for European citizens and a 'passport union'. . . . The notion of citizen thus turned into a new informal resource of the acquis communautaire. (Wiener, 1997, pp. 538–9)

As Bo Stråth (2002) has suggested, the appeal to identity has in some ways replaced appeals to the notion of integration as a self-evident good. How far these centralized initiatives amount to the emergence of a genuine European identity, assuming such a thing is anyway important, is of course open to question.

European society in the modern world

We have learned from thinkers such as Elias, Touraine, Giddens and Beck to avoid thinking of 'societies' as if they were individuals, capable of thought and action, defined by the boundaries of particular states, and it is no less important to avoid applying the same thinking to 'Europe'. It is clearly an entity with fuzzy edges, and not just

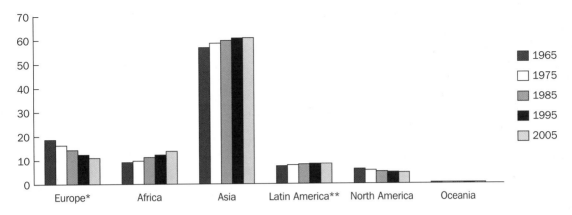

* Includes all of Russian Federation.
** And Caribbean.

Figure 7.2 Population of major regions as % of total world population, 1965–2005

because some European states include overseas territories or because Turkey and Russia stretch into Asia.

What can be said in the end about the residual distinctiveness of Europe as a region of the modern world? A familiar theme, invoked even in an advertising series by Shell some years ago, is diversity, notably the diversity of languages. Compared with the largely Anglophone societies of North America or the area sharing Chinese pictograms, or even large regions such as India or the former USSR with an established lingua franca, Europe looks rather a mess. We may wonder how far such a perception rests on overlooking linguistic diversity elsewhere in the world, but it is at least true that in the European case a pattern of linguistic variation, largely coexisting with the boundaries of developed modern states, creates powerful entrenched structures and interests which, in turn, act as obstacles to cultural and political integration. (It is obvious, at least to this particular English speaker, that the official language of the EU ought to be English, just as it is obvious that its principal institutions should all be centralized in Brussels, but hardly anyone quite dares to say so.)

The contours of Europe's main divisions are shifting in dramatic ways. It is not just that the old political East/West division has now been replaced by an economic one. The cultural North/South divide within Europe remains important, but is changing in many ways, with the modernization of

(parts of the) southern European societies. It is now, for example, Italy, rather than the Protestant northern countries, which (in the absence of adequate child-care provision) apparently puts work before having children. The North–South religious divide remains an important structural principle in Western Europe, as does, further east, that between Orthodox Christianity and Islam. The East–West line also remains crucial, as Germans on both sides (but especially the East) will confirm, and many Central Europeans would also continue to stress the distinctiveness of their societies from 'Eastern' Europe as well as from Russia. There are also many similarities between Scandinavia and parts of East-Central Europe in terms of attitudes to secularism and welfare, despite their diverse political histories for much of the twentieth century.

Göran Therborn's book on European modernity (1995) is an exceptionally useful attempt to document these and other variations across post-1945 Europe, showing how the country and broader regional groupings vary according to the dimension chosen. This discussion is heavily indebted to his pioneering work, and I shall be guided by the questions which he poses: 'Have the societies of Europe become more similar to others on the globe? More distinctively European? More differentiated or more similar among themselves?' (Therborn, 1995, p. 30).

A clear area of difference from most of the rest of the world concerns population. Several

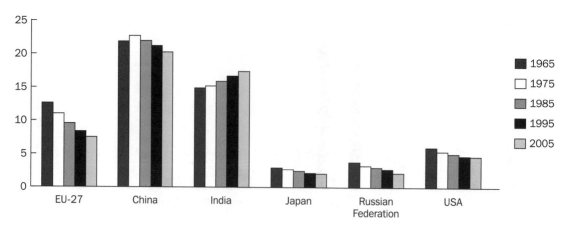

Figure 7.3   Population of EU-27 and some major countries as % of total world population, 1965–2005

Source: Data compiled from Eurostat Newsrelease STAT/08/119 (26 August 2008).

European countries have indulged in panics about their low rates of reproduction – France more or less endemically. Europe as a whole has become a low-growth area (see Figures 7.2 and 7.3), an effect mitigated by immigration and the greater fertility of the small immigrant populations. Although these populations have been relatively small overall, their concentration in particular regions, notably in the larger cities, and in manual occupations, has increased their visibility.

Expected population changes by the middle of the twenty-first century are extremely uneven across Europe (see Figure 7.4).

On 2008 projections (see Figure 7.4), *all* post-communist states currently in the EU, including Germany, are expected to decline by 2035, while *all* other European states experience modest or in some cases, notably the UK, quite substantial increases. (For excellent surveys of these and other issues to do with family structures, see Therborn, 2004, 2011) The above estimates include expectations about migration, and for this as well as other reasons should be treated with extreme caution. Post-communist countries may not be seen as attractive intra-EU migration destinations, except perhaps for retirement migration, but they may well attract migrants from further east.

Migration has in fact been an extremely important feature of recent European history. Europe is not a largely settler region like North America or Australia, but it has seen considerable flows of migrants within Europe and from elsewhere. In the twentieth century, there were essentially four combined and overlapping processes. First, economic migration *out* of Europe to the settler regions of the world, particularly North America. Second, a largely East–West migration *within* Europe of refugees or, as they were called after the Second World War, 'displaced persons' – fleeing anti-semitic pogroms or other forms of political persecution at the turn of the twentieth century and political and boundary changes in the aftermaths of the two world wars. Third, a largely South–North economic migration in the twentieth-century boom years, both within Europe and even within states (for example, from southern Italy to northern Italy or Northern Europe) and from outside – especially from the European states' colonies or former colonies. Fourth, and continuing into the present century, a confusing combination of labour migration within the EU and/or the Schengen area, residual economic migration from outside Europe, much of it illegal, and some continuing migration into Europe by refugees and asylum seekers. Russell King and Marco Donati (1999, pp. 136, 143) contrast the 'migration divide' of the 1960s with that in the last two decades of the twentieth century. Whereas in the 1960s the divide ran horizontally through Europe between the north and the south, it now follows the southern and eastern Mediterranean coastline, with only the former Yugoslavia (excluding Slovenia),

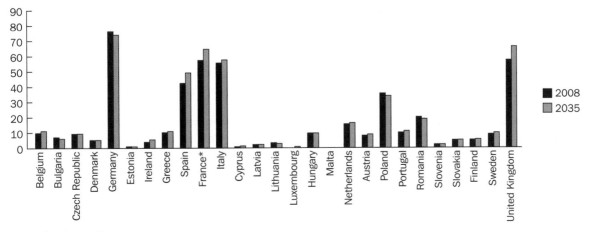

* Metropolitan France only.

Figure 7.4   Population of the EU-27, 2008 and projected 2035 (millions)

Source: Data compiled from Eurostat Newsrelease STAT/08/119 (26 August 2008).

Albania and Turkey on the 'sending' side of the line.

All the categories used in migration studies (economic/refugee, legal/illegal) are of course falsely precise attempts to capture a more complex reality, but the European situation is essentially shaped by two paradoxes. First, Europe is not a settler region but contains substantial numbers of settled migrants from outside. Second, it now forms essentially a single economic area, like the USA, but with much *less* internal migration. On the first point, there has of course been a huge amount of confusion and double-think in Europe around issues of immigration and ethnic relations. Many European countries which had not had substantial colonial empires persisted in the pretence that they were merely receiving temporary 'guest workers' rather than immigrants and that they were not 'countries of immigration'. State policies switched abruptly from active recruitment to attempts to stem the migrant flows; a second wave of immigration occurred in the 1990s with immigrants from the former communist countries and refugees from there and elsewhere. Some ethnic minorities were largely invisible, like Irish citizens in Britain or English people in Scotland; others became and remain the objects of racism and moral panics such as 'Islamophobia'. Similarly, attention focused more on immigration than emigration, even where rates

were similar. Finally, some traditionally 'exporting' states like Ireland or the Nordic countries became importers. On the second issue of the European economic and social space, the pan-European legal and social framework intersects with Europe's political and linguistic divisions. The free movement of labour was one of the core principles of the European integration process over the past 50 years, yet most migration in practice has been driven by necessity rather than the kind of free-moving wanderlust envisaged by the founding fathers of modern Europe. The formal obstacles to cross-border migration (passport controls, work permits, and so on) have been removed, but others remain. In Switzerland and Germany, for example, it is hard for long-term foreign residents to become citizens if they wish to, and voting rights are not transferable in most EU states except for local and European elections. Most important, perhaps, are the more informal obstacles in the diversity of administrative and cultural practices across Europe. Even for the young affluent mobile and polyglot professionals described as 'Eurostars' by Adrian Favell (2008: 222),

[Europe's] countries and its cities are not interchangeable, its states are nations, and Europe is not America . . . So the myth of the free European market bumps up again and again to the residual power of national and local cultures . . . They hold back the boundary crossing opportunities that would flow in a Europe in which social and professional currencies were truly mobile, interchangeable and convertible from place to place.

We are unlikely, then, to see a massive increase in migration *within* Europe; the increase of 10 per cent per year in around 2005 (Herm, 2008) is unlikely to continue. Two exceptional cases however deserve attention. One is retirement migration (Oliver, 2008), largely though not exclusively from north to south and focused particularly on Spain. In this case, residents may be able to live in a semi-ghetto serviced by other expatriates or intermediaries, thus mitigating difficulties of adaptation and producing something more like conditions for US pensioners moving from snowbelt to sunbelt. The other case is that of relatively short-term flows such as that of Eastern Europeans, particularly Poles, for a time after 2004. Many of these migrants returned as the Polish economy advanced and then the credit crunch closed down opportunities in Western Europe. Flows of this kind might occur again, reflecting continuing inequalities in European labour markets. Overall, then, migration has continued to change European society, though perhaps the most important feature of the past decades is that *all* European states have been shaped by immigration, whereas its impact in the mid-twentieth century was much more uneven.

The differences between European countries in their labour-force structures are substantially explained by their positions on the historical trajectory from agrarian to industrial and post-industrial society (Therborn, 1995, pp. 65ff). Europe was unique in the thoroughgoing nature of its industrialization and the primacy for a time, in many countries, of industrial employment. As Therborn (1995, p. 70) notes, 'Sixteen out of . . . twenty-five European countries had a period of (relatively) predominant industrial employment. Outside Europe this has only happened in Taiwan.' This to some extent cuts across the East/West divide; some communist and now post-communist countries have large agricultural populations and others do not. The gender division of labour is fundamentally

shaped by economic factors, in the sense of predominant types of production, but with significant differences between countries which one might expect to be more similar in their structures and attitudes. Conversely, the former state socialist societies of Eastern Europe, though they had much higher rates of female participation in paid work than *most* Western societies, averaged similar rates to Finland and Sweden (Therborn, 1995, p. 63); Eastern rates have now dramatically declined.

Working practices and workplace cultures display considerable diversity in Europe. Broadly speaking, the contrast between corporatist Rhineland capitalism and the neo-liberal British version (Albert, 1991) intersects with that between managerially top-heavy and authoritarian French (and other Latin) enterprises and those in Germany or Scandinavia, where workers have tended to be more skilled, participation more institutionalized and managers less numerous (Therborn, 1995, p. 79; cf. Lane, 1989). How far these differences will persist, against a background of globalization of both economic structures and managerial cultures, is an open question, as is the future shape of Eastern Europe in the European and world division of labour. Here, of course, EU membership in the short, medium or long term is a crucial factor. But if there is, as Colin Crouch (1993) has suggested, a European model or set of models of industrial relations, this may well appeal to other regions of the world.

Welfare-state structures again display a clear contrast between Scandinavian and Eastern European patterns of state-based provision on the one hand and insurance-based private or semi-private systems in most of the rest of Europe, with the UK, Ireland and Italy in an intermediate position. On the whole, the state-based systems provide more as a proportion of gross domestic product (GDP), though the insurance-based systems in France, Belgium and the Netherlands are also major providers. Generally speaking, Europe is characterized by generous welfare states, partly though not exclusively because it tends to be rich. 'In three countries', Therborn (1995, pp. 155–6) notes (the Netherlands, Norway and Sweden, with France close to the same position), 'the welfare state has become more important than private property as a source of household income.'

European welfare states by and large survived the twin onslaughts of neoliberal reforms in the West, associated with the Thatcher and Major governments in the UK in the 1980s and early 1990s but with parallels elsewhere, and of post-communist transition in the East, which tended to replace universalistic state provision with a move to insurance-based systems. They confront, however, a time-bomb in the form of ageing populations, meaning that the economically active will be less and less able to fund the growing state pension bill for the retired, combined with the more recent impact of the 2008 financial crisis, which has led states to cut back on welfare provision. (In late 2009 and early 2010, for example, Latvian pensioners had to sue the Government in the face of threatened cuts in pensions.)

The EU, as we saw in the introductory section of this chapter on 'contemporary Europe' has always avoided grasping the nettle of social policy, leaving this instead to the member states and concentrating instead on relatively minor issues of the transferability of entitlements for migrants between historically entrenched and often incompatible national systems. A concern with the risk of 'social dumping', the ability of states with low wages and poor benefits to undercut those with more generous regimes, was reflected in the 'Social Chapter' of the ill-fated European Constitution. This provoked resistance from the UK, which was allowed to 'opt out' from some provisions concerning the protection of workers' rights. Meanwhile, however, the European Court has undercut this whole area by supporting the rights of contractors to operate across the Union with their own labour, recruited in, and operating according to the provisions of their home states, at the expense of local wage rates and other regulations. This may be countered by new legislation, but at the beginning of the 2010s it still threatened a 'race to the bottom' *within* the EU, which had previously aimed to resist similar pressures at a global level.

The fate of European welfare states is in turn, of course, related to broader issues about forms of production, private versus public ownership, and class relations in European states (Therborn, 1995, pp. 123–6). Europe comes out as relatively equal, compared with North America and Australia, but with significant variations between the egalitarian north-west and east and the unequal south (Therborn, 1995, p. 153; see also Bailey, 1992, 1998; Lenoir, 1994). An interesting difference between east and west is that in the east's criticism of social inequalities correlates positively with the objective degree of inequality as measured by the Gini coefficient, whereas this association is lacking in the west. In other words, the more unequal societies in the east seem to be correspondingly more concerned about inequality, whereas in highly unequal Western European societies such as Britain it is less of a topic of concern. (See Jan Delhey's work (2001), based on data from the International Social Survey Programme.)

Social mobility has attracted a great deal of often technical social research, though within Europe the differences between countries are not particularly dramatic, with structural changes such as the disappearance of peasantries and the increase in white-collar and service jobs accounting for much of the mobility in European societies. In terms of social openness or fluidity, there are not particularly significant differences between countries. The former socialist countries, which of course actively pursued redistributive policies in the 1950s, have remained rather more open than capitalist Western Europe, but not dramatically so. Partial exceptions to this trend in their respective camps are Sweden, where mobility is relatively high, and Hungary, where it is relatively low. Japan, the USA and Australia all score higher for openness than any of the major European countries except Czechoslovakia (Therborn, 1995, p. 174; Eriksson and Goldthorpe, 1992, p. 381). Another important parallel between Eastern and Western Europe is the importance of 'cultural capital' in the transmission of advantage. Whereas the children of the traditional European bourgeoisies might hope to inherit land, factories or large amounts of monetary wealth from their parents, in the twentieth century what has been called the 'service class' of professional and managerial employees in public service and the private sector tended to transmit their advantages through the educational system, by

---

● **Social mobility**: The 'upward' or 'downward' movement from one position in a social scale to another, e.g. from 'working class' to 'middle class' – either within an individual's lifetime or from one generation to another.

paying for their children to attend exclusive fee-paying schools or by pushing them into and through elite establishments like some of the French *lycées* and *Grandes Écoles* – open to all, but in practice heavily populated by bourgeois Parisians (Bourdieu, 1970; Marceau, 1977). Initiatives in France and elsewhere to widen access to the more privileged actors of higher education seem likely to fall victim to the growing marketization of tertiary education, as universities across Europe consider introducing tuition fees, where they have not already done so. A US model of high fees whose inegalitarian effects are partly mitigated by scholarships seems likely to prevail, in an increasingly globalized sector. In Eastern Europe, once again, the threat to traditional forms of inheritance, family succession and educational privilege was more drastic under Communist rule, but old elites often managed to preserve a privileged position through the years of high Stalinism into advanced socialist and then again capitalist conditions (Szelenyi, 1988; Eyal, Szelenyi and Townsley, 1998).

Looking more broadly at the cultural sphere, it is clear that Europe's continuing position as a major cultural producer is one of the effects of its previous world hegemony, partly preserved in that of its world languages: English, French, Spanish, Portuguese and to some extent even Dutch. It has also stood up in many ways to the challenge of North American imports. This applies not just to cultural commodities such as films but also to material aspects of life such as the car-based civilization; despite everything, most European cities remain less car-based and suburbanized than US ones. For a time these might have seemed like cultural lags. Now, however, it appears that in many ways parts of the USA are returning to more 'European' modes of life, including railways and urban mass-transit systems, delicatessen food (even cheese) and niche markets for cult movies in the larger cities.

It is clear that human societies are much more ingenious in their cultural pick-and-mix or *bricolage* than we can predict (see, for example, Gilroy, 1993). It seems fair to expect, however, that despite the Americanizing pull of the mass media, reflecting and reinforcing the appeal of North America and to some extent Australia to many young Europeans, Europe will remain culturally distinct from other world regions. There may be a certain drift away from North American models, with local differences persisting against a background of common European and global systems. The washing powder, for example, may have instructions in many languages and contact addresses in half a dozen countries, but the fine detail of domestic work will continue to display interesting differences across the continent. The interrelations between post-conventional post-national identities, themselves competing with more atavistic traditional national identities, and a European identity whose ambivalence Gerard Delanty (1999) and others have rightly stressed, will form the broader social and cultural background to the ups and downs of the political and economic project of European integration in the rest of the twenty-first century. The political project of a truly united Europe may be distant or even unrealistic, but it is important to remember that Europe *has* been united since 1989 in many important ways (Outhwaite, 2010c). The fact that one can travel, say, from the far west of Europe to the formerly Soviet Baltic states, without passport controls or visas, and find much the same political and legal structures there, indicates a massive achievement for Europeans as a whole.

SUMMARY

- This chapter has attempted to situate Europe and its distinctive patterns of social structuration in its historical and geographical context, focusing in particular on the specific character of European capitalism, the European constitutional state, the emphasis in many parts of Europe on individualism and the processes of systematization and calculation summed up in the term 'rationalization'.

- I have tried to bring out the commonalities as well as the differences between the component states and regions of contemporary Europe, which is perhaps not yet 'a society' in the usual sense of the term, but which may be on the way to becoming one.

QUESTIONS FOR DISCUSSION

- What is distinctive about modernity in its contemporary European forms?

- What are the main distinctive features of European social structures?

- Have north/south differences within Europe become as important as east/west ones ?

FURTHER READING

Crouch, C. (1999) *Social Change in Western Europe* (Oxford: Oxford University Press). A comprehensive analysis of Western Europe.

Crouch, C. (2008) 'Change in European Societies since the 1970s', *West European Politics* 31(1): 14–39. The update includes Eastern Europe.

Delanty, G. and Rumford, C. (2005) *Rethinking Europe: Social Theory and the Implications of Europeanization* (London: Routledge).

Hudson, R. and A. M. Williams (eds) (1999) *Divided Europe: Society and Territory* (London: Sage). A creative exploration of economic, political, spatial and social divisions in contemporary Europe.

Outhwaite, W. (2008) *European Society* (Cambridge:

Polity Press). Focuses on the similarities and diversity of European political, economic and social structures, defending the relevance of the notion of society.

Roche, M. (2010) *Exploring the Sociology of Europe* (London: Sage). A wide-ranging historical sociology of Europe, focusing on the interplay of 'deep social structures' and contemporary transformations, notably of the European welfare state.

Rumford, C. ed. (2009) *The Sage Handbook of European Studies* (London: Sage).

Therborn, G. (1995) *European Modernity and Beyond: The Trajectory of European Societies, 1945–2000* (London: Sage). A brilliant combination of bold theorizing and often surprising empirical documentation.

The European Economy 1950 to 2010: the Miracle of Growth and the Sources of Wealth

VIVIEN A. SCHMIDT

The annual labour of every nation is the fund which originally supplies it with all the necessaries and conveniencies of life which it annually consumes, and which consist always either in the immediate produce of that labour, or in what is purchased with that produce from other nations. According, therefore, as this produce, or what is purchased with it, bears a greater or smaller proportion to the number of those who are to consume it, the nation will be better or worse supplied with all the necessaries and conveniencies for which it has occasion.

Adam Smith, *An Inquiry Into The Nature And Causes Of The Wealth Of Nations*, 1776, Introduction

This chapter considers the growth of the European economy from the 'post-war miracle' of the first 30 years, through the oil shocks of the 1970s, to the stepped-up pace of globalization and European integration beginning in the 1980s and the collapse of communism in the early 1990s, to the dotcom boom and bust of the early 2000s through to the credit boom and bust of the late 2000s. It will examine the different ways in which economic life and systems of social security have been organized in the various countries since the Second World War, and how they have changed over time. For Western Europe, the chapter will discuss three ways in which countries organized their economies. These are, first, the liberal market economy characteristic of Britain and Ireland, second, the 'coordinated' market economy of German and many smaller Western European countries, and third, the state-influenced market economy of France, Italy and Spain. For Eastern Europe, the chapter will discuss the state-led command economy found in Communist-controlled central and Eastern Europe before the collapse of communism and the dependent market economies that subsequently emerged. The chapter also outlines the three main ways in which social security and welfare systems are structured in Europe generally, including the liberal welfare state of Britain and Ireland, the social-democratic welfare state of Scandinavian countries, and the conservative welfare state of continental and southern Europe, as well as Eastern Europe following the fall of the Wall. The chapter shows that although the pressures for change have produced greater market orientation in all the various national versions of capitalism and belt-tightening in all the social security and welfare systems, significant differences in both economic organization and welfare systems remain between European countries.

The miracle of post-war economic growth

After 1950 European countries experienced phenomenal growth and, as Adam Smith predicted in the passage cited at the head of the chapter, their populations benefited from tremendous improvement in their standard of living, although growth was faster between 1950 and the mid-1970s than after. In

Western Europe, wealth provided people not only with the basics, such as running water and flush toilets, but also with the amenities to make every-day life easier – televisions, telephones and cars, followed by mobile phones and even personal computers. Eastern European countries, having grown at much the same pace as the West until the 1970s, suffered a major economic slowdown there-after, and by the 2000s were lagging behind in providing the basics, let alone the amenities, for their citizens.

The increase in wealth

The period of the 1950s and 1960s up until the mid-1970s were the years of the 'post-war miracle,' the 'golden age', or the *trente glorieuses* ('thirty glorious years'), when countries grew exponen-tially as they rebuilt and expanded their economies following the devastation wrought by the Second World War (see Figure 8.1). In the early 1950s, in fact, Europe was not much richer than it had been in 1913, just prior to the First World War, having had a mean annual growth rate of 1.2 per cent between 1913 and 1950. By the early 1970s, by contrast, all Western European countries had at least doubled their wealth compared to the 1950s, with a mean annual rate of growth between 1950 and 1973 of 3.8 per cent. Southern European countries such as Spain, Portugal and Greece, although starting and ending poorer, had an even higher mean rate of growth, at around 6 per cent annually, as opposed to a 0.7 per cent rate earlier. Eastern Europe also showed a high mean annual rate of growth: at 4 per cent annually between 1950 and 1973, by contrast with the 1 per cent annually between 1913 and 1950 – higher than Western European countries although lower than Southern European ones (Maddison, 1995, Table 3–2).

Between the 1970s and the mid-2000s, growth in gross domestic product (GDP) was more highly differentiated (see Figure 8.1). All countries had to struggle with the two oil crises in the mid- and late 1970s, when the price of crude oil skyrocketed, producing inflation and raising the production costs for all goods, while the collapse of the Bretton Woods agreement on a fixed dollar exchange rate spelled increasing currency volatility for the West of

Europe. By the 1980s and 1990s, moreover, global-ization, understood as the growing international-ization of the financial markets and trade, brought intensifying competitive pressures to the West's product and capital markets. However, the increas-ing integration of European economies through the single market and the single currency (see Chapter 4) served not only as a further conduit for such globalization but also as a shield against it for the European countries that joined the EU in successive waves (see Schmidt, 2002, ch. 1).

Although the rate of growth generally slowed as countries tried to adjust to the much more compet-itive environment, with a 1.8 per cent mean annual rate of growth (in real GDP) between 1973 and 1992 for Western European countries and 2.2 per cent for Southern European countries, these rates still resulted in a considerable increase in wealth. By the early 1990s, almost all Western European coun-tries had more than tripled their GDP per capita compared to the 1950s while Southern European countries had quintupled theirs. Through the 1990s, moreover, growth continued, with an average annual rate of 1.9 in real GDP between 1993 and 1999 for the 15 members of the European Union (EU) (OECD, 2001). Growth rates between 2000 and 2007 were more highly differentiated. While the UK and Ireland averaged around 2.75 per cent and 6 per cent, respectively, France and Germany were much slower, producing average annual growth rates of between 2.0 and 1.7 per cent. Sweden and Norway, by contrast, had average annual growth rates of between 2.5 and 3 per cent (OECD, 2009).

The story was quite different for the countries of Eastern Europe across this same time period, however. Most of these countries started out in 1950 with a GDP per capita similar to the Southern European countries, grew less quickly yet still impressively to 1973, but then really slowed down between 1973 and 1992, falling back in 1992 to below their 1973 level with the collapse of their economies following the fall of the Berlin Wall. They only slowly recovered, with annual per cent increases in real GDP often higher than those of EU countries, such as Hungary at 2.7 per cent and Poland at 5.4 per cent between 1993 and 1999 (OECD, 2001). Between 2000 and 2007, however, growth rates were much higher, generally outstrip-

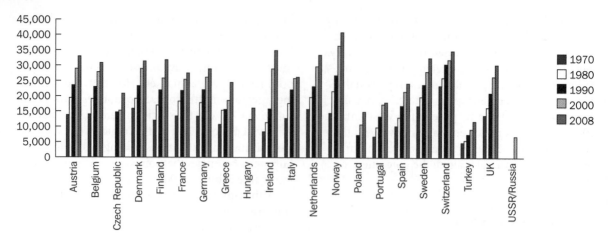

Notes: GDP per head, US$, constant prices, constant PPPs, reference year 2000.

Figure 8.1   GDP per capita of 21 European countries, 1970–2008

Source: OECD Statistics online (2010).

ping Western European countries. Hungary had an average annual growth rate of 3.95 per cent, Poland's was above 4 per cent, and Estonia's average annual growth rate was still higher (8.2 per cent), reaching a peak in 2006 with an annual growth rate of 10.4 per cent (OECD, 2009).

Once the economic crisis hit, growth declined precipitously for all European countries. But now, there were tremendous differences among countries in both East and West. In the East, which was hit first by the crisis, Poland was the only country to post a positive growth rate, at 1.4 per cent in 2009, while other Eastern European countries, namely Latvia, Hungary and Romania, had to go to the International Monetary Fund (IMF) for a bailout in 2008. In the West, Greece had to go to the EU (joined by the IMF) for a major loan in 2010, which the EU then granted, followed by a massive loan-guarantee fund for the other Southern Mediterranean countries after they (and the euro) came under massive pressure from the markets. This stabilization fund seemed to calm the markets, but only momentarily, as the euro slid in value on concerns that the new austerity measures announced by Southern Mediterranean countries, among others, would stymie growth, and that the new debt that the EU was potentially taking on was unsustainable. By the end of 2010, as the markets

continued to pummel vulnerable member states with increasingly high interest rates for their bond issues, Ireland followed with a request to the EU and IMF for a bailout, and Portugal in early 2011. By summer 2011, Greece was again in the headlines, in need of a further loan bailout, which was complicated by German demands that the European bank lenders participate, a Greek conservative opposition unwilling to vote for another austerity package, and massive protests in the streets.

As of mid-2011, then, it remained unclear what the prospects for growth would be, with markets asking the EU to square the circle by demanding sound economic fundamentals attainable only through austerity measures to reduce deficits and public debt at the same time as they expected sustainable growth – which is impossible in the short term, given austerity measures.

The rise of consumerism: from flush toilets to mobile phones

With the extraordinary growth in Europe beginning in the 1950s came a dramatic improvement in the quality of life. Living conditions at the end of the war were often quite stark for many in continental Europe, with large numbers of people living in dwellings with no running water and no flush toilets. According to United Nations (UN) statistics, only Britain had more than nine in ten dwellings equipped with both running water and flush toilets in 1951. But this changed rapidly during the post-war period for most other Western European countries. For example, whereas in the first half of the 1950s only half of French dwellings had running water and only a third in Italy, by 1968 almost all French dwellings and 60 per cent of Italian dwellings did. By contrast, whereas half the households in Germany already had flush toilets in 1954 and almost all did by 1968, in France only half of all households had flush toilets by this later date (UN, 1972). By the 1990s, however, over nine in ten dwellings across Western Europe were equipped with running water and flush toilets (UN, 2001, Table 7.5).

Along with the basics in terms of comfortable living came all the other household amenities that added to ease of existence, such as refrigerators and washing machines. To take only one example, in France, under 10 per cent of the population lived in dwellings with refrigerators or washing machines in 1954, whereas close to 90 per cent had refrigerators and 70 per cent washing machines by 1974 (INSEE, 1990, Tables 33, 34).

Televisions, telephones, and personal computers followed suit (see Table 8.1). By the late 1970s, over one in every three adults had television sets and telephones in most Western European countries and by the late 1990s, over one in every two adults – and thus most households. By this time, moreover, at least one in every five adults had mobile phones and personal computers (PCs), although in Scandinavian countries it was one in every three adults. By 2008, the numbers for both mobile phones and PCs had jumped dramatically, with almost all adults having at least one mobile phone and close to four out of five with PCs. Southern European countries, by contrast, started much lower, but they largely caught up with their richer neighbours by the late 1990s in everything but PCs, owned by only two out of five adults.

Conditions did not improve as rapidly for the Eastern and Central European countries. In the 1990s, only in the Czech Republic, Slovakia, Slovenia and Estonia were more than nine in ten

dwellings equipped with both running water and flush toilets. But the poorest countries were much less well equipped, such as Romania, where in 1992 only five in ten had running water and four in ten flush toilets (UN, 2001, Table 7.5). By 2008, however, conditions had improved, even if in Bulgaria 29 per cent of the population still lacked indoor flush toilets for sole household use, while in Romania that number was at 41 per cent (Eurostat, 2010).

Similar variations were apparent in the ownership of televisions, telephones, and PCs (see Table 8.1). In the more affluent Eastern European countries, such as Czechoslovakia in the late 1970s, one in every four adults had televisions and one in five telephones whereas by the late 1990s the ratios were closer to one in two with televisions and more than one in three with telephones, while close to one in ten had mobile phones and PCs. In poorer countries such as Bulgaria in the late 1970s, by contrast, only one in every five adults owned televisions, and one in ten telephones. The proportions went up to over one in three for televisions and telephones by the late 1990s, although not even one in fifty for mobile phones. By the late 2000s, however, all of these countries had caught up with regard to mobile phones, which helps explain the fact that the number of telephones remained low, while they were close to the numbers for Southern Europe with regard to PCs per adult (see Table 8.1).

Perhaps the most impressive figure in terms of improving living standards and consumption for all of Europe has been the rise in the number of cars. Car ownership jumped dramatically between 1955 and 1970, increasing three, four, or fivefold in most Western European countries, and continued to grow significantly thereafter. By 1998 close to one in every two or three adults owned a car. By the late 2000s, there was only minor change in the numbers for most countries with the exception of Ireland, the 'Celtic Tiger,' which went from 374 cars per thousand population in 2002 to 437 cars per thousand in 2007 (UN, 2008).

Southern European countries like Spain, Portugal and Greece lagged behind the other Western European countries in the 1970s, however. But by 1985, a few years after the end of the dictatorships, at the time these countries joined the EU, we see the same kind of jump in ownership that

Table 8.1   Televisions, telephones, mobile phones and personal computers in selected European countries, 1997–2008 (% of population)

	Televisions			Telephones				Mobile phones			Personal computers		
	1977	1998	2000	1977	1998	2004	2008	1998	2005	2008	1998	2007	2008
France	36	58	63	33	57	56	56	19	79	93	21	69	71
UK	33	65	65	42[a]	56	58	54	25	109	126	26	78	80
Germany	31	58	59	37	57	66	62	17	96	128	31	78	80
Denmark	34	59	81	54	66	65	46	36	101	116	39	84	86
Greece	12	47	49	25	52	57	54	20	92	124	5.2	40	44
Czechoslovakia/													
Czech Republic	25	45	51	19	36	34	22	9	115	133	10	55	63
Bulgaria	18	36	45	11	33	35	29	1.5	80	138	—	35	40
Romania	:	:	38		16	20	24	3	62	115		34	35

Sources: United Nations, *Statistical Yearbook* (New York and Geneva: UN, various years); UN Economic Commission for Europe, *Trends in Europe and North America 2001* (New York and Geneva: UN, 2001), Tables 11.1, 11.2; Eurostat 2007; International Telecommunication Union 2010.

other Western European countries experienced in 1970. Only in Greece does car ownership continue to be low at only 251 cars per thousand in 1998 – but that figure does not, of course, include the number of individually owned boats that substitute for cars on many of the islands. By 2007, however Greece was up to 429 cars per thousand (UN, 2008).

In the Eastern and Central European countries, the lag in car ownership was greater. In the 1970s, car ownership was lower than in west Europe in 1955. By 1998, although the increase was significant, it was still not as great as in the West, the level having only reached 257 cars per 1000. A decade later, most Central and Eastern European countries had gone up by at least fifty if not one hundred cars per thousand. For example, while the Czech Republic went from 358 cars per thousand in 2002 to 414 in 2008, Latvia jumped from 265 cars per thousand in 2002 to 398 in 2007 (UN, 2008).

The explanation of growth

How do we explain this amazing increase in material wealth and quality of life, especially in the West of Europe? For the early post-war years, the tremendous spurt in growth can be explained by the surfeit of pent-up demand – first for the basics of life (the flush-toilet factor) and then increas-

ingly for the luxuries that became everyday necessities. If you could produce, you could sell. Moreover, people had the money to buy – at least in the West.

More money in peoples' pockets

Wages increased dramatically from the 1950s on, in particular in the manufacturing sector. For example, workers' hourly pay in manufacturing more than doubled in each decade between 1960 and 1980, and continued to increase significantly after that, if somewhat more slowly. The differences among countries were more pronounced in the early years, in which German manufacturing workers clearly earned a lot more than their counterparts in France, let alone in Italy, the UK or Sweden. By 2009, however, the differences among countries were marginal compared to the past, although still important with regard to the price-competitiveness of their products. But now, German workers were paid somewhat less than their counterparts in the other countries. This said, while hourly earnings for manufacturing workers may have gone up significantly, growth in real wages for the labour force as a whole, meaning the comparative amount of money in workers' pockets, declined significantly, as salaries for the average earners saw little increase. What is clear is that

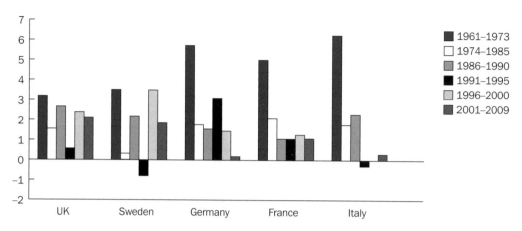

Figure 8.2   Growth in real wages in five European countries, 1961–2009

Source: European Economy' Spring 2008 Statistical Appendix, http://ec.europa.eu/economy_finance/publications/publication12534_de.pdf.

while growth in real wages was tremendous the 1960s, the oil crises of the 1970s through to the mid-1980s brought a dramatic drop in increased earnings for everyone, while in subsequent years these countries had different trajectories. Most notably, French workers' earnings remained pretty flat from the mid-1980s on, with an increase from 2001 to 2009 of only 1.12 per cent, whereas Germany saw greater wage progression between the mid-1980s and the early 2000s, at which point it then saw a massive decline, with increases of only 0.19 per cent in real wages between 2001 and 2009 (see Figure 8.2). Workers' purchasing power remained, however, due to cheap credit from the financial markets and cheap imports from the East, whether Eastern Europe or East Asia, and especially China.

As average wages remained relatively stable in the 2000s, however, income at the highest levels benefited from astronomical jumps in salary. In the 1960s the ratio of the average European Chief Executive Officer (CEO) to manufacturing worker pay was not that excessive, although significantly lower in Europe, and in particular Finland, than in the USA, even then. By the mid-2000s, this had changed dramatically, with the USA again in the lead, followed closely by the UK. By 2008, however, French CEOs led Europe in compensation, with average salaries of €5.87 million, ahead of the British, at €5.85 million, but nowhere near the Americans, at €12.97 million (HayGroup study

cited in La-Croix.com, 2 May 2009). Investment bankers did even better, such as the head of the Deutsche Bank, who received €14 million in 2007, although only €1.4 million in 2008. And we have not yet mentioned the megabonuses of financial market traders, or the windfalls, such as the sale of ABN Amro, a Dutch banking institution, which netted the ABN chairman around $34 million upon his retirement after the sale. Although the financial crisis beginning in 2008 may have slowed the progression in big salaries and bonuses for top managers and bankers, in particular for banks that were granted massive government loans, they have not produced a significant reduction in pay, nor have the wage inequalities between the highest and lowest paid changed. Thus, it was not just football heroes and movie stars who earned mega-millions. CEOs did as well. As a result, at the same time that demand held steady not just for cars, televisions and telephones but for mobile phones, computers, CD players and DVD players, demand was also generated for high-ticket luxury items such as Armani suits, Hermès scarves and Vuitton luggage, not to mention Ferrari sports cars and yachts.

Growth was fuelled not only by more money in peoples' pockets but also by the opening European economies gained from the globalization and European integration of trade and of the financial markets, while pre-1989 the command economies of Eastern Europe benefited from the large market led by the Soviet Union.

Expanding markets through globalization and Europeanization

At the end of the Second World War, policy-makers in Europe and the USA were convinced that the only way to promote peace and prosperity was through the internationalization of trade. This was to bring business efficiencies, investment opportunities and competitiveness while providing consumers with a greater variety of higher-quality products at lower prices. Multinational corporations were to be the vehicles for growth while new international institutions such as the General Agreement on Tariffs and Trade (GATT) – which became the World Trade Organization (WTO) in 1995 – were to help reduce barriers to trade while ensuring a fair playing field. In the early years, moreover, with countries devastated by war and without the means to rebuild, the Marshall Plan instituted by the USA provided the kick-start to growth, with a vast infusion of money for all in Europe who asked – which they did in the west of Europe, but not the east. Financial market stabilization was also supported early on by international institutions, such as the IMF and the World Bank, as well as by the Bretton Woods system of fixed dollar exchange rates. Liberalization of the financial markets came later, following the collapse of the Bretton Woods system in the early 1970s, with the progressive removal of capital controls along with the deregulation of currency and capital markets. Since then, the twin processes of the internationalization of trade and of the financial markets (sometimes regarded as the essential elements of globalization) have been characterized by the exponential growth of international trade dominated by seemingly 'stateless' multinational corporations and by the tremendous expansion of the financial markets dominated by new, non-governmental actors in the form of institutional investors (see Held et al., 1999).

In Europe, trade regionalization through the European integration process, which meant an end to borders and the free movement of capital, goods, people, and services (see Chapter 4), was a complement to trade internationalization. European integration helped improve competitiveness not only through the reduction in tariff and non-tariff barriers but also through the economies of scale afforded by the single European market and the savings ensured by the single currency (see Chapter 4). It also protected European economies from the costs of inefficient regulation by providing common health, safety and environmental rules, harmonized product standards, and deregulation of financial markets, telecommunications, electricity and transport. And it shielded them from the dangers of unfair competition through competition policies, anti-dumping measures, multilateral as well as bilateral trade agreements and common agricultural and fisheries policies.

The combined impact of the internationalization and Europeanization of trade was dramatic: tariff barriers went down from levels as high as 30 per cent or more in the early 1950s to under 6 per cent by the 1990s. By 2005, the EU had the world's largest share of the world market in merchandise, at 19.6 per cent, compared to the USA at 13 per cent, Japan at 9.5 per cent and China at 14 per cent and, together with Japan, was also most prominent in world trade in the manufacturing sector, in particular in upmarket products.

Moreover, European firms have been major world players in international investment. In 2000, a top year for foreign investment, EU member states alone were responsible for 67 per cent, or $770 billion, of world foreign direct investment outflows, while they attracted 50 per cent, or $617 billion, of world foreign direct investment inflows. In 1999, a year that saw particularly strong merger and acquisition activity (M&As), European cross-border M&As accounted for close to half of all global cross-border M&A-related sales and 70 per cent of purchases. Thus, for example, while European car manufacturers sought new partners in the USA – Daimler with Chrysler – and in Japan – Renault with Nissan, the big German banks bought themselves instant investment expertise and entrée into the financial markets by acquiring British and American investment houses, such as Deutsche Bank's acquisition of Morgan Grenfell and later of Bankers' Trust.

The most spectacular M&As at this time, however, were in services, most notably the takeover by the British mobile phone company Vodaphone of the German manufacturing company Mannesmann in 2000 at a cost of € 204.8 billion. And the most significant fiasco was the

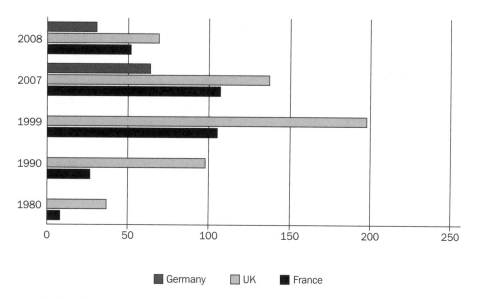

Figure 8.3   Capital value of shares traded on the stock exchange in three European countries, 1980–2008 (as % of GDP)

Source: World Bank, various years.

French media giant Vivendi, which had gone on such a massive buying spree, with $77 billion-worth of takeovers, including Pathé and Universal Studios, that, once the dotcom crisis hit in 2001, it ended up on the brink of bankruptcy. Subsequently, as the European economy recovered from the dotcom crash, came the mega-bank mergers, resulting in banks 'too big to fail' such as the British HBSC, the Spanish Santander and the French Paribas.

Financial market internationalization followed upon trade internationalization, beginning in the 1970s. The rapid expansion of the currency markets came first, as a by-product of the break-down of the Bretton Woods system of fixed exchange rates, while capital mobility also increased as countries gradually abolished capital controls. Whereas the currency markets traded around $10–20 billion in the 1970s, close to $500 billion in 1988, by 1998 they were at $1.5 trillion, while by 2007, just before the beginning of the financial market crisis, they were trading at $3.98 trillion.

Stock market liberalization came next – with the USA leading deregulation in 1979 followed by Britain and France in 1986 and Germany much later, only in 1995. The effects of stock market liberalization have been perhaps most impressive in France, with Germany providing a notable contrast (see Figure 8.3).

In all this, the impact of EU integration has not only acted as a complement to globalization, by promoting openness in the currency markets through reductions in national capital controls along with the liberalization of the capital markets. It has also served to soften its effects by reducing European member states' exposure to the currency markets through convergence in the monetary policy arena. Coordinated action through the European Monetary System (EMS) began in 1979. On the basis of the Maastricht Treaty convergence criteria (see Box 4.3) the drive towards a single currency within the context of European Monetary Union (EMU) was undertaken. This was intended to provide greater protection against speculative forces as well as greater currency stability and a euro that would rival the dollar in its use as a world reserve currency.

Since its introduction, the euro has proven itself as a credible international currency, despite its initial unexpected weakness in 2002, its subsequent overvaluation compared to the weakening dollar, and then its precipitous weakening in 2010, followed again by major overvaluation in 2011. This said, the financial crisis beginning in 2008 tested the eurozone most severely. It passed that test in 2008 with flying colours, as the ECB intervened in coordination with other central banks to stabilize world currency markets while the member states, led by the UK and France, followed with national actions to rescue banks and inject major stimulus spending into the economy.

But in 2010, when Greece was under immense market pressure beginning in February because of fears of a sovereign debt default, the EU dithered, letting the problem fester as the costs of Greek government borrowing went up and up, so much so that even once the EU approved a loan of €110 billion (of which €30 billion came from the IMF) on 3 May, it was not enough to calm the markets, now worried about sovereign debt default of other Southern European member states. The EU was therefore forced six days later to come up with the €750 billion loan guarantee fund, called the EFSF (European Financial Stability Facility), of which €250 billion came from the IMF. This was because of the continued slide in the value of the euro on worries about the contagion effects on other Southern European countries with fragile finances. The subsequent loan bailouts of Ireland in December 2010 and Portugal in May 2011 under the EFSF were negotiated with shorter delays, although here the hesitations came from the countries themselves, as increasingly unpopular governments were loath to impose further austerity on increasingly unhappy electorates – who in elections shortly after the bailouts punished their governments by ejecting them.

In the case of Ireland, the bailout came on the heels of the decision of the EU, under German insistence, to create the ESM (European Security Mechanism), which was scheduled to take over from the EFSF in 2013, and which would be able to impose 'haircuts' – or losses – on the private banks. Misunderstandings in the markets about when such losses would be imposed led to a massive increase in interest rates on Irish debt issues, forcing it to ask for a loan under the EFSF; a few months later, similar pressures on Portugal led it, too, to ask for protection, with a loan agreed in May 2011. Moreover, by late spring 2011, the Greek tragedy replayed itself, now because of debt coming up for renewal, which required yet another round of EU and IMF meetings on a second loan bailout,

and yet another cliff-hanging vote in the Greek parliament on yet another round of austerity measures.

In short, capital markets, just like product markets, grew exponentially from the 1950s to the 2000s. There was more money in people's pockets, in their bank accounts, and in their brokers' accounts, all of which fuelled economic growth – until the financial crisis beginning in 2008. But even then, major economic disruption was avoided, although growth slowed, in particular in Latvia, Romania and Hungary under IMF rule beginning in 2008, and in Greece, Ireland and Portugal under EU rule beginning in 2010 or 2011.

Technological innovation and the shift in productive activities

But however large the product and capital markets, demand would quickly have been exhausted had it not been for the technological innovations that generated new products and services. This included not only the DVDs that replaced the CD players that themselves had replaced phonographs and gramophones, but also the robots that increased productivity while decreasing the numbers of workers needed on the shop floor and the computerized stock-trading systems that replaced hand bids, making trillion-dollar money flows possible.

Technology had already produced the earlier industrial revolutions that had raised productivity in agriculture, thus bringing about the rural exodus that had provided the unending supply of labour for the factories in urban areas. By the first half of the twentieth century, manufacturing had clearly replaced agriculture as the most important basis for wealth creation, even though some countries were already much further down the road to industrialization than others. By the 1990s, however, it had become clear that yet another technological revolution had taken place, this time from industrial manufacturing to services and knowledge-based industries (see Figures 8.4, 8.5 and 8.6). Whereas in the 1950s, the most productive jobs were those in which workers were mostly concentrated on making things, by the 2000s, they were ones focused on handling information and providing services. There has been an explosion in jobs both

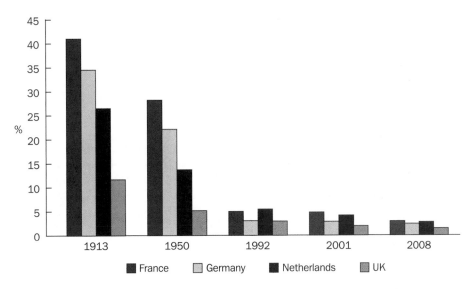

Figure 8.4   Employment in agriculture in four European countries, 1913, 1950, 1992, 2001 and 2008

Source: Angus Maddison, *L'Économie Mondiale 1820–1992, Analyse et Statistiques* (Paris: OECD, 1995), Table 2–5; Eurostat 2002; OECD 2009.

at the low end, in fast-food outlets and pizza-delivery services, as well as in the caring industries, and at the high end, in information technology and financial services, as well as in professional services of all kinds. The big growth industries were no longer manufacturing – or hardware – but software, services and the entertainment industry.

Also, whereas employment in services increased exponentially, employment in industry eroded while employment in agriculture plummeted – down to the single digits in all Western European countries (except Portugal) (Maddison, 1995, Table 2–5). Manufacturing jobs declined because of technological innovations that increased productivity rates while decreasing the number of workers needed per task, through the automation and robotization of factories and computer-linked just-in-time inventory-control systems. However, industrial employment also dropped because of rising competition from developing countries, where wages remain much lower but skills have been growing. Industrial jobs in particular started to move offshore from the 1980s and picked up steam in the 1990s with outsourcing to Asia, accompanied from the mid-1990s by 'near-sourcing' to Central and Eastern Europe. In the 2000s, outsourcing of service jobs followed, in particular

through call centres and technical support, which sparked an increasingly vociferous polemic about the dangers of 'globalization,' especially in continental European countries like France. Near-shore 'insourcing,' following the accession of Central and Eastern European countries to the EU in 2004, became the next focus of public concern, with images of the 'Polish plumber' coming to take French jobs a factor in the negative vote in the French referendum on the Constitutional Treaty in 2005. By 2008, the Netherlands had gone the furthest among West European countries towards the service industries, even outdistancing the UK. Germany remained more present in industry. Spain had made the most dramatic transition since the 1970s while Greece, by contrast, continued to have a larger agricultural sector (see Figure 8.7).

In Eastern Europe, industry remained stronger, despite the collapse of many communist-era industrial firms. This was the result of large foreign direct investment from multinational firms – most of them Western European – looking for low-wage but high-skilled industrial labour, although the transition to a service economy was also under way in Eastern European countries along with the reduction in agricultural workers. In 2001 the Czech Republic was down to only 5 out of every

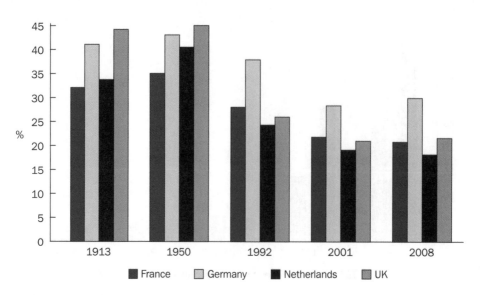

Figure 8.5   Employment in industry in four European countries, 1913, 1950, 1992, 2001, and 2008

Source: Angus Maddison, *L'Économie Mondiale 1820–1992, Analyse et Statistiques* (Paris: OECD, 1995), Table 2–5; Eurostat 2002 ; OECD 2009.

100 workers in agriculture (from 12 in 1990), while in Poland 19 out of every 100 workers were employed in agriculture – down from 25 in 1992 (OECD, various years). By 2008, the Czech Republic was down even further in agriculture, to 3.3 workers for every 100 workers, but had held steady in industry and in services. In Poland, employment in agriculture had also decreased, but not nearly as much as in the Czech Republic (OECD, 2009) (see Figure 8.7).

Investment in Physical and Human Capital and the Rise in Productivity

While technological innovation, with the attendant shift in productive activities from agriculture through industry to services, helps explain the continued demand that fuelled growth, it does not explain Europe's capacity to meet those demands. Investment in physical capital – including new commercial buildings, machinery and equipment – as well as in human capital, through education for the young and skills for workers, were additional factors in growth. These were key elements in the increases in productivity that enabled the bulk of workers to move out of agriculture into industry,

then out of industry into services.

Productivity, much like GDP, grew exponentially in the post-war period compared to the past, and continued to grow, but at a slower pace from the mid-1970s on. In Western Europe, the most spectacular rate of growth was that of Germany, while Britain, by contrast, had the slowest rate of growth in productivity in the post-war years. Among Southern European countries, Spain grew fastest. In the East, productivity growth was lower than in most of the West of Europe other than Britain, but still impressive between 1950 and 1973. But productivity gains virtually stopped between 1973 and 1992 for Central and Eastern European countries before, however, subsequently picking up significantly these countries, It also continued for the West, albeit more slowly, into the 2000s.

In Western Europe, one of the most important factors in the increases in productivity was the extraordinary rate of investment in physical capital between the 1950s and the 1990s. In this period, it largely managed to close the gap with the world's economic leader, the USA. In 1950, the average amount invested in equipment and machinery per employee by France, Germany, the Netherlands, and the UK was relatively low, at a ratio of approximately 1 to 4 with the USA. It was still behind in

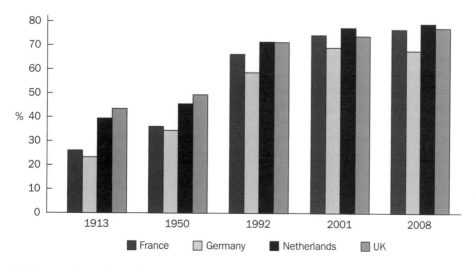

Figure 8.6   Employment in services in four European countries, 1913, 1950, 1992, 2001 and 2008

Source: Angus Maddison, *L'Économie Mondiale 1820–1992, Analyse et Statistiques* (Paris: OECD, 1995), Table 2–5; Eurostat 2002 ; OECD 2009.

1973, but the gap was down to a ratio of 2 to 3, as these four countries had increased their physical capital fourfold. By 1992, the gap had narrowed even further, as the four had close to doubled their investment yet again, with the ratio with the USA now only 3 to 4 (Maddison, 1995, Table 2–2). In the 2000s, when considering capital investment more generally, we continue to see steady improvement in the amount countries invested (in terms of gross fixed capital formation); but the differences among European countries increased as France continued to inch its way up to Germany, which was significantly higher than all the other countries, while Britain lagged behind and CEECs showed significant increases in what was naturally a much lower amount of investment, given country size.

The catch-up in investment in physical capital was reinforced by major investments in human capital with regard to education and skills. All European countries greatly improved their educational systems. In the three largest EU member states, the general population's years of schooling increased from around 10 in the early 1950s to 12 in Germany, 14 in Britain, and 16 in France by the early 1990s (Maddison, 1995, Table 2–3). Germany more than made up for its lower rate of schooling, moreover, with apprenticeship and vocational training programmes that ensured its workers the

highest levels of technical skills in Europe and its manufactured goods a higher price/quality ratio than France or Britain, even into the late 1990s (*World Competitiveness Yearbook* 2000). France's longer years of schooling, instead, ensured its students had the administrative skills that served to increase its productivity to the highest rate in Europe by the late 1990s (although mainly because the German productivity figures now included the formerly Communist eastern *Länder*). Britain, by contrast, was way behind on skills training, which in the 1990s showed up not only in its lower price/quality ratio but also in its relative unit labour costs in manufacturing. Britain's move to the service industries was thus perhaps propitious. By 2009, Britain had again become more competitive in what manufacturing was left to it, with relative unit labour costs lower than other EU member states (at 86), followed by Ireland (92) and the Czech Republic (94). Germany (at 96), however, was also highly competitive, more so than France (at 102), although it was nevertheless still below the eurozone average (of 108) along with Scandinavian countries like Sweden (99) and Denmark (103). This was in great contrast to southern European countries like Italy (117) and Spain (115), along with a CEEC like Slovakia (113) (OECD 2010 – 2005 = 100).

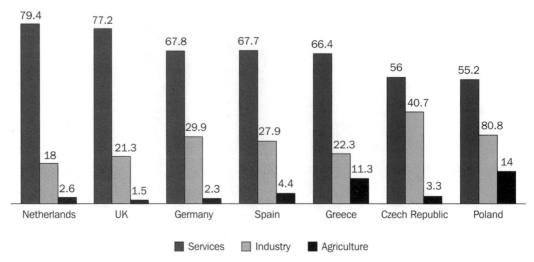

Figure 8.7   Employment in services, industry and agriculture in seven European countries, 2008 (%)

Data source: OECD 2009.

To see what this all means for business competitiveness, it is useful to consider perceptions of European countries in the comparative world surveys related to the ease of doing business in the world (World Bank, 2010), to perceptions of corruption (Transparency International, 2009) and to assessments of countries' world competitiveness (*World Competitiveness Yearbook* 2009) (see Table 8.2). On all three of such assessments, Anglophone and Scandinavian countries plus Switzerland come out closest to the top, with the Anglophones winning on ease of doing business, and Scandinavians and Switzerland on (least) corruption perception and world competitiveness. Continental Europeans follow behind, closely shadowed by the Baltic States, who are the champions among Central and East European countries, despite the fact that Estonia fell dramatically by eight ranking levels in competitiveness between 2008 and 2009. The Southern Mediterranean states come in last compared to other Western European countries and are on a par with the rest of the CEECs on all measures.

These figures, including levels of investment in capital, of productivity and skills, business competitiveness and corruption, go some way towards explaining why it was that, when the economic crisis hit in 2008, countries like Romania and Hungary had to go to the IMF for a bailout – although it does not explain Latvia, which was suffering under the weight of euro-denominated loans. It also helps explain why two years later Southern European countries like Greece had to be bailed out by the EU while a massive loan guarantee fund was created for the other Southern European countries. But of course, a lot more was at play: for Greece, market concerns about its high debt and deficit, joined with the fact that it had cooked its books not once, to gain accession to the euro, but twice, to hide the size of its EU rule-busting deficit – upon the advice of Goldman Sachs. For Spain, despite its good track record on government deficit and debt, the problem was the size of its real-estate bubble, and how quickly its economy deteriorated. Portugal, by contrast, was plagued by low growth, while Ireland was similarly troubled by its massive real-estate bubble, and the fact that the government had, in one ill-conceived move, transferred private debt to the public side by pledging to guarantee the banks at the height of the crisis and in fear of a run on those banks.

Other factors are also important to understanding not only the crisis but also countries' trajectories over time, involving the governance of the economy, both in terms of work and welfare. For this, we need to consider the ways Western

Table 8.2 European country rankings on various business and competitiveness measures (clustered in geographical areas/varieties of capitalism)

Country	Ease of doing business (ranked from 1 down)	Corruption Perception Index score (top score 9.4 out of 10)	World Competitiveness Scoreboard ranking 2009/08
Anglophone			
UK	5	7.7	21 /21
Ireland	7	8.0	19 /12
Scandinavian			
Denmark	6	9.3	5 /6
Sweden	18	9.2	6 /9
Finland	16	8.9	9 /15
Norway	10	8.6	11 /11
Continental			
Switzerland	21	9.0	4 /4
Germany	25	8.0	13 /16
Netherlands	30	8.9	10 /10
Austria	28	7.9	16 /14
Belgium	22	7.1	22 /22
Luxembourg	64	8.2	12 /5
France	31	6.9	28 /25
S. Mediterranean			
Portugal	48	5.8	34 /37
Spain	62	6.1	39 /33
Italy	78	4.3	50 /46
Greece	109	3.8	52 /42
Eastern Europe			
Estonia	24	6.6	35 /23
Latvia	27	4.5	——-
Lithuania	26	4.9	31 /36
Hungary	47	5.1	45 /38
Poland	72	5.0	44 /44
Czech Republic	74	4.9	29 /28
Slovakia	42	4.5	33 /30
Slovenia	53	6.6	32 /32
Bulgaria	44	3.8	38 /39
Romania	55	3.8	54 /45

Sources: World Bank, 'Doing Business' 2010, http://www.doingbusiness.org (based on period June 2008–May 2009); Transparency International Corruption Perceptions Index 2009, http://www.transparency.org; *World Competitiveness Yearbook 2009*, http://www.imd.ch/research/publications/wcy/upload/scoreboard.pdf.

European countries adjusted their post-war economic systems in response to the changing economic environment from 1973 onwards and how East European countries adjusted after 1989.

The challenges of growth

European economic development is best divided into two periods. For Western Europe, there is the 'golden age' between the 1950s and the early 1970s when all countries prospered, whatever the structure of their systems of work and welfare, and the period of adjustment since then, when countries responded in different ways at different times, with differing results, to the increasing economic pressures on their economic governance systems. For Eastern Europe, following the Communist era that ended in 1989, formerly closed command economies were hit with the full force of globalization and Europeanization as they sought to institute greater openness while converting to market economies.

Systems of Work and Welfare in the Post-war Period

From the early post-war years until the 1970s, European countries were able to consolidate very different systems of economic management and development, all with rapid economic growth – in the West under the protective barriers of capital exchange controls, fixed but adjustable exchange rates and optional barriers to trade; in the East, behind the protective barrier of the Iron Curtain. Moreover, in both the West and the East, populations all came to expect certain basic entitlements such as the right to an education when young, a job when full-bodied, health care when sick, social assistance when poor or disabled and a pension when old.

In the West, countries such as Germany, the Netherlands, Denmark and Sweden were characterized by coordinated market economies in which businesses cooperated with one another through mutually reinforcing networks and with labour through centrally organized negotiation systems. Countries such as Britain and Ireland, by contrast, were characterized by liberal market economies in which the state had a more hands-off approach to both business and labour, businesses were more

individualistic in their interrelationships, and labour–management relations were often adversarial. Countries such as France, and Italy to a lesser extent, instead had state-led market economies in which the interventionist state sought to direct business investment and to impose management–labour cooperation, although often without much success, given adversarial interrelationships. Spain, Greece and Portugal were authoritarian dictatorships with state-controlled market economies in which the interventionist state centrally controlled business and organized corporatist labour–management relations. Countries such as Czechoslovakia, Hungary and Poland, finally, were characterized by state-controlled command economies in which the interventionist state centrally organized the distribution system, owned all businesses, and controlled labour.

But whatever the economic governance system, all countries did quite well in this post-war period, and all developed welfare states that sought to guarantee full employment, a decent pension, universal health care and education for all. But here again, there were significant differences among countries in how welfare was provided and how it was financed. A number of types can be distinguished. In 'liberal' Anglo-Saxon countries (the UK and Ireland), welfare was assumed to be a matter of individual responsibility, provided by the state on the basis of needs, and primarily for the poor, with a comparatively low level of benefits and services (other than in health and education). In 'social-democratic' Scandinavian countries, by contrast, welfare was assumed to be a collective responsibility, equally accessible to all citizens, and a universal right provided by the state for all at the highest level of benefits and services. In 'conservative' continental Europe, however, welfare was for the most part understood as a matter of family responsibility available at variable levels according to gender and social status, based on work history, and provided by intermediary groups and the state, with a reasonably high level of benefits but not of services. Mediterranean countries are sometimes seen as a subset of the Conservative, sometimes as a type on its own, in which welfare was even more dependent upon the family, with lower levels of benefits and almost no services. Finally, in Communist Eastern European countries, welfare

Key Figure 8.1

John Maynard Keynes (1883–1946)

A UK economist whose major work, *The General Theory of Employment, Interest and Money*, written in 1936, departed significantly from neoclassical economic theories, and went a long way towards establishing the discipline now known as macroeconomics. In recasting traditional laissez-faire principles, Keynes contended that full employment led to high consumption and increased productivity. He provided the theoretical basis for the policy of demand management, a policy of governmental manipulation of taxation and expenditure, which was widely adopted by Western governments in the early post-Second World War period. Keynesian theories have had a profound effect upon both modern liberalism and social democracy.

was a matter entirely for the state, which provided jobs, housing, health care and education, as well as basic pensions for everyone at a comparatively low level of benefits and services.

West European countries' differing post-war configurations of work and welfare worked, for better or for worse – better for Germany, worse for Britain – in ways which were relatively unconstrained by major external pressures from the 1950s to the 1970s, with all experiencing steady growth in national wealth, rising living standards for their populations, and more money in people's pockets to fuel the consumer society. Such unconstrained growth came to an end beginning in the 1970s, when the collapse of the Bretton Woods system of fixed exchange rates followed by the two oil crises produced growing currency volatility, rising inflation and declining competitiveness. The challenges of the 1970s, moreover, were followed in the 1980s and 1990s by increasing pressures of globalization, with the rising internationalization of national markets for goods, capital and services. European integration, moreover, represented an arguably even greater economic challenge than globalisation, since it involved integrating in a single market – and not simply opening to external competition – national markets for goods, capital, services *and* labour in addition to eliminating national currencies in favour of a single currency, the euro.

In response to the pressures of globalization and EU integration, then, Western European countries adjusted their systems of work and welfare. For

Eastern European countries, the moment of reckoning came in the early 1990s, when the end of communism spelled the entire collapse of their command economies and their conversion to market economies. But whenever the moment of reckoning, governments' responses seemed very similar.

Governments of the left as much as the right tended to focus on globalization as the driving force for change, portraying it as prescribing certain policies – primarily the low government deficits, debts and inflation that are the cornerstones of monetarist economics as well as liberalization of financial markets, deregulation of business, privatization of nationalized enterprise, decentralization of labour markets and retrenchment of the welfare state. And it was understood to proscribe others, in particular neo-Keynesian monetary policy, government interventionism, high taxes and high welfare-state spending (see Key Figure 8.1).

Scholars differ over whether government policies have produced convergence in national economic governance systems or have allowed for continuing divergence. For some scholars, globalization has pushed all national economies in a more market-oriented direction, spelling the beginning of the end of the generous post-war welfare state and the victory of a single neo-liberal or 'Anglo-Saxon' model of capitalism, in particular as states have liberalized, deregulated and privatized, as firms have turned more and more to the financial markets for capital in place of the banks or the state (Cerny, 1994) and as multinationals have become increasingly 'stateless' through the internationalization of their operations (Stopford and Strange, 1991). Others argue that, rather than convergence on one neo-liberal model, two of the three post-war economic governance systems are still viable: the liberal market economies characteristic of Britain and Ireland and the coordinated market economies of Germany, the Netherlands, Denmark and Sweden (Hall and Soskice, 2001). Others, including this author, still see a third variety, pointing to the continuing differentiation of countries that in the post-war period were characterized by state-led or state-controlled market economies but that have subsequently developed into 'state-influenced' market economies, including France, Italy, Spain and Greece (Schmidt, 2002, 2009). Yet others consider no generalizations possible in terms of one, two or three varieties of capitalism, given the extent to which contemporary capitalism is embedded in institutional arrangements that differ from country to country (Hollingsworth and Boyer, 1999). Still others maintain that developments in response to globalization have even produced a hybridization in national capitalisms (Streeck and Yamamura, 2001) – and that this is also a trend seen in Central and Eastern Europe.

Finally, although welfare systems have also reformed as governments have sought to cut costs and reduce services in response to social security deficits and demographic pressures, they also continue to differ in basic configuration. This is a result of continuing differences in philosophy and purpose and in overall levels of generosity of benefits and provision of services, as well as in the problems they confront today (Esping-Andersen, 1999, 2009; Scharpf and Schmidt, 2000; Huber and Stephens, 2001). The 'European Social Model', which has recently been frequently invoked by EU and national officials in the 2000s (Barbier, 2008), is not a term used to describe any common reality but rather to demonstrate a commitment among the member states of the EU to common goals for basic social benefits and services, such as ensuring that all citizens have access to social assistance, pensions, employment, education and health care.

Responses to the Challenges to Growth in the West

In Western Europe, all countries sought to adjust their systems in the face of increasing competitive pressures, some employing radical therapy early on, others making more incremental policy changes over time, but all in a more market-oriented direction. Changes in monetary policy came first, as governments confronted with rising inflation, little growth and increasing currency volatility decided that the only way to reassure the currency markets and restart growth was to switch from expansive policies to more restrictive ones focused on fiscal austerity and monetary stability, or 'hard money' policies (for a major influence on the underlying theories see Key Figure 8.2)

These monetarist policies began in the mid-1970s in Germany and Switzerland, followed by Britain in the late 1970s, with France holding out until relatively late, to 1983, when its 'great U-turn' in monetary policy occurred, while Sweden was the only one to buck the trend, and switched only in the early 1990s. For members of the EU, moreover, monetary integration, especially in the 1990s with the push for the single currency, added further budgetary discipline in exchange for greater protection from the most detrimental effects of global financial market speculation. This applied not only to eurozone members but also to the Central and Eastern European countries left in the waiting room to the EMS, which pegged their currencies to the euro as well as to the countries who had opted out, such as the UK and Denmark or Sweden, which was resisting entrance despite not having an official opt-out.

Changes in industrial policy followed those in monetary policy, as countries switched from demand-side policies to supply-side ones, and as privatization and deregulation became the watchwords of reform. Across Europe, countries with large numbers of public enterprises sold them off. In Britain, privatization began in the early 1980s, and encompassed not only firms in the competitive sectors but also public utilities, such as British Telecom and British Gas. In France, where privatisation started with a bang in 1986, a vast number of firms, banks and insurance companies, as well as industrial firms, were sold in full or in part, raising

Key Figure 8.2

Friedrich Hayek (1899–1992)

Born and educated in Austria, Hayek moved in 1931 to the London School of Economics, thence to Chicago in 1950 and finally to Freiburg and Salzburg. He was awarded the Nobel Prize for economics in 1974. He argued, against Keynes (see Key Figure 8.1), that government intervention to deal with recession and unemployment by stimulating demand would cause inflation. He argued strongly against centralized planning, partly on the basis that only the free market generates the data people need to make economic decisions.

In the 1940s he widened his arguments into the field of political theory, arguing, in *The Road to Serfdom*, against socialism as a form of totalitarian control. In *The Constitution of Liberty* (1960) he set out further his wide-ranging liberal principles, and included an essay on 'why I am not a conservative', which did not deter the British Conservative Party in the 1980s and 1990s from citing him as a major influence on their thinking. His work in technical economics on the business cycle, capital, investment and monetary economics has had considerable influence on the development of economic theory.

a total of €70 billion in public share offerings by 2002. Other countries followed suit, with Italy one of the last to start. Deregulation, moreover, whether stemming from countries' own initiatives or pushed by the EU, opened up increasing numbers of sectors to competition, especially in the formerly protected markets of telecommunications, electricity and transport.

Changes in labour-market policy often came in conjunction with the changes in monetary and/or industrial policy. Such changes differed greatly from country to country, although they generally went in the direction of greater labour-market flexibility. While countries such as Britain and France radically decentralized their wage-bargaining systems, moving to company-level agreements and individualized contracts, others, such as the Netherlands and Denmark, increased the flexibility of their centrally coordinated systems, allowing for regional and even plant-level agreements, while yet others, most notably Italy and Ireland, constructed new centrally coordinated systems. In the late 1990s, moreover, the EU itself began to engage member states in a joint effort to improve their employment outlook, for example by greater labour flexibility through part-time and temporary jobs, and by improving 'employability' through new training and education initiatives.

For some countries, these changes in monetary, industrial and labour policies simply reinforced long-standing economic governance practices. This was largely the case of the UK's liberal market economy, in which business interrelationships became even more individualistic, the state even more liberal, and labour–management relations more neutral, given the reduction in union power (King and Wood, 1999). Moreover, business has become even more market driven as financial markets with 'impatient' capital push firms to pay greater attention to profits in the short term in order to maximize 'share-holder value,' or risk takeover (Hall and Soskice, 2001). This, added to employment systems with low levels of employment protection, comparatively short-term employment, and individual responsibility for education and training, has tended to promote high responsiveness to changing market conditions and comparative advantage in two very different areas: first where radical innovation is the key to market dominance – bio-technology, the new economy, and high-end financial services – and, second, low-end services and low-tech industries in which workers' low wages, low skills and scant vocational training makes for competition on the basis of price rather than quality.

For other countries, in particular those characterized by coordinated market economies such as Germany, the Netherlands, Austria, Sweden and Denmark, by contrast, the traditionally collaborative inter-firm relations and cooperative labour management relations supported by an 'enabling' state continued, despite liberalizing reforms that served to improve competitiveness. Moreover, even with the turn to the financial markets, firms tend to be less exposed to financial market pressures because providers of finance still take a long-term view on return on investment, while the higher concentration of share-ownership through strategic investors protects firms better against takeover, and insulates them more against pressures to make short-term profits to the detriment of more long-term goals such as firm value or market share. As a result, corporate governance continues to be more driven by a wider range of 'stakeholder values' – including employees, suppliers, clients and shareholders – than in liberal capitalism. All of this, moreover, added to an employment system with high-wage labour, long-term employment and high investment in vocational training by firms and the state, leads to a comparative advantage in sectors such as high-precision engineering and high-value-added manufacturing, which depend upon a more stable, long-term investment environment where highly paid, technically skilled workers ensure the incremental innovation necessary to the production of high-quality products with high value-added (Hall and Soskice, 2001).

Finally, for countries characterized by state-led market economies in the post-war period, the traditionally 'interventionist' state has given up its leadership of business and labour for a more market-oriented, 'influencing' role which may be either 'enhancing', mostly the case in France and Spain, or 'hindering', in the case of Italy (Schmidt, 2002, 2009). This means that although the state has given up attempting to lead, it has not stopped it from continuing to intervene strategically where it sees the need, mainly to protect business and/or labour from the worst effects of the markets – whether this means bailing out firms in difficulty, 'moralizing' the labour markets through the 35-hour working week, as in France, or engineering corporatist agreements in wage-bargaining and pension reform, as in Italy or Spain (Molina and Rhodes, 2007). Firms in those countries, moreover, are much more autonomous than in the past, as the state has loosened its ownership and control through privatization and deregulation, while they are also less pressured by the financial markets than British firms, since they enjoy more concentrated share-ownership which reduces takeover risks, and they are less constrained by the 'stakeholders' than German firms, given the lack of coordinated, network-based relationships. For France, all of this, added to an employment system that sits somewhere between those of Germany and Britain in terms of worker pay, job protections, skills and training, makes it better than Germany but behind Britain in radical innovation, and better than Britain but behind Germany in incremental innovation – except in traditionally state-dominated sectors such as telecommunications, electricity, rail transport and aerospace, where radical innovation has come from state-financed, high-profile *grands projets*.

The changes in policies and practices in all the European varieties of market economy had a positive impact on growth across Western Europe – at least up until the economic crisis of the late 2000s. With inflation increasingly under control, countries' investment environments improved and consumption took off again. In a more deregulated environment, private and privatized, as well as still public, firms were better able to do what they found necessary in order to generate profits. But this included restructuring and rationalizing operations as well as providing for the 'renewal of the workforce' – all essentially code words for, among other things, firing workers, generally older workers with outdated skills, and hiring others, most often younger workers. Although this was a boon to productivity and growth, it generated major problems for social policy, mainly as a result of rising unemployment. Moreover, some of the solutions to these problems, such as generous early retirement programmes in France and Germany or disability programmes in the Netherlands, only added to the burdens of the welfare state, already under stress as a result of the demographic pressures related to the ageing of the population that have made pay-as-you-go systems increasingly unsustainable.

By the 1990s, most countries' welfare states were in trouble, and reforms were therefore attempted to make them more sustainable. These were focused not only on the 'old social risks' for which the post-war welfare state was designed – e.g. pension systems, health care and unemployment compensation – and involved partially privatizing pensions, introducing user fees and reducing benefits and social services. They also targeted the 'new social risks' that affected those who benefited the least from the post-war welfare state: the 'outsiders' who tend to be younger, female or immigrant, without work, without skills or on welfare, as well as older workers who had lost their jobs. Reforms here encompassed labour-activation policies providing education, training and job-seeker aid as well as welfare-to-work programmes for the young and the long-term unemployed or child-care services (and to a lesser extent elderly care) for women, to free them up for work (Taylor-Gooby, 2004). But although all countries engaged in these reforms, this in no way suggests the end of the welfare state, or its convergence on a single, more liberal model. Countries continue to differ widely in what they spend, how much they spend and in how they spend it, and they face different problems as a result.

The 'liberal' Anglo-Saxon welfare systems became even less generous as they reinforced individual responsibility for welfare provision above a certain basic minimum and privatized pensions, retaining only a rather minimal basic pension. Poverty therefore remains a problem in 'liberal' Anglo-Saxon countries, where social transfers have traditionally not brought the poverty level down as much as in the more generous continental and Scandinavian countries. But interestingly enough, the UK, under the Labour government from the late 1990s until the economic crisis of 2008, had actually managed to bring poverty down, with redistribution 'by stealth' (since the government never talked about it), in great contrast to Ireland, where poverty remained comparatively highest, despite the countries' economic miracle (see Figure 8.8). For the UK, however, the figures are likely to go down again as a result of the massive cuts in public spending – much of which are targeted on the welfare state – under the government of David Cameron, elected in May 2010.

'Social-democratic' Scandinavian welfare systems have continued to maintain a high level of generosity despite cuts in benefits/or services and the introduction of user fees. Sweden also marketized pensions, but placed these in public funds administered by the state as opposed to private fund managers, as in Anglo-Saxon countries. For the 'Scandinavian' countries, the challenge has been maintaining the welfare system at such a high level (Scharpf and Schmidt, 2000).

Although 'conservative' or 'Bismarckian' continental European countries have reformed to varying degrees in different ways, all have retained their reasonably high level of benefits even as they have introduced some degree of recourse to individuals' own resources through pension reform. Here the problem has long been unemployment, due to much greater labour-market rigidities than in 'Anglo-Saxon' countries, where unemployment has dropped significantly over time, or in Scandinavian countries, where it has always remained low (see Figure 8.9). The remedies to unemployment, through the institutionalization of greater flexibility by way of temporary and part-time work – only sometimes with security, to guarantee 'flexicurity' – have produced another problem with the dualization of labour markets (Palier, 2010). This is because core 'insider' workers in manufacturing industries continue to have job security and high pay while 'outsiders', whether also in manufacturing or at the low end of the services industry, have little job security, low pay and often few benefits. But we can add poverty alongside unemployment and dualization as the problems for Mediterranean countries like Italy, in which very low employment rates add to high poverty, in particular in the south of the country.).

There were also other challenges to the post-war systems of work and welfare, in particular those related to changing family patterns, with women eager to enter the workforce and increasingly needed, given more precarious employment conditions for all. But accommodating women's entry into the workforce came more easily to some countries than others (see Figure 8.10). This depended not only upon the structure of the labour market, in particular the availability of part-time and temporary jobs, but also on the very structure of the welfare system, for example whether pension arrangements could act as disincentives to entry into the labour market because of low benefits for anything other than full-time employment over a

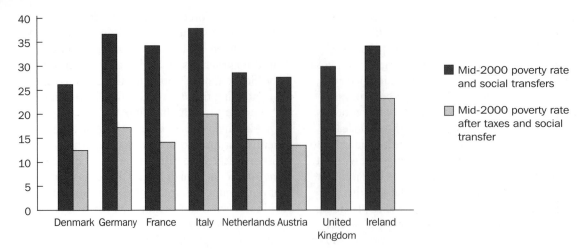

Figure 8.8   Poverty levels and the effects of social transfers in selected EU welfare states, 2005

Source: Eurostat 2007.

lifetime, whether fiscal policies taxed a second income at the same rate as the first, or whether there was provision of day-care for children or services for the elderly.

Women's entry into the workforce has been easiest in Scandinavian countries, given that they enjoy welfare systems that already had long-standing commitments to equality in work and to the public provision of caring services. It has not been that much more difficult in Anglo-Saxon countries, since although the welfare system did not do much in the way of public provision of caring services, the liberal market economy had spurred on the growth of private-sector service jobs. This provided women with private caring services as well as jobs, even if many were part-time and low-paid. Women had the hardest time in continental and Mediterranean Europe, given welfare systems based on the family that had all the structural disincentives to women working suggested above. But while some, such as Germany or Italy, did little to change this, other countries either already had a high level of public caring services that eased entry, as France did, or engaged in major reforms, as did the Netherlands, which underwent a veritable revolution in gender relations due to a very large rise in part-time and temporary employment, including in private caring services, as well to changes in pension arrangements.

Responses to the Challenges to Growth in the East

In Eastern Europe, the history was quite different. Women's participation rates had always been high, since all women were expected to work just like men, and the state provided caring services for the children and the elderly. The command economies, however, having worked relatively well in the post-war period, started grinding to a halt in the 1970s and the 1980s.

This can be explained by a combination of factors. The lack of investment in physical capital – buildings, machinery and equipment – was a great problem for productivity improvements, as was the lack of investment in human capital, notably worker training (in contrast to education more generally). Eastern European industrial goods remained more low-tech than high-tech, and did not benefit from most of the computer-based production systems that had raised labour productivity in the West. What is more, the centralized distribution system through Moscow stifled demand as well as technological innovation, by seeking to define the market and consumer needs, instead of allowing the market to define itself and industry to innovate in response to consumer wants. The fall of communism could be seen as the product of a consumer revolt – in response to the

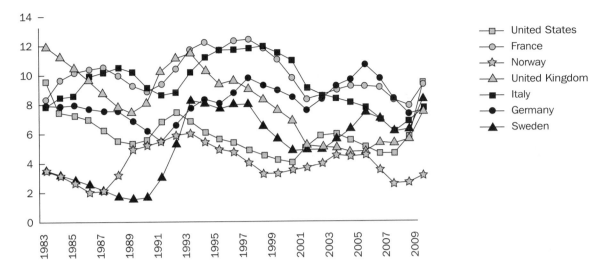

Figure 8.9   Harmonized unemployment rates in six European countries, 1983–2009

Source: OECD Statistics 2010, http://stats.oecd.org/index.aspx.

pent-up demand – as much as of a political one.

With the end of communism in the early 1990s, most countries underwent an overnight transformation, although some went through a shock-therapy conversion to capitalism whereas others took the transition period more slowly. All experienced transition-related recessions from which many took a decade or longer to emerge, as they privatized many if not most of their formerly state-owned industries – with Western European firms often the acquirers – and deregulated various sectors of their economies. Moreover, they have all been subject to the discipline of the eurozone monetary policies, either because they have already entered, the cases for Slovenia, Slovakia and Estonia, or because they are in the antechamber, and peg their currencies to the euro. Most of their labour-management systems bear some resemblance to the corporatist relations of coordinated market economies, but labour tends to be weak, in particular in sectors where foreign multinationals are predominant, so that agreements tend to be dominated by management. In addition, the state's influence is strong not because the state exercises significant leadership but because societal interests and organizations tend to be weak – with corruption rampant in some countries, in particular Bulgaria and Romania. As a result, it is difficult to

slot these countries easily into any one of the three Western European varieties of capitalism discussed so far. While some scholars therefore call them hybrids, others refer to them as systems of 'embedded neo-liberalism', meaning that these countries seek to create institutions of social protection even as they follow the neo-liberal tenets. The most recent label is 'dependent market economy', which highlights the ways in which these countries are dependent on foreign capital for investment and growth (Nölke and Vliegenthart, 2009).

The welfare system has naturally also been transformed since the Communist welfare system died along with guaranteed jobs and pensions. Although there is great diversity in welfare provisions, most Central and Eastern European countries tend to resemble a somewhat less generous version of the continental welfare state, in particular with regard to pensions and social services (Cerami and Vanhuysse, 2009). The result has been that the family has generally taken over from the state – and where there is no family to supplement meagre incomes, poverty is the outcome.

Finally, just as most Central and Eastern European countries began to achieve high rates of growth and productivity, with major gains in national standards of living, the global crisis hit. Some countries managed to weather the storm

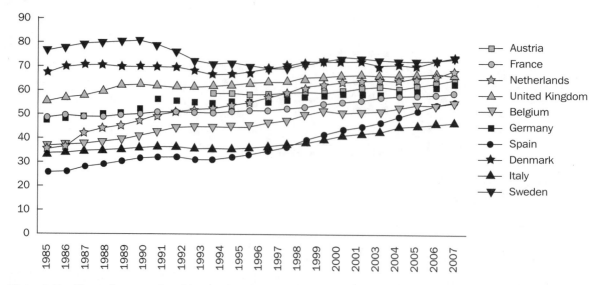

Figure 8.10   Share of women of working age (15–64) in employment in ten European countries, 1985–2007

Source: OECD Factbook 2009: Economic, Environmental and Social Statistics.

reasonably well – Poland in particular. But for those countries most reliant on foreign direct investment, with high rates of borrowing in euro-denominated bonds, the crisis spelled disaster, as they found themselves highly vulnerable to economic downturn and capital flight (Orenstein, 2009). For Hungary, Romania and Latvia, the difficulties of servicing their debts and the dangers of sovereign debt default meant that they had to turn to the IMF. And because they chose not to give up their currencies' peg to the euro, they could not devalue their currencies in order thereby to grow their way out of recession via less expensive exports and lower comparative labour costs. Instead, they had to cut spending in the public sector, closing schools and hospitals, reducing benefits and public-sector salaries and pensions and raising taxes. Thus, at a time when the rest of Europe, and in particular the richer countries, were encouraged to 'spend, spend, spend' to avoid recession and maintain employment, those Eastern European countries in trouble were plunged into deepening recessions and rising unemployment. The result has been increasing differentiation among Central and Eastern European countries, with some becoming more and more prosperous as potential members of the eurozone, such as Slovenia and Poland, while others languish.

Conclusion

In sum, economic expansion in Europe, although varied depending upon the country and subject to stops and starts depending upon the time period, has nevertheless been nothing short of spectacular. Affluence has gone hand in hand with the technological advances that have ensured that people in any productive activity, whether agriculture, industry or services, have had greater money to spend not just on necessities but on luxuries. Moreover, although the organization of national economies and the configuration of welfare states have undergone significant change in response to the challenges of globalization and Europeanization, there is no convergence to a one-size-fits-all neo-liberal model. Instead, national patterns of economic organization and national welfare systems remain quite different, even as governments seek to reform in ways that make their national economies more competitive and welfare systems more sustainable.

The question, given the global economic crisis beginning in 2008 and the EU's own sovereign debt crisis beginning in 2010, is how well European countries, not to mention the EU itself, will continue to perform in an increasingly economically uncertain world. The problem here is that as the EU moves into austerity mode, with countries across Europe tightening their belts, one needs to ask where growth will come from. The answer from the countries of Northern Europe, led by Germany, has been in their models of export-led growth, which do well with the 'culture of stability' promoted by Germany in particular – so long as the Chinese markets for high-quality manufacturing goods, and cars in particular, remain strong. But these current account-surplus countries – whose publics save more than they spend – need the current account-deficit countries of Southern and Eastern Europe to continue to spend – which they are less likely to do, given recessionary trends on top of across-the-board cuts in public budgets, especially in countries that have EU loan bailouts. Moreover, the Anglo-Saxon countries are also in for hard times, with Ireland under EU-mandated austerity budgets and the UK under self-imposed austerity, and with little credit available for their models of credit-fuelled growth. As this book goes to press, France and Germany are the only countries that have posted significant gains in growth. Whether they pull the EU out of the doldrums, or the other European countries pull them down, as the eurozone crisis continues to fester, remains in question.

SUMMARY

- The European economy grew in a 'miraculous' way in the first thirty years after 1945, resulting in increased wealth and, in Western Europe, substantial increases in the ownership of consumer goods. Living standards and possession of consumer goods in Eastern Europe lagged behind until the 1990s, but caught up rapidly in the first decade of the twenty-first century.

- Growth has been fuelled by rising wages and the expansion of markets through globalization and increasing European integration. Moreover, technological innovation produced a shift in productive activities towards the service sector and investment in physical and human capital enhanced productivity, if at markedly different rates in different countries.

- The differential impact of the economic crisis that began in 2008 can in part be explained by these differences, as also by the variations in structures of work and welfare. There is substantial academic debate over whether there has, since the early twenty-first century, been convergence in national economic governance systems or whether differentiation continues, for example between liberal, state-led and state-influenced market economies.

- All types of economy faced adjustments in monetary, industrial and labour-market policies in the wake of the 1970s oil-price shock. In Western Europe, whilst these adjustments supported growth in the 1990s, by the 2000s welfare states were facing major challenges. In Eastern Europe the command economies disappeared, to be replaced by forms of capitalism and transformed welfare systems. The impact of the global crisis since 2008 has been to increase differentiation between Eastern European economies. The longer-term impact of the crisis across all of Europe remains uncertain.

QUESTIONS FOR DISCUSSION

- What were the main drivers of the development of the consumer economy in Europe in the second half of the twentieth century?

- What meaning, if any, does the notion of a European social model have?

- What is the future outlook for the different types of welfare state found across Europe?

- What have been the main drivers and impacts of the economic crisis since 2008?

- Can the eurozone survive?

FURTHER READING

Gamble, Andrew (2009) *The Spectre at the Feast* (Basingstoke: Palgrave Macmillan).

Locke, Richard (1995) *Remaking the Italian Economy* (Ithaca, NY and London: Cornell University Press).

Mishel, Lawrence, Jared Bernstein, and Heidi Shierholz (2009) *The State of Working America 2008/2009*. (Ithaca, NY: ILR Press/Cornell University Press).

CHAPTER 9

Regions and Regional Politics in Europe

JÖRG MATHIAS, WITH ANNE STEVENS

In order to promote its overall harmonious development, the Union shall develop and pursue its actions leading to the strengthening of its economic, social and territorial cohesion.

In particular, the Union shall aim at reducing disparities between the levels of development of the various regions and the backwardness of the least favoured regions.

Consolidated version of the Treaty on the Functioning of the
European Union, Article 174

Many substantial changes in the structures and procedures of territorial governance are occurring at present in many European states. These changes are primarily aimed at shifting state responsibilities to lower levels of government, notably to the regional level. These shifts have appeared rather suddenly almost everywhere across the European continent since the mid-1980s. For the member states of the European Union (EU), it was particularly significant that these changes took place at the same time as significant shifts of state responsibility to the European level (commonly referred to as European integration) also occurred. However, such changes were not limited to EU member states. Following the end of the Cold War, significant territorial governance reform processes took place in the previously Communist countries in Central and Eastern Europe, as part of their wider political and economic reform efforts to develop Western-style democracies and market economies. All these reform processes not only took many different pathways across the continent, but also led to a diversity of outcomes: there are examples of secession, of federation-building, of new models of regional autonomy, of devolution, and of massive administrative reform. In the context of a Europe where identity (including the identity conferred by a sense of geographical belonging) is to some extent replacing ideology, this chapter looks briefly at the interlocking relationships between notions of nation, state and governance, and then turns to a more specific consideration of one aspect of state evolution: the emergence of regions as a significant level of governance.

Nations, state and identity

It was in Europe that the nation-state emerged, its attributes were defined and the system of relations between states that has now become the worldwide system first developed. Several key moments can be identified in this process. The 1648 Peace of Westphalia ushered in the so-called 'Westphalian' system of relationships between states, which recognizes the distinction between internal and external affairs and the position of states as equal actors within a system, maintaining relationships of trade, diplomacy and sometimes war with the other actors in the system. For practical purposes most of the time such relationships were in fact personal relationships between the rulers, cemented, for example, by strategic marriages.

Nevertheless the ruler was becoming the embodiment of the state, conceived of as a larger and more abstract entity.

A second key moment was the French Revolution. The absolutist monarchs of France had sought to weld together their disparate domains. Loyalty to the monarch could no longer be the glue holding the state together when his position and authority was contested. Instead the idea of the nation was invoked; this brought together the notion that it was the people (or at least the male population) from whom authority derived with the sense that the people of a particular territory shared values which needed to be defended – in this case the values of revolutionary citizens fighting against reactionary and foreign enemies. However, when the tide turned and Napoleonic conquests brought revolutionary values and French ways of doing things to territories which had not been part of the realm of the kings of France, resistance ensued. What was provoked was the beginning of a modern form of nationalism, which appealed to language, to culture, including the 'folk' culture of music and tales, to history, to literature, in some cases to religion, to create a sense of mutual belonging and difference from outsiders. As opposed to the universalism of the ideals of the French Revolution, the nationalist ideologies of the Romantic reaction of the early nineteenth century appealed to particularism and difference, above all as embodied in idealized versions of the nation.

Another key moment came in 1870, which saw the unification of both Italy and Germany. By 1918 the sprawling and diverse empires which had provided a framework for the ordering of much of Europe south of Scandinavia and east of France had finally collapsed (see Chapter 2). The peace settlement redrew the map of Europe, and emphasized 'national self-determination' – Woodrow Wilson's idea that 'every little language should have a state all of its own' – as the basis on which this should be done. In practice the principle proved unworkable. By and large the jumble of languages, religions, cultures and senses of identity across much of Europe, especially Central and Eastern Europe, was not organized along geographically neat lines. Governments attempted to enhance the cohesion of their territories and peoples by the promotion of a sense of national identity common

to all of them. As an Italian politician remarked in the opening session of the new Italian Parliament in 1861: 'Now that we have created Italy we must start creating Italians' (Davies, 1996, p. 814). By the end of the second decade of the twentieth century Europe was organized, as it had never previously been, entirely on the basis of autonomous states, most of which claimed to be 'nation-states' – that is, to be constituted not merely by governmental arrangements, but by a shared sense of the identity among the inhabitants. Nationality and citizenship became largely conflated. Only in the Soviet Union, itself a union of republics, where the core of identity was class – the republics were 'people's' or 'proletarian' republics – was the glue of state nationalism formally repudiated. Informally, and politically when necessary, as the experiences of the Second World War and of the break-up of the Soviet Union in the 1990s revealed, a sense of national identity was never very deeply buried.

In the modern world the state – as the sovereign body within a defined territory – is taken for granted as setting the parameters for both internal and external politics. The modern state has emerged as a highly multifunctional entity, and as its organizational complexity increased and its activity extended, it had to become more coherent, more uniform and hence in some senses more coercive. The consent of its population to an increasing role was usually ensured through the functioning of democracy, which allows for reciprocity of rights and powers between a sovereign state and a sovereign people (Schöpflin, 2000, p. 38.) but the sovereign people in any given territory was itself not a uniform or homogeneous mass. But if all the people are to consent to be governed, then there must be some kind of solidarity, based on a common identity, a common sense of values and a sense of sharing 'certain key moral aims and obligations' (Schöpflin, 2000, p. 40). This sense of solidarity has generally had a national – that is, at least implicitly, an ethnic – content and, as we have seen, states have had an interest in protecting and promoting it. '[U]sually the one dominant ethnic group imposes its vision on the state … and that is imposed in turn on all the ethnic groups in that territory' (Schöpflin, 2000, p. 41). For these reasons it has become axiomatic, though not always entirely correct, to talk of Europe as consisting of nation-

Key Figure 9.1

Jordi Pujol (1930–)

Jordi Pujol was born in Barcelona, and became active in agitation for the rights of Catalan language, culture and politics under Franco's dictatorship, when such activities were prohibited. He was imprisoned for his activism for two and half years. In 1974, just before Franco's death, he was involved in founding a Catalan political party, Convergència Democràtica de Catalunya (CDC: Democratic Convergence of Catalonia), which was legalized in 1977 as the transition to democracy got under way. He became a member of the Spanish national Parliament between 1977 and 1980, but from 1980, when the first elections to the regional assembly in Catalonia were held, until his retirement in 2003 he was the President (first minister) of the Catalan government (Generalitat de Catalunya). Pujol did not seek independence for Catalonia, but worked for full recognition of its identity and responsibilities as a component of an essentially federal Spanish state. He was able to exploit the Olympic Games in Barcelona in 1992 while he was President of the Catalan Government to enhance the image and regeneration of Catalonia. He pushed hard for recognition of the role of major regions like Catalonia within the EU, for example through the lobbying group the Assembly of European Regions, and became prominent as one of the leading European politicians at sub-national level.

states. They remain key entities in determining almost everyone's sense of identity and belonging, not only by conferring nationality upon them, but also through the role they play in all public affairs.

We are arguing for the continued crucial importance of individual states as the framework both for internal policy-making and for international relations. Interdependence, or even pooled sovereignty, and diffused authority (see Chapter 4 and below) are inescapable features of the environment to which states are adapting (see below). But there is no sign of the emergence of any real alternative to the nation-state as the main unit which provides for the organization of society and the provision of key collective services.

Moreover, nation-states are the main units between which international relations are conducted. This is because despite the movements towards a common EU foreign and defence policy it is the nation-states that control the two key resources, force and money. It is by and within the nation-states that armies and police forces are raised and commanded, and it is nation-states who raise and spend large, and not diminishing, proportions of gross domestic product (GDP). Over recent years, indeed, there has been an increasing tendency for relatively decentralized states to seek to recentralize

expenditure. While it is understandable that since the 2008 financial crisis it may suit local government to try to locate responsibility for difficult decisions and cuts in spending away from themselves, in fact this tendency pre-dates the crisis. It can be seen in the German labour market and social security reforms implemented between 2003 and 2005 and known as Hartz I–IV. A similar trend is currently observable in Spain. Even Catalonia and the Basque countries, which since the 1970s have insisted on asserting their regional cultural and political autonomy (see Key Figure 9.1) now want to recentralize (i.e. offload upward) health and education expenditure (but preferably while retaining the old influence over policy contents).

Spain thus constitutes an example of a perhaps more general trend of contradictory tensions – between a sense of identity related as much to subnational or even ethnic allegiances as to the nation-state on the one hand, and the centralizing tendencies of modern politics on the other. Sometimes (as in the case of the Basques, in both France and Spain, or the Bosnian Serbs) the issues spill across national boundaries. Sometimes they result in substantial devolution (Scotland) or the more or less forcible creation of new states (Slovakia, potentially Kosovo).

Key Figure 9.2

Alex Salmond (1954–)

Alex Salmond became the fourth 'first minister' of the devolved Scottish government in 2007. As the leader of the largest party in the Scottish Parliament, the Scottish National Party (SNP), though without an overall majority, he led a minority government, supported by the Scottish Green Party, though without any formal coalition. In the 2011 Scottish Parliamentary election the Scottish National Party was returned with an overall majority of seats and Salmond continued as First Minister. Salmond is an economist by training and professional career. He joined the Scottish National Party as a student and in 1990 was elected as its leader. He stood down as party leader in 2000, but was again, successfully, a candidate for the leadership in 2004. He was a member of the Scottish Parliament from its first election in 1999 until 2001 and has been again since 2007, and a member of the UK Parliament from 1988 to 2010. Salmond is a shrewd, skilful and ruthless politician, whose political stance has moved towards the centre from his youthful far-left position. His major commitment, however, is to independence for Scotland, and the SNP remains committed to public spending in Scotland, pledging, for example, to retain free tuition for Scottish university students at Scottish universities and free social care for the elderly.

These tensions are frequently embodied in political parties and groupings, arguing (see below) for better recognition of their group's social and cultural specificity. Belgium is a particular case of acute tension. Two different views can be discerned among such groups – either that statehood is something worthwhile striving for – the position, for example of the Scottish National Party (see Key Figure 9.2) – or alternatively that nationhood should carry the same rights (but not necessarily the same obligations) as statehood, which is broadly the approach of the Welsh party Plaid Cymru.

Some commentators now argue that the two decades since the end of the Cold War (see Chapter 2) have seen the re-emergence of nationalism in new forms shaped by a new globalized context. It tends nowadays to find its political outlet in far-right or populist groups and parties such as the National Front in France or, more recently, the English Defence League. While there is some blurring at the edges, such parties and groups can be distinguished from both the violent, anti-parliamentary movement of the pro-fascist extreme right and from the more or less secessionist regional parties described above. These new forms of nationalism can be called 'neo-nationalisms'. In contrast to earlier nationalisms, their opposition is not usually to domination by a different ethnic group or a remote state government; rather it is to much broader trends: for example to globalization, to human migration resulting in new influxes of population from different cultural and ethnic backgrounds, or to the process of European integration. Interactions with, and reactions to, these new phenomena constitute, according to Gingrich and Banks (2006, p. 2), 'the most visible "new" aspects in current European nationalisms'. But while neo-nationalism is not an 'isolated phenomenon' and indeed seeks to root itself in populist mass culture, neither is it 'internally coherent' (Gingrich and Banks, 2006, p. 3).

Within contemporary Europe the various forms of nationalism are most visible on the Asian borders, where acute tensions exist, for example in Georgia, Ossetia and Chechnya, and at Europe's western edges, where some strong, but largely non-violent, secessionist parties continue and populist neo-nationalism also flourishes. Clearly Europeanization in various guises has an impact on developments in nationalism. It may be that the relatively low salience of secessionist and neo-nationalism in much of the core of Europe has to do, as Tony Judt hinted (Judt, 2005, ch. 24), with the existence of what is sometimes conceived of – mostly in opposition to the 'American model' – as a specifically 'European' model of society and politics, combined (see Chapter 8), with the determined survival of intergovernmentalism as a key characteristic of the EU.

Equally, and in contrast, for the secessionists maybe it is less risky to envisage a brand new state when it will fall under the sheltering umbrella of potential EU membership. The pressure from these movements is one of the many factors to explain other significant developments since the late 1980s: the strengthening of the regional level in the domestic political arena alongside the establishment of regions as political actors on the European level.

A typology of regions

Since the 1980s it has become clear that regional economies were changing and developing, and interacting in new ways with their social and political environment. Moreover, as regions changed, people interested in regionalism as expressed in sociocultural ways found that economic and political changes provided a new underpinning for their activities. These activists focus on historical territorial roots, regional community languages, typical territorial patterns of predominance of religious beliefs, and expressions of cultural heritage in a broad sense, and seek to foster popular mass involvement, for which sociocultural activities provide a somewhat more accessible vehicle compared to political and economic activities, which usually require a far higher level of personal commitment by individuals.

The region as a political, economic and sociocultural space now offers to some extent a viable alternative to the dictum of state supremacy in matters of governance and public policy-making, which had been largely uncontested until the 1980s. This raises serious questions about the scope and purpose of the reforms. Were the proponents of the changes enemies of the state? Could they possibly even succeed in challenging the state? Some empirical evidence from the early 1990s seemed to point in that direction, and some very enthusiastic debates on a 'Europe of the Regions' as an alternative scenario to the existing Europe of the States

added weight to these concerns, which were particularly grave in regions which regard themselves as nations, so that it seemed that regionalism was about to combine forces with minority nationalism. State responses were swift and, to the credit of most state governments involved, modern and constructive rather than reactionary and suppressive. Therefore, in most countries new systems of territorial governance emerged, over a relatively short period of time, aimed at accommodating regional interests and improving functional efficiency, while barring from access to political decision-making the more extreme, destructive forces of regionalism – in particular those employing the use of political violence to further their ends.

So why has regional politics taken on this new significance? The aim of this chapter is to present the process of regions emerging as significant political actors in today's Europe, the increasing role which regions are playing in European politics, and the changing nature of territorial politics in many European countries because of the intertwined processes of regionalism and regionalization. The chapter aims to introduce the key concepts and themes of regional studies as they have emerged in recent years, and to provide an overview of current political activities of regional actors. Finally, some likely future developments are considered.

What, exactly, are regions? The answer to that question varies widely: geographers, economists, politicians, governments, and individual citizens may hold different and potentially contradictory notions of what constitutes a region. What we are dealing with in this chapter are sub-state regions – regions within states. However, it should be noted that in some academic literature, in particular on International Relations, the term 'regions' is also used in reference to larger geopolitical entities, such as Western Europe, Sub-Saharan Africa or the Pacific Rim.

Academic researchers in regional studies tend to use functional definitions of the term 'region', geared towards their specific research interest. A very comprehensive attempt to classify concepts of regions was undertaken by Keating and Loughlin (1997, pp. 6–8; see also Loughlin, 1996, pp. 147–8). They distinguish between (i) economic regions, (ii) historical regions, (iii) administrative regions, and (iv) political regions. Each of these classes of

Table 9.1   A functional classification of regions

Class of region	Typical features	Examples
Economic regions	Population clusters Predominant patterns of economic activity	Greater London, Île de France, Barcelona *Ruhrgebiet* (manufacturing, technology), Costa del Sol (tourism)
Historical regions	Regional language Major geographical features shaping historical settlement patterns Predominant religious patterns Sometimes historically contested between states	Wales, Catalonia, Basque Country Regions along the River Rhine the Alps (Swiss Cantons, South Tyrol) Hadrian's Wall (English border) Welsh Free Churches, Scottish Presbyterians, Calvinist Swiss Cantons Alsace, Upper Silesia, Northern Ireland, Gibraltar
Administrative regions	Conglomerations of smaller territories with different histories (More or less) ruler-straight borders between neighbouring territories Economic governance by local (rather than regional) governments and semi-public agencies	Languedoc-Roussillon, Baden-Württemberg Mecklenburg-Vorpommern Nevada (USA), Saskatchewan (Canada), Norrbotten (Sweden) English regions and regions in the Republic of Ireland
Political Regions	Regional legislative assemblies Regional government/executive Regional political parties	Scottish Parliament, National Assembly for Wales, German *Landtage* *Junta/Gobierno* (Spain) *Président de Region* (France) *Landesregierung* (Germany) *Landeshauptmann* (Austria) Mayor of London (only UK example) SNP, Plaid Cymru, PNV (Basque Country), CiU (Catalonia), CSU (Bavaria), Lega Nord (Northern Italy)

regions is characterized by a number of typical features on which the classification is based. Some key characteristics and examples are outlined in Table 9.1.

Obviously, these classifications, broad as they are, cannot be utilized easily. First, two or even three of the categories may be applicable to the same region. Current economic homogeneity might coincide with historical patterns of settlement, and such a region might also have its own government. This situation, however, must be regarded as the exception rather than the rule. Cultural distinctiveness, vociferously proclaimed by one group of people within a region, might not be taken seriously – or even be regarded as offensive – by another group now living within the same region. Insensitive state governments of the past might have created administrative regions regardless of economic and sociocultural criteria, and their present-day successors might be unwilling to abandon that practice. On the other hand, even in cases where no ethnic consideration needs to be taken into account, historical sensitivity might have its own pitfalls. Had, for instance, the Germans in the post-war reconstruction period insisted on following the traditional pattern of political regions of the eighteenth and nineteenth centuries, they would have created an instant administrative nightmare, with the establishment of possibly as many as 50 mini-regions, all historically distinct, instead of the mere dozen political regions actually created at the time. Following the country's unification in 1990, modern Germany now has 16 political regions.

This apparent lack of clarity in the definition of the term 'region' is to some extent unavoidable. In today's Europe, regions, which have grown over long historical periods and been reformed over and over again by changing governments, now resemble a patchwork of territorial units. The political powers held by regional governments, their relationships with the state to which the regions belong, and the level of interest in regional matters displayed by the regional populations and elites all vary widely across Europe – and in some states even from region to region within the same state.

This latter phenomenon is known as **asymmetric government** (Keating, 1998b, p. 195), and applies to a situation where the constitutional, legal, institutional and procedural arrangements for governing a region vary from the arrangements in other regions within the same state. However, the practical political and administrative problems associated with such regional imbalances are not always particularly helpful in establishing and running an efficient system of territorial governance in the whole country. Enshrining such asymmetries formally as part of the rules by which the polity concerned is governed has therefore to be regarded as something of a stop-gap solution. The political systems of states where such asymmetric structures are in operation are often characterized by prolonged political debates involving the state

government and all the regional governments, in search of a negotiated settlement that accommodates conflicting interests as far as possible, while at the same time ensuring the establishment of a flexible and efficient system of decision-making and interest representation. These problems are more pronounced in multi-national states, such as Spain and the UK, where the interests of different national or ethnic groupings have to be accommodated. Over the last decade or so, both countries have seen numerous reforms of their territorial governance, with mixed success in terms of accommodating regional interests and improving public policy-making in and for the regions. In Spain, the trend of maximizing regional autonomy, prevalent from the late 1970s to the late 1990s, has recently shown signs of slowing down, or even reversing towards centralization, mainly due to economic constraints (Maiz, Caamano and Aspitarte, 2010, pp. 63–82). In the British case, perhaps the most significant development since devolution began in 1998/99 was that a Nationalist (SNP) government took office for the first time in Edinburgh in 2007, and returned with an overall majority in May 2011. The whole UK devolution system has not yet been tested under a Conservative–Liberal Democrat government in London. Since the early 2000s, Italy has also become a case of asymmetric government. The rise of the Lega Nord, with its distinct agenda of desolidarization with other parts of the country, combined with strong yet somewhat divisive centre-right governments in Rome, contributed to an oscillating devolution-centralization cycle, with its most tangible outcome so far being the establishment of higher levels of autonomy for five of the 22 Italian regions.

The use of a particular descriptive term for certain regions may also indicate the pursuit of a specific agenda by the authors or speakers concerned. For example, a persistent reference to a historical or ethnic region as a 'nation' or 'stateless nation' often implies that the user of this concept is of the opinion that such nationhood still lacks adequate recognition in political and socioeconomic terms. On the other hand, the UK government's use of the 'Standard Region' system in England indicates that region-making to suit administrative convenience is still very much in evidence in England, despite the significant

---

● **Asymmetric government** In some countries, the political powers and the degree of autonomy from the central government enjoyed by regions, vary from region to region. One example of such a scenario is the UK, where, for instance, the powers of the Scottish Parliament and the powers of the National Assembly for Wales are not identical.

progress towards devolution in other parts of the country. Not until 1999 was the English problem tackled by the introduction of a 'tripartite' regional government structure involving government offices, Regional Development Agencies and Regional Assemblies comprising delegates from existing local authorities in the region (Sandford and McQuail, 2001, pp. 26–35). A further step towards devolution in England, the creation of elected Regional Assemblies, was envisaged by the Labour government from about 2000 on, but in 2004 a referendum in one of the regions concerned, the North-East, saw an overwhelming public rejection of this idea, putting at least a temporary halt to plans for holding further referendums in other English regions. In other countries such as Ireland, Greece, Hungary and Romania, the creation of administrative or planning regions in recent years has often been associated with the need to provide a suitable administrative infrastructure for the management of economic development tasks, in particular in regions where EU funding was available for development projects. Faced with similar problems in their early years of EU membership, both Poland and the Czech Republic have gone one step further and established fully functional political regions instead of mere administrative regions.

Region-building: the interaction of regionalism and regionalization

Since the mid-1980s, many European countries have experienced political developments which addressed the issue of territorial governance. Regional politicians, business elites and also, in some regions, popular mass movements started to express demands for greater regional self-determination in political decision-making and economic and social development, as well as an enhanced status for social and cultural expressions of regional identity, including – where they exist – regional languages. Three key reasons can be distinguished for the increased interest in regional self-determination: (1) dissatisfaction with the current relationship between the regions and the state, (2) perceived external threats to the development of the regional economy and (3) a desire to strengthen a region's social and cultural identity.

The first reason is regional dissatisfaction with the treatment and/or services received from the state, which can be found in particular in less developed, geographically remote and economically poorer regions. Examples of such regions include Puglia, Calabria and Sicily in southern Italy; Mecklenburg-Vorpommern, Saxony-Anhalt and Thuringia in eastern Germany; Andalusia, Extremadura and Galicia in Spain; the North-East and the North-West of England, and also Wales. Citizens of such regions may feel that living in that region has a negative impact on their ability to exercise their political rights, on their socioeconomic prospects, or on their quality of life. On the political side, typical complaints include the lack of effective regional political institutions such as a well-functioning regional government and regional executive, or the lack of real decision-making powers for existing institutional structures, the external domination – usually by the central government – of regional institutions, and a perceived lack of interest in, or even bias against, the region in the political institutions of the state, e.g. under-representation in Parliament. Other causes for concern may include a perception that the central government underspends public funds in the region compared to other regions, or ignores a region's specific needs when formulating the country's public policies, including foreign policy.

The list of potential economic, social and cultural ailments which may give rise to demands for greater regional self-determination is even longer: the most common complaint is about a lack of effort on the part of the state to combat urgent economic problems in the region, e.g. high unemployment, or a lack of opportunities for young people who are about to enter the workforce. Almost equally frequently complaints are made about education systems that are perceived as inadequate, about an insufficiently developed transport infrastructure, and not least about the lack of modern cultural and leisure facilities. In all these cases, the underlying assumption is that people in other regions of the same country experience a better service by the state, or at least have better opportunities to manage their own affairs.

The second reason for demanding greater regional self-determination is predominantly socioeconomic in nature. It can be described as a 'circling-of-the wagons' effect in the face of actual or perceived threats to the regional economy, such as globalization, with its tighter competition for job creation and retention, cheap goods and services, and inward investment. It is often the economically better-developed, better-off regions who take this approach. Examples include Lombardy, Emilia-Romagna and Tuscany in Northern Italy; Bavaria, Baden-Württemberg and Saxony in Germany; Catalonia in Spain; Flanders in Belgium; and also Greater London and the South-East of England in the UK. Such regions tend to show a significant reluctance to share their relative wealth in the name of solidarity with their fellow citizens in the poorer regions. Regional politicians, as well as business elites, are concerned that a persistent outflow of resources, such as taxes raised in the region, would undermine their own future prospects of maintaining their strong economic status. Regions which hold such fears may also turn to stating political demands for rights to engage in external interest representation, in particular within the EU. Central governments are often not trusted to be capable or willing to provide sufficient protection for the region against these perceived external economic threats, and regional politicians may well start to believe that they would be better able than the central government to ensure a stable and secure future for the region. Therefore, they usually demand a greater and more direct influence in shaping fiscal policies on the domestic side, and in shaping the country's external interest representation, e.g. in EU negotiations on regulatory policies.

Thirdly, regions undergoing radical changes in their social and demographic structures often also experience a heightened awareness of the region's distinctiveness and identity. This awareness in turn often leads to demands for greater regional self-determination in order to prevent the possible loss of such distinctiveness and identity in an increasingly mixed multicultural, multi-religious and generally libertarian and laissez-faire European society – in short, a sociocultural 'circling of the wagons'. Thus, regional governments and other regional activists are prepared to expend resources on cultural institutions and symbols, not only protecting the regions' heritage but also instigating new initiatives to add to the region's stock of cultural features. Where a regional language other than the official language of the country exists, initiatives to promote that regional language are often regarded as central to the preservation of regional identity, as is for instance the case in Catalonia, the Basque Country and Wales. Other approaches include the preservation of the architectural heritage, of traditional economic features (e.g. a former mine being turned into a mining museum), and the promotion of regional arts – old and new.

All three types of interest in the region not only as a mere territory but as a vibrant political, economic and cultural public space may – and often do – lead to the rise of regional movements: groups of people who actively engage in sustained efforts to promote their regions through all available channels of political interest representation as well as in economic and cultural activities. This phenomenon is usually called **regionalism**. The aims of regionalism vary from region to region, and are dependent on the nature of the perceived problems and the level of aspiration displayed by the groups engaged in it. Thus, the size and structure of regionalist movements also varies – from small, informal groups of members of regional political and business elites on the one hand, to mass movements involving large sections of the population and a number of social institutions in the society, including political parties, unions, religious groups and other interest organizations, on the other hand. In the latter case, it is justified to speak of not merely regionalist movements but of **regional mobilization**, where more or less the whole regional civil society is engaged in a region-building project in all three areas: political, economic and cultural.

● **Regionalism** is the active promotion of regional interests in political, economic, social and cultural terms. A wave of vociferous regionalism has swept all over Europe since the mid-1980s, which has been labelled New Regionalism.

● **Regional mobilization** denotes a situation where large sections of a region's civic society are engaged in a co-coordinated effort to develop the region and to further all the region's interests. It brings together the political, business and social elites with mass movements, and is characterized by large-scale public debates on regional matters, by networks of cooperation between regional political economic and social actors, and by a sharing of resources between these regional actors for mutual benefit.

The aims of such region-building projects range widely in terms of scope, ambition and the intensity of effort put into the region-building projects by the people engaged in regionalism. A fairly mild and often low-intensity form of regionalism consists of demanding equal treatment with other regions in the same country ('state-citizenship' or 'Jacobin' regionalism; Loughlin, 1996, p. 13). Regions where this approach can be observed include the Italian region of South Tyrol/Trentino, Mecklenburg-Vorpommern and Schleswig-Holstein in Germany, Brittany in France, the North-East of England, Andalusia in Spain, and the Alentejo in Portugal. On the other end of the scale, we find outright demands – not necessarily shared by all inhabitants of those regions – for secession from the country to which the region currently belongs, either with a view to establishing an independent state (e.g. the Basque Country, Corsica, Scotland), or with a view to joining a different country (e.g. Northern Ireland, Kosovo, South Ossetia). In most regions, the actual level of regionalist aims can be located somewhere in between these two extremes, and constitute a broad-ranging set of aims and ambitions which can be termed 'moderate' or 'autonomist regionalism' (Loughlin, 1993, p. 13). Proponents of this form of regionalism are aiming for varying degrees of autonomy for their region within the political structures of the state to which the region belongs. In these regions, regional self-determination is often understood to mean having sufficient 'access to authoritative decision-making' within the polity (Marks, 1996, p. 22–3). Authoritative decision-making, in this sense, comprises both the formal constitutional, legal and institutional structures of the governmental system, and informal channels of influence and interest representation in all public policy-making. The ultimate aim of gaining access to authoritative decision-making is to gain access not just to practical decision-making processes in the day-to-day management of public affairs, but access to decision-making on the rules, formal and informal, by which the polity is governed. The pursuit of these aims does not automatically make all regionalists enemies of the state, although some regionalists – especially those who resort to the use of politically motivated violence to further their aims – are often portrayed as such. Yet in the vast majority of cases

where regional mobilization takes place it is the wish to enhance the democracy, transparency and accountability of the state through the active involvement of its constituent parts which is at the heart of regionalists' political ambitions.

Since the late 1990s, however, it has become obvious that, for the reasons outlined above, most states are faced with strong regionalist challenges to their systems of territorial governance which were developed during the nineteenth and twentieth centuries. In response to these challenges, state governments may decide to become proactive in this process and instigate territorial governance reforms themselves. This transfer of powers and functions from central governments to the regions is known as **regionalization**. Gary Marks (1996, pp. 25–33) envisaged three approaches to regionalization which central governments may take. (1) A minimalist approach, possibly motivated by little more than administrative convenience, may be to off-load state responsibilities to regional political institutions (e.g. France since 1982, Romania since 2007), or, for economic development purposes, to semi-public regional agencies (e.g. Ireland, Greece, Hungary and England since the 1990s). (2) In cases where autonomist regionalism is present, state governments may wish to act pre-emptively to appease regionalists. One example of this is the UK government's offer of devolution to Scotland and Wales in 1998; another is the preparedness of successive post-Franco Spanish governments to negotiate ever-changing arrangements of autonomy to accommodate different regionalist demands from the different regions and autonomous communities. (3) In extreme cases, central governments may have no choice but to act – against their own preferences – to prevent secessionist scenarios, such as the possible break-up of Belgium in the early 1990s.

In all three cases, the emerging results are usually significant territorial, institutional and procedural (decision-making) reforms, ranging from simple administrative decentralization via

---

● **Regionalization** is the active engagement by state governments in processes of region-building. This may include the transfer of political powers and functions to the regional level, the granting of greater degrees of regional autonomy, and the acceptance of greater regional influence on public policy-making for the whole country.

political devolution and the creation of asymmetric structures to fully-fledged federalization. If even the latter fails, however, a secession solution may be inevitable; hopefully a peaceful affair like the break-up of Czechoslovakia, where the Czech and Slovak regions amicably negotiated their separation into two sovereign countries. The three Baltic countries Estonia, Latvia and Lithuania also gained or regained their statehood quite recently after having been treated as mere small regions of the old Soviet Union since the 1940s. At the end of the Cold War, Yugoslavia was faced with an all-encompassing secessionist situation based on ethno-national tensions, which resulted in civil war in many parts of the country, before its former regions were able to reconstitute themselves as states, leaving virtually no trace of the old state. So far, the countries with longer traditions of adequate regional or federal structures, such as Italy and Germany, have escaped the need for massive institutional reform, but even there emerging socioeconomic imbalances have required a number of adjustments to accommodate diverging interests between the regions, such as the above-mentioned move towards some asymmetric arrangements in Italy, or the lengthy German federalism reform process of 2004–08.

Regional activists and movements

Regionalism and region-building cannot exist without active, vociferous and sustained support by at least some sections of the population in a region. Even in government-driven regionalization initiatives the central government needs reliable political and economic partners at the regional level to implement the intended reforms of territorial governance and to take over the functions and responsibilities the central government wishes to devolve. In short, regional interests, desires and ambitions need protagonists who actively promote these interests and engage in political dialogue with other political institutions and organizations, as well as with the other economic, social and cultural interest groups which form the civic society of a regional polity.

Regionalist movements have developed a multitude of organizational forms, depending on the nature of their specific regionalist motivations, on the nature of their demands, on the degree of

popular support they enjoy, on the nature and extent of the resources – ranging from money via seats in parliaments to arms – to which they have access, and not least on the degree of radicalism prevalent among their members. There is no easy way to classify the various organizational arrangements of regionalist movements, as these movements are often heterogeneous in their composition and often comprise several individual organizations. However, three elements are typically present in all regionalist movements: a leadership elite, a political organization, and a mass organization.

The first element is a regionalist leadership elite. These are the actual regionalists, who are fully committed to the regionalist cause and are determined to do everything they can to promote the region's interests. Indeed, it is often they who decide what the region's interests are – or ought to be – and then try to persuade others to follow their lead. Such leadership elites are often not highly visible and may operate quite informally. Members of regional business elites often feature in these regionalist leaderships, though the public face of the leadership is more likely to be composed of senior politicians, academics, clergy, other professionally qualified people, or celebrities from the arts and sports. In a few extreme cases, where regionalism has turned to armed struggle, senior paramilitary commanders are often the most influential members of the leadership elite, though thankfully most regionalist leaderships in present-day Europe have not seen the need to establish paramilitary wings in their regionalist movements. Therefore, business suits, traditional regional dresses and clerical robes, rather than camouflage jackets and balaclavas, tend to be the usual attire of regionalist leaders.

The second key ingredient of any regionalist movement is the presence of at least one regionalist political party or party-like political wing. The task of these political parties is to make regionalism politically visible, in particular by formulating policies, participating in elections, issuing political statements and declarations, and sending representatives to political negotiations with the government or other political institutions. Political parties also have the task of generating political support for regionalist demands among the population of the region. This has the effect of forcing all political parties operating in the region to develop a policy stance towards regionalist claims, even if they do not particularly wish to do so (e.g. the Conservative Party in Scotland and Wales). Furthermore, the need to formulate regional policy agendas in competition with regionalist parties may cause difficulties for established state-wide parties, or even force them to take over the regionalist agenda – as the Labour Party more or less successfully did in Scotland and Wales from 1998 on. However, on a number of occasions it became evident since 2000 that the regional party leaders in Edinburgh and Cardiff were not singing from the same song-sheet as the central party leadership and government in London.

The third element of regionalist movements is the presence of one or even several organizational vehicles for mass involvement, such as social or cultural organizations, religious organizations, or linguistic community organizations. Here, the level of commitment required of individual members is usually lower than in the other forms of organization, and the main tasks conducted by these organizations are the generation of further mass appeal through charitable activities, the staging of social and cultural events within the region, and the promotion of the region outside its borders. The sociocultural organizations also usually act as a recruiting ground for the other forms of organization, such as the leadership elite, the political parties, and – where they exist – the paramilitary organizations.

Present-day Europe comprises a vast array of regional parties and movements, which can be classified by their degree of radicalism, ranging from the most settled, most accommodated ones such as the Südschleswigscher Wählerverband, representing the Danish minority in northern Germany, to violent secessionists such as Herri Batasuna, the political wing of the Basque Euskadi Ta Askatasuna (ETA). Between these two extremes, there are a number of shades and motivational backgrounds, including socioculturally driven parties like the Welsh Plaid Cymru. The vast majority of regionalist political parties are driven by a desire to develop the region economically and socially through the acquisition of a greater degree of political autonomy from the central government. Typical examples include the Scottish National Party, the Bavarian Christian Social Union, the Catalan Convergencia i Unio, the Flemish Volksunie and the Walloon Rassemblement Wallon. There are also some movements for whom regionalism is essentially a vehicle to promote their right-wing populist and/or separatist political agenda of de-solidarization with the rest of the country, such as Vlaams Berlang in Flanders, the Union Corse in Corsica or the Lega Nord in Northern Italy.

Ethnically and culturally motivated regionalists in particular are often portrayed as reactionary, hyper-conservative, xenophobic and narrow-minded. While some regionalist movements comprise such elements, this is not the typical world-view of regionalists, and one has to be careful in assessing the reasons for such phenomena. One case in point was the Vlaams Blok in Flanders, which had to be formally disbanded by order of the Belgian Supreme Court in 2004, due to the organization's apparently excessively xenophobic policies and rhetoric. However, this political movement, which was at the time supported by about a quarter of the Flemish electorate, immediately reconstituted itself under the new name Vlaams Berlang (Flemish Interest). Simply outlawing political convictions which are shared by a very large percentage of the electorate and which are represented by the strongest political party in a region cannot be the answer to a problem of territorial governance in a democratic state. Nor is radical right-wing populism the exclusive preserve of regional parties. In the late 1990s and early 2000s, the whole of Europe experienced a rise of right-wing populist movements such as those of Jean-Marie Le Pen (France), Pym Fortyn (the Netherlands), Ole Rasmussen (Denmark), Jörg Haider (Austria) and the Kaczyński brothers (Poland). Radical right-wing populism usually utilizes political opportunities arising from popular dissatisfaction with the incumbent mainstream political establishment (Rydgren, 2006, p. 9). Therefore, in all these scenarios, mainstream political parties – national as well as regional – need to take a serious look at the root causes which lead to such political stances, and need to develop appropriate public policies and, if necessary, institutional reforms.

In general, there is nothing sinister in wishing to be assured of one's own identity before engaging in intercultural social exchange. Such assurance is of particular importance in regions which regard themselves as nations and/or have a history of social and cultural suppression at the hands of previous state regimes which engaged in creating strong nation-states or 'empires' by trying to eradicate 'deviant' narratives of history, tradition and sociocultural identity. While probably the most pronounced twentieth-century example of such a policy is the Franco dictatorship in Spain, most pre-1990 Communist regimes in Eastern and Central Europe took a similarly strong-armed approach to territorial governance, as did Victorian Britain with regard to Wales and Ireland (and to a lesser extent Scotland). France, the centralized state par excellence since even before the 1789 revolution, remained in denial about the need for meaningful territorial governance until as late as 1982, preferring instead to develop an extensive and robust administrative structure designed to ensure uniformity of policy implementation throughout the country. Since 1982, however, France has embarked on a significant process of regionalization, with the creation of political regions and a significant transfer of economic development functions to the regional level.

Regions and the European Union

The predominance of states, whether in the form of nation-states or in the form of multi-national political unions and federations, as the key actors in European politics left the regions in a fringe position for much of the nineteenth and twentieth centuries in terms of their participation in European political developments. During its early years, the EEC/EC followed this trend, as member states displayed little or no interest in making territorial governance a European issue, although economic policy-making by the new supranational institutions did affect some regions more than others – in particular industrial regions where coal and steel were key products, and also many rural regions which benefited from the introduction of a Common Agricultural Policy (CAP). However, this lack of interest among member states in dealing with regional development at the European level resulted, until the mid-1970s, in the absence of a distinct EEC/EC regional policy beyond some general provisions, designed to facilitate economic cohesion as planned and implemented by the member states' governments.

This situation changed considerably in the wake of the publication of the *Report on the Regional Problems in the Enlarged Community* (the 'Thomson Report'), which showed patterns of enormous regional disparities in terms of economic development throughout the then nine member states, and identified these disparities as a main obstacle to the development of a Common Market (Bache, 1998, pp. 38–9). Subsequent policy negotiations at the European level led to the establishment of the *European Regional Development Fund* (ERDF), designed to help less developed regions to overcome their economic difficulties, thus not only enhancing the competitiveness of these regions but also contributing to a harmonization of markets and living conditions throughout the EC. However, in these early days the regions remained more or less passive objects of policy-making by EC institutions and member-state governments, with the latter being responsible for identifying eligible regions as well as for implementing regional development strategies in the member states. The overall financial commitment of the EC to regional development was initially quite small, comprising only 4.8 per cent of the EC's budget in 1975, the ERDF's first year of operations (Bache, 1998, p. 62).

During the 1980s, a number of reforms took place in EC regional policy-making aimed at harmonizing the use of the EC's Structural Funds (the ERDF, the European Social Fund and the Guidance Section of the European Agricultural Guarantee and Guidance Fund) in all member states, and to target these funds at specific economic problems encountered by the eligible regions. Therefore, it became the EC's responsibility to identify regions eligible to receive funds by means of harmonized, EC-wide (rather than national) economic criteria, and to determine both the general economic aims ('Objectives') to be achieved by spending EC money in the regions concerned, as well as to negotiate specific priorities and types of development projects to be supported in each eligible region, in the form of Operational Programmes. Yet it was still the member-state governments which negotiated on behalf of the regions – much to the dissatisfaction of regional and local politicians, in particular in regions where their regional development ideas did not coincide with the member-state government's visions of overall development in the whole country. Scotland and Wales in the Thatcher era were very good examples of such a situation.

It was not until 1993, however, that the regions were at last recognized by the EU institutions as political actors within the EU. The two main steps in that direction were included in the Treaty on European Union (TEU). The first step was the introduction of a requirement in the management procedures for the Structural Funds that sub-national decision-makers must be consulted in the process of negotiating the contents of Operational Programmes for each eligible region. This step was designed to be a practical application of the principle of partnership, although who exactly the sub-national decision-makers to be consulted are still varies considerably from member state to member state. Where they exist, regional governments normally send delegates to the appropriate Monitoring Committees. Where no regional government is present, the regional representatives may be delegates drawn from local authorities in these regions, or delegates from semi-public Regional Development Agencies (RDAs). In the latter case, the agencies have a specific regional brief, but may still be under the political control of the member state's central government, as is the case in Greece, Ireland, and Hungary. The EU nevertheless accepts this practice in the absence of any better alternatives.

The second, and possibly more important step taken in the TEU was the establishment of the Committee of the Regions (CoR) as an institution of the EU. It provides a route for interest representation at the European level, not only for regions which receive Structural Funds, but also for those regions – usually the economically better-developed ones – whose main EU-related interests are in the field of regulatory policy concerning their key economic affairs. The CoR offers exactly this kind of access to EU policy-making, as the institution's main task is to comment upon proposed new EU legislation from a regional perspective. While the CoR is not formally endowed with any policy-making role or veto power, the other EU institutions (Council, Commission, European Parliament) have started to value the CoR's advice. However,

this has not been an easy learning process, not least since the membership composition of the CoR is very heterogenous, with representatives from both regional and local governments. A Prime Minister of a German *Land* and a local Mayor from Luxembourg have vastly different responsibilities and political interests. Following various attempts at organizing the CoR's work effectively, and taking into account the considerable rise in membership from 189 members at the start in 1994 to 344 members since the 2007 EU enlargement, the CoR has now settled down to an organizational structure not dissimilar to that of the European Parliament. Within the current CoR we find four party-political groups: the European People's Party (EPP; Conservatives/Christian Democrats), the Party of European Socialists (PES; Socialists/Social Democrats), the Alliance of Liberals and Democrats in Europe (ALDE; Liberals/Centrists), and the Union for Europe of the Nations–European Alliance (UEN–EA; Nationalists/Eurosceptics). The practical work is organized into six permanent Commissions along broad thematic lines:

1. Citizenship, Governance, Institutional and External Affairs
2. Territorial Cohesion
3. Economic and Social Policy
4. Education, Youth, Culture and Research
5. Environment, Climate Change, and Energy
6. Natural Resources.

When required, the CoR also establishes a Temporary ad-hoc Commission on the EU Budget. Finally, there is also a permanent group dealing with CoR-internal 'housekeeping' matters, the Committee for Administrative and Financial Affairs.

Despite this apparent progress in terms of regional engagement at the EU level, or 'vertical' interest representation (Hrbek and Weyand, 1994, p. 82), EU regional policy-making has also led to what appears to be a disadvantage for regional policy-makers. The present EU system seems to focus on economic cohesion by all means, including political integration. This is an important reason why regions which are seemingly quite different in their identity, political and economic history, and political culture nevertheless appear to produce some surprisingly similar policy output in terms of regional development practices, patterns of political behaviour, and community development (Mathias, 2004, p. 144). The EU's drive to bring about integration 'from above' has given rise to suspicions among a considerable number of regional actors from different national backgrounds that in a European 'super-state' regional interest representation might be more difficult to achieve than within the nation-states of old. These immediate political concerns are partially based on a lingering suspicion, in particular among culturally motivated regionalists, that European harmonization may in itself be detrimental to efforts to uphold regional identities and expressions of distinctiveness – despite the new-found status of regions as political actors in Europe, and despite the explicitly pro-European stance of most economically motivated regionalists.

Therefore, since the early 1990s we have seen increasing demands in many EU regions to establish a 'Europe of the Regions' to counterbalance the 'Europe of the Bankers' designed in Brussels and the capitals of the more influential member states. While at present hardly any regionalists would go so far as wishing that regions rather than states should replace the member states as the 'building blocks of European integration' (Hrbek and Weyand, 1994, p. 13), three typical demands are regularly made by representatives of the regions concerning the future directions of EU regional policy-making. The first demand focuses on further enhancement of access to decision-making – not only via the CoR but increasingly also through the involvement of regional representatives as part of their national delegations in the Council, through a stronger territorial representation aspect in the work of Members of the European Parliament, and through increased direct dialogue between regional representatives and the Commission. The second demand is for a continued commitment on the part of the EU to support regional economic development. While most regions in the EU-15 accept that the bulk of the resources available for this purpose will have to be targeted at regions in the new member states for the foreseeable future, support for regional development should at least remain the second largest item in the EU budget (or possibly even overtake CAP funding), and

ailing regions in the 'old' member states should not be excluded from access to Structural Funds altogether. In addition, the EU should keep up its policy of promoting cross-border interregional cooperation through the European Region (EUREGIO) and similar programmes. The third demand aims at the enhancement of recognition for regional cultures. The EU should celebrate its rich diversity of cultures and languages through promotional activities (e.g. the Cultural Capital of Europe programme), and support for regional and local initiatives.

It is likely that all three demands will be met by the EU to some extent, though not to a degree that will satisfy all regionalists. Much will depend on the preparedness of member-states' governments to cooperate in these processes. Such cooperation is absolutely essential for any regional representatives' involvement in the work of the Council, which is explicitly designed as an institution of the governments of member states, not regions. Only in the cases of Spain, Germany and Belgium do regions have legal entitlements to such representation enshrined in domestic legislation. UK Labour governments in recent years have allowed such representation in practice from time to time, yet have stopped short of providing such legal entitlements to the regional governments in Scotland, Wales and Northern Ireland.

The degree of financial provision for the Structural Funds also largely depends on the Council – and to some extent the European Parliament. While the settlement for the previous funding period (1999–2006) in effect operated a dual system which compromises between the established support patterns of the EU-15 and the immediate special needs of the new members, the current funding period (2007–13) saw the introduction of a unified system of eligibility rules and objectives throughout the EU-27, which required – and will continue to require significant adjustments in supported regions in both the old and the new member states. However, the overall demand for regional support funding has become so great that even the traditionally 'untouchable' CAP funding has become a potential source of funds to meet these demands – resulting, among other problems, in a conflict of interest for predominantly agricultural regions.

Celebrating cultural diversity, by contrast, can be regarded as the icing on the cake. In most member states the issue is not, in principle, politically controversial, and the only question is the extent of the EU's financial support for these activities. Culturally motivated regionalists, however, are likely to use the extent of this support as a yardstick by which to measure how serious the EU is in its recognition of regions as valuable members of the European polity: is 'united in its diversity' really on the agenda, or just a catch-phrase to alleviate Eurosceptic fears of an 'ever closer union'?

Interregional cooperation

Structural changes encountered by regions in EU member states in the processes of European integration, globalization, and technological advancements challenging traditional socioeconomic regional patterns of development have forced regions to develop appropriate political response strategies, seeking new ways and means of governance (Kohler-Koch, 1998, pp. 17–19). One focus of these changes was on institutional reform and on developing new policy-making procedures and styles (Knodt, 1998, pp. 13–21). These are essentially internal regional reform and mobilization processes.

The other focus, which has particularly come to the fore in recent years, is an increased level of interest and activity in the field of interregional cooperation and external interest representation, or 'horizontal integration' (Hrbek and Weyand, 1994, p. 43). This has been the most recent growth area of regional activities, with plenty of future potential. It is based on a recognition by political regions that there are joint interests between them, expressed in three different ways: (1) domestic interregional cooperation, (2) cross-border interregional cooperation, and (3) joint pursuit of interests.

Domestic interregional cooperation may develop when neighboring political regions within a country recognize that they in fact form an economic region and hence start co-coordinating their regional development strategies. This is in particular the case where political borders between regions have been drawn up in the past based on patterns of economic development which no longer exist, or based on outdated historical patterns of political separation. The development of highly industrialized super-regions since the Industrial Revolution has taken little note of political boundaries. One example of this is the English South-East, stretching its tentacles ever further away from London and as far west as Bristol and Cardiff. Another example is the German industrialised and urbanized area along the rivers Rhine and Ruhr, covering large sections of three political regions (North Rhine-Westphalia, Rhineland-Palatinate and Hesse). The governments of these German *Länder* have no choice but to cooperate in shaping their regional development strategies. However, since 1969 all German *Länder* coordinate their regional development strategies and operate a system of transfer payments between richer and poorer regions, in an effort to equalize socioeconomic living conditions throughout the country (Anderson, 1995, pp. 28–30).

Cross-border interregional cooperation is essentially based on the same principles as domestic interregional cooperation, namely economic regions fostering economic development despite being split into neighbouring political regions. The key difference is that the political borders in question are not merely regional borders, or outdated historical borders, but actual borders between sovereign states. This fact brings with it a number of political consequences. Today's state borders are largely a product of Europe's violent political history. They also often – but not always – denote ethnic and linguistic boundaries; therefore border regions often carry a historically rooted potential for ethno-territorial conflict (Wolff, 2003, pp. 4–15). This forces the political regions on either side of the border to engage in new forms of external interest representation, which have been termed '**paradiplomacy**' (Cornago, 1999, p. 40). In essence, political regions have started to run low-key foreign relations of their own, entering into formal partnerships with regions from abroad, sending trade

---

● **Paradiplomacy** is the generic term for activities of external political interest representation by Non-Central Governments (NCG), i.e. regional governments and also some local governments. The NCGs may enter into formal cooperation agreements with NCG from abroad, or occasionally even with foreign state governments, and generally conduct foreign representation activities such as, for instance, running an embassy-like representation office in Brussels.

delegations, encouraging and supporting cross-border joint-venture business developments, and co-coordinating their political interest representation activities at the European level. Technically, these activities constitute a breach of the foreign policy monopoly which states – but not regions – enjoy as part of their sovereignty. Therefore, many European states, including France, Spain and the UK, were initially very reluctant to allow regions to engage in paradiplomacy. Only in Germany has this not been a big issue, as the *Länder* enjoy a constitutional right to external interest representation provided these activities do not undermine federal foreign policy (which itself is shaped with the active involvement of all the *Länder*). Nevertheless, in practical terms paradiplomatic engagements by regions are now usually tolerated by all EU member states because of the evident economic benefits. Moreover, the EU itself has helped to foster such cross-border partnerships through the EUREGIO and INTERREG programmes.

Joint pursuit of common political, economic, social and cultural interests is, however, not limited to regions located in close geographical proximity. Regions separated by longer distances may nevertheless recognize that they share certain economic and/or political interests and therefore wish to cooperate in various ways: engaging in economic cooperation, sharing experience in policy-making, and/or jointly defining and pursuing political interests (Eißel et al., 1999, pp. 23–7). This can be done in the form of bilateral partnerships between regions, but in practice the more usual forms are multilateral partnerships involving regions which share certain economic and social characteristics, regardless of their national background and different political structure. Examples of such partnerships include the Conference of Peripheral Maritime Regions (CPMR), the Association of European Regions of Industrial Technology (RETI) and the 'Four Motors' Consortium, a partnership between four of Europe's strongest regions, Baden-Württemberg, Lombardy, Catalonia and Rhône-Alpes. In addition, in recent years we have seen a proliferation of partnerships based on sociocultural interests, such as the partnership between Scotland, Wales and Galicia, based on the common Celtic heritage, and the partnership between Catalonia and Wales, focusing on regional language issues

and policies. The whole scope of partnership activities is completed by regional support for existing and new bilateral and multilateral relationships at the local level. Since the mid-1980s there has been a new wave of town-twinning and similar arrangements, adding to the already comprehensive European network of twinned cities, towns and local government districts which evolved in the 1950s and 1960s.

Interpreting regional developments and predicting the outlook for regions in the coming decade

Those who have been attempting to analyse and explain the developments described above have found the concept of 'New Regionalism' (Keating, 1998a, pp. 7–13), which is one of the most recent, but also one of the most important of developments in modernizing European politics, of particular explanatory power. It attempts to identify and encapsulate the many recent changes. Moreover, New Regionalism thinking has not been limited to the political scene. Economists dealing with regional economic development, spatial planning and meso-level economic systems have started to utilize the New Regionalism concept in almost a paradigmatic way, on the one hand finding it a useful tool to analyse the political and social environment in which regional economies function, and on the other hand adding much needed economic and social empirical evidence to the analysis of regional political-interest formation and representation. At the same time the sociocultural regionalists found in New Regionalism a new rationale for their activities, and a modern way of linking them with ongoing developments in other – i.e. political and economic – spheres of human activity, while adding a significant new dimension.

Indeed, as we have seen, the practical implementation of New Regionalism in Europe took a variety of shapes, customized to the specific circumstances of the individual polities. The constitutional, legal and administrative solutions employed in the countries concerned were manifold, though normally with three characteristic features: (1) a greater emphasis on regional self-determination for key political, economic and social policy-making issues; (2) improved relations between state governments and regional governments, with a proliferation of decision-making institutions and organizations, which may involve asymmetric solutions for different regions within the same country; and (3) wider, more formalized and more stable recognition and access to decision-making for non-public actors, not only through more widespread use of partnerships between public authorities and regional businesses communities, but also for social and cultural interest groups.

At present, this can probably be regarded as the 'paradigmatic' core of New Regionalism, in so far as it is appropriate to speak of paradigms in political science. However, one needs to be careful with this label, in two respects: first, it is debatable to what extent such a wide range of multi-faceted empirical examples as have developed across the continent of Europe can – and should – be pressed into a rigid, ill-fitting theoretical straitjacket. Secondly, New Regionalism, while perfectly capable of analysing and comparing general trends in region-building processes, is not a tool for predicting specific outcomes in and for specific countries or regions. Instead, it is a tool for promoting policy learning, providing important empirical evidence on key political, economic, social and cultural factors in processes of comprehensive regional development. New Regionalism researchers engage in a vast array of qualitative and quantitative research on individual regions, analysing their cases in great detail, as well as providing comprehensive comparisons between cases, developing the methodological arsenal to do so as they investigate new phenomena and new territories. This research, therefore, is not only at the forefront of political science research in Europe at present, but also at the forefront of developing interdisciplinary cooperation across the social sciences. In this sense, New Regionalism is not a paradigm, but a 'broad church'.

There is, in essence, no end-game scenario. No one envisages that a predictable and uniform 'Europe of the regions' will one day emerge as the outcome of the processes and developments described above. Nevertheless, regions as political actors and key instruments of territorial governance are here to stay, and are likely to develop further. Four areas of development will be of particular interest in the foreseeable future:

1. Completing the recent reform processes which began in the 1990s, by making the new structural, institutional and procedural arrangements work and filling them with suitable political content, is a challenge for the majority of European countries, both in Western Europe and in Central and Eastern Europe.

2. Political accommodation of dissatisfied regions remains a continuing problem to which there is no easy solution. This is particularly relevant for the Spanish, Italian and Belgian constitutional reform processes, and also for the real 'problem regions' in this respect (the Basque Country and Corsica, and to a lesser degree nowadays, Northern Ireland).

3. The development of suitable regional economic infrastructures – technical as well as human – remains a continuing task, in particular in regions which have recently undergone significant economic changes. This of course includes most regions in the new EU member states.

4. A key factor for the future will be further realization and utilization of the full potential of interregional cooperation: at present only a quarter of EU regions participate fully in such partnerships, and they do so with varying degrees of intensity and economic success. Yet this is the everyday 'low politics' groundwork upon which the ideals of 'high politics', such as 'ever closer union' are going to depend in practice.

Therefore, it is essential that regions and regionalists are taken seriously by other political actors and institutions, and it is equally essential to maintain an active involvement of individual citizens in the affairs of their regions. The democratic future of Europe depends on it.

SUMMARY

- As identity, not least national identity and nationalism, has to some extent replaced ideology, the relationships between local populations, the nations of Europe and the state, and the nature of governance have all become more complex.

- Nation-states continue to be crucially important as the framework for internal policy making and external relations.

- The nation-state is, however, under strain, and since the 1980s regions have emerged as increasingly important political actors.

- This growing importance has been reflected in political arrangements for territorial governance, which have altered in response to requests from the regions.

- The EU has become heavily involved in relationships with the regions, attempting to produce more harmonized levels of economic development across its territory.

- Regions will certainly continue to be a key arena for the exercise of citizen's democratic activity.

QUESTIONS FOR DISCUSSION

- How can we explain the persistence of nationalism in the era of globalization?

- What constitutes a region? Which different classes of regions do we find in Europe at present?

- What is the difference between regionalism and regionalization, and how are the two phenomena linked to each other?

- Who are regionalists, and what do they stand for?

- To what extent have regions become significant actors in the politics of the EU?

- Are regional and national borders still relevant in today's EU?

- How would you characterize your home region in terms of political significance, economic and social development, and sociocultural identity?

FURTHER READING

Aldecoa, Francisco (1999) *Paradiplomacy in Action* (London and Portland, OR: Frank Cass). Introduces the concept of paradiplomacy and provides a range of practical examples.

Anderson, James, Liam O'Dowd and Thomas M. Wilson (eds) (2002) *New Borders for a*

Changing Europe (London and Portland, OR: Frank Cass). Discusses the continued significant role of political borders as barriers for economic and social integration between neighbouring regions and states in Europe.

Bache, Ian (1998) *The Politics of European Union Regional Policy* (Sheffield: Sheffield University Press). A short history of EU Structural Funds policy development from the 1970s to the 1990s.

Balme, Richard (ed.) (1996) *Les Politiques du Néo-Régionalisme* (Paris: Economica). Explores New Regionalism as a political concept, as well as a Europe-wide movement.

Batt, Judy and Kataryna Wolczuk (eds) (2002) *Region, State and Identity in Central and Eastern Europe* (London and Portland, OR: Frank Cass). A concise assessment of the arrival of New Regionalism in the CEE countries.

Deffner, Alex, Dimitrios Konstadakopulos and Yannis Psycharis (eds) (2003) *Culture and Regional Economic Development in Europe: Cultural, Political and Social Perspectives* (Volos: University of Thessaly Press). A comprehensive reader outlining the three pillars – political, socioeconomic and cultural – of regionalism in Europe. Contains several case studies and examples from Southern Europe.

Hooghe, Lisbeth and Gary Marks (2001) *Multi-Level Governance and European Integration* (Boulder, CO, New York and Oxford: Rowman & Littlefield). Already recognized as a classic text on MLG; also contains an appendix specifically addressing the role of regions in MLG.

Hrbek, Rudolf and Sabine Weyand (1994) *betrifft: Das Europa der Regionen* (Munich: C.H. Beck). Introduces and explains the concepts of vertical and horizontal interregional integration; a complimentary view to MLG.

Keating, Michael (1998) *The New Regionalism in Western Europe: Territorial Restructuring and Political Change* (Cheltenham: Edward Elgar). A specific look at Western Europe, tracking the 'wave of regionalism' sweeping the continent since the 1980s.

Keating, Michael, and John Loughlin (eds) (1997) *The Political Economy of Regionalism* (London and Portland, OR: Frank Cass). Now also recognized as a classic text, it introduces various definitions and classifications for types of regions as well as for regional movements, which are now widely accepted throughout the other literature in the field.

Loughlin, John (ed.) (2010) *The Oxford Handbook of Local and Regional Democracy in Europe* (Oxford: Oxford University Press). The most comprehensive and up-to-date coverage of the regional/local question across the continent, covering 29 states.

Minahan, James B. (2000) *One Europe, Many Nations. A Historical Dictionary of European National Groups* (Westport, CT and London: Greenwood Press). A comprehensive overview of national groupings, large or small, key to understanding identity formation.

Warleigh, Alex (2002), *The Committee of the Regions: Institutionalizing Multi-Governance?* (London: Kogan Page). A critical account of the 'birth' of the CoR and its first two mandate periods.

European Security

MIKE BOWKER

Let me say ... that the security agenda we face is large and complex. There must be collective action. We in Europe can and should play our part. It is what European citizens want. And it is what partners around the world expect.
Catherine Ashton, EU High Representative for Foreign Affairs and Security Policy at the Munich Security Conference, 6 February 2010

This chapter provides a general overview of European security in the contemporary period. First, it will show how the security agenda has changed since the **Cold War**. Then, it will outline the main threats to European security today, before describing the current security architecture in Europe which has been set up to try to deal with the new and more unpredictable challenges of the post-Cold War period.

Security during the Cold War

Realist thinkers, who dominated the debate on international relations during the Cold War, argued that security was predominantly about the defence of the state from military attack by another state (see Morgenthau, 1978; Waltz, 1979). For a state to feel secure, they argued, it needed to build up its military forces, either alone or in alliance with others, to deter, and if necessary repel, any potential aggressors. This is what happened during the Cold War as the USA and the USSR, the leading countries in their respective blocs, spent unprecedented sums of money on defence. History shows that an arms race often leads to war, but in this case direct superpower conflict was avoided. Realists argued this was so for two interrelated reasons. First, a balance of power emerged after the end of the Second World War which meant that neither side could be sure of victory in the event of war. Second, this doubt was greatly reinforced by the invention of nuclear weapons. So powerful were these weapons that by the early 1970s, both the USA and USSR had accumulated sufficient to destroy each other and much of the rest of the world. This destructive capability, known as Mutually Assured Destruction (MAD), changed the fundamentals of military strategy. For MAD had rendered meaningless any concept of victory in a superpower conflict. As a result, military strategists in Washington and Moscow no longer focused on how to win a war, but on how best to avoid one. This was the basis of nuclear deterrence.

● **The Cold War** was a result of ideological and military rivalry between two blocs – East and West – led by the USA and the USSR. There were many crises and conflicts during the Cold War, but war between the two superpowers was avoided, many people believing because of the balance of terror.

● **Realism**: Realist thinkers argue that states always pursue their own national interests in the world, both to maximize their own power and to defend their own territory.

In certain respects at least, Europe could be viewed as a beneficiary of MAD. In the first few years after the war, crises in the divided German capital of Berlin always looked the most likely to escalate into a major confrontation. Yet after Moscow built the Berlin Wall in 1961 and consolidated its position in East Germany, there were no more East–West crises in Europe. A form of stability emerged which was based on an increasing acceptance in the West of Germany as a divided country and Europe as a divided continent. The academic, John Lewis Gaddis, was so convinced by the stabilizing factors inherent in the structures of the Cold War that he wrote an article in 1986 referring to the East–West rivalry as 'the long peace' (Gaddis, 1986). However, only three years later, in November 1989, the Berlin Wall fell and the Cold War was over.

Critics argued that Gaddis and others had not predicted the end of the Cold War because they had largely ignored internal factors within the Soviet bloc. For stability in Europe was based on a fundamental injustice. While the people of Western Europe had prospered, those on the other side of the iron curtain suffered political repression and relative economic deprivation under a system imposed on them by Stalin after the war. As there was a lack of legitimacy, Moscow could only maintain its position in Eastern Europe through force or the threat of force. Thus, as the reformist Soviet leader, Mikhail Gorbachev, withdrew the threat of force from 1985, the people gained confidence and rose up against the Communist system. Moscow withdrew from Eastern Europe and the Soviet Union itself collapsed as a state in December 1991. The Cold War had come to a remarkably abrupt and peaceful end. It was greeted with a feeling of euphoria. The people of Eastern Europe had been freed from Communist oppression and the constant fear of nuclear Armageddon had been lifted from the continent as a whole.

The Cold War had been a system based on division and fear, but as Gaddis had said, it was also one that had created stability in Europe. Was there a danger that this stability would be lost? Whilst politicians struggled to adjust to the new realities, international relations theorists put forward different ideas on what the post-Cold War world might look like and the possible consequences for state security.

Theories of the post-Cold War system

Realists tended to be pessimistic about the future. The ideological rivalry of the Cold War might have gone, but they expected new rivalries to emerge. John Mearsheimer (1990), for example, argued that national and ethnic difference would deepen in the absence of the stabilizing features of the Cold War. This would represent a return to the international politics of the past. New powers would arise to challenge the dominance of the USA as the sole superpower in the post-Cold War world. This process would be highly destabilizing, but even if a multipolar system were to emerge, Mearsheimer predicted it would be less stable and more war-prone than the bipolar, Cold War system which preceded it. In fact, America's dominance has proved more durable than Mearsheimer might have expected, in part because Washington has proved willing to maintain its military advantage in the world at great cost to its finances. Its economic dominance, however, has been reduced. The European Union (EU) has roughly the same total output as the USA, whilst the economies of China, India and even Russia are growing at impressive rates. There are predictions, therefore, that China will overtake America in gross domestic product (GDP) terms within a generation as the West suffers continued decline.

Samuel Huntington (1996) did not disagree with much of Mearsheimer's analysis, but argued that cultural difference, with religion at its core, was more likely than ethnicity to lead to conflict and major war. This claim was based on two main propositions. First, Huntington argued that culture was deeply rooted in a person's identity. This made it particularly difficult for different parties to compromise and make concessions on religious and cultural issues. This, in turn, greatly increased not only the likelihood of conflict, but also its subsequent intensity. Second, Huntington claimed that those of the same culture would stand by each other in times of crisis and form coherent entities which he called civilizations: 'kin would stand by kin' (1996, p. 217). Therefore, he argued that major wars were most likely to occur between great civilizations rather than great states. Much of Huntington's book was devoted to a consideration

BOX 10.1

The end of history

Francis Fukuyama wrote an article in 1989 called 'The End of History?' It argued that the end of the Cold War represented a victory for liberal democracy. This was accepted by many, but more controversially Fukuyama went on to argue that liberal democracy was the best possible political system and there would be no more ideological challenges to it.

of the clash, which he seemed to predict, between the Western and Muslim civilizations, and the West's necessary response. Like realists, Huntington emphasized the need for the West to maintain its defences if it wished to protect its current position in the world. Huntington's ideas attracted a great deal of attention, but it was always a controversial theory. Many critics were ready to acknowledge the increased importance of culture and religion in the post-Cold War world, but doubted that they were the cause of war. Furthermore, he appeared to exaggerate the supposed unity of different civilizations and their ability to supplant the state and act effectively on the international stage.

Radical theorists, such as Eric Hobsbawm (1994) and Noam Chomsky (1994), agreed with realists that divisions remained in the post-Cold War world, but argued that the fundamental divide in the world was economic. Hobsbawm acknowledged that the capitalist system had proved more effective than the communist alternative in generating wealth, but argued it was singularly unable to distribute it equitably. Inequalities in wealth will persist because radicals perceive it to be inherent to the capitalist system. Unlike the realists, therefore, the radicals do not believe that security is best preserved through military preparedness and the balance of power, but through the radical redistribution of wealth, which may well require the dismantling of the capitalist system. Conservative critics would acknowledge the importance of poverty as an issue in international relations, but most doubt that it is a root cause of war. They would certainly not advocate the overthrow of capitalism, believing that the market and good governance are the only way to raise the develop-

ing countries out of their poverty (World Bank 2002).

In contrast to the realists and radicals, liberals were amongst those celebrating the end of the Cold War (Fukuyama, 1989) (see Box 10.1). Without dismissing the problems outlined above, liberals argued that the end of the Cold War represented a great opportunity to create a more stable and peaceful international system based on liberal values and principles. The extension of the market and free trade would lead to greater prosperity, they claimed, while the extension of democracy would deliver not only greater liberty and a more accountable government, but also enhanced security across Europe. For liberals argue that democracies are less war-prone than dictatorships. Democracies do fight wars, but the proposition advanced by the academic, Michael Doyle (1986), is that democracies do not fight each other. This became known as the 'democratic peace' theory. Thus, security was perceived to be dependent on the democratization process and liberals actively sought to promote democracy across Europe and the world.

Liberals also wanted international law to govern the behaviour of states. States generally see the advantage of acting in line with international law, but the international community would be expected to act in the case of any violations. In most cases, this would involve nothing more than diplomatic pressure, but if faced with a recalcitrant regime or the most blatant of breaches, the international community might decide to impose sanctions or even use military force. One such extreme case involved Saddam Hussein's Iraq when it invaded and annexed Kuwait in August 1990. When Saddam refused to withdraw, the United Nations

(UN) approved the use of force to drive Iraq out of Kuwait. Known as collective security, this concept argues that states should act collectively for the common good (in this case in defence of Kuwait's right to sovereignty), rather than alone or in blocs to protect narrow national interest. Ultimately, liberals argue that it is better to base peace and stability on international law rather than on division and nuclear deterrence.

Finally, another important aspect of liberal thinking is the emphasis placed on international and regional organizations as a means of extending security. Most liberals agree with realists that the state remains the most important actor in international relations, but argue that organizations, like the UN and the EU, can play a positive role in the world. For example, they can provide forums for states to communicate, build up trust, and peacefully resolve disputes. Liberals, therefore, promoted the extension and enlargement of such organizations across the world.

While liberal concepts of security have not been adopted worldwide, they became the guiding force in Europe in the post-Cold War period. Thus, Europe signed the Charter of Paris in 1990 and the Charter of European Security in 1999, both of which emphasize key liberal concepts, such as equal security, respect for international law and the non-use of force to resolve disputes.

The new security agenda

Although liberal and realists theorists had different ideas on how to maintain security, their priorities remained the same – the defence of the state against military attack. The radicals, on the other hand, did not take such a state-centric view and argued that security was better served by spending on economic development rather than the military. Although the radicals were on the periphery of the security debate during the Cold War, some of these basic ideas were taken up by a new generation of writers who sought to develop a new agenda (see Buzan, 1991).

First, it was agreed that the focus of security studies should shift from states to the people and groups living within them (Waever et al., 1993). In realist theory, the state was the key unit of analysis because its primary duty was seen to be the protection of its citizens. However, it became increasingly obvious that this was not always happening. In more repressive states, the government was commonly perceived to be a bigger threat to the life and well-being of its citizens than foreign countries and outside powers. In other cases, central authority might have broken down, and the state would, in those circumstances, be unable to protect the interests of its own citizens (even if it wanted to). In such failed states, citizens might face a variety of possible security threats, including the breakdown of law and order, warlordism, and even civil war. Indeed, in recent times, the traditional security threat of interstate war, the central focus for realists, has become comparatively rare. Civil war is far more common and, not unconnected to this fact, civilians rather than the military tend to be the greatest casualties of modern warfare (Kaldor, 1999). Of the over four million people killed in wars since 1990, 90 per cent were civilians (Solana, 2003, p. 3).

Another feature of the post-Cold War period which undermined the state-centric view of the world relates to the emergence of international terrorism as a major security threat. Whatever our views of the terrorist threat today, it is clear that al-Qaeda is not a state, but a loosely organized, transnational body with informal links to like-minded bodies across the world (Burke, 2004). Therefore, it poses a very different sort of threat than the Soviet Union during the Cold War. The Soviet Union was a state with legitimate leaders with whom it was possible to negotiate and reach agreement on a variety of issues. For the most part, the Soviet Union also recognized the rules of the international game, which helped make the Cold War more predictable and stable. Al-Qaeda, on the other hand, is a truly revolutionary organisation, in the sense that it has no respect for the sovereignty of states, international law or diplomatic conventions. In sum, international terrorism poses a new kind of security threat to the world. Although there might be a role for the military to combat terrorism, it is widely recognized that a political strategy of 'hearts and minds' has become at least as important (English, 2009).

Finally, an increasing number of writers have not only criticized the state-centric emphasis of traditional security theorists but also its concentration on the military. Barry Buzan (1991), among others, has sought to broaden the concept of security to include non-military threats, such as pandemics, resources, environmental degradation and climate change – all of which can threaten the lives of citizens and the ability of states and societies to maintain functional integrity. This new security agenda has not been accepted by all theorists. Some traditional theorists have stated their concern that such an approach broadens the concept to such an extent that almost anything could be classified as a security issue, thereby undermining its analytical utility (Paris, 2001). There is no doubt that the threat of military intervention and climate change are very different and require very different responses, but a growing number of academics, governments and institutions alike have acknowledged the need to extend the concept of security beyond the traditional realist and liberal concerns.

Contemporary European security threats

When the Cold War ended, the most immediate security threat appeared to be uncertainty over the future of the Soviet bloc, and most particularly post-Soviet Russia. Although most communist states were successful in transforming their societies, there were conflicts on the territory of the former Soviet Union and Yugoslavia. In both cases, the West struggled to readjust its policy towards Moscow and bring peace and stability to the Balkans. However, since the terrorist attacks on America on 11 September 2001, a new security challenge, originating from beyond the continent of Europe, arose in the form of Islamist militancy, while non-traditional security issues have also risen up the political agenda in recent times. We will consider these security risks in turn.

Post-Soviet Russia

The West feared the consequences of a military superpower breaking up. However, Russia acted as the successor to the Soviet Union. It took over the treaty obligations of the USSR and its permanent seat on the UN Security Council. The military was split up between the 15 successor states but unequally, with Russia emerging as the dominant power. It was also agreed that all remaining nuclear weapons in the Soviet Union would be put under Russian control, which averted the threat of nuclear proliferation at a stroke. However, the collapse of the economy across the former Soviet Union led to a cash-starved military at a time when Russia faced new security concerns. Russia had to get used to living within new borders at a time when it faced unrest and instability amongst many of its neighbours.

Initially, President Boris Yeltsin adopted a pro-Western foreign policy in an attempt to gain aid and support for the transformation process, but public backing for the reforms declined steeply as living standards collapsed and crime and corruption soared. When Vladimir Putin (see Key Figure 10.1) succeeded Yeltsin in 2000, he captured the public mood by calling for a stronger state, law and order and a revival of Russian patriotism. As the economy boomed for much of the decade, in large part due to the steep rise in energy and commodity prices, Putin's popularity rose and the political situation stabilized. Putin was able to increase defence spending significantly, and even though it remained well below that of the USA, it recovered to levels similar to those of Britain and France (see Table 10.1). The militarization of Russian policy has led to widespread concerns over Moscow's intentions. There are fears that Moscow wants to re-create the old Soviet Union and even reimpose its influence over the former Warsaw Pact countries in Eastern Europe (Lucas, 2008). This view gained greater credence when Putin (2005) described the end of the Soviet Union as 'The greatest geopolitical catastrophe of the twentieth century', and his successor, Dmitry Medvedev (2008b), argued in the aftermath of the war in Georgia in 2008 that Russia had 'privileged interests' in the former Soviet space, which it had a duty to defend.

In fact, the idea of Russia claiming privileged interests in the former Soviet space is not really new. For Moscow has always been willing to act within the former Soviet Union and, on occasion, it has resorted to military force, for example, in Moldova, Tajikistan and, in more recent times, in Chechnya and Georgia. The conflict in Chechnya started in 1994 when Moscow intervened militarily

Table 10.1   Five countries with the highest military spending in 2008

Rank	Country	Spending ($bn)	World share (%)	Spending per capita (%)	Share of GDP (2007)	1999–2008 (%)
1.	USA	607.0	41.5	1967	4.0	66.5
2.	China	84.9	5.8	63	2.0	194.0
3.	France	65.7	4.5	1061	2.3	3.5
4.	Britain	65.3	4.5	1070	2.4	20.7
5.	Russia	58.6	4.0	413	3.5	173.0

Note: Estimated figures for Russia and China.

Source: SIPRI Yearbook 2008, *Armaments, Military Expenditure: Disarmament and International Security* (Oxford: Oxford University Press, 2008).

to prevent the republic gaining independence from Russia. The war was brutal, with heavy casualties on both sides. Russian troops committed war crimes and numerous human rights violations, while Chechen militants used ever more violent forms of terrorism. After Ramzan Kadyrov became Chechen President in 2007, a relative stability returned to the republic, enabling Moscow to declare victory (not for the first time) in April 2009. However, the rest of the northern Caucasus remains highly unstable and as terrorist attacks on Russia continue, fears remain that war could return to Chechnya itself.

When Moscow fought to defend its territorial integrity in Chechnya, there was criticism in the West for its methods but general sympathy with its war aims. There was less sympathy when Russia used military force against the sovereign state of Georgia in August 2008. Against a background of escalating tension between Moscow and Tbilisi, war broke out over the autonomous republic of South Ossetia which, like Chechnya, sought independence. On this occasion, however, the republic wanted secession from Georgia and was acting with Russian support. Tbilisi initiated the assault on Tskhinvali, the capital of South Ossetia, on the night of 7–8 August, ostensibly to reintegrate it into Georgia. A military response from Moscow was widely perceived to be legitimate but, in the words of an independent report, it went 'far beyond the limits of defence' (IIFFMCG, 2009, p. 24). For Russian troops not only drove Georgian forces out of South Ossetia, but also took over strategic points in Georgia itself and threatened to march on Tbilisi

and overthrow the pro-Western leader, Mikheil Saakashvili. EU diplomacy prevented this and Russian troops later withdrew, but many commentators in the West perceived Moscow's military intervention as a challenge to the prevailing security order in Europe. According to this view, Russia had acted, not to defend South Ossetians, as Moscow suggested, but to protect its economic interests in the Caucasus and to curtail the West's growing influence in the region. Russia was accused of seeking to build a new iron curtain in Europe and to carve out its own sphere of influence on former Soviet territory (Asmus 2010). While some in Europe, most notably France and Germany, acknowledged that the Saakashvili administration had acted irresponsibly in attacking Tskhinvali, critics in the West felt that Moscow's disproportionate response in Georgia was symptomatic of an increasingly aggressive Russian foreign policy which coincided with Russia's drift towards authoritarianism under Putin's presidency.

Russia's more assertive foreign policy has not only revealed itself in military terms, but Moscow has also shown itself willing to use its dominance of the European energy market as a political bargaining chip. It has suspended or threatened to suspend supplies to Georgia, Ukraine and Belarus, all of which are transit states for oil and gas to the rest of Europe. Such a policy may be counter-productive in the longer term since it only increases suspicion of Moscow and encourages states to diversify sources of supply and increase efforts to develop alternative forms of energy. This recognition might have played a part in recent improvements in rela-

Key Figure 10.1

Vladimir Vladimirovich Putin (1952–)

Vladimir Putin was a late child, born to elderly parents, a family of workers, on 7 October 1952 in the centre of Leningrad (now St Petersburg). In 1970 he entered the Law Faculty of Leningrad State University, while at the same time continuing to become a master at sambo and karate. On graduating in 1975 he entered the KGB (Committee for State Security), and in 1985 he was posted to Dresden. There in 1989 he saw communism collapse, an event that marked his political personality. Back in Russia, he joined the office of the liberal mayor of what had become St Petersburg, Anatoly Sobchak, and quickly rose to become first deputy mayor of the city. Soon after Sobchak's defeat in the 1996 elections, Putin moved to Moscow and began a rapid advancement in the Presidential Administration in the Kremlin under President Boris Yeltsin, and became prime minister in August 1999. On Yeltsin's resignation on 31 December 1999, Putin became acting president, was elected to the post in March 2000, and was subsequently re-elected for a second four-year term in 2004. His presidency was characterized by 'stabilization', but this was accompanied by restrictions on the riotous pluralism of the 1990s. In 2008 he gave up office, as stipulated by the 1993 constitution, but returned to the premiership, where he became part of the 'tandem' with his nominated successor, President Dmitry Medvedev. In 2012 he returned to the presidency for a third term.

tions with the West. Barack Obama has talked of the need to 're-set relations', and President Medvedev has shown signs of wishing to reciprocate. As a first sign of a thaw, the two sides signed a follow-up to the Strategic Arms Reduction Treaty (START), the treaty on long-range nuclear weapons, in 2010. Europe, for its part, remains more divided over its relationship with Moscow, but a form of economic interdependence has evolved which tends to encourage dialogue rather than isolation.

The wars in Yugoslavia

The wars in the former Yugoslavia provided Europe with its first major security problem in the post-Cold War era. As the Yugoslav state broke up in 1991, there were a series of secessionist wars with Belgrade. They started in Slovenia and Croatia but extended to Bosnia in 1992. The war in Bosnia was the most brutal, where religious differences appeared to add to the intensity of the conflict. Pictures in the media of ethnic cleansing and concentration camps seemed more reminiscent of the Second World War rather than the liberals' New World Order. The EU was wholly unprepared to

either prevent or manage the war in Bosnia. It was divided over policy and lacked the military capability or political will to intervene effectively. The UN, for its part, deployed peacekeepers on the battlefield to monitor the conflict and provide humanitarian aid, but it too was unable to mediate any peace settlement. In fact, it was only when the USA intervened and the North Atlantic Treaty Organization (NATO) acted more robustly that the war in Bosnia was finally brought to a conclusion in 1995. In the Dayton peace agreement, Bosnia gained its independence, but it was effectively partitioned on an ethnic basis, with the Serbs in possession of half the country with the Muslims and Croats sharing the remainder.

However, the West was unable to prevent war returning to the Balkans in 1999 when Kosovo took its turn to seek secession from Serbia. The West had learnt some of the lessons of Bosnia, however, and was quicker to respond to Serb attacks on the Kosovar Albanians. When the Serb leader, Slobodan Miloševi , refused to withdraw his forces from Kosovo, NATO carried out its threat and from March 1999 launched a bombing campaign against Serb positions. A peace settlement was finally agreed with Belgrade in June after 78 days of

BOX 10.2
The Washington Treaty of NATO: Article 5

'The Parties agree that an armed attack against one or more of them in Europe or North America shall be considered an attack against them all, and consequently they agree that, if such an armed attack occurs, each of them, in exercise of the right of individual or collective self-defence recognized in Article 51 of the Charter of the United Nations, will assist the Party or Parties so attacked by taking forthwith, individually, and in concert with the other Parties, such action as it deems necessary, including the use of armed force, to restore and maintain the security of the North Atlantic area.'
NATO Handbook, NATO Information Service, Brussels, 1989, p. 14.

---

bombing, which led to Serb troop withdrawal from Kosovo and the return of refugees to their homes. Miloševi was subsequently removed from office in a popular uprising in October 2000 after he tried to rig election results in his favour, and he was then turned over to an international war crimes tribunal in The Hague. Miloševi died in his cell in March 2006 before a final judgement was passed, but the West saw its intervention in Kosovo as a success, especially in comparison to the delayed and muddled reaction to the earlier crisis in Bosnia. The trial of Miloševi also seemed to imply that the West's commitment to liberal principles, including international law, human rights and collective security, had not been completely forgotten in the secessionist wars of Yugoslavia.

International terrorism

International terrorism was not new, but it moved to the top of the political agenda after al-Qaeda's attack on New York and Washington on 11 September 2001. Almost 3000 people lost their lives, making it the most devastating terrorist atrocity in history. It was an attack aimed at America, but the targets - the World Trade Center and the Pentagon – also symbolized an attack on the West as a whole. European leaders were quick to condemn the attack and publicly support the USA. Prime Minister Tony Blair declared that Britain would 'stand shoulder to shoulder with America' in its moment of need (Blair, 2001, p. 2). For the first time in its history, NATO invoked Article 5 of its Washington Treaty to declare the attack on the USA an act of war and, in so doing, pledged a collective commitment to use force in defence of one of its member states (see Box 10.2).

However, President Bush initially chose not to act through NATO. Instead, the USA led a so-called 'coalition of the willing' in a war in Afghanistan against al-Qaeda and the Taliban government. There was widespread support for Washington when the war began on 7 October 2001, but some strains emerged in the US–EU relationship as concerns over collateral damage rose. These soon subsided, however, when the war came to an apparently speedy end. The Taliban was overthrown on 7 November and Mullah Omar's stronghold in Kandahar was overrun in the following month. Neither Osama bin Laden nor the Mullah were captured, but al-Qaeda's headquarters and terrorist training camps in Afghanistan were destroyed and many al-Qaeda operatives captured. A new pro-Western government was put in place in Kabul by December 2001 and there were hopes that the war in Afghanistan had been won.

Victory allowed President Bush to extend his war on terror to Iraq. This war, however, was far more controversial both amongst the public and political leaders in Europe. There were doubts over Saddam Hussein's connection with al-Qaeda and fears over the possible long-term consequences of military intervention. Formally, Bush went to war against Iraq in 2003 because Saddam had continued to defy the UN since the first Gulf War in 1991 – especially in relation to his retention of weapons of mass destruction (WMD) – and remained a destabilizing force in the region. Bush and his allies, however, were unable to convince the UN of the need for military intervention, a case that was further weakened after the war when it was discovered that Iraq had no WMD after all. The allies were also unprepared for the long and difficult task of replacing Saddam's brutal dictatorship with a functioning alternative. As a result, Iraq was plagued by anarchy and spiralling levels of terrorism which reached a peak in 2004 and 2005. The situation stabilized somewhat after Bush backed a military surge in 2007, but America's final withdrawal seemed far off even though Barack Obama announced that it would start in 2011.

Critics have argued that the USA adopted the wrong policy in the war on terror with an over-emphasis on the military (Rogers, 2008). The wars in Afghanistan and Iraq have alienated much Muslim opinion, while the revelations about Guantánamo Bay, Abu Ghraib and extraordinary rendition have undermined the West's claim to the moral high ground. A growing number of commentators, however, have started to argue that al-Qaeda's position is weakening in the world (Cronin, 2009). A war against terrorism might never end in a conclusive way like more conventional conflicts, but opinion polls in Muslim countries and the decline in attacks on Western targets suggest that the balance of power, at least, might have shifted (see Table 10.2).

Non-traditional security threats

Climate change

Although there are many potential non-traditional security threats, as stated earlier, we will concentrate on two interconnected issues – climate change and energy security – which are currently the most important facing Europe. Climate change, in particular, is an issue which has risen to the top of the political agenda in Europe. Although there are some dissidents, scientists are generally agreed that human activity has been instrumental in producing changes in the climate which potentially threaten our way of life on the planet. According to their research, global warming will result in rising sea levels, melting glaciers, increased desertification, and the extinction of many species. Hundreds of

Table 10.2   Confidence in Osama Bin Laden, May–June 2009 (%)

	No confidence	Confidence
Jordan	61	28
Egypt	68	23
Pakistan	47	18
Turkey	77	3
Lebanon	98	2

Source: Pew Global Attitudes Project, http://pewglobal.org/2010/02/04/mixed-views-of-hamas-and-hezbollah-in-largely-muslim-nations, accessed 13 May 2010.

millions of people will face food shortages, flooding and reduced access to drinking water. The main reason for climate change has been identified as the increasing concentration of greenhouse gases in the atmosphere, notably by the burning of fossil fuels. The average temperature of the earth has risen by 0.7 degrees centigrade since 1900 and is expected to rise between 1.1 and 6.4 degrees centigrade by the end of the century (IIPCC, 2007, p 13). The scientists argue that any rise over 2 degrees centigrade is potentially catastrophic.

Climate change clearly poses a major challenge to the international community. It is the kind of challenge that cannot be tackled effectively by individual states on their own. Climate change is a global phenomenon which requires cooperation among states at both the international and regional level. Although political leaders were slow to grasp the implications of climate change, this has changed in recent times. A number of international treaties have been agreed, including the Kyoto treaty of 1998, which committed the signatories to reduce or limit their greenhouse gas emissions by various amounts dependent on existing emissions, level of economic development and their ability to act. Some progress has been made to reduce emissions globally, although some of the biggest polluters, such as the USA and China, have sometimes been reluctant to sign binding treaties which could adversely affect their economies.

The EU, on the other hand, has been a leader in the green movement. The EU is a major producer of greenhouse gases, but it signed up at Kyoto to reduce the levels of greenhouse gas emissions by an average of 8 per cent – the highest amongst the signatories. However, in an unprecedented move, the EU agreed in December 2008 that the danger of climate change was so great that it would go further and unilaterally set itself targets to reduce greenhouse gases by at least 20 per cent from 1990 levels by 2020. It also agreed to raise renewable energy's share of the market to 20 per cent and cut overall energy consumption by 20 per cent. The EU continues to believe that international action is the most effective means of halting climate change, but favoured a policy of 'leadership by example', in the hope of encouraging other states to take similar action. The EU also introduced the world's first emissions trading system (ETS) in 2005. Under the system, limits on the amount of carbon dioxide emitted by certain energy intensive industries are set by the EU. Companies can only exceed their quota if they buy permits from others which have not been so profligate. The idea is to reward companies which successfully reduce their emissions and penalize those which do not achieve their targets.

The EU has used its considerable soft power to promote the need to address the issue of climate change. One problem is that although all countries are affected, not all are affected equally. Some countries within Europe, such as the low-lying Netherlands, are more vulnerable to the consequences of climate change than others, but in general, the poorest countries are at greatest risk. On occasion, this has made agreement, and more importantly implementation, more difficult. Politics is also notoriously short-term in its thinking. Yet a growing number of countries have come to accept the need for the world to confront the issue of climate change and the EU has played a significant role in this shift in attitude.

Energy security

The EU is a major consumer of energy and it has become increasingly concerned in recent years over a number of issues, including the possibility of supplies running out, rising prices and its heavy dependence on imports. According to official reports, over 50 per cent of the EU's energy is imported, and this figure is predicted to rise over the coming years (EU, 2010). This is particularly problematic because of the concentration of oil and gas reserves in a limited number of places – Russia, the Middle East and parts of Africa – all of which are viewed as politically volatile, increasing concerns over regular supply. The EU has adopted a number of strategies to try and deal with such problems. First, the EU has sought to diversify the number of sources of supply. To this end, the EU has helped fund exploration, extraction and the distribution of energy in countries which do not dominate the energy market. As part of this process, a gas pipeline was built from Baku on the Caspian Sea to Turkey, which circumvented Russian territory. The EU, however, has not always been consistent in its policy, for another major project is under way which will take gas across the Baltic Sea directly from Russia to Germany and bypass the transit states.

A second strategy is to diversify the forms of energy used. Thus the EU is emphasizing the need to move towards more sustainable forms of energy, such as sun, wind and wave power. More controversially, some countries rely on nuclear power as a clean alternative to oil and coal. France already generates over 40 per cent of its energy this way, but the public in Germany remains strongly opposed to nuclear power, largely on the grounds of safety. Natural gas is another source of energy which is increasingly being used as a greener way of generating electricity. However, this only increases the problem of the EU's overdependence on Russian energy, for Russia possesses almost 50 per cent of known natural gas reserves. Although the EU recognizes the benefits in all sorts of ways of adopting a common policy on energy – not least in terms of dealing with suppliers, like Russia, and keeping down costs – the differences over each country's dependence on coal, oil, gas, nuclear and green energy has made this difficult to achieve.

Security architecture in Europe

This section will consider the structures that have been put in place to deal with the security challenges of the post-Cold War period. Most attention will be paid to the regional organizations, especially NATO and the EU, but it should be noted here that the nation-state remains the most important actor in defence policy. However, even the bigger

European states, like Britain, France and Germany, recognize that they can only protect themselves in alliance with others. Most also recognize that this means a continuing role for the USA. As Bosnia and Kosovo showed, without the USA, the Europeans are unable to mount anything other than a fairly low-level military operation. Today, only the USA can think in terms of unilateral military action. It is the sole remaining superpower in the world and spends almost double the combined defence budget of the EU. It can also boast a substantial advantage in all the most important areas of modern warfare - most notably, precision weaponry, intelligence, communications and logistics. Washington, therefore, has less need of international organizations and alliances than the Europeans. So, when America joins any international organization, it is very reluctant to be constrained by it. This unilateralist trait was more apparent than ever under the leadership of President George W. Bush, although it may wane to some extent under Barack Obama (Peterson and Pollack, 2003, p. 9). Many Europeans are uncomfortable with US dominance, but there is no doubt that European security would be severely undermined if America pulled out of NATO and ended its long-standing commitment to Europe. As far as traditional security matters are concerned, the USA remains central. In large part, it was this understanding that led Tony Blair to support President Bush in the war on Iraq in 2003.

North Atlantic Treaty Organization (NATO)

The main regional organization dealing with traditional security matters in Europe is NATO. It was formed by the Washington Treaty in April 1949, and its main purpose during the Cold War was to contain the Soviet Union and deter any Soviet attack on Western Europe. Its credibility relied on the commitment in Article 5 to collective defence and the membership of the USA as a counterbalance to the growing military power of the USSR. However, when the Cold War came to end, inevitably NATO's future was hotly debated. After the collapse of the Soviet Union and the dissolution of the Warsaw Pact, what was the purpose of NATO?

In fact, NATO survived and, if anything, its position was strengthened in the immediate post-Cold War period. Spain joined its integrated military command, France rejoined the Military Committee, and the transatlantic alliance began to enlarge its membership to include former Soviet-bloc countries (see Table 3.1). Why, then, has NATO prospered? First, as indicated earlier in the chapter, it soon became apparent that all security issues had not disappeared along with the Cold War. As a result, there was still room for a multinational military alliance like NATO with an integrated military command, which could offer its members the security of collective defence. This was a particular attraction to East European countries, which continued to fear expansionist tendencies in Russia. Second, Europe recognized that it still needed the USA to contribute to its security, and the best way to ensure a continued American commitment was through NATO. Finally, NATO could continue to serve a stabilizing function. Through its integrated military command, it could prevent the renationalization of the military in the different states of Europe and the possibility, as outlined by John Mearsheimer (1990), of new power blocs forming.

Even though NATO won the argument for its continued existence, it had to change radically to meet the new challenges of the post-Cold War world. This required smaller, more flexible and more mobile forces to deal with the less predictable security concerns of the modern era. Another key debate revolved around 'out-of-area' operations. It has become ever clearer since the end of the Cold War that the primary security threats to both Europe and the USA no longer lie only on the continent of Europe. International terrorism stems from instability in the Middle East, the Caucasus and Asia. Washington is keen for NATO to project its power into these areas to fight terrorism, while some European member states are more cautious. NATO agreed at the Istanbul Summit in June 2004 to increase its deployment of peacekeepers in Afghanistan, but Chirac resisted the plan for NATO to become involved in peacekeeping operations in Iraq. Chirac's position underlined continuing divisions within the transatlantic alliance which have long frustrated Washington. *The Wall Street Journal* epitomized this frustration in its editorial of 28

BOX 10.3

The Common Foreign and Security Policy (CFSP)

The CFSP was created with the entry into force of the Treaty on the European Union (at Maastricht) in 1993. Article 11 of Title V sets outs its five main principles:

- to safeguard the common values and fundamental interests of the Union

- to strengthen the security of the Union
- to preserve peace and strengthen international security
- to promote international co-operation
- to develop democracy and rule of law, including human rights.

June 2004 by casting doubt on the value of NATO to the USA and suggested that the American taxpayer may no longer be willing to foot the bill for European security if the Europeans continue to behave in this uncooperative way.

The other major debate revolved around the issue of enlargement. NATO favoured expanding its membership because it not only offered security to former communist states but also helped to reintegrate those countries into the community of Western states. Enlargement was permitted according to Article 10 of the Washington Treaty and a number of states, including Germany, Turkey and Spain, had joined long after NATO was founded in 1949. If former communist states wanted to join the alliance, it was difficult to see how that could be ruled out, at least in principle. However, NATO did lay down conditions – the new members should be democratic; they should allow transparency and civilian control over their military; they should have no outstanding border or ethnic disputes with their neighbours; and they should be in a position to contribute militarily to the Atlantic Alliance. At the Madrid summit in 1997, it was decided that Hungary, the Czech Republic and Poland had satisfied these conditions and were invited to become members of NATO on its fiftieth anniversary in 1999. By April 2009, NATO membership had increased from the original 12 countries to 28, with Albania and Croatia the latest to join.

Although enlargement was perceived by many to be part of the project for democracy promotion, there were some dissenting voices. For example, the distinguished academic and diplomat, George

Kennan, described NATO enlargement as a 'fateful blunder' (*International Herald Tribune*, 6 February 1997, p. 8). There were a number of reasons for his concern. First, many believed that enlargement was unnecessary. It was generally agreed that the threats to Central and Eastern Europe had disappeared or been greatly reduced when the Soviet Union collapsed and the Warsaw Pact was abolished. Why then the need to offer membership to these countries and the guarantee of Article 5? Second, what would happen to those states excluded from membership? Was there a danger of creating new divisions in Europe as those left outside NATO sought new alliances to ensure their own security? Third, there was a fear that enlargement could weaken NATO, which operates on the basis of consensus. Consensus in an enlarged NATO would be more difficult to achieve and, as a result, NATO might be less able to act decisively in times of crisis.

However, the biggest concern related to Moscow, which has always opposed enlargement. Yeltsin feared it would lead to Moscow's exclusion from discussion on important security matters in Europe. Such concerns were partly overcome through the signing of the Founding Act in May 1997 between Moscow and NATO which established the Russia–NATO Permanent Joint Council (PJC). In the words of President Clinton, this body would give Moscow a voice in NATO but, in recognition of particular concerns in Eastern Europe, not the right of veto. However, the limits of the consultation process in NATO were revealed by the war in Kosovo, when Moscow felt its views had been ignored. As a result, Moscow withdrew from

BOX 10.4
High Representative of Foreign and Security Policy

The post was set up by the Amsterdam Treaty in 1997. Javier Solana was the first holder of the position, which he held for ten years from 1999. Its duties were expanded by the Lisbon Treaty in 2007, and the High Representative now sits in the European Commission and chairs meetings of Council of EU foreign ministers. The current holder of the position is Catherine Ashton from Britain.

the PJC, only returning after Putin became Russian President in 2000. At the Rome Summit in May 2002, further attempts were made to heal the rift. Amongst declarations of partnership and friendship, the PJC was abolished and replaced by the NATO–Russia Council (NRC), which allowed for broader and deeper discussion of general security issues at the level of ambassadors, foreign and defence ministers and, when necessary, between heads of state. The limitations of the NRC, however, were revealed when it was not consulted prior to Russia's war with Georgia in August 2008, and meetings of the NRC were suspended by the West until December in protest over Russia's actions.

It appeared that Moscow had accepted the principle of NATO enlargement by 2000, but this was mistaken. Increasingly, Putin argued that NATO was a potential threat to Russia. It had ceased to be just a collective defence organization for Europe, as was revealed in the war over Kosovo when NATO went to war despite no member country being threatened, and was continuing to expand its area of operations. It was acting increasingly out-of-area too, while NATO was perceived to be a Trojan horse for the pursuit of American interests at a time when Putin increasingly believed that Russian and American interests had diverged. When Bush promoted the idea of NATO membership for Ukraine and Georgia at the Bucharest summit in April 2008, Putin spoke out against it in the strongest terms. Many believe that Russia acted so forcefully in Georgia later that summer to prevent it joining NATO and becoming fully integrated into the West. NATO sees enlargement as a means of stabilizing countries and ensuring borders are secure; Moscow perceives it as an attempt by the USA to encircle Russia and undermine its influence in areas of perceived vital interest.

The European Union (EU)

The governments of the EU have long recognized the virtue of a Common Foreign and Security Policy (CFSP). Yet, progress has been extremely slow and it has proved difficult to reach agreement amongst the different governments within the union. As a result, foreign and security policy has remained largely outside the formal institutions of the EU. However, a series of events, including the end of the Cold War, Europe's inadequate response to the conflicts in the former Yugoslavia and the emergence of international terrorism, made some progress on the issue imperative. Finally, the 1992 Maastricht Treaty established the CFSP, which was reinforced and extended by the Amsterdam Treaty of 1997 (se Box 10.3). It was also at Amsterdam that it was also agreed to create the post of High Representative of Foreign and Security Policy which was intended to improve the coherence and credibility of the CFSP (see Box 10.4).

The EU has no standing army, but it has built up a limited capacity under the auspices of the European Security and Defence Policy (ESDP). The two leading military powers in Europe, Britain and France, agreed at St Malo in 1998 that the EU should develop 'a capacity for autonomous action backed up by credible military forces, the means to decide to use them, and a readiness to do so, in order to respond to international crises' (*NATO Handbook*, 2001, ch. 4, p. 1). The EU was charged with being able to carry out the so-called

Petersberg tasks, which included humanitarian and rescue missions, as well as crisis management and peacekeeping. Since 2003, the EU has carried out a series of operations, including peacekeeping and police missions in the Balkans – the most demanding being the replacement of NATO forces in Bosnia in 2005. The EU has also deployed in the Congo in 2003 and on the border areas of Chad and the Central African Republic in 2008 to protect refugees displaced by the fighting in Darfur. The EU was also involved in a three-year police mission in Afghanistan from 2007 and played the leading role in mediating a settlement to the war in Georgia in August 2008, where it provided observers to monitor the peace and helped organize humanitarian aid. It is clear, therefore, that the EU is slowly becoming more of a military actor on the international stage. Yet, it is not in a position to supplant NATO as a security organization. Even to carry out the Petersberg tasks, the EU is reliant on US assets. There is also the problem of a lack of leadership, which Washington provides in NATO. The Iraq War revealed once more how deep the divisions in Europe can be on some major issues. These divisions have made progress in the field of foreign and security policy particularly difficult, and it remains one area where essential authority remains with EU governments.

Although individual states take the lead in the war on terrorism, the EU has attempted to act more decisively in this area. Crucially, the EU has sought to enable cooperation amongst states and to coordinate the war on terrorism. Thus, after the Madrid bombings, the EU agreed to the Hague Programme in November 2004. It included sharing intelligence and improved police and judicial cooperation across borders. The EU also sought to restrict the financing of terrorist organizations and introduced a European Arrest Warrant in 2005 to speed up extradition. The EU has also emphasized the need to deal not only with the threat of terrorism, but also its causes. As a result, the EU has argued for the need to tackle poverty and promote good governance in countries which have become centres for radicalism.

It is in these areas of so-called soft security that the EU is particularly well placed to make a difference. It has enlarged its membership to promote democracy and enhance security across Europe, but

this has been far less controversial than in the case of NATO. The EU is not primarily a military organization and, crucially, the USA is not a member. Furthermore, as mentioned earlier, the EU has been more successful in promoting non-traditional security issues, most notably, climate change, the environment and energy.

Pan-European organizations

The Organization for Security and Co-operation in Europe (OSCE). The OSCE is less well known than either NATO or the EU, but it has played an important if less visible role in European security. The original Conference on Security and Co-operation in Europe (CSCE) was set up by the 1975 Helsinki Final Act. The CSCE was unique for the Cold War period because it was a genuinely pan-European institution which also included the USA and Canada as members due to their membership of NATO. The original act covered a number of issues, including security, trade and human rights. The CSCE itself was tasked to monitor the implementation of the act and extend it where possible.

In the immediate aftermath of the Cold War, Moscow wanted the CSCE to replace NATO and the Warsaw Pact and to become the main security organization in Europe. It was not tainted by the ideological divisions of the Cold War and had the advantage of having all European states as members. The CSCE was institutionalized in 1994 and became the OSCE, but it never took up the role Moscow had wanted, for a number of reasons. First, there was a persistent suspicion of Russia which meant the former Soviet bloc countries, in particular, did not want to base their security on an institution which had Russia as a member. Second, its size (there were 56 members in all) and the fact that decisions were made on a consensus basis weakened its ability to act effectively. Third, there was little desire in the West to dismantle NATO and risk a reduced commitment from the USA to Europe's defence. This does not mean that the OSCE has no role to play in European security matters. As a genuinely pan-European body, it was viewed generally as an independent body, which meant it was particularly well suited for soft security issues, including mediating disputes, monitoring peace agreements

BOX 10.5
UN Security Council (UNSC)

There are 15 members on the UN Security Council, the top decision-making body. Five are permanent members and they have the right of veto on all decisions. They are: the USA, Russia, China, France and Britain. The other ten members are elected for two years. They have the right to vote, but not the right of veto.

and various democracy promotion measures such as observing elections.

The Medvedev proposal. As Russia's foreign policy shifted towards a more anti-Western posture under Putin, Moscow became more openly suspicious of the OSCE's claims to neutrality. Thus, Moscow insisted the OSCE withdraw from its monitoring role in Chechnya in 2003 and restricted its rights to observe the parliamentary election of December 2007 and the presidential election of 2008. As a result, President Medvedev put forward a proposal in November 2009 for a new security treaty for Europe (Russian Ministry of Foreign Affairs, 2009). In this proposal, the parties to the treaty would be roughly the same as those in the OSCE (although there was a suggestion of including China too), and the principles underpinning the treaty were those agreed in Helsinki in 1975 and the Charter for European Security in 1999. Thus, security of the parties in Medvedev's draft treaty, was based on respect for the sovereignty of states, international law and the non-use of force. In the case of a breach of these principles, a conference would be convened to consider the action to be taken. The conference would be considered quorate if two-thirds of the membership was present, decisions would be by consensus and would be binding on all members (Article 6). Like NATO's Article 5, the treaty stated that an attack on one member would be perceived to be the equivalent of an attack on all members. Such an attack, however, would not trigger an automatic military response, although it might be approved by the conference under Article 51 of the UN Charter on the right of self-defence (Article 7). The treaty makes it clear that the UN continues to bear primary responsibility for maintaining peace and

stability in Europe, which would effectively give Russia a further right of veto over any military actions, since it remains one of the five permanent members of the UN Security Council (see Box 10.5).

Medvedev was right to point out the deficiencies of the current security architecture in Europe. As he said in a speech in Berlin in 2008, there were real dangers in marginalizing and isolating countries like Russia and creating zones in Europe with differentiated levels of security (Medvedev, 2008a). Russia, may exaggerate its isolation at times, but French President, Nicolas Sarkozy, welcomed Medvedev's initiative as a sign of Russia's willingness to act more constructively in Europe. The majority of European leaders, however, remained sceptical. There was still no appetite for replacing existing security institutions, such as NATO, especially when the proposed security structures looked weaker than those already in place. There was also distrust of Moscow after the war in Georgia. Critics argued that Moscow had violated the key principles outlined in Medvedev's own proposal when Russia invaded Georgia in August 2008. The problem is that Russia is perceived by many – principally Soviet successor states and parts of Eastern Europe – as the main security threat in Europe today. There are, however, divisions over how the West should respond. While there is concern over allowing Russia to fully integrate into European institutions, the majority acknowledge it is potentially very destabilizing to leave such an increasingly powerful state out of key discussions on security matters.

Conclusion

The security threats today are more unpredictable and multifaceted than during the Cold War, and

European leaders recognize that individual nation-states alone can no longer protect their citizens. Europe still needs the alliance with America, but the majority of European leaders tend to have a more liberal view of security. They are less willing to use the military to resolve security challenges and are more willing to work through international organizations than the Americans. They are also more open to the idea of describing non-military threats as security issues. These differences have caused a certain amount of friction in transatlantic relations in recent times, although the election of Barack Obama as US President has given hope of greater agreement and co-operation across the Atlantic.

SUMMARY

- In the Cold War period, European security was mainly concerned with the containment of the Soviet Union. After the collapse of the USSR in 1991, however, this changed. The threat of nuclear war faded, but other security risks emerged.

- Europe faced security threats as a result of the transition process in post-communist states, like the former Soviet Union and Yugoslavia, but international terrorism was perceived to be the major new threat after September 11, 2001.

- The military still has a large role to play in maintaining stability in Europe, but non-military aspects of security are becoming more important, such as economic aid, the promotion of democracy and the closer integration of Europe.

- The US and NATO are still vital in preserving peace and security in Europe, but the EU and the OSCE have an important role to play in less traditional security matters.

QUESTIONS FOR DISCUSSION

- Did nuclear deterrence keep the peace in Europe during the Cold War?

- Is Russia a security threat in the post-Cold War world?

- Should we view climate change as a security issue?

- Why did Yugoslavia break up violently?

- How do you win a war on terror?

- Would you abolish NATO?

FURTHER READING

Asmus, Ronald D. (2010) *A Little War That Shook the World: Georgia, Russia and the Future of the West* (New York: Palgrave Macmillan).

Burke, J. (2004) *Al-Qaeda: The True Story of Radical Islam* (Harmondsworth: Penguin).

Buzan, Barry (1991) *People, States and Fear*, 2nd edn (Hemel Hempstead: Harvester Wheatsheaf).

Dalby, Simon (2009) *Security and Environmental Change* (Cambridge: Polity Press).

English, Richard (2009) *Terrorism: How to Respond* (Oxford: Oxford University Press).

Hughes, James (2007) *Chechnya: From Nationalism to Jihad* (Philadelphia: University of Pennsylvania Press).

Mankoff, Jeffrey (2009) *Russian Foreign Policy: The Return of Great Power Politics* (Lanham, MD: Rowman & Littlefield).

Park, William and Rees, G. Wyn (1998) *Rethinking Security in Post-Cold War Europe* (London and New York: Addison Wesley Longman).

Peterson, John and Pollack, Mark A. (2003) *Europe, America, Bush: Transatlantic Relations in the Twenty-First Century* (London: Routledge).

Rief, David (1994) *Slaughterhouse and the Failure of the West* (London: Vintage).

Williams, Paul (2008) *Security Studies: An Introduction* (Hoboken, NJ: Taylor & Francis).

The Cultural Dimension

JOHN COOMBES

> Je ne peins pas l'être; je peins le passage.
> (I do not show being. I show movement.)
>
> Montaigne, *Essais*

The problems of giving a comprehensive account of twentieth-century European **culture** are considerable: first, when we remember that twice as many books (in which, until recently, culture was principally lodged) were published in the 25 years after 1960, as in the whole previous recorded history of humanity; and secondly, when we reflect that culture is less satisfactorily defined as a series of isolated and conspicuous activities (concerts, exhibitions – though these definitely have their place) than, more widely, as the means by which humanity seeks to define itself and its relation to the world.

The scope of such an inquiry becomes even more daunting when we recognize that cultural history (if it is to be more than a mere series of facts and dates) always demands antecedents to its own starting point; and that its materials, in order to be explained, have to be placed in a context with which they may be contrasted. Much recent postmodernist thinking has attacked 'dualism' (the opposition of 'past' and 'present', 'fact' and 'fiction', 'subject' and 'object'). It has sought to replace it, and indeed notions of determination and contrast, with a kind of universal, random present without a history. Yet these contrasts, and their interaction, would seem to explain more about culture than a repeated statement of their absence. Such contrasts cannot, of course, be seen as consisting of *abstract* elements eternally ranged against each other, in some strange Tom and Jerry conflict of the world of ideas. They are better seen as forming a kind of web or network, each of whose components acts upon, and moves away from, its neighbours by turns.

Clearly no account of the cultural production of a whole century – let alone one as brief as this – can hope, so to speak, to unweave the web entirely and to lay bare all its constituents and their articulations. Rather, certain contrasting tendencies may be singled out, and their affinities, at various historical moments, with others, more or less overtly suggested. Three such contrasts – perhaps the most widely recognized of all – have already been instanced. Among others of specific relevance to the twentieth-century experience we might add:

realism/modernism
selfhood/collectivity
convention/subversion
aesthetics/politics

● **Culture**: The relationship between ideas, connections and institutions, reflection on the nature of which enables us to understand our relationship to the world.

denotation/connotation
structure/chance
rationality/**unconscious**
capital/labour
politics/mysticism.

The tendencies of any cultural product of the twentieth century can probably be charted along more than one of these lines – and with more profit to the understanding of it than if it were to be represented as an ideal form and located exclusively along, or at the extremity of, any one of them. We shall not attempt to cover all areas of cultural endeavour but will try to indicate the main themes through analysis of the media, education, architecture and cinema.

Romanticism and positivism

Such tendencies – whether perceived *within* the cultural item or activity itself, or in its relation to the world which it inhabits – must be understood (unless we subscribe to an excessively simple notion of time and history as an eternal present) as, at any time, part of a complex process. What they are is to be understood as deriving from, and referring to (whether consciously or implicitly), the cultural moments which preceded them; and as in some sense meeting the cultural world which we, their interpreters, inhabit.

Here again, ways of connecting historical epochs are myriad. But when, in particular, we look back over the twentieth century as a whole, it is apparent that – turbulent and sanguinary though it has been – the period has not been, in the final analysis, a **revolutionary** one. In terms of the transformation of social relations and of ways of seeing, rather, we observe the global domination – in 2000 as in 1900 – of liberal capitalism. In

● **Denotation**: The act of marking or distinguishing something as separate or distinct.

● **Connotation**: The process of noting something together with something else, the implication of something besides itself.

● **Unconscious**: Simply, those operations of the mind of which we are not immediately aware. By extension, a reservoir of drives and motives which may run counter to, or threaten, the operations of the rational consciousness.

oblique and dependent relationship to this multi-faceted phenomenon – as 100 years ago – remain a variety of archaic and/or authoritarian regimes; more directly subordinate to it, now as then, are the countries of the developing world of the South.

The dominance of liberalism – and its engagement with a series of powerful threats to it throughout the century – is, then, the context within which the culture of our times must be viewed. By comparison, the transitions effected from 1789 to 1911 – from France to Mexico and China, and from *ancien régime* and still more archaic forms to, at least, proto-democratic liberalism – mark out the nineteenth century as, indeed, a revolutionary epoch. It is not, then, surprising that the cultural movements of world-historical significance to which, more than to any other, subsequent developments in European intellectual life can be related, are the intellectual trends which attained dominance between 1800 and 1850: *romanticism* and *positivism*.

For most people *romanticism* evokes, quite appropriately, sexual passion – but there is more to it than that. In contrast to the world of classical values which it opposed, and which was centred on fixed forms and 'rules', whether political, social or aesthetic, romanticism lays stress on the authenticity and variability of personal experience – and indeed of the self both as a focus for human experience and in its changing relation to nature and to society. Rather than the human being seen as the measure of all things, as in the world of the classics, romanticism lays continual stress upon otherness, upon the questionability of apparently fixed forms of existence (it is in this sense that Marx and Engels may be seen as Romantic thinkers as much as political economists). This is especially apparent in the mode, much used by Romantic writers and their successors, known as 'Romantic irony', whereby the text avows its own artificiality and questionability. The Romantic interrogation of the relationship of consciousness and the world (articulated in German idealist philosophy, notably by Hegel)

● **Revolutionary**: In its strictly political sense, whatever furthers the transfer of power and wealth in society from one class to another; in artistic and cultural affairs, by analogy, whatever transforms the established patterns of aesthetic production and their recognition or consumption.

Key Figure 11.1

Pablo Ruiz Picasso (1881–1973)

By perhaps the most prolific and versatile artist in history and certainly in the twentieth century, Picasso's work suggests from the outset a critical fusion of various painterly elements. If the works of the early Blue Period seem mawkish, this is perhaps because their debt to Gauguin and Toulouse-Lautrec is still offset by that of El Greco and a Christian ideology with which their author had nothing directly to do. The slightly later Rose Period bears the imprint of Picasso's writer friends in Paris, Max Jacob and Guillaume Apollinaire – both concerned with manipulating words and typography to new, disruptive effect, and Gertrude Stein, whose modernist prose is considerably more impenetrable than even Picasso's most innovatory forms. His great early cubist work *Les Demoiselles d'Avignon* (1907) continued fragmentations of planes and surfaces with a representation of the whores portrayed as sordid, appealing and vulnerable in their necessarily fragmented lives. Picasso's cubist painting – whether mono- or polychromatic – tends subsequently to increasingly radical fragmentation. Its effects are often heightened by the use of collage; related effects are achieved in experiments with sculpture, and with other 3-dimensional constructions which look forward to 1960s pop art. In the early 1930s Picasso's cubism goes through a particularly erotic phase (his women, however weird to some, are always lively and sexy in appearance). The Spanish Civil War ensured that joy in painting gave way to the grim panorama, combining dislocated elements of cubism and allegorical realism, of Picasso's most famous painting, *Guernica* (1937). The same intensity is caught in the smaller anti-American painting of the Korean War, *Massacre en Corée* (1951). Much of the production of Picasso's last years consists of reworkings of paintings by the great artists of the past, from Velázquez to Monet – not as imitations or embellishment but as a continuing dialogue.

provides the basis for *phenomenological* thinking, whether in Wordsworth's poetry or in Marx's interrogation of the social order.

This latter suggests an alternative to both idealistic and positivistic modes of thought, which propose, respectively, that it is the mind which constructs the world or that it is the world which determines the mind. Phenomenology opposes to these the proposition that mind and world, as interdependent elements, determine each other; it is thus closely related to *dialectics* (the investigation of forces in their conflict and possible resolution). It will be apparent that the effects of these conceptual derivatives of romanticism were potentially (and have been effectively) tremendously far-reaching, putting into question, as they do, fixed and traditional notions of personality and collectivity; text and reader; self and world.

Resonances of Romantic questioning are, as we shall see, to be perceived throughout the twentieth century. They are most generally apparent in revolutionary crises, from St Petersburg to Barcelona,

and from Mexico City to Shanghai. In every area of artistic practice, **modernism** – seeking as it does, whether in architecture or in drama, to display self-consciously both its contemporary nature and its situation within continuing history – has expanded the practices of Romantic irony. Movements such as *cubism*, *Dada*, **futurism** and **surrealism** have worked on the notion of the work of art (and by implication that of our conscious-

---

● **Modernism**: An aesthetic tendency which contrasts with realism (q.v.) in that, rather than an art work purporting to show an aspect of the world external to it, it draws attention to the devices by which it attains to that world.

● **Futurism**: An Italian aesthetic movement which rejected values of reason and progress in favour of the veneration of speed, violence and war; one of the early constituents of fascism.

● **Surrealism**: An aesthetic movement which originated in France after the First World War; it was/is principally concerned with the dual (sur-real) possibilities of perceptions in life and art, and with the exploration of the unconscious (q.v.) in the form of automatic writing.

Key Figure 11.2

Jean-Paul Sartre (1905–80)

Philosopher, novelist and playwright, Jean-Paul Sartre is arguably the most prominent figure in twentieth-century French intellectual life. He first achieved recognition with *La Nausée* (1938), a novel whose central focus was the question of contingency (the apparent formlessness and lack of necessity of the world), which had been a preoccupation for him since the mid-1920s. The 1940s were a particularly productive period for Sartre, his brand of existentialism being elaborated both in his seminal philosophical work *L'Être et le néant* (1943), his novel cycle *Les Chemins de la liberté* (1945–9), his plays, notably *Les Mouches* (1943), *Huis clos* (1945), and *Les Mains sales* (1948), and through the controversial journal *Les Temps Modernes* (1945–   ), which he inaugurated and edited. Sartre's existentialism of the 1940s, which came to characterize French existentialism in general, stressed individual choice and responsibility based ontologically on an affirmation of human freedom (at the level of the analysis and evaluation of being). Although a declared socialist by the 1940s, Sartre's emphasis on subjectivity brought him into conflict with his Marxist contemporaries and, following an abortive attempt to initiate a left-wing group in 1948, Sartre spent much of the next decade in an awkward position politically, at times close to communism whilst strongly critical at others. *La Critique de la raison dialectique* (1960), in which he sought to reconcile the concerns of subjectivity with a Marxist analysis of history and society, did much to dispel the tension between his philosophy and his politics. His last major work, *L'Idiot de la famille* (1971–2), was never completed; a study of the novelist Flaubert, it brings together many of his major concerns. His last years were mainly taken up with radically anti-authoritarian political activism.

---

ness itself) as fragmented and diverse rather than as fixed and unitary (see Key Figure 11.1). The philosophy of *existentialism* continues romanticism's rejection of pre-cast forms in its insistence on man's responsibility to make sense of the world through the exercise of conscious choice, rather than through dependence on any more reassuring notion of intellectual tradition or inheritance (see Key Figure 11.2). Even such widely divergent intellectual phenomena as *socialist realism* and *absurdism* show signs of a common Romantic ancestry; the former in its optimism as to the capacities of mankind to overcome its past; the latter in its notation of human experience as a performance generating – from moment to moment – its own meaning.

The contours of *positivism*, by contrast, are possibly easier to delineate. Its authority – even, its notoriety – derives in the main from two nineteenth-century thinkers, Auguste Comte in France, and Herbert Spencer in England. Whilst romanticism cannot be imagined apart from a context of

revolutionary change in Europe, positivism represents the consecration of the newly established bourgeois order: it is, accordingly, as much a plan for the implications of philosophy as a network of philosophical concepts in themselves. The implications of positivism are – in distinction from the linguistic, formal and often political libertarianism of the Romantics – in many respects authoritarian; Comte's political and social thinking was hierarchical, and notably placed thinkers at the apex of the hierarchy. Further conceptual elements confirm this underlying tendency: the positivistic preoccupation with the cult of the fact (*le culte du fait*) with its tendency to limit the possibilities of human action to conformity to what is, rather than to a search for change; an epistemology, similarly, which asserts the determination of the mind, unilaterally, by the world, and likewise limits the possibility of the transformation of either; an unimaginative and arbitrary division of knowledge into the 'known' and the 'unknowable' (*l'inconnaissable*) which similarly forecloses the limits of mental progress within the bounds of established utility; and an inordinate preoccupation with taxonomy – the ordering and classification of knowledge, by which those who have accumulated most may, in effect, transform its quantity into quality and secure their intellectual and social power.

Positivism's concern with regularity, order and classification of course predisposed it to absorption into the 'official' art of the twentieth century in many of its contexts and into forms of cultural production whose function was the legitimation and perpetuation of the status quo. At its most extreme this could lead back beyond romanticism to a reversion to classicism as a supposedly 'objective' aesthetic yardstick; the trend was most consistently imposed in architecture by the fascist regimes, and subsequently, half-heartedly sustained by Anglo-Saxon conservative practitioners working for regimes sympathetic to aesthetic and political repression. But positivism's stress on linearity and clarity meant that artistic discourses could emerge from positivism which were not constrained by a tedious conformity to authority. After all, nineteenth-century **naturalism** – as variously exemplified by the novelist Émile Zola, the dramatists Henrik Ibsen and (the earlier) August Strindberg, and the polymath George Bernard Shaw – often demonstrates the contradictory workings of positivism in practice; and the philosophy's connections with the extensive and varied world of pre-First World War social democracy (which comprised such diverse figures as Jean Jaurès, Karl Kautsky, Rosa Luxemburg and Lenin) generated a massively influential body of political, but also of politically committed, painting and fiction – notably in the *roman fleuve* (saga fiction) tradition, and somewhat later in the various manifestations of socialist realism throughout Europe. Our two major cultural tendencies in the modern world should not, then, be seen as confrontational opposites, nor as complementary forces; but rather as tendencies which, by turn, implicitly comment on, negate and confirm each other. The demands of both are so enormous that

● **Naturalism**: A late nineteenth-century aesthetic movement which combines minute depiction of the external world with a wide preoccupation with the operation of heredity and environment as understood by nineteenth-century science.

twentieth-century experience cannot possibly ignore them.

The media

Relatively speaking, the greatest rate of growth of all cultural forces in the twentieth century has been that of the electronic media, transmission and recording. Here it is easy to forget – in a world of satellites and internet – that the quantum leap in mass communication was the invention of 'broadcasting' radio itself, of which subsequent inventions are mainly, after all, only sophisticated developments: the social and political organization of radio thus merits particular attention.

First, however, some reference needs to be made to some of the social attitudes attendant upon the rapid technical advances of the twentieth century in general and their effects on culture. Opposition to them, it may be said, has tended to come in Europe from more or less marginalized groups – factions of the aristocracy, gentry and intelligentsia – for whom culture was their only capital and who, thus, felt disproportionately threatened by its wider dissemination. More rational fears concerning the dilution of artistic quality through its mass dissemination have largely proved unfounded; recorded music has neither, as was feared, killed off live music nor has it blighted the careers of practising musicians. Rather, throughout Europe and beyond, it has stimulated a widespread musical enthusiasm previously restricted to the geographically and financially privileged.

If there are indeed negative aspects to such cultural shifts, they are hardly new. The world-wide success in the 1990s of the three tenors – Carreras, Domingo, Pavarotti – was deplored by nostalgics for cultural privilege on account of its transmission to the masses of opera arias out of context; and (more perceptively) by those who suggested that the inflatory effect of the vast investment and huge fees involved would eventually put opera still further out of the reach of the masses. But it should be remembered that attentive reverence for singing within the opera house only dates from the age of Wagner (the 1860s); and that commercialization of single arias dates back to the invention of the gramophone record and its exploitation by Caruso (*c*.1900) – the first recording star to become a millionaire.

The dissemination of all these cultural activities involves, of course, a range of electronic media activities whose development has, throughout the twentieth century, increased, stimulated and been stimulated by their interpretation in ways unthinkable in the epoch of European classicism, but which have considerable affinities with the world of romanticism, especially with the Wagnerian mixed-media total work of art (*Gesamtkunstwerk*); and paradoxically (in form though obviously not in scale) with the carnivals of late medieval and early modern times. (Then the major ideology which dominated them was the Church; now it is the logic and function of the media themselves.)

The process of such cultural production has in the twentieth century become increasingly self-referential and self-parodic. A contemporary manifestation of a mixed-media show may well arouse admiration for including a computer-generated image of Donald Duck – a simulation, in effect, of a 1930s simulation drawn with little concern for verisimilitude – not for its precise resemblance to its model, but for the technical achievement involved in – after all – an aesthetic banality.

Radio was of course the first means of simultaneous communication to a mass audience. In 1922, when the BBC, the first regular radio service, began, the cinema – its only mechanized rival – could, owing to the high cost of film, only reach a small audience simultaneously. There was until relatively late in the century a lack of homogeneous cinema audiences even in small, densely populated countries such as Britain and Belgium; populations which radio (and later TV) were later to homogenize. Again, film distribution (even with films, later, existing in multiple copies) remained decentralized; in Britain until the 1960s and in much of the rest of Europe throughout the century, small, independently owned cinemas and chains of cinemas were the norm, and ensured a multiplicity of viewing choice.

In the last quarter of the twentieth century, however, power over cinematic distribution – and thus consumption – became especially concentrated in agglomerative chains of cinemas; uniformity of programmes ensued. Britain was especially vulnerable to this development, which had, as did many others, its origins in the USA – on account moreover of similarity of language, and thus, supposedly, of cultural identity.

The same tendencies – to homogenization resulting from capital agglomeration in the interests of large US or multinational concerns – are to be observed (especially but not solely in Great Britain) both in publishing and in the sale of books. In publishing, the 'gentleman' individual publisher has been replaced as decision-maker by the accountant; in distribution, guaranteed prices, profit-margins and choice have been cut, and turnover has increased, to the advantage of major capital and the disadvantage of independent ownership. The trend has continued in all areas of media sales, whether prices (with their effect on public access) have relatively increased (books, cinema entrance) or decreased (recorded music) in the latter part of the century.

The development of radio (and later TV) throughout the twentieth century has been more complex. Whilst the production and circulation of books, recorded music and other materials (CD-Roms etc.) has in general become increasingly dominated by unambiguous market considerations (the origins of all these products were, after all, commercial if in varying ways), radio has seen the intersection of three basic models of organization. These – the public-service, the commercial and the totalitarian – are not always as self-explanatory as this nomenclature may seem.

The major and innovatory example of public-service broadcasting, the BBC, initially gained its reputation from being the world's first public radio service. Afterwards to be partially imitated outside Europe in some of the countries of the British Empire/Commonwealth (especially Canada), and in the liberal democracies of Europe (notably being transplanted to the British zone of Germany after the Second World War), its ethos – imposed on the British Broadcasting *Company* (1922–6) by its first director-general, John Reith – was initially one of, largely, benevolent authoritarianism. This was manifest as an elitism through which the cultural monopoly of a **Fabian**, liberal and conservative upper middle-class oligarchy, preserved by the absence of competition, was imposed on the nation as a whole.

● **Fabian**: Fabianism was a tendency in British socialism dating from the 1880s, advocating the total but gradual transformation of society by administrative action under, largely, the control of the enlightened middle classes.

Many of the BBC's earlier practices now seem ludicrously archaic – with their instigator Reith a bizarre as much as a benevolent despot – and its overall political practices (for at least half a century) seem to have been over-submissive to established power. The value of the model, however – easy clichés about its generating a sense of 'national community' apart – has resided in its durability and, eventually, its ability to develop and provide a natural forum for political and cultural discussion more effectively than other systems (in so far as these have not themselves imitated its forms). Further, the BBC TV – especially since the 1960s – has managed to produce 'quality' programmes which are also highly saleable overseas. And its radio World Service – directly funded by the government, antique in presentational format, radically independent (more so than its internal services) in its coverage of world affairs, and universally respected – reflects the paradoxes of the BBC's origins and subsequent development.

The commercial model of radio developed rapidly throughout Europe in the later 1920s, and again in the years since 1945. More recently its practices have been, of course, taken up increasingly by cable, satellite and other forms of commercial television. In essence the antithesis of BBC broadcasting, it was from the outset populistic, imposing on its mass public a diet of what was then called 'light music' as remorseless as the BBC's uplifting material; designed, with its rapid alternation of recorded music and adverts, for brief and casual attention; and of course cheaply produced, being financed from fluctuating advertising revenues as against the public service's relatively massive income from licence fees. In the television era, commercial broadcasting seemed, in the third quarter of the twentieth century, and in those countries (Britain, Holland, Italy, West Germany) with a relatively strong public broadcasting tradition, to attempt to imitate it. Later technical developments – satellite and cable broadcasting and the consequent multiplication of channels – led to a proliferation of viewing modes. Many channels do little but recycle programmes from the major producers; others – just as cheaply – run perpetual talk shows. Most of these are no doubt harmless enough, and undoubtedly viewed by their audience at home with a humorous distance which may be associated with the late twentieth-century postmodern condition in general.

More sinister implications of what can easily become a disquieting manifestation of manipulative populism – indeed brainwashing, as was apparent in Italy in the 1990s when the massive broadcasting apparatus of Silvio Berlusconi undoubtedly led to the political success of his Forza Italia movement – are shown in an apparently unstructured anti-intellectualism, the harbinger of a return to a politics of the extreme Right. In the English-language popular press, preoccupation with right-wing politics and with profits has been more evenly balanced, if to some extent similar in effect.

Public broadcasting systems in continental Europe have in general withstood these pressures less adequately than the BBC (which it is not unduly Anglocentric to characterize, with all its faults, as the flagship of twentieth-century broadcasting). Contrasting the history of the RTF – subsequently ORTF – in Europe's other major traditionally liberal democracy, France, with that of the BBC is instructive here. Before the Second World War, French broadcasting, unlike British, was largely commercial – stations like Tour Eiffel broadcasting notably in English on Sunday to circumvent the sabbatarian gloom imposed on Britain by Reith's BBC. The war and the subsequent occupation of France (1940–4) convinced the politicians, both those of the Resistance in London and those of Vichy and the collaboration, of the importance of radio as a source of information and of propaganda. Accordingly the establishment of the RTF at the liberation was accompanied by that of a Minister of Information to control it; acceptance was general (amongst the political class at least) that the business of the RTF – apart from a genuine diversification of cultural activity modelled largely on the BBC – was to present the viewpoint of the government of the day.

This caused little concern so long as, under the Fourth Republic, the government changed fairly regularly every two or three months. With the 1960s however, two related phenomena became apparent: the advent of television with its greater possibilities of ideological impact; and the durability of the de Gaulle government, whose power to control the media – although the product of a previous dispensation – now gave it quasi-totalitarian potential. Freedom of the media from government control was a major demand of the workers' and students' movement of 1968; the subsequent relaxation of controls evolved until it coincided with the Socialist victory of 1981. For some years after this – until, in the late 1980s, its effectiveness was undermined by the dual process of partial denationalization and the development (as elsewhere) of satellite and cable networks – the televisual production of the (by now) ORTF was equal in quality to any other.

Political pressures such as these were, of course, minor, compared with those operated in the totalitarian countries, and especially in the most efficiently organized of them, Nazi Germany. Here, totalitarian intensity was compounded by the absence of TV (the country's subjects being absorbed into the visually spectacular by obligatory attendance at rallies instead of receiving their impact passively at home – the technical lack doubtless proving ideologically effective); and especially by the relentless unity of the electronic message – the 'people's receiver' (*Volksempfänger*), commonly known as the 'Goebbels gob' (*Goebbelsschnauze*) – its price subsidized, and only capable of receiving one programme.

The 'Goebbels gob' – produced by the million – stands as a powerful symbol of what fascism threatened: the destruction altogether of politics, culture and technology. It may be seen as a grotesque parody of the early ideology of broadcasting, with its hope of imposing a national community. The other extreme alternative to that mode – random consumption, postmodern fragmentation – hardly empowers its recipients. Rather than mindless aggression, it stimulates inertia. Other developments in the media highlight perennial arguments, less about culture itself than about its valuation (in so far as the two can be separated). Rapid advances in the recording and reproduction of music have vastly increased its availability and simultaneously reduced its significance. The increasing tendency of radio stations to play single movements of classical works again puts the listeners, effectively, back into the position of their predecessors at the eighteenth-century court, socially absorbing a few bars of Telemann or Vivaldi.

Finally, many of the developments which we have noted as achieved in the latter years of the twentieth century could hardly have come about without tremendous achievements in the field of cybernetics – after the revolution of steam around 1800 and that of electricity around 1880, the third great stage in the industrial revolution. Since the 1980s there has been talk of the 'revolutionary' impact of these developments for personal life, of 'empowerment' through their articulation with the individual subject through the internet. Yet whilst there is so far the sense that possibilities of communication have increased exponentially, it is not as yet clear how these processes have come to constitute a genuine popular force for recognisable change. As in other areas of the media – and indeed in most areas of cultural production – the technical is rarely harmonized with its use and administration.

Education

Educational theorists of the nineteenth century found themselves, in seeking to maintain the regular functioning of the societies in which they were operating, confronted by a paradox. First, these societies in the main were – since the industrial revolution – mass-societies in the sense of their modes of operation, production and (increasingly in the latter part of the century) dissemination of knowledge and information; yet secondly, in a period prior to the establishment of political (let alone social and economic) democracy, control of all these practices was restricted to a small minority of the population.

From this followed the contradictory motivation of all proposals for educational innovation which did not rest on more or less total opposition to the established nature of society. Education for the masses had to be developed broadly, to ensure their greater capacity, in literacy and numeracy, to operate the productive systems in which they were involved. Yet it had, as far as possible, to offset, notably through systems of moral education, the propensity of the increasingly stimulated mental capacities of the masses to question their ascribed place in the social order.

Outside the activities of such ruling-class educationists – whose theories, aptly summarized by Dickens's Mr Gradgrind in *Hard Times* as the exclusive domain of 'facts', impress us today principally by their monotony – there grew up in the nineteenth century a varied body of radical and working-class educational thinking. Whether inspired by Chartism, trade unionism or aesthetic socialism in Britain, by Marxism in Russia, Germany and Denmark, or by varieties of socialism and anarcho-syndicalism in France and Spain, questioning of the narrow norms of bourgeois utility in education had, by 1900, become extremely forceful. It could ensure that, in the European liberal (and subsequently social) democracies of the twentieth century, there continued an implicit negotiation between the elements of inherited utilitarianism and its radical critics.

Such utilitarianism has frequently manifested itself across Europe as an educational vulgarization of what we have termed the 'positivist' tradition. International in scope and linear in its objects and progress, it has throughout the twentieth century been a force for standardization and measurement of achievement, for – at best – rationality and conscious purpose; and – at worst – for the monotonous subjugation of education to the supposed needs of industry and business. Nor are the modern reverberations of the Romantic tradition necessarily more inclined to see education as, fundamentally, the production of knowledge. More diverse (and notably more subject to national variation) than the modes of positivism, romanticism rejects its tendency to systemization – often in the name of childhood spontaneity, but also in the name of tradition, heritage, and exclusive notions of **Literature** and Culture. In educational (as in other) politics, positivism tends in general to support of the status quo; whilst romanticism can move, sometimes bafflingly, between Left and Right.

Democratic advances in education – both to ensure its availability to the masses, and to maintain it as a critical function not pre-ordained to serve any particular group or social order – had quite a strong basis in previous practice in France. Revolutionary projects for the interrelation of educational and social transformation had been

considerably cut back by Napoleon I, but the legislation founding the *Université* in 1808 had at least established the principle of a total exam-based state **meritocracy**, and the abolition of all vestiges of *ancien régime* educational privilege. Throughout the nineteenth century the principle had been reinforced by the universalization of primary education, and (in the 1880s) its patriotic extension through a system of scholarships to the secondary and higher sphere. The unequal nature of society, however, continued to ensure that the system, though rigorously uniform, only benefited a minority; and a growth of political awareness ensured, in the early years of the century, the development of a workers' educational movement, the *Universités Populaires*, of considerable breadth and vitality – though unlike its British equivalents, the Workers' Educational Association and the National Council of Labour Colleges, riven with internal dissension.

Initiatives in French education have in general been particularly dependent on general political developments; thus we observe, as consequences of moderate left-wing governments of the 1920s, an extension of possibilities for secondary education, the first steps towards comprehensive secondary education and the massive investment in sport, leisure and cultural facilities under the *Front Populaire* government of 1936. The politicization of education and culture had its reverse side under the Vichy regime (1940–4). This attempted a total reversal of French educational history. First, it reinstated the dominance of the Church. Finally excluded from state schools by the law of separation of Church and State of 1904, the Catholic Church had maintained its own schools throughout the Republic; 'private', basically, in their religious teaching and finances – though state subsidy for Catholic schools will always be a contentious issue in French politics – they have necessarily always followed the State curriculum for the *baccalauréat*. Under Vichy, every opportunity was used for the indoctrination of Pétainist, anti-Semitic and a bizarre ruralist propaganda which may well appear more laughable to those reading it today than to those who fell foul of it at the time.

● **Literature**: Its definition will probably be forever a vexed question, but *literature* may perhaps be defined as what is written and read, and *Literature* as those texts which, for whatever reason, have remained continuously (or nearly) in print since their first publication.

● **Meritocracy**: Rule by those deemed to be the most deserving, the brightest and/or the most successful.

Since the liberation, France has continued to develop, in common with much of western Europe, an increasingly egalitarian education system. As we have noted, the independent Church sector has continued to flourish; though, given its basis in belief rather than in class and money, it has very little of the aura of snobbery and privilege which still surrounds its counterpart in Britain. Though educational selection has increasingly been delayed to 16+, the subsequent distinction between *Collèges d'Enseignement Général* and *Lycées* has to some extent affinities with the division in higher education between universities and *Grandes Écoles*. These latter, highly competitive, Napoleonic institutions represent the pinnacle of the State elitist system: they are, together with its evident centralization, the aspect of French education which makes it closest to that of the USSR.

By comparison with such schematization (positivist both in its negative rigidity and in its positive ability to organize knowledge effectively) the British educational system seems difficult to delineate. It has shared with the French system some notable similarities, such as the strange belief (held possibly later in Britain's public schools than in France) that a thorough knowledge of the Classics was the best possible preparation for a life in public affairs, and, more generally, a spasmodic commitment to the delay, at least, of selection to a later age. As in France, access to secondary education became more widely available between the world wars – though in keeping with a British propensity for hierarchical decentralization, it was (until 1945) controlled in country towns largely by grocers rather than by ministry officials.

Since Britain's major reorganization of education at the end of the Second World War – positivist, quite possibly without knowing it, in its division of 11-year-olds into the academic, the technically gifted (at 11!), and the rest – the tendency has, as in France, been until recently towards the progressive elimination of these distinctions and a realisation that they involve social as well as academic factors; albeit, as with much in the British educational system, on a local and arbitrary basis. In recent years, partial maintenance of 11+ selection has combined with increased dependence on commercial funding to slow down, if not to reverse, the trend. The relationship of these factors to the imposition since 1986 of a national curriculum is

problematic; whereas in France a uniform syllabus is largely accepted, its introduction in Britain has proved politically contentious, both to those who resent the disappearance of their ancient local privileges, and to those who object to its reversion to utilitarianism.

The principal curiosity of British education is, however, the continued dominance of the private sector. The so-called 'public' schools constitute a hegemonic bloc not to be found elsewhere in Europe, and one which manages still to extract deference from other sectors (selective and even non-selective state schools) in terms of imitation of its organization, nomenclature, and attitudes. Whilst certain areas of the French system embody elitism, the 'public' schools represent a privilege subject to virtually no external intellectual control, a dominance which quite probably goes back to 1688, of gentry, upper professional classes, business and – residually – aristocracy.

German education before 1914 reflected, as in France and Britain, the norms of a rigid social hierarchy, as well as the undemocratic hierarchies of the Wilhelmine state, with military academies as a more savage version of the British private sector. The transformations effected by the Weimar Republic, accordingly, going as they did further than contemporary Britain or France in terms of comprehensivization and sexual equality at all levels, aroused ferocious opposition from nostalgics for 1900 and anti-Republicans in general. The clock was comprehensively put back by the Nazis, with selection reintroduced on traditional as well as political and racial grounds; abolition of 'modern' subjects like 'civics'; confusion of teaching the national literature with Nazi sloganizing; garbled teaching of the Classics; an increase of rote-learning, and so on.

After 1945, and until reunification, the Federal Republic took as its model the less archaic aspects of the Second Empire; and the Democratic Republic, the advanced social-democratic ideology and practices of the Weimar Republic. Thus the nature of West German education could vary (though rather less than in Britain) from *Land* to *Land*: in the social-democratic (urban) *Länder* there might be experiments in comprehensivization; in the Christian-democratic areas, selection – and the concomitant social distinctions – were

Key Figure 11.3

Anatoli v. Lunacharsky (1875–1933)

Lunacharsky is principally remembered for his activities as People's Commissar for Education, from the moment of the Bolshevik Revolution in 1917, to 1929. His project during this period was unique in the twentieth century: extensively, to increase literacy in the new Soviet Union to the level of Western Europe (in which he sowed the seeds of considerable success), and intensively, to further new developments in Soviet literature, music and the visual arts. Here too, Soviet production in the 1920s was remarkable – modernist drama and the novel, acmeism and constructivism in painting, the engagement of Shostakovich and others with jazz, etc. But with the rise of Stalin and the officially sanctioned doctrines of socialist realism, Lunacharsky's positive attitude to modernism was given a hostile definition as collusion with formalism and he was sent into semi-exile as ambassador to Spain.

His earlier periods of exile (under Czarism) had been more productive; after 1905 he had edited the Bolshevik journal *Vpered* (Forward) and had developed a reputation as a publicist, orator and historian of literature and art. Later, in exile with Gorki on Capri, he wrote *Outlines of a Collectivist Philosophy* (1909) and, interestingly, planned an advanced school for a select élite of workers, which Lenin opposed. After the 1917 Revolution he also wrote dramas for the atheist theatre, *Oliver Cromwell* (1920) and *Campanella* (1922), and again with Gorky was involved in preserving art works during the Civil War. Lunacharsky's career and its eclipse may be seen to furnish an instance of the critical confrontation of Enlightenment values with radically new twentieth-century political and social forms.

rigorously preserved (especially by the Catholic middle classes).

In East Germany, revival of the educational practices of Weimar were of course combined with political and cultural affinities with the USSR. The virtual absence of a Soviet-style *Nomenklatura*, however, had the result that universal (and centrally determined) comprehensive secondary education did not tail off, at higher-education level, into a 'partially exclusive' 'private domain' for those with influence, as in the Soviet Union. The social constitution of the universities in the GDR was more socially comprehensive – certainly than that of their West German counterparts, but also than, for instance, those in Poland, where (even under the People's Republic) they remained largely colonized by nostalgics for the pre-war regime. In short, the norms of education in the GDR would seem closer to those of France than to those of other comparable countries.

Since reunification the GDR has been totally incorporated into the Federal Republic of Germany (FRG), and most aspects of GDR culture, from their origins in the Berlin Enlightenment to the present, have been subordinated to those of the West. Division of the former unitary Republic into *Länder* has led to the reintroduction of selection in many areas; the teaching of literature has changed from relating text and context, to the immediate interpretation of texts ('practical criticism' on the Anglo-Saxon model); history is no longer social history but narrative history, paradoxically a new manifestation of positivism.

For all the tendencies manifested, essentially in its latter years, towards appropriation of educational and cultural (as well as other) power by corrupt officials, the educational achievements of the USSR cannot but appear impressive. It was long fashionable amongst – especially British – superior people to mock the Soviet passion for 'culture'. But the preoccupation becomes more accessible when we reflect that the Bolshevik founders of the Soviet Union were taking over a country of relative backwardness and one of enormous diversity (Soviet newsreel films show literacy classes for the women of Central Asia – one of the regime's proudest achievements). From this, Soviet education achieved – in less than 50 years – parity with the nations of the West (see Key Figure 11.3), before declining to some extent under the dual pressures of changes in the terms of world trade, and the cost of the Cold War. It can hardly be maintained that conditions have improved since the fall of the Soviet Union. In educational terms this has meant the diminution of higher educational opportunities for all but a wealthy few, and a disastrously under-funded system.

In the first half of the century we can see (with the exception of the fascist states) a general tendency for governments to incorporate workers' demands – familiar since the nineteenth century – into their practice. Since then a combination of factors – political reaction against social democracy, the collapse of regimes and currencies under external (and internal) pressure – has reversed the tendency. The consequences for the world may be incalculable.

Architecture

European architecture between 1880 and 1920, in common with other domains of artistic production, seems a tangle of conflicting impulses from which, none the less, two major tendencies dominate: construction in the image of the past (a tendency not entirely without affinities with various kinds of representational **realism**); and modernist construction, which in many ways asserts its own independence of the past and the self-sufficiency of its own forms.

To the first type may be ascribed the massive German neo-Gothic bourgeois villas constructed in the expansionist years of the Wilhelmine Empire. Similar edifices – of the same period, though rather more slender and less overpowering – are to be found in what were, at the time, the more prosperous regions of Britain. Throughout western Europe at the time, however, the dominant architectural style – for official construction and for the housing of the prosperous – occasioned a kind of classicism so diluted that it has rapidly come to be considered as a form hardly to be noted in any particular way:

● **Realism**: An aesthetic which seeks to engage with the external world both in the depiction of its appearances and in an investigation of their history.

the habitat of a middle class whose increasing social diversity was, for most of the period, only matched by its growing political dominance. Significantly, its principal exponent in Britain, Edwin Lutyens, is remembered chiefly for a complex where such 'normality' asserts itself as extraordinary: the official British government buildings in New Delhi, whose arrogant disregard of their 'native' surroundings symbolizes the motives of Imperial power.

Different, though analogous, reflections are provoked by the town of Metz in eastern France. Annexed into the German Second Empire from 1871 to 1918, the town was largely reconstructed in accordance with contemporary nationalist ideology and resembles a fascinating architectural icon, with a neo-Gothic Wilhelmine centre, surrounded by untouched French neo-classical building of the late eighteenth and early nineteenth centuries and, on the outskirts, all the eclectic paraphernalia of post-1918 construction.

The architecture which sought, against all this, to articulate new forms (and which accordingly figured in architectural textbooks) constituted a minority of building construction. Of most significance in the years before the First World War was the international movement known as *art nouveau* (in French and English) and as *Jugendstil* (in German). It flourished, mainly, far from the major cities of Europe – in Brussels and in Helsinki, in Prague and in Barcelona, where the unfinished *Sagrada Familia* temple by Antonio Gaudí has a claim to be seen as its principal monument. As in the similarly florid Parisian domestic architecture and Metro entrances of Hector Guimard, the reaction against rectilinear classicism could not be more pronounced; the decorated, intertwining, curving lines immediately evoke the Gothic Middle Ages and Grimm's fairy tales, yet are evidently supported by the most modern iron and steel construction. To some extent consequent upon the earlier painting and graphics of the English Pre-Raphaelites, and with roots in the contemporary writing of the Catholic revival in France – most notably in the dramas of Paul Claudel – *art nouveau* presents us not with an ideology of medievalism but with a 'false middle ages' (*faux moyen âge*), evoking distance from the present rather than identification with the past.

Its affinities are, in Britain, with the work of Charles Rennie Mackintosh – principally in Glasgow rather than in London, reinforcing the impression of a movement largely confined to the peripheries of Europe by the force of metropolitan eclecticism – and the Arts and Crafts Movement. This was more concerned with design than with architecture, but derived significantly from the concerns of William Morris, probably the greatest British socialist thinker of the nineteenth century, with the identity of social and aesthetic transformation.

Yet for all of Morris's massive influence, both on thinking about aesthetics and on socialism, such innovatory architecture was only for a privileged few. Until the years following the First World War, innovations in housing for the masses were largely restricted to arranging a rapidly increasing urban population in such a manner as most efficiently to maximize profits. Increasingly, across Europe as a whole, working-class housing came to be indistinguishable, from the outside at least, from the barracks – or indeed the prison. The oppressiveness of such conditions at their worst is represented in a scene in the Soviet film *Strike* (1925) by Sergei Eisenstein (1898–1948) where the Czarist mounted police ride up the staircases of the apartment block in pursuit of the workers. Of course there were exceptions, of which the Karl Marx Hof in Vienna – designed and constructed for the workers by their own organizations – is the most famous. But in general the benefits of new design, with its additional demands on both time and space for construction, remained marginal.

During the decades after 1918, however, the relationship between economics, class and design altered considerably. The middle classes and the possessors of capital across Europe maintained, in general, their economic advantages to a greater degree than has commonly been supposed – but the social and political adjustments of the post-war period included, to the advantage of the working classes, certain areas of social democracy of which publicly subsidized housing was one of the most significant.

It is in this context that new developments in modernist architecture emerged, with the work of the *Bauhaus* (c.1922–33) and Walter Gropius in Germany, and that of Le Corbusier in France. The collective political and aesthetic philosophy of the *Bauhaus* was close to that of the German Communist Party (its preoccupations having much in common with those of Morris 50 years earlier), whilst Le Corbusier's authoritarian individualism in many ways brought him close to fascism; the two centres of architectural activity had together an impact across Europe – in Italy, Britain and elsewhere.

The functionalism of *Bauhaus* architecture – with its steel-framed windows, flat roofs and rectilinear white-covered outer wall surfaces whose bevelled corners alone offset the effect of a cubic 'living machine' (to use Le Corbusier's phrase) – combined frequently, in western Europe between 1920 and 1940, with the superficially similar 'Spanish colonial style'. The effect was a large volume of production of small box-like suburban dwellings whose inspiration was modernist, but whose living arrangements essentially differed little from the cottages of previous centuries. The mass of housing for the Western European upper working and lower middle class would seem, however, to have struck a lifeless compromise between such (modest) modernism, and other styles of architecture favoured by the dominant upper middle classes of the period. In the 1930s, Nazism (having banned the *Bauhaus* in 1933) favoured the revival of traces of the Gothic; in Britain mock- (or as it became vulgarly known, 'stockbroker') Tudor building, complete with fake beams and mullioned windows, perhaps testified to a longing for past stability, as did the widespread imitation of the Norman manor-house in northern France.

Outside the liberal democracies at the time, non-domestic architecture was the centre of attention. Unlike Hitler (and in line with a general policy less dominating of business enterprise than the Third Reich), Mussolini, once sponsored by the futurists, permitted a limited amount of modernist activity, mainly in the private sector. Nazi architecture, however, seems to have been entirely preoccupied with its own giganticism: above all, the designs by Hitler and Speer for a new Berlin (Germania), with its physically impossible Assembly Hall (*große Halle*), and plans for new railway stations with doors (presumably to be opened by hand) 8 metres high. These were characterized by an uneasy mix of cultural indicators: primeval Germanic myth, the historic authority of classicism, the contemporary miracles of technology.

Soviet architecture of the Stalinist period (*c*.1932–53) has often been compared to this – and undoubtedly, in their shared neo-classicism and in the often injudicious decoration of buildings with monumental sculptures, there are notable similarities. But the differences are also to be noted; architectural production in the Soviet Union was less monolithic than in Nazi Germany and in spite of its increasing control in the 1930s by the Central Committee of the Party, modernist impulses (dominant in the previous decade) survived to co-exist with 'official' classicism. From their co-existence emerged, on occasion, buildings far from the more bizarre excesses of Nazism and largely comparable with certain major Western European enterprises of the interwar period (such as the principal buildings of London University, and Cambridge University Library) – austerely functional and not without a certain drab grandeur.

In the 30 years after 1945 – in what may be termed the period of European reconstruction and social democracy – it now appears that, in both East and West Europe, the principal influence on housing styles for most people – whether acknowledged or not – was, especially for the public sector (and posthumously), the *Bauhaus*. Its stress on uncluttered functionalism was particularly appropriate to an era where speed of construction was essential; stress on utility of form rather than decoration was also suitable to a democratic age. Other contemporary developments in mass housing were noticeable – new versions of the perennial cottage, particularly in Great Britain, but also in the North of Europe generally, from northern France to Scandinavia – but remained overall a minority phenomenon.

Meanwhile housing for the more prosperous tended, through virtually all the rest of the century, to national – or at least regional – stereotypes. In France an attenuated classicism mostly prevailed, with smaller houses – especially those built identically on small estates, a tendency only to emerge in the last third of the century – affecting a self-conscious prettiness, presumably redolent of the eighteenth-century cottage. In Austria and Germany, and to some extent in Poland and even Scandinavia, architectural style often recalls the aristocratic past of hunting lodges and the cosy rusticity of the *White Horse Inn*. Most intriguingly of all, perhaps, there emerged around 1980 in Britain a kind of diluted resurrection of the interwar mock-Tudor style – now an imitation not so much of the sixteenth century as of the 1930s, a truly postmodern parody of a parody.

The last decades of the century produced little in the way of noteworthy monumental and public architecture. The reconstruction of Berlin after German reunification from 1989 onwards was notable, in a climate more in accordance with profit than with aesthetics, mainly for a style of office building which, whilst incorporating some modernist elements, might be termed international–bureaucratic, and for little else.

A contrast might be drawn, finally, between the two grandiose Paris edifices evolved in, respectively, the 1970s and 1980s – the *Centre Pompidou* of Richard Rogers and the *Pyramide du Louvre* of I. M. Pei – and the recent extension to London's *National Gallery*, an ill-proportioned work of neo-classicism, parasitic upon the elegant 1820s neo-classicism of the main building, which it seems to mimic ineptly. The difference is here extremely evident between an aesthetic activity which aims to see beyond the limitations of the present, and one which, necessarily engaged in that present as all art must be, immerses itself in a reversion to a falsely imagined past. A contrast which appears most visibly in architecture – but is by no means restricted to it.

Cinema

Together with jazz (principally a North American phenomenon and thus not a subject for this volume), cinema is the quintessentially twentieth-century art form. Its history, from its beginnings in Paris with the Lumière brothers in the late 1890s to the present day, is dramatic, as is its rise from side-show curiosity and simple item in a music-hall programme to gigantic mechanism for mass entertainment, dramatic enlightenment and propaganda. Then follows its relative decline (first the diminution of its audiences – from the 1950s – through the competition of television; secondly, the dispersal of cinema audiences themselves – from the 1980s – by the use of video). Yet in spite of these vicissitudes it remains the most powerful force for the dissemination of culture in the world.

Technical advances in the industry have been prodigious. Yet, as opposed to many which have proved relatively short-lived (Cinerama, Todd-AO, 3-D etc.), only two innovations can be confidently stated to have had a significant and long-lasting effect on cinematic form as a whole – the introduction of sound (1928–9) and, soon after, that of colour (*c*.1935). Use of sound had the effect – principally in Hollywood but also in the European cinema – of effecting a reversion to the representational naturalism from which, paradoxically, the European theatre was at almost the same time emerging. Colour took much longer to catch on, and it was almost 30 years after its first use that it became, as now, practically universal. Partly this was due to the crudity of North American colour systems (licensed throughout western Europe); in the early post-war decades its indiscriminate use was partly responsible for the division of cinema production (and presumably its hitherto relatively heterogeneous audiences) into two categories: light comedy and 'spectacular' (in colour), and 'serious' or 'intellectual' films (in black and white). It is difficult to judge the original impact of films of the silent/black and white era; as ever, we can only attempt a relation of our contemporary reactions with our general aesthetic and historical preoccupations. However, it can be safely assumed that the element of the extraordinary in early cinema must have militated against any simple, realist response to screen images as a 'slice of life'; both the gestures of the actors and the insertion of captions (from which Brecht borrowed for the theatre) must have given, as to some extent they do now, the effect of opera rather than anything more everyday, whatever the ostensible setting.

The effectiveness of these conditions for the 'de-realizing' drama of the early 1920s – for German expressionism and French surrealism – is apparent in films such as Robert Wiene's *Dr Caligari's Cabinet* (*Das Kabinett des Doktor Caligari*, 1919). Here the strangeness of the youthful medium is correlated with bizarre distortions of plot and of visual perspective – and Caligari emerges as the manipulator of these distortions, but in a lunatic asylum – a prescient foretaste, perhaps, of the Third Reich. René Clair's *Entr'acte* (1929) and Germaine

Dulac's *The Seashell and the Clergyman* (*La Coquille et le Clergyman*, 1928) both involve a ludicrous dreamlike chase – the mourners after a runaway coffin, the unfortunate portly clergyman along a beach. Each film thus celebrates modernism (the speed of the camera a source of the futurism from which surrealism derived) whilst simultaneously rendering it ludicrous.

The vicissitudes of German cinematic expressionism are, of course, tortuous. Fritz Lang, whose *Metropolis* (1926) is supremely cinematic in that the class and social conflicts it shows occur within a gigantic closed, 'layered' townscape, emigrated to Hollywood in 1933 and subsequently produced films closer to the US social realist norm of the period. Leni Riefenstahl, the best known Nazi filmmaker, incorporated expressionist elements (choric unison, rapidly clashing images) in her film of the Nazi Party rally, *Triumph of the Will* (*Triumph des Willens*, 1934). The progress of French surrealism through the century has been more serene: elements of it subsist in Jean Cocteau's *Orphée* (1950) and *Le Testament d'Orphée* (1960) and in the comic-satirical mode of Jean-Pierre Mocky's *Snobs* (1961).

Affinities can be observed between the work of German expressionists and that of their Soviet near-contemporary Sergei Eisenstein. The revolutionary impact of his films – e.g. *Battleship Potemkin* (1925) and *October* (1928) – is of course much more direct, but not, for that matter, simple. Notably Eisenstein's innovatory use of *montage* (cutting rapidly from scene to scene, image to image) builds a complex network of representations of political conflict, of which the film may be seen, retrospectively, as the resolution.

The 1930s look now like the period when the centre of world film production moved to Hollywood (though this was not to be a permanent development); when the 'dream factory' seemed capable of producing a virtually inexhaustible supply of comedies, fantasies and social dramas – still of course the case today. One factor in this was, of course, the emigration not just of German directors, but of actors, administrators and technicians of all sorts. What was now produced in Germany was not, in the main, direct fascist propaganda on film (and this was true of fascist Italy too): apart from the notorious Riefenstahl and one or two others, production centred on banal 'feel-good' comedies and mediocre musicals – the 'dream factory' of Hollywood without the imagination or the tools.

The British film industry of the time – without suffering the repressions of its German counterpart – hardly survived the world economic crisis much better. Emigration to Hollywood was, unlike that from Germany, more economic than political – but virtually as disastrous. Severity of censorship, extraordinary for a supposedly liberal democracy, was also doubtless to blame. When Alfred Hitchcock left in 1939, he was only continuing an established trend. Meanwhile, the production of comedies, versions of that British speciality the comedy murder mystery (satirized indeed by Hitchcock in *The 39 Steps*, 1935), Gracie Fields and George Formby musicals, and the historical biographies of Alexander Korda, produced material now principally of antiquarian interest. One field of film-making was, however, genuinely innovatory – the documentaries of Herbert Grierson, which incorporated into their dramatic investigations of British working life not only music by Benjamin Britten but texts by W. H. Auden.

The only European country to come near to rivalling Hollywood in technical and discursive cinematic power, at this period, was France. The legacy of surrealism was extended with the Prévert brothers' *It's Buttoned Up* (*L'Affaire est dans le sac*, 1932) and with Jean Vigo's hilarious and bizarre *Nought for Behaviour* (*Zéro de Conduite*, 1933) and off-beat, lyrical *l'Atalante* (1934). In addition there evolved a series of subtly argued and brilliantly shot films of critical social realism – of which the most striking were those of Jean Renoir: *The Great Illusion* (*La Grande illusion*, 1937) and pre-eminently *The Rules of the Game* (*La Règle du Jeu*, 1939), the free adaptation of an early Romantic comedy by Alfred de Musset. The genre, with its epic range and persistent interrogation of social relationships, has, though not continually dominant in French cinema, continued to produce isolated masterpieces ever since – the panoramic history of nineteenth-century art and politics in Marcel Carné's *Children of the Gods* (*Les Enfants du Paradis*, 1944) and Claude Berri's Zola adaptation, *Germinal* (1992).

After the Second World War, epic realism emerged as the dominant mode in much of Europe.

In the Soviet Union, Eisenstein's *Ivan the Terrible* (1945–58) showed a narrative more monumental than his earlier work, as in a different register did Sergei Bondarchuk's *War and Peace* (1966–7), which outgunned in every way the 1956 US version by King Vidor. In Eastern and Southern Europe, in countries where hitherto political circumstances had largely excluded the possibility, film dramas of epic proportions concerned with the interplay of historical and personal forces were dominant for at least a quarter-century. In Poland, Andrzej Wajda's trilogy (*A Generation*, 1954; *Kanal*, 1957; *Ashes and Diamonds*, 1958) chronicled the Occupation and Resistance with both respect and scepticism; later, his *Man of Marble* (1977) gave an account – dynamic and panoramic – of a whole society with few equivalents in the West. In Hungary something of a similar epic breadth and intensity was manifest in Miklós Jancsó's accounts of successive moments in Hungarian history: pathetic in *The Round-up* (1965); heroic in *Reds and Whites* (1967); ironic in *The Confrontation* (1969). And from Greece, where the national culture was twice virtually destroyed by the pre-war and post-war dictatorships, came one of the most remarkable films of this type: Theodor Angelopoulos's *The Travelling Players* (1975) not only chronicled more than two critical decades of Greek history, but the changing relation to them of Greek classical and artistic performance in general, through the varying stories of the actors in the title.

But it is in Italy that the most varied developments from French critical realism are to be found. Italian neo-realism dates from the decline and fall of Mussolini, and is largely defined through the work of two directors: the former fascist Roberto Rossellini, whose major contribution to the movement, *Rome, Open City* (*Roma, Città aperta*, 1945) is none the less remarkable for its combination of fluid actuality with denunciation of repression and torture; and Luchino Visconti, a Communist whose more consistent work in the idiom began with *Ossessione* (1942). This version of the James M. Cain story *The Postman Always Rings Twice* is distinguished from the three Hollywood versions (1944 [as *Double Indemnity*], 1946 and 1981) by its treatment of its characters as social agents rather than as individual demons. Visconti's later films – *The Earthquake* (*La Terra Trema*, 1948) and *Rocco and his Brothers* (*Rocco e i suoi fratelli*, 1960) –

developed these tendencies on a wider canvas; *The Damned* (*Götterdämmerung*, 1969), on an industrial dynasty in early fascist Germany, contrives to combine them with an appropriately Wagnerian intensity.

In contrast to the uncompromising depiction of conflict in Visconti stand the films of Federico Fellini. Though *La Strada* (1954), with its peasant girl dominated by a circus strong-man, may be seen as an allegory of Italy under fascism, later films – *Satyricon* (1969), *Fellini's Rome* (*Roma*, 1972), *Amarcord* (1973) – deploy a somewhat unctuous political ambiguity, together with cynical manipulation of images of the cruel and the bizarre. The latter characteristics are also prominent in the work of Pier Paolo Pasolini, but with a very different accent. *The Gospel According to St Matthew* (*Il Vangelo secondo Matteo*, 1964) gives – partly through the distanced sound of the Bach *Passion* which accompanies it – a sympathetic atheist version of the Gospel story, of poor peasants in social and existential isolation; and *The 120 Days of Sodom* (*Salò*, 1975) conflates the imagined horrors of de Sade with those of the last days of Italian fascism, to an extent that until recently ensured its prohibition in Britain.

Most affinities with the work of Visconti, however, are to be found in that of Bernardo Bertolucci. *The Conformist* (*Il Conformista*, 1970) examines, in the mode of a thriller, the relation between mythology, sexuality and fascist repression; and the gigantic *1900* (*Novecento*, 1976) explores twentieth-century Italy – in a way which also recalls Wajda and Angelopoulos – through the changing terms of class and personal relations represented by the two protagonists, landowner and labourer.

To turn from the violent drama of Italian history and cinema to the work of Ingmar Bergman in the relative isolation and apparent calm of Sweden seems to involve a vast transition. True, Bergman's early films, especially, seem claustrophobic by comparison with the Italian panoramas of Visconti or Bertolucci; but their preoccupation with Protestant guilt (as early as *Frenzy* [*Hets*], 1944, the issue is of ethical collusion with Nazism), personal violation and the failure of transcendental mythologies achieves – in films such as *The Seventh Seal* (*Det Sjunde Inseglet*, 1957),

Winter Light (*Nattsvardsgästerna*, 1962) and *The Silence* (*Tystnaden*, 1963) – a discursive intensity comparable with their more expansive Italian contemporaries; subsequently Bergman moved to wider political scenes, as in the denunciation of the Vietnam War, *The Shame* (*Skammen*, 1968), and to family dramas.

The relationship between fantasy and politics, and between 'personal vision' and social realism, is, as we have seen it in Italy and elsewhere, a complex one in which no rigid dividing lines can, ultimately, be drawn. In Germany (East and West) the tremendous influence of Brecht on all subsequent artistic production has ensured that the treatment of 'social' topics in the cinema was achieved through a cinematic rhetoric which induced the spectator to see the circumstances of those topics as strange and questionable. This is the case in the work of Rainer Werner Fassbinder, about racism and political persecution – *Fear Eats the Soul* (*Angst essen Seele auf*, 1974) and *The Marriage of Maria Braun* (*Die Ehe der Maria Braun*, 1979). It also characterizes Margarethe von Trotta's feminist *The German Sisters* (*Die Deutsche Frauen*, 1980). On the other hand, the more 'personal' dramas of Werner Herzog's films – *Aguirre the Wrath of God* (*Aguirre der Zorn Gottes*, 1973) and *Fitzcarraldo* (1982) – often concerned with demented and marginal characters, have a social reference of violence and oppression which evidently reaches back, implicitly, into a recent political past.

The most prominent cinematic phenomenon of the latter half of the twentieth century, the French *nouvelle vague* of the late 1950s and 1960s, seems, in retrospect, to have initiated the formulation of ambiguities. It was never clear what constituted the *ancienne vague* which the young directors and critics of *Cahiers du Cinéma* were (if only in terms of journalistic speculation) to reject. A 'staged' romantic panorama like Carné's *Children of the Gods* maybe (though obviously they could not dismiss it as negligible)? But other 'monuments' of older French cinema – parts of Renoir's *The Rules of the Game* and particularly his *A Day in the Country* (*Une Partie de Campagne*, 1936) – had the inconclusive thematics and close depiction of character and situation through intimate camera-work which the *nouvelle vague* generation were to take up.

Claude Chabrol's thrillers and dramas of the everyday – *The Girls* (*Les Bonnes Femmes*, 1960), *The Butcher* (*Le Boucher*, 1969) – have much in common with these antecedents, as they do with the *film noir* productions of Henri-Georges Clouzot during and after the war period – *The Raven* (*Le Corbeau*, 1943), *The Wages of Fear* (*Le Salaire de la Peur*, 1953), *Diabolique* (*Les Diaboliques*, 1951). François Truffaut, similarly, made his name with *The 400 Blows* (*Les 400 Coups*, 1959), a semi-autobiographical narrative of the problems of an isolated and increasingly delinquent boy, which now seems more innovative for its understanding of its subject than for its cinematography, which is not radically distinguishable from that of 'old wave' directors such as Claude Autant-Lara – *Thou Shall Not Kill* (*Tu ne tueras pas*, 1962). Later, Truffaut was to direct a series of films continuing the life-story of his first protagonist, Antoine Doinel – sympathetic without being condescending, but essentially repetitive.

The most contentious and varied of the *nouvelle vague* directors are Louis Malle and Jean-Luc Godard. Malle's achievements have included a combination – in *The Lovers* (*Les Amants*, 1959) – of sexual intensity and direct evocation of place which seemed to fuse the archetypal with the local; *Lacombe Lucien* (1973) maintained a dispassionate lucidity in its account of a young French farm boy drifting into collaboration with the Gestapo. The work of Godard, the most avowedly 'Brechtian' of the group, has ranged from the confrontational, anti-elitist satire of *Les Carabiniers* (1963) to the consideration of the interplay of cinema illusion and natural reality as expressive of a world without values in *Contempt* (*Le Mépris*, 1963). *Two or Three Things That I Know About Her* (*Deux ou trois choses que je sais d'elle*, 1967) gave brief presentations of part-time prostitutes as characteristic of contemporary relations; *Weekend* (1968) went further, in presenting universal carnage on the roads and comic cannibalism as the essential reality of social life.

Meanwhile, the social realism which had been, ever since the war, the strength of the British cinema was renewed in the 1960s. Its greatest achievements in the epoch of post-war social democracy had been transformations of nineteenth-century texts from Dickens to Stevenson (notably David Lean's unsurpassed *Great Expectations*, 1946, and Byron Harkin's *Treasure Island*, 1950). Now Karel Reisz (*Saturday Night and Sunday Morning*, 1960) set a trend which had many undistinguished imitations (for instance, John Schlesinger's *A Kind of Loving*, 1962) and some less literal-minded successors capable of uniting the bizarre and the fantastic in a project of social denunciation, as in Reisz's *Morgan – A Suitable Case for Treatment* (1966) and Lindsay Anderson's *If* (1968).

But the innovatory impact of this British 'new wave', as it soon became known, was to a large extent, like that of its French counterpart, the effect of its contrast with the anodyne nature of the cinema immediately preceding it. Just as there are major affinities between French cinema of the 1940s and 1960s, so in Britain identical themes emerge. The disaffection of youth from the inauthentic routine of society, the oppressiveness of the urban scene and yet the impossibility of escape – all of this is to be found in films such as Robert Hamer's *It Always Rains on Sunday* (1947) or Charles Crichton's *Dance Hall* (1950).

These films are nowadays forgotten: I cite them in conclusion, not as a display of erudition, but to make the point that the cinema is not just a series of 'masterpieces' (which will, by reason of their continued availability, none the less continue largely to determine our view of its evolution) but, like other cultural forms, a network of relationships across theme and technique, geography and time.

Postmodernism and deconstruction: towards the beginning of the twenty-first century

We have examined some cultural tendencies – whether we designate them by turns as realism or modernism, representation or self-questioning, harmony or dissonance – whose meanings are, by and large, within the conceptual limits set by the European Enlightenment of the eighteenth century. That is to say, both the cultural products of the first two-thirds of the twentieth century and the efforts of interpretation directed at them have, in the main, inhabited a mental universe in which reason and the viability of the search for truth went together with notions of the mutual determination of phenomena in the context of historical progression.

These principles (or conventions, according to preference) have, in the last third of the twentieth century, been increasingly challenged by tendencies in thinking variously known as post-structuralism, postmodernism or deconstruction. These share characteristics which, though hardly novel in themselves, have seemed, in a new configuration, to dominate European intellectual life at the expense of more established models of thinking, whether positivist, Marxist or aesthetic. Their effect would appear to derive from a combination of the following: an irrationalism which comprises a denial not just of the supremacy of human reason, but also of the validity of the notions of historical determination or of progress; a radical scepticism which denies both the significance of the thinking subject and the attainability of truth; an extreme eclecticism which sees all phenomena as of equal importance and the relations between them as infinite – thus seeing our world as a location of indifference, where choice and value are ultimately of no significance.

The proponents of this thinking have been mainly French, although it has been taken up enthusiastically by some others elsewhere. At the risk of conglomerating figures from varying intellectual spheres (but who none the less seem to have a great deal in common, in both their actuality and their effect) we might single out four thinkers. Michel Foucault's preoccupation with the relationship between intellect and power (*The Birth of the Clinic* [*Naissance de la clinique*], 1963; *Discipline and Punish* [*Surveiller et punir*], 1977) led him to apparent revulsion from the notion of power in itself, from the general reforming tendencies of the Enlightenment and after, and towards the supposition that viable political activity could only consist in little local struggles for power, in minor agitation against universal, large-scale domination. His anti-intellectualism was effectively underwritten by Jean-François Lyotard (*The Post-modern Condition* [*La Condition postmoderne*], 1982), whose project of combating what he termed the 'grand narrative' of history (*le grand récit*) was to reduce the understanding of society and the past to moments of insight rather

than any wider speculation. Jean Baudrillard (*The Mirror of Production* [*Le Miroir de la production*], 1973) has more recently reflected this scepticism in his affirmation that the Gulf War never happened (that is to say, because we cannot distinguish between a plethora of media images of a phenomenon, its particular significance is to be discounted); the perception coincided to some extent with Baudrillard's fascination with the 'emptiness' of the USA. The radical scepticism of Jacques Derrida (*De la grammatologie* [*Grammatology*], 1967; *Spectres of Marx* [*Les Spectres de Marx*], 1993) seeks to dismiss logocentrism (the functional centrality of language and reason) as well as the phenomenon, supposedly associated with it throughout modern history, of binary thinking (thinking in terms of contrasts). These he characterizes (fallaciously) as specifically European modes of thinking, and he proposes a preoccupation with language, centrally, as a system of displacements, its relation to its objects infinitely questionable and obstructive of any notion of truth.

It is hard not to see the political consequences of such thinking. The relationship of the self to the world is in many respects radically questioned and – so the proponents of the new thinking would assert – opened up. Yet in the absence of any preoccupation with the determination – or the mediation/transformation – of one phenomenon by another, the possibilities of any substantive change in a world which seems effectively to be there as it is, nowhere and everywhere at once, are small.

What results is a kind of universal conservative inertia. In speaking briefly of postmodern artistic production it is not appropriate to generalize in the same way as in discussing the legislative statements of postmodern philosophers. We may, however, note, finally, that a significant tendency in postmodern art is towards minimalism. Yves Klein painted one-colour canvases around 1960; in 1978 Carl André achieved notoriety by arranging a row of bricks in London's Tate Gallery; in 1998 Per Kirkeby's *Brick Work* repeated the exercise. It rather looks as if the tendency of postmodern art may take us back to the naturalism with which we started at the beginning of the century – always different, yet always the same.

SUMMARY

- Culture may perhaps be stated to be the way in which humanity defines itself in its relation to the world; the statement may then be broken down into further contrasts manifest as those between aesthetics and politics, personality and collectivity, etc.

- Twentieth-century cultural developments may be charted in many ways; one is to examine the effects of the intellectual relations of romanticism (which stresses personal feeling over general structure, a sense of distance from established reality, the possibility of otherness and revolt and the interrelation of mind and world); and positivism (the practical philosophy of the nineteenth-century dominant classes, stressing intellectual and social order, the significance of facts, categorization and classification, the determination of mind by world).

- In the media, the new organization of technical advances (notably in the field of electronic reproduction) has brought the most ambitious romantic forms (the total work of art) closer to a mass audience; their administration has, however, shown conflict between fixed attitudes inherited from the nineteenth century and the rise of new forms of organization appropriate to such wider audiences.

- Education is evidently the crucial site for the transmission of knowledge and for the generation of conditions for the furtherance of cultural activities. The relation between the authority of knowledge and the possibility of its free development is always a complex one, never separable from political conditions.

- In architecture a contrast is evident between work which evidently recapitulates past forms, and that which aims to be of its own time and to display its own processes of construction – a contrast which indicates similarly a complicated series of relationships to history and power.

- The conditions of cinema were set in the first third of the twentieth century through the eventual relation of early silent film (often fantastic, quasi-abstract) and sound film (for some time exclusively preoccupied with the chronicle of external reality). Out of these tendencies various forms of modern cinema have emerged.

- So far we have counterposed general cultural tendencies in terms of the rational analysis of opposing and inter-determining forces, as practised in European thought since the Enlightenment. In the last third of the twentieth century influential thinking has emerged (postmodernism, deconstruction) which is radically eclectic and sceptical and which negates the possibility of determination, truth itself and, presumably, judgement.

- It is too early to say whether such thinking will outlive the immediate historical circumstances that engendered it. At any event, the details which such thinking examines are infinite; what it derives from them is always the same.

QUESTIONS FOR DISCUSSION

- Explain the difference between Romantic and positivist approaches to culture.

- What have been the main tendencies in the development of the media?

- Can the educational system of a country be politically 'neutral'?

- Is architecture a good case study demonstrating the tension between romanticism and positivism?

- How has film been used for propaganda purposes?

- What are the distinctive features of the postmodern approach to culture?

FURTHER READING

Barthes, Roland (1992) *Mythologies*, trans. Annette Lavers (London: Jonathan Cape). Barthes generates a vivid field of experience for us between theories of society and images of everyday life.

Benjamin, Walter (1982) *Illuminations*, ed. Hannah Arendt (London: Fontana). Quirky and stimulating; reflections on what and how we think by the most visionary Marxist of them all.

Bloch, Ernst (1991) *Heritage of our Times* (Cambridge: Polity Press). Meditations on culture and history, progress and barbarism by one of the most strenuous of Central European thinkers.

Camus, Albert (1969) *The Rebel* (Harmondsworth: Penguin). Liberal thought at its defining moment of crisis in mid-20th century.

Gasset, José Ortega y (1972) *The Dehumanization of Art* (Princeton, NJ: Princeton University Press). An elegant summation of conservative thinking.

Harby, Howard (ed.) (1961) *European Music in the Twentieth Century* (Harmondsworth: Penguin). Music, the least referential of the arts, seems difficult to connect with other art forms. A careful and comprehensive work such as this helps.

Hughes, Robert (1991) *The Shock of the New – Art and the Century of Change* (London: BBC/Thames and Hudson). Determined in its opinions, wide-ranging and with an eye for significant detail.

Hughes, Stuart (1961) *Consciousness and Society – The Reorientation of European Social Thought, 1890–1930* (New York: Alfred A. Knopf). Undogmatic, perceptive and inclusive – an attractive introduction to the history of twentieth-century thought.

Krakauer, Siegfried (1979) *Theory of Film: The Redemption of Physical Reality* (New York: Oxford University Press). The daddy of all film theorists – sophisticated, embattled and lucid.

Sartre, Jean Paul (1976) *Critique of Dialectical Reason: I* (London: Verso). The paradoxes of personality, society and history and our need to articulate them.

Tompkins, Calvin (1968) *Ahead of the Game: Four Versions of Avant-Garde* (Harmondsworth: Penguin). An enthusiasm which provides a way in to sometimes the most obscure of twentieth-century artistic production.

Williams, Raymond (1996) *Keywords* (London: Fontana). Not just a lexicon of intellectual terms but a means to their critical evaluation.

CHAPTER 12

Conclusion: Endings and Beginnings

RICHARD SAKWA AND ANNE STEVENS

Contemporary Europe presents a picture of complexity and challenges. Europe is no longer the measure of modernity and a synonym for progress. Longstanding risks persist, arising from imbalances in the mechanisms for political participation (Chapter 6) and accountability (Chapter 5), of difficulties in the processes of integration (Chapters 3 and 4), or of unpredictable but possibly violent risks to security (Chapter 10). To these must be added newly perceived dangers, of economic collapse arising from global instability in the financial system and massive indebtedness (Chapter 8), of political and social extremism and unrest spurred on by the policies adopted to deal with economic crisis, and of the consequences of the geographical and ecological change produced by climate change.

Some form of representative democracy and an economy 'run on the basis of a competitive capitalism which looks to the market for its instructions' may indeed be 'the only viable options for modern society' (Beedham, 1999). However, not only is democracy far from axiomatic or inevitable in Europe (Mazower, 1998), but it is in itself not always a bar to more or less authoritarian rule (Zakaria, 1997). As Thomas Saalfeld and Dieter Rucht both remind us (Chapters 5 and 6), a wider process of political participation than the mere casting of a vote may be required, even where political competition is relatively unfettered, if individuals and minorities are to be confident that their contribution to debates will not go unheeded and their rights will be respected.

Many of the cleavages identified in Chapter 1, which have shaped the identity of Europe, continue to run very deep. Some of them were for much of the twentieth century overshadowed by the monolithic ideologies which underpinned so many of the bloody conflicts of the period. Two of the most influential of these, fascism and communism, have greatly diminished and no longer enjoy political dominance anywhere. Ideologies which proclaim a total and all-embracing world-view – religious fundamentalism is another – have not altogether disappeared as political forces within as well as outside Europe. Secularization, democracy and liberal values, on the other hand, are more pluralist. But that in itself opens up the possibility of widespread, if less total and bloody, conflict.

In facing these risks Europe is confronted with the question of what it is becoming and what it should be. Are there distinctively 'European' models of protectionism, taxation, economic organization and welfare-state provision? How should they be preserved, if at all, in the face of the challenges outlined above? What does it mean to be 'European' in a globalized world, and what role can Europe play in a world which is no longer bipolar (dominated by two great powers, the USA and the USSR) but in which new powers – above all China and India – are emerging both as nuclear powers and as major economic players, together with a range of emerging economies such as Brazil, Indonesia, South Africa and Nigeria?

A globalized world

Globalization is a contested (Held, Goldblatt, and Perraton, 1999, p. 1), not to say muddled and ambiguous (Hurrell and Menon, 2003, p. 399) concept, if not indeed a cliché. What the concept seeks to capture is the sense that relationships and transactions are being conducted across continents and regions, producing very widespread networks and flows of activity. Debates continue about whether the concept is simply descriptive, or whether it is also explanatory, concerned not just with processes but with their outcomes. Moreover, is the term describing something decisively different and new, or are we witnessing today simply the current version of types of relationships that have long existed? Writers in the eighteenth and nineteenth centuries were predicting the impact of what we now call globalization (Hurrell and Menon, 2003, p. 398). There is nothing particularly new about widespread networks and flows of activity: for example the so-called 'world religions' spread fast – Christianity from India to Rome and beyond within a century, Islam very speedily outwards from Arabia as far as northern Spain and China. In the fifteenth century Magellan's expedition circumnavigated the globe, in the eighteenth century the slave trade took a triangular transcontinental course from Britain to Africa to America, while the empires, trade and investment of the nineteenth century can be described as global. However, what is new is that, whether the relationships are those of trade, investment, finance, culture or migration, they are intensifying – there are more of them, more closely interconnected; they are happening faster, as a result of new technologies of transport and communication; and the impact of distant events becomes deeper – a bomb in Bali affects families in Australia and the UK; it becomes almost a domestic event. An outbreak of disease in Mexico in spring 2009 resulted, by early 2010, in some 50 countries worldwide experiencing more than 40 fatalities (European Centre for Disease Control, 2010), and the declaration by the World Health Organization (WHO) of a pandemic. The patterns of migration discussed by William Outhwaite in Chapter 7 can certainly be seen as one manifestation of globalization.

For many commentators and critics, however, globalization is a word that describes not just the number and speed of transactions and flows, but also their characteristics, nature and implications. For some – Held and McGrew (2001) call them 'hyperglobalists' – the implications of what is happening is the emergence of a single global economy – 'supra-territorial capitalism' – so that global finance and corporate capital control economic power and wealth, removing the management and regulation of national economies, including welfare states, from national governments. And in seeking its own interests, this capital is perceived to require – and hence coerce, states which wish their economies to be competitive and flourishing to provide – a liberal, deregulated, unprotected economic environment.

Alongside this, the argument goes, is a burgeoning of the extent to which states are linked into intergovernmental organizations, whether for security (e.g. NATO), for development and global finance (the World Bank and the International Monetary Fund, IMF), for the regulation of trade (the World Trade Organization, WTO) or for many other common purposes; according to Held at the beginning of the twentieth century there were 37 such organizations. At the start of the twenty-first century there were nearly 300 (Held and McGrew, 2001). International non-governmental organizations have proliferated alongside these, rising in the same period from about 371 to perhaps 25,000. Increasingly, therefore, states are answerable to, or influenced by, bodies which extend well beyond their territorial borders. Their autonomy of action, some feel, is thereby compromised. Moreover, national identity is perceived to be compromised by aspects of cultural globalization: the emergence of English as a worldwide common language; the global circulation of Hollywood films and TV programmes produced in America; shared adulation of footballers and pop stars; the ubiquity of certain types of fast food.

Critics of these perceptions of globalization argue that territorial and national divisions may be reconfigured, but they are not diminishing, and that states continue to be the key actors in internal and international politics. States increasingly choose pooled sovereignty and interdependence, if with chosen partners. But they can equally, as the division in Europe over support for the American coalition of forces in Iraq in 2003–4 demonstrated, diverge in their actions, and (as in the case of the Euro stability and growth pact) repudiate obligations. Multinational corporations bring powerful economic arguments to bear, but states still can and do make choices about regulation and welfare provision. Technological developments, not least satellite phones and the internet, bring very distant events very close in time and may magnify their impact. Nevertheless, power politics persist, even if some of the future patterns, even within Europe, are far from determined.

Public perceptions of globalization are understandably affected by diverse political reactions to its impact. Campaigners readily seek to persuade governments to act together on issues which they understand are beyond the control of any one government and express disappointment and disillusion when the conflicting interests of states produce lesser results than they have been pressing for, as in the case of climate-change protesters at the Copenhagen summit in December 2009 (*Guardian*, 12 December 2009; BBC, 2009). Governments, which defend some actions on the grounds of the pursuit of national interest, are equally quick to deny collective responsibility for the adverse impact of events that can be blamed on 'outsiders', as in the case of the 2008 bank crisis (see Chapter 8) or the 2010 oil spill in the Gulf of Mexico. Moreover 'Globalization' becomes both the umbrella under which governments shelter from hostility to decisions which they have regarded as desirable but know will be electorally unpopular and a scapegoat for trends which citizens find disturbing or unwelcome.

Europe today

Many of the contributors to this book have stressed the plurality and variety of Europe, which has caused the historian Tony Judt, for example, writing about the 'varieties of Europe', to conclude that '[t]here is little to be gained by seeking to distil the essence of "Europe" . . . today's Europeans are more numerous and heterogeneous than ever before' so that 'European experience and identity' involves faultlines and overlapping contours (Judt, 2005, p. 752). Historians of Europe have recently become increasingly 'cautious in their assumptions about a continuity or a narrative based on the advancement of civilization' (Delanty, 2010, p. 1). Nevertheless, it can be argued that even in an 'an increasingly post-European age' (Delanty, 2010, p. 18) there are a number of trends, tensions and reinterpretations that are distinctive and important.

This book has in general focused upon the period since 1989, and more specifically since 1945, a year which saw the end of a period of particular violence and savagery. While an atmosphere of threat, menace and foreboding certainly did not disappear, interstate war ceased in Europe. For some forty years, up to 1989, interstate relations within Europe were characterized by the frozen version of peace known as Cold War. This condition, rather like the artificially induced coma of a person with serious injury, was maintained by a number of specific devices (Judt, 2005, p. 750), including the 'outsourcing' of extreme political conflict to other parts of the world (e.g. Korea, Malaya and Angola) and the internal repression – Judt calls it 'a distinctive form of permanent warfare upon their own societies' – practised by Communist regimes in Central and Eastern Europe. It did, however, allow for the inception of a number of healing processes, including the integration which meant that the question of the role of Germany in Europe would not again be the trigger for war as it had been in 1914 and 1939, and economic reconstruction alongside the emergence of welfare states. But the metaphor of a patient in a coma must not be pressed too far. When the patient revived some healing had undoubtedly occurred, but equally, old wounds opened up and new diseases manifested themselves.

Any attempt to identify the major trends of internal development in Europe since 1945 and more especially since 1989 must inevitably be subjective and partial, since a main element of European distinctiveness is constituted by a process of reinvention. As Outhwaite points out (Chapter 7), the values which took shape in particular during and after the sixteenth century and as a consequence of the French Revolution were widely exported through the processes of empire-building and colonization, and are, in some forms, now being re-imported. So Europe can claim no exclusive ownership. It is not attachment to the so-called 'Western' approach to liberal democracy, the role of the market, economic forces and human rights, which distinguishes the nation-states of Europe from much of the rest of the world. They are distinguished rather by the scope and scale of the transformations that they have undergone in the last 60 years, and their ability to adapt to these.

Some of these transformations are social, some political. In particular the end of colonialism and empire, the passage from fascism or autocracy for Italy, Germany, Greece, Spain and Portugal, and the 'triple transformation' (political, social and national) after communism in Central and Eastern Europe, have required greater or lesser adjustments in all European states. In comparison, other 'Western' countries, and especially the USA, fixed as it is within the firm corset of its constitutional discourse and values, seem more static and less flexible.

The trends referred to above are discernible chiefly with the illumination of hindsight and the benefit of comparison. Each is associated with its own particular challenges. Our partial and subjective list includes, first, the complex evolution of the place of religion in society, described in Chapter 7, so that European society can, as Outhwaite argues, be described as both secular and post-secular and is grappling with the challenges involved in the accommodation of diverse manifestations of religion within a society that is now very diverse. Recent moves, in France, Belgium and Catalonia, to ban the wearing of the face-covering veil in public reflect this. Equally, since the proponents of the ban frequently, if contentiously, argued that the veil indicates a repressive and demeaning approach to women which is inconsistent with the modern recognition of the equality in rights and status of men and women, this move also reflects a second major trend, the changing position of women. In this there have been very substantial shifts over the last 40 years, and younger people today can and do make everyday assumptions about women's position that would have seemed at best highly radical and at worst unimaginable only a few decades ago. After 1945 women had the right to vote in all European countries except Switzerland, where this was gained in 1971. They have increasingly become as willing as men to exercise this right, although the extent to which this is reflected in the composition of legislative assemblies is variable: in 2010, on average, 42 per cent of the members of the national parliaments of the Nordic countries were women, while the average proportion of women members in all the other European countries was only 20 per cent (Interparliamentary Union, 2010). The UK has had a woman Prime Minister and Germany a woman Chancellor. However, despite undoubted progress, not least in the extent to which the presence of women, combined with legislative frameworks, has in many countries made the public and formal expression of prejudice unacceptable, optimism can only be cautious. Rising affluence and the acquisition of consumer goods (Chapter 8) have had an impact upon the nature of the domestic labour which, however, still falls predominantly to women (Stevens, 2007, p. 87), and gender pay gaps stubbornly persist. The differences in the ways in which political and social trends affect women and men mean that all generalizations have to be taken with care. This is particularly true for the ex-Communist countries of Central and Eastern Europe where the post-1989 transformations had profound but paradoxical effects (Einhorn, 2006). It may also be true for the austerity forecast in response to the sovereign debt crises of 2010 (Chapters 2 and 8), where public spending cuts are likely to have particularly harsh effects upon women (*Guardian*, 5 July 2010).

The evolution of the welfare state (Chapter 8) can be seen as a third crucial trend. Underlying this evolution is the struggle for social justice which, Gerard Delanty argues, is a particularly distinctive feature of European modernity.

> Certainly when one looks at Europe from a global perspective, it is the struggle for social justice that stands out as the most prominent feature of Europe's political heritage and a key characteristic of the formation of modernity. Modernity evolved in Europe, unlike in other parts of the world, in [such] a way that capitalism and state formation were constrained by the taming influences of civil society, including social movements concerned with social justice. (Delanty, 2010, p. 12)

The welfare state in Europe exists in a profusion of varied forms (Ferrera, Hemerijk, and Rhodes, 2003), which have, at least until the onset of the global financial crisis in late 2007, proved rather resistant to 'Europeanizing' harmonization even within the eurozone. Income disparities persist, indeed within individual countries have tended to widen (Chapter 8), but nevertheless European welfare states are expected to, and do, provide health care, sound education, and at least minimal income provision for the sick, the unemployed and the aged. One consequence is that all 15 of the pre-2004-enlargement members of the EU rank above the USA for infant mortality and life expectancy at birth (*CIA World Factbook*, 2010; World Health Organization, 2006). Critics of the 'European social model', which, in all its many variations, has provided most citizens, in the name of civic solidarity and collective responsibility, with some sense of protection against serious risks, argue that it does so in ways that may be both unfair and unsustainable; unfair because they tend to result in economic rigidities that constrain both employment and growth, and unsustainable because a declining birth rate and ageing population are increasing the proportion of the elderly who require pensions and care, and decreasing the proportion of the active citizens whose labours must pay for these.

The continent-wide unification poses another challenge. With the accession of a large bloc of eastern European countries to the EU in 2004 and 2007, with some more enlargement also in prospect in the Balkans, the political division of the continent is beginning to be transcended (see Chapter 3). This is reinforced by the enlargement of NATO to the region in two main waves of enlargement in 1999 and 2004 (see Chapter 10). Various solidarity programmes are also beginning to reduce the wide gap in standards of living and patterns of social consumption between the two parts of the continent (see Chapter 8). Nevertheless, historical divisions are not so easily overcome, and in terms of security perceptions there remains a gulf between the two regions. Eastern Europe was particularly badly hit by the global financial crisis from 2008, which set back many countries' ambitions fully to integrate with the global economic system. Above all, there remain seven countries to the east of the current EU whose status is ambiguous in terms of existing models of European integration. For six of these countries (Belarus, Ukraine, Moldova, Armenia, Azerbaijan and Georgia) the present position of enlargement fatigue and geopolitical indeterminacy is clearly unsatisfactory, caught as they are between two blocs, while for the seventh (Russia) the situation is also fraught with dangers and risks. It is for this reason that commentators in

Moscow are now calling for a visionary new approach to continent-wide integration in some form of 'union of Europe', bringing together the EU, the 'lands in between', and Russia (Sakwa, 2010).

Chapter 9 identified a further set of problems, those associated with adjustment to the demands of regions and communities. The challenge is linked to those of welfare, since in most nation-states there are transfers, sometimes substantial ones, of public funds between geographic areas, whether planned and formulaic, as in the transfer of resources to the eastern *Länder* of Germany, or automatic, through the taxation of the employed in prosperous regions with the payment of benefits to those in poverty elsewhere. But such arrangements become more visible and salient when times are hard. The accommodation of dissatisfied regions, as Jörg Mathias argues, involves delicate political arrangements. The period since 1989 has already seen the political map of Europe change, and a number of countries, most notably Belgium, seem to live with perpetually unstable political architecture.

Set against these centrifugal pressures is the centripetal pull of integration described in Chapters 3 and 4. In a globalizing world this process, which more than any other single factor has shaped the nature of intra-European relations and the way in which 'Europe' is perceived from outside, remains paradoxical and ambiguous. Many of the founding ambitions of the originators have been achieved. While Europe has not been without small wars within its boundaries in the past half-century, a major European civil war that wrought such havoc twice in the first half of the twentieth century now seems unthinkable. The maintenance of internal peace can by and large be taken for granted, but the second main objective – that of increasing prosperity – has increased in importance. The EU is now large and very internally diverse, and that increased diversity has provoked a 'deep dispute' (*Economist*, 10 July 2010) about what the prime purpose of the EU now is. Is it to promote the mobility of trade and labour that will exploit the comparative advantage of each part of the EU – cheaper labour in the east, for example – and thus bring increased competition, flexibility and dynamism: 'globalism within its own borders'?

Or is it to repel or at least to blunt the impact of globalization, to do what no single nation-state is big enough to contemplate on its own and 'assert the supremacy of political will over market forces' so as to protect wages, living standards, security of employment, and the welfare safety net, with all their underlying values? (*Economist*, 10 July 2010). This dispute has rumbled on more or less openly at least since the 'widening versus deepening' debates of the 1990s. The attempts in the early 2000s following the Treaty of Nice to initiate wide political discussion of the future of Europe followed by the constitutional convention were an ultimately futile attempt to resolve the question: these ambiguities were amongst the many, and sometimes contradictory, considerations that resulted in the rejection of the draft Constitutional Treaty in France and the Netherlands (Taggart, 2006). It has not been resolved by the technical tidying-up of the Treaty of Lisbon, and continues to bedevil intra-EU relations, whether over the measures to be taken to deal with heavy indebtedness in some eurozone countries, or over the possible enlargement of the EU, especially to Turkey (Chapter 3).

Europe in the world

The question of future further enlargement of the EU (Chapter 3) raises the issue of the borders of the EU, its relationship to the concept of Europe and its coexistence with its neighbours. The current extent of the EU, the candidacies of Iceland, Albania and the states in the territory of the former Yugoslavia, and the close involvement of Norway and Switzerland in the EU single market and the Schengen agreement make the conflation of the terms 'EU' and 'Europe' almost justifiable. Almost but not quite. Tony Judt's illuminating discussion insists that the borders between 'East and West, Asia and Europe, were always walls in the mind at least as much as lines on the earth' and that it may be more helpful to think of fluid and indeterminate border zones (Judt, 2005, p. 752). Wherever these walls in the mind are mapped on the globe, however, it is clear that, alongside enlargement (and especially the question of the future status of Turkey, see Chapter 3), one of the key challenges faced by Europe is coexistence with close neighbours whose territories lie wholly or in part outside the European borderlands, in particular the states of the Middle East, of North Africa and Russia (Chapter 10). As Mike Bowker points out, the recognition of the consequences of economic interdependence, especially in energy, may recently have helped to soften Russian foreign policy, but even in energy the interests of the EU member states may point in different directions, and the formulation of a common stance is far from easy.

In a number of respects integrative projects in Europe have reached a plateau, and in some aspects there has been a noticeable decline. The 2009 Lisbon Treaty within the EU represented a significant watering-down of some of the ambitions vested in drafts of the European constitution that it came to replace. Russia's relations with the EU are characterized by a lukewarm embrace that at times becomes a chilly estrangement. No common language or common purpose has been found in relations between the two regions. The enlargement agenda is no longer the focus of relations with neighbours, and although in the Balkans it remains an important tool, with the exception of Croatia growth will be a long-term process. The prospects of Turkish membership are receding, while the EU aspirations of Ukraine and other Eastern European countries have been placed on indefinite hold.

Europe has traditionally been defined in terms of inclusion and exclusion, and European identity has been forged in contrast to number of 'others', although the object of this otherness has varied over time. The 'other' variously encompassed Asia, Africa and even an image of America, and in particular the peoples of these continents. Countries like Germany and Spain have not been immune to being 'othered', and the French saying that 'Africa begins at the Pyrenees' reflects a concise idea of the spatial extent of Europe. The traditional 'other' in the European state system has been 'the Turk', on the margins of Europe and for a long period in a state of decline as the 'sick man of Europe'. But it was Russia that was not only the constitutive 'other'; its entrance into the European state system and politics was considered a threat to the constitution of Europe itself. Today the challenge is to find a way of overcoming this internal 'othering', while avoiding the danger of building internal pan-European unity on the foundations of 'othering' some external force or country.

In a certain sense all of Europe is becoming a global outsider. While the Russians now talk of 'greater Europe', this is taking place precisely at a time when the continent as a whole is becoming a 'lesser Europe'. When the idea of a European constitution was first mooted it was intended to provide a formal framework for European ascendancy. However, the bruising experience followed by the adoption of the rather modest Lisbon Treaty appears now to be a response to relative decline. The Lisbon Treaty, moreover, appears to have done little to remove confusion about leadership in domestic and foreign policy in the EU. Although the EU has a total combined GDP equal to that of the USA ($14.5 trillion), its strategic marginalization derives not just from a lack of unity but also from the absence of common resolve. Both Russia and the EU begin to suspect that they are on a relative downward slope in terms of global power, and that the continent as a whole is in danger of being marginalized.

Much attention has been focused on the rise of the so-called BRIC countries (Brazil, Russia, India and China), a term invented in a report by Goldman Sachs in 2003. In fact, nothing unites these countries other than their common status as 'emerging economies'. Above all, the rise of China has mesmerized the rest of the world. This was vividly in evidence at the World Economic Forum in Davos in January 2010. Coming in the wake of the greatest economic crisis since the great depression of the 1930s, the 'masters of the universe' (as the financiers on Wall Street once dubbed themselves) were in a chastened mood, and more attentive to the real balance of power. As Larry Elliot, economics editor of the *Guardian*, vividly describes, there was a new power in the land:

The flipside to the waxing of China has been the waning of Europe. Sessions on China were packed; a session on the future of the Eurozone was half full. For the Asian and the American contingents in Davos, the crisis in Greece was very much a local affair in a part of the world that matters less than it once did. A declining population and sluggish growth mean that this trend is likely to continue. While there is no immediate prospect of Greece leaving the Eurozone, the creation of the single currency

may prove to be the zenith of Europe's influence. (Elliott, 2010)

China's rise has been accompanied by a flood of literature suggesting that it represents 'the end of the western world' (Jacques, 2009), although there are some more sceptical views (Hutton, 2008). Thus not only Russia and Europe are entering, according to some commentators, an era of unaccustomed marginality, but the whole epoch is becoming 'post-European'.

In this context, Europe (the whole continent, east and west) is increasingly faced with the challenge of taking responsibility for its strategic security needs, and indeed, its role in Eurasia and the world. Instead, Europe's identity crisis is reflected in the development of a siege mentality lacking a coherent response to the challenges of immigration, terrorism, human trafficking, and energy issues. The various problems on Europe's periphery reflect Europe's identity crisis, incoherent foreign policy and elements of institutional paralysis. Too often the EU's default position has been little more than a pale mirror image of American policy, with deleterious consequences for both. When Europe has tried to define its own position or to take the lead, as in climate change, it has not been able to find a clear way of achieving its goals. The marginalization of the EU at the Copenhagen climate change summit in December 2009 was clear evidence of this unwonted marginalization.

The achievements of the European 'project', however, should be stressed. Europe retains the ability to regenerate and reinvent itself. Official Europe has made the historic choice to focus on peace and development, and although this risks complacency, it has helped tame the continent's history of internecine and external warfare. While still at an unacceptably high level, deaths in Europe from war and violence have amounted to only one million in the second half of the century compared with 60 million in the first half (Mazower, 1998). The 'muddling through' that a pluralistic society has preferred is producing in contemporary Europe notable progress in cross-border trade and movement, in economic stability, in the development of welfare states and of human rights, and in the creation of a single European people referred to above. There is still a chance that the reinvention of the nation-state and of Europe will result in the gradual evolution of a set of political relationships of a new sort: functional, complex, multilingual, geared to supporting economic development and controlling it, attentive to the social dimension, and concentrating at interstate level on the management of tasks which transcend the local, whether – to take examples amongst many others – the movement of people or trade, or facing environmental issues and threats. The achievement of this new set of relationships, which will be both unprecedented and unparalleled elsewhere, will depend upon the ability of the states of Europe, within the EU and outside it, to manage conflict without resorting to violence. Peace, even if sometimes a partial and punctured one, and despite all the disappointments and setbacks, may still be a realistic vision and hope for a united Europe.

References

Chapter 1

Beck, Ulrich (1992) *Risk Society: Towards a New Modernity* (London: Sage).

Bernstein, Eduard ([1899] 1961) *Evolutionary Socialism: The Classic Statement of Democratic Socialism* (New York: Shocken Books).

Diamond, Jared M. (1997) *Guns, Germs and Steel* (London: Jonathan Cape).

Friedrich, C. and Z. Brzezinski (1966) *Totalitarian Dictatorship and Autocracy*, rev. edn (New York: Praeger).

Garton Ash, Timothy (1999) *History of the Present: Essays, Sketches and Despatches From Europe in the 1990s* (London: Allen Lane).

Gellner, Ernest (1983) *Nations and Nationalism: New Perspectives on the Past* (Oxford: Basil Blackwell).

George, Stephen (1998) *An Awkward Partner: Britain in the European Community*, 3rd edn (London: Oxford University Press).

Hayek, Friedrich A. von (1944) *The Road to Serfdom* (London: Routledge).

Huntington, Samuel (1993) 'The Clash of Civilizations?', *Foreign Affairs* 72(3): 22–49.

Huntington, Samuel (1996) *The Clash of Civilizations and the Remaking of World Order* (New York: Simon & Schuster).

Keane, John (ed.) (1988) *Civil Society and the State: New European Perspectives* (London: Verso).

Kennedy, Paul (1987) *The Rise and Fall of the Great Powers: Economic Change and Military Conflict from 1500 to 2000* (New York: Random House).

Lewis, Bernard (1982), *The Muslim Discovery of Europe* (New York: Norton).

Lieven, Dominic (2003) *Empire: The Russian Empire and its Rivals from the Sixteenth Century to the Present* (London: Pimlico).

Marquand, David (2004) *Decline of the Public: The Hollowing out of Citizenship* (Cambridge: Polity Press).

Mastny, Vojtech (1993) 'The Helsinki Process and a New Framework of European Security', in Jonathan Story (ed.), *The New Europe* (Oxford: Blackwell), pp. 421–42.

Mazower, M. (1998) *The Dark Continent: Europe's Twentieth Century* (London: Allen Lane/Penguin).

Mestrovic, S.G. (1994) *The Balkanization of the West: The Confluence of Postmodernism and Postcommunism* (London: Routledge).

Paasi, Anssi (1996) *Territories, Boundaries and Consciousness: The Changing Geographies of the Finnish-Russian Border* (Chichester: John Wiley).

Przeworski, Adam (1991) *Democracy and the Market: Political and Economic Reforms in Eastern Europe and Latin America* (Cambridge: Cambridge University Press).

Sassoon, Donald (1996) *One Hundred Years of Socialism: The West European Left in the Twentieth Century* (London: I.B. Tauris).

Scott, James C. (1996) *Seeing Like a State: How Certain Schemes to Improve the Human Condition Have Failed* (New Haven, CT & London: Yale University Press).

Therborn, G. (1995) *European Modernity and Beyond: The Trajectory of European Societies, 1945–2000* (London: Sage).

Tilly, Charles (2004) *Contention and Democracy in Europe, 1650–2000* (Cambridge: Cambridge University Press).

Zielonka, Jan (2006) *Europe as Empire: The Nature of the*

Enlarged European Union (Oxford: Oxford University Press).

Zweig, Stefan (1943) *The World of Yesterday* (London: Cassell).

Chapter 2

Bell, Daniel (1960) *The End of Ideology: On the Exhaustion of Political Ideas in the Fifties* (New York: The Free Press).

Carr, E.H. (1939) *The Twenty Years' Crisis of 1919–1939: An Introduction to the Study of International Relations* (London: Macmillan).

Fukuyama, Francis (1992) *The End of History and the Last Man* (New York: The Free Press).

Chapter 3

Ágh, Attila (1998) *The Politics of Central Europe* (London: Sage).

Bicchi, Federica (2010) 'The Impact of the ENP on EU–North Africa Relations: The Good, the Bad and the Ugly', in Richard G. Whitman and Stefan Wolff (eds), *The European Neighbourhood Policy in Perspective: Context, Implementation and Impact* (Basingstoke: Palgrave Macmillan), pp. 206–22.

Blazyca, George (2003) 'Managing Transition Economies', in Stephen White, Judy Batt and Paul G. Lewis (eds), *Developments in Central and East European Politics* (London: Palgrave Macmillan), pp. 213–33.

Booth, Jenny (2005) 'Bush hails Georgia as a beacon of liberty', *Times Online,* 10 May 2005, available at http://www.timesonline.co.uk/tol/news/world/article520811.ece, accessed 15 March 2010.

Commission of the European Communities (2003) *Communication from the Commission, Wider Europe–Neighbourhood: A New Framework for Relations with our Eastern and Southern Neighbours* (Brussels) COM(2003) 104 final.

Commission of the European Communities (2004) *Communication from the Commission to the Council and the European Parliament: Recommendation of the European Commission Turkey's progress towards accession* (Brussels) COM (2004) 656, p. 3.

Commission of the European Communities (2006) *Communication from the Commission: Monitoring report on the state of preparedness for EU membership of Bulgaria and Romania* (Brussels) COM (2006) 26 September.

Commission of the European Communities (2007) *Communication from the Commission: A Strong European Neighbourhood Policy* (Brussels) COM (2007) 774 final.

Commission of the European Communities (2008a) *Communication from the Commission to the European Parliament and the Council: Barcelona Process: Union for the Mediterranean* COM (2008) 319 final, Brussels, 20 May.

Commission of the European Communities (2008b) *Communication from the Commission to the European Parliament and the Council: Eastern Partnership* (Brussels) COM (2008) 823 final, Brussels 3 December.

Council of Europe Directorate of Communication (2010) 'Council of Europe condemns executions in Belarus', press release 248(2010).

Council of the European Communities (1993) *Presidency Conclusions: Copenhagen European Council* (Brussels: CEC).

Council of the European Union (2010) *EU–Turkey Association Council,* Brussels, 10 May, 9687/10 (Presse 116).

Dannreuther, Roland (ed.) (2004) *European Union Foreign and Security Policy: Towards a Neighbourhood Strategy* (London: Routledge).

Dannreuther, Roland (2006) 'Developing the Alternative to Enlargement: The European Neighbourhood Policy', *European Foreign Affairs Review* 11(2): 183–201.

Edwards, Geoffrey (2008) 'The Construction of Ambiguity and the Limits of Attraction: Europe and its Neighbourhood Policy', *Journal of European Integration* 30(1): 45–62.

European Commission (2010) *Eurostat: GDP per capita in PPS,* http://epp.eurostat.ec.europa.eu/tgm/table.do?tab=table&init=1&plugin=1&language=en&pcode=tsieb010

European Council (2003) *EU-Western Balkans Summit – Declaration,* Thessaloniki, 21 June, 10229/03 (Presse 163).

Featherstone, Kevin and Radaelli, Claudio, M. (eds) (2003) *The Politics of Europeanization* (Oxford: Oxford University Press).

Freedom House (2004) *Freedom in the World 2004: The Annual Survey of Political Rights and Civil Liberties* (Lanham, MD: Rowman & Littlefield), http://www.freedomhouse.org/.

Freedom House (2009) *Freedom in the World Comparative and Historical Data,* http://www.

freedomhouse.org/template.cfm?page=439, accessed 5 April 2010.

Freedom House (2010) *Freedom in the World 2010: Erosion of Freedom Intensifies*, http://www.freedomhouse.org/template.cfm?page=505, accessed 15 April 2010.

Gallagher, Tom (2003) 'The Balkans since 1989: The Winding Retreat from National Communism', in Stephen White, Judy Batt and Paul Lewis (eds), *Developments in Central and East European Politics* (Basingstoke: Palgrave Macmillan).

Grabbe, Heather (2006) *The EU's Transformative Power: Europeanization through Conditionality in Central and Eastern Europe* (Basingstoke: Palgrave Macmillan).

Hill, Fiona and Taspinar, Omer (2006) 'Turkey and Russia: Axis of the Excluded?', *Survival* 48(1): 81–92.

Huntington, Samuel (1991) *The Third Wave Democratization in the Late Twentieth Century* (Norman and London: University of Oklahoma Press)

Jasiewicz, Krzysztof (2003) 'Elections and Voting Behaviour', in Stephen White, Judy Batt and Paul G. Lewis (eds), *Developments in Central and East European Politics* (London: Palgrave Macmillan).

Ladrech, Paul (2004) 'Europeanization and the Member States', in Maria Green Cowles and Desmond Dinan (eds), *Developments in the European Union 2* (Basingstoke: Palgrave Macmillan).

Millard, Frances (2003) 'Poland', in Stephen White, Judy Batt and Paul G. Lewis (eds), *Developments in Central and East European Politics* (London: Palgrave Macmillan).

Millard, Frances (2004) *Elections, Parties, and Representation in Post-Communist Europe* (Basingstoke: Palgrave Macmillan).

Offe, Claus (1991) 'Capitalism by Democratic Design? Democratic Theory Facing the Triple Transition in East Central Europe', *Social Research* 58(4): 865–92.

OSCE (2010) *International Election Observation Mission, Ukraine – Presidential Election, Second Round, 7 February 2010, Statement of Preliminary Findings and Conclusions*, available at http://www.osce.org/documents/odihr/2010/02/42679_en.pdf, accessed 20 April 2010.

Pankowski, Rafal (2010) *The Populist Radical Right in Poland* (London: Routledge).

Pridham, Geoffrey (2002) 'EU Enlargement and Consolidating Democracy in Post-Communist States – Formality and Reality', *Journal of Common Market Studies* 40(4): 953–73.

Prodi, Romano (2002) *A Wider Europe – A Proximity Policy as the Key to Stability,* Brussels, 6 December, SPEECH/02/619.

Rose, Richard (1997) 'Rights and Obligations of Individuals in the Baltic States', *East European Constitutional Review* 6(4): 35–43.

Sakwa, Richard (2008) *Putin: Russia's Choice*, 2nd edn (London: Routledge).

Sasse, Gwendolyn, (2010) 'The ENP and the EU's Eastern Neighbours: Ukraine and Moldova as Test Cases', in Richard G. Whitman and Stefan Wolff (eds), *The European Neighbourhood Policy in Perspective: Context, Implementation and Impact* (Basingstoke: Palgrave Macmillan).

Smith, Julie and Jenkins, Charles (eds) (2003) *Through the Paper Curtain: Insiders and Outsiders in the New Europe* (Oxford: Blackwell).

Szczerbiak, Aleks and Hanley, Seán (eds) (2005) *Centre-Right Parties in Post-Communist East-Central Europe* (Abingdon: Routledge).

World Bank (2002) *Transition: The First Ten Years. Analysis and Lessons for Eastern Europe and the Former Soviet Union* (Washington, DC: IBRD/World Bank).

Chapter 4

Balme, Richard, and Woll, Cornelia (2005) 'France: Between Integration and National Sovereignty', in S. Bulmer and C. Lesquesne (eds), *The Member States of the European Union* (Oxford: Oxford University Press), pp. 97–118.

Best, Edward, Christiansen, Thomas and Settembri, Pierpaolo (2009) 'Effects of Enlargement on the EU's Institutions and Decisionmaking – The EU Institutions after Enlargement: Not Quite Business as Usual', in G. Avery, A. Faber and A. Schmidt (eds), *Enlarging the European Union: Effects on the New Member States and the EU* (Brussels: Trans European Policy Studies Association), pp. 112–24.

Bomberg, Elizabeth, Cram, Laura and Martin, David (2003) 'The EU's Institutions', in Elizabeth Bomberg and Alexander Stubb (eds), *The European Union: How Does It Work?* (Oxford: Oxford University Press), pp. 43–68.

Bulmer, Simon, and Radaelli, Claudio (2005) 'The Europeanisation of National Policy', in S. Bulmer and C. Lesquesne (eds), *The Member States of the European Union* (Oxford: Oxford University Press).

Cassese, Sabino (2009) 'Introduction: Im Zweifel für Europa', in S. Micossi and G.L. Tosato (eds), *The European Union in the 21st Century: Perspectives from the Lisbon Treaty* (Brussels: Centre for European Policy Studies).

Church, Clive (2009) Watching the ratification of the Treaty of Lisbon. Unpublished paper available via the author at http://www.kent.ac.uk/politics/about-us/staff/members/church.html

CIA (2010) *CIA World Factbook*, available at https://www.cia.gov/library/publications/the-world-factbook/index.html, accessed 5 April 2011.

Council of the European Union (2009), The Treaty of Lisbon: Information Note, December.

Cram, Laura (1989) 'The Commission', in Laura Cram, Desmond Dinan and Neill Nugent (eds), *Developments in the European Union* (Basingstoke: Palgrave Macmillan), pp. 44–61.

De Porte, A.W. (1979) *Europe between the Superpowers: The Enduring Balance* (New Haven, CT and London: Yale University Press).

Dinan, Desmond (1994) *Ever Closer Union? An Introduction to the European Community* (London: Macmillan).

Eising, Rainer (2007) 'Interest Groups and the European Union', in M. Cini (ed.), *European Union Politics* (Oxford: Oxford University Press).

European Commission: Employment, Social Affairs and Equal Opportunities Directorate General (2010) [cited 10 April 2010], available from http://ec.europa.eu/social/main.jsp?langId=en&catId=750.

European Commission (2010) *Mechanism for Cooperation and Verification for Bulgaria and Romania* 2010 [cited 3 May 2010], http://ec.europa.eu/dgs/secretariat_general/cvm/progress_reports_en.htm.

Eurostat (2010) Tables, graphs and maps: total population at 1 January. Table code tps 00001 at http://epp.eurostat.ec.europa.euhttp://epp.eurostat.ec.europa.eu, accessed 25 August 2011.

Falkner, Gerda, and Treib, Oliver (2008) 'Three Worlds of Compliance or Four: The EU 15 Compared to the New Member States', *Journal of Common Market Studies* 469(2): 293–313.

Garton-Ash, Timothy (2010) 'You can see why Berlin has cut the motor, but now Europe is stalled', *Guardian*, 1 April.

Grabbe, Heather (2010) 'We've Got to Get the EU's Balkans Enlargement Back on Track', *Europe's World Online Journal* 4.

Grabbe, Heather, and Sedelmeier, Ulrich (2009) 'The Future Shape of the European Union', in M. Egan, N. Nugent and W.E. Paterson (eds), *Research Agendas in European Studies* (Basingstoke: Palgrave Macmillan).

Hix, Simon (1999) *The Political System of the European Union* (Basingstoke: Palgrave Macmillan).

Hyde-Pryce, Adrian (1998) 'Patterns of International Politics', in S. White, J. Batt and P.G. Lewis (eds), *Developments in Central and East European Politics 2* (Basingstoke: Palgrave Macmillan), pp. 255–75.

Ivaldi, Gilles (2006) 'Beyond France's 2005 Referendum on the European Constitutional Treaty: Second Order Model, Anti-establishment Attitudes and the End of the Alternative European Utopia', *West European Politics* 29(1): 47–69.

Kurpas, Sebastian, Grøn, Caroline, and Kaczy ski, Piotr Maciej (2008) 'The European Commission after Enlargement: Does More Add Up to Less?' Brussels: Centre for European Policy Studies.

Laffan, Brigid (1992) *Integration and Cooperation in Europe* (London: Routledge).

Lubbers, Marcel (2008) 'Regarding the Dutch "Nee" to the European Constitution: A Test of the Identity, Utilitarian and Political Approaches to Voting 'No'', *European Union Politics* 9(1): 59–86.

Mayhew, Alan (1998) *Recreating Europe: The European Union's Policy towards Central and Eastern Europe* (Cambridge: Cambridge University Press).

Moravcsik, Andrew (1998) *The Choice for Europe: Social Purpose and State Power from Messina to Maastricht* (London: University College London Press).

Nugent, Neill (1999) *The Government and Politics of the European Union*, 4th edn (Basingstoke: Palgrave Macmillan).

Peterson, John, and Elizabeth Bomberg (1999) *Decision-making in the European Union* (London: Macmillan).

Picq, Jean (1995) *Il faut aimer l'État* (Paris: Flammarion).

Quaglia, Lucia, Holmes, Peter and Eastwood, Rob (2009) 'The Financial Turmoil and EU Policy Co-operation in 2008', *Journal of Common Market Studies* 47 (Annual Review): 63–87.

Radaelli, Claudio (1999) *Technocracy in the European Union* (London: Longman).

Rehn, Olli (2008) Interview. *Euractiv*, http://www.euractiv.com/en/enlargement/commissioner-rehn-am-just-factory-manager/article-177381.

Szczerbiak, Aleks, and Taggart, Paul (2008) *Opposing Europe? The Comparative Party Politics of*

Euroscepticism, Vol. 1 (Oxford: Oxford University Press).

Vachudova, Milada Anna (2009) 'Corruption and Compliance in the EU's Post-communist Members and Candidates', *Journal of Common Market Studies* 47 (Annual review): 43–62.

Wallace, Helen (2005) 'An Institutional Anatomy and Five Policy Modes', in H. Wallace, W. Wallace and M.A. Pollack (eds), *Policy-making in the European Union*, 5th edn (Oxford: Oxford University Press).

Wallace, Helen (2007) 'Adapting to Enlargement of the European Union: Institutional Practice since May 2004' (Brussels: Trans European Policy Studies Association).

Watson, Rory, and Michael Shackleton (2008) 'Organised Interests and Lobbying in the EU', in E. Bomberg, J. Peterson and A. Stubb (eds), *The European Union: How Does it Work?* (Oxford: Oxford University Press).

Chapter 5

Andeweg, R.B. (1997) 'Collegiality and Collectivity: Cabinets, Cabinet Committees and Cabinet Ministers', in P. Weller, H. Bakvis and R.A.W. Rhodes (eds), *The Hollow Crown: Countervailing Trends in Core Executives* (Basingstoke: Palgrave Macmillan), pp. 58–83.

Bobba, G. and Seddone, A. (2011) 'Personal and Personalized Party: Notes on a Theoretical Framework', unpublished paper for the Political Studies Association annual conference, London.

Budge, Ian et al. (1997) *The Politics of the New Europe: Atlantic to Urals* (London and New York: Longman).

Crick, Bernard (1970) 'Parliament in the British Political System', in Allan Kornberg and Lloyd D. Musolf (eds), *Legislatures in Developmental Perspective* (Durham, NC: Duke University Press), pp. 33–54.

De Winter, L. (1991) 'Parliamentary and Party Pathways to the Cabinet', in J. Blondel and J.-L. Thiébault (eds), *The Profession of Government Minister in Western Europe* (Basingstoke: Macmillan), pp. 44–69.

Duverger, M. (1980) 'A New Political System Model: Semi-presidential Government', *European Journal of Political Research* 8: 165–87.

European Commission (2010) *Eurostat, Government Finance Statistics,* http://epp.eurostat.ec.europa.eu/portal/page/portal/government_finance_statistics/data/main_tables

Hague, R. and Harrop, M. (2004) *Comparative Government and Politics: An Introduction*, 6th edn (Basingstoke: Palgrave Macmillan).

Hague, R., Harrop, M. and Breslin, S. (1988) *Comparative Government and Politics: An Introduction*, 4th edn (Basingstoke: Palgrave Macmillan).

Hailsham, Lord (1976) *Elective Dictatorship* (London: BBC).

Heywood, A. (1997) *Politics* (Basingstoke: Palgrave Macmillan).

Huber, E., Ragin, C. and Stephens, J.D. (1993) 'Social Democracy, Christian Democracy, Constitutional Structure and the Welfare State: Towards a Resolution of Quantitative Studies', *American Journal of Sociology* 99(3): 711–49.

Ismayr, W. (2004) 'Die politischen Systeme der EU Beitrittsländer im Vergleich', *Aus Politik und Zeitgeschichte* B 5-6: 5–14.

King, A. (1976) 'Modes of Executive–Legislative Relations: Great Britain, France and West Germany', *Legislative Studies Quarterly* 1: 11–36.

Kuntz, P. and Thompson, M.N. (2009) 'More Than Just the Final Straw: Stolen Elections as Revolutionary Triggers', *Comparative Politics* 41(3): 253–72.

Lijphart, A. (ed.) (1992), *Parliamentary versus Presidential Government* (Oxford: Oxford University Press).

Lijphart, A. (1994) *Electoral Systems and Party Systems: A Study of Twenty-Seven Democracies,1945–1990* (Oxford: Oxford University Press).

Lijphart, A. (1999) *Patterns of Democracy: Government Forms and Performance in Thirty-Six Countries* (New Haven, CT: Yale University Press).

Linz, J.J. (1992) 'The Perils of Presidentialism', in A. Lipjhart (ed.), *Parliamentary versusPresidential Government* (Oxford: Oxford University Press).

Lupia, A. and McCubbins, M.D. (1998) *The Democratic Dilemma: Can Citizens Learn What They Need to Know?* (Cambridge: Cambridge University Press).

McCubbins, M.D. and Schwartz, T. (1984) 'Congressional Oversight Overlooked: Police Patrols Versus Fire Alarms', *American Journal of Political Science* 28: 165–79.

Mezey, M.L. (1998) 'Executive–Legislative Relations', in G.T. Kurian (ed.), *World Encyclopaedia of Parliaments and Legislatures*, Vol. II (Washington, DC: Congressional Quarterly), pp. 780–6.

Möckli, S. (1988) 'Direktdemokratische Einrichtungen und Verfahren in den Mitgliedsstaaten des

Europarates', *Zeitschrift für Parlamentsfragen* 29(1): 90–107.

Pharr, S.J. and Putnam, R.D. (eds.) (2000) *Disaffected Democracies: What's Troubling the Trilateral Countries?* (Princeton, NJ: Princeton University Press).

Scharpf, F. W. (1993) 'Coordination in Hierarchies and Networks', in F.W. Scharpf (ed.), *Games in Hierarchies and Networks: Analytical and Empirical Approaches to the Study of Governance Institutions* (Frankfurt/M.: Campus and Boulder, CO: Westview Press).

Shugart, M.S. (2001) 'Electoral "Efficiency" and the Move to Mixed-member Systems', *Electoral Studies* 20: 173–93.

Shugart, S. and Carey, J.M. (1992) *Presidents and Assemblies: Constitutional Design and Electoral Dynamics* (Cambridge: Cambridge University Press 1992).

Siaroff, A. (2003) 'Comparative Presidencies: The Inadequacy of the Presidential, Semi-presidential and Parliamentary Distinction', *European Journal of Political Research* 42: 287–312.

Strøm, K., (1995) 'Parliamentary Government and Legislative Organisation', in H. Döring (ed.), *Parliaments and Majority Rule in Western Europe* (Frankfurt/M.: Campus and New York: St Martin's Press), pp. 51–82.

Strøm, K., Müller, W.C. and Bergman, T. (eds.) (2003) *Delegation and Accountability in Parliamentary Democracies* (Oxford: Oxford University Press).

Taagepera, R. and Shugart, M.S. (1989) *Seats and Votes: The Effects and Determinants of Electoral Systems* (New Haven, CT: Yale University Press).

Chapter 6

Bachrach, Peter (1967) *The Theory of Democratic Elitism* (Boston: Little, Brown).

Barber, Benjamin (1985) *Strong Democracy: Participatory Politics for a New Age* (Berkeley: University of California Press).

Barnes, Samuel, Kaase, Max et al. (1979) *Political Action: Mass Participation in Five Western Democracies* (Beverley Hills and London: Sage).

Bomberg, Elizabeth (1998) *Green Parties and Politics in the European Union* (London: Routledge).

Borg, Sami (1995) 'Electoral Participation', in Jan W. van Deth and Elinor Scargrough (eds), *The Impact of Values: Beliefs in Government*, Vol. 4 (Oxford: Oxford University Press), pp. 441–60.

Bowles, Samuel and Gintis, Herbert (1986) *Democracy and Capitalism: Property, Community and the Contradictions of Modern Thought* (London: Routledge & Kegan Paul).

Brannan, Tessa, John, Peter and *Stoker, Gerry* (2007) *Re-energizing Citizenship: Strategies for Civil Renewal* (Basingstoke: Palgrave Macmillan).

Budge, Ian et al. (1997) *The Politics of the New Europe: Atlantic to Urals* (London: Longman).

Crewe, Ivor and Denver, David (eds) (1985) *Electoral Change in Western Democracies: Patterns and Sources of Electoral Volatility* (London: Croom Helm).

Dahl, Robert A. (1994) 'A Democratic Dilemma: System Effectiveness versus Citizen Participation', *Political Science Quarterly* 109: 23–34.

Dalton, Russell J. (1996) *Citizen Politics: Public Opinion and Political Parties in Advanced Industrial Democracies*, 2nd edn (Chatham, NJ: Chatham House).

Dalton, Russell J. (2004) *Democratic Challenges, Democratic Choices: The Erosion of Political Support in Advanced Industrial Democracies* (Oxford: Oxford University Press).

della Porta, Donatella, Kriesi, Hanspeter and Rucht, Dieter (1999) *Social Movements in a Globalizing World* (London: Macmillan).

della Porta, Donatella and Reiter, Herbert (eds) (1998) *Policing Protest: The Control of Mass Demonstrations in Western Democracies* (Minneapolis and London: University of Minnesota Press).

Downs, Anthony (1957) *An Economic Theory of Democracy* (New York: Harper & Row).

Dryzek, Jon S. (1996) 'Political Inclusion and the Dynamics of Democratisation', *American Political Science Review* 90(1): 475–87.

Fuchs, Dieter (1991) 'The Normalization of the Unconventional: Forms of Political Action and New Social Movements', in Gerd Meyer and Franciszek Ryszka (eds), *Political Participation and Democracy in Poland and West Germany* (Warsaw: Wydawca), pp. 148–65.

Greenwood, Justin and Aspinall, Mark (1998) *Collective Action in the European Union* (London: Routledge).

Gundelach, Peter (1995) 'Grass Roots Activity', in Jan W. van Deth and Elinor Scargrough (eds), *The Impact of Values: Belief in Government*, Vol. 4 (Oxford: Oxford University Press), pp. 412–40.

Habermas, Jürgen (1992) *Daktizität und Geltung* (Frankfurt/M.: Suhrkamp).

Hay, Colin (2007) *Why We Hate Politics* (Cambridge: Polity Press).

Hildebrandt, Kai and Dalton, Russell J. (1977) 'Die neue Politik – Politischer Wandel oder Schönwtterpolitik?', *Politische Vierteljahresschrift* 13(2): 165–77.

Hirst, Paul (1994) *Associative Democracy: New Forms of Economic and Social Government* (Cambridge: Polity Press).

Inglehart, R. (1977) *The Silent Revolution: Changing Values and Political Styles among Western Publics* (Princeton, NJ: Princeton University Press).

Inglehart, Ronald (1981) 'Post-Materialism in an Environment of Insecurity', *American Political Science Review* 75(4): 880–9.

Jennings, Kent M., Van Deth, Jan W. et al. (eds) (1990) *Continuities in Political Action: A Longitudinal Study of Political Orientations in Three Western Democracies* (Berlin and New York: de Gruyter).

Katz, Richard S., Mair, Peter et al. (1992) 'The Membership of Political Parties in European Democracies, 1960–1990', *European Journal of Political Research* 22: 329–45.

Keim, Donald W. (1975) 'Participation in Contemporary Democratic Theories', in J. Roland Pennock and John W. Chapman (eds), *Participation in Politics* (New York: Lieber, Atherton), pp. 1–38.

Key, Valdimer O., Jr (1958) *Politics, Parties and Pressure Groups*, 4th edn (New York: Crowell).

Khan, Usman (1999) *Participation beyond the Ballot Box* (London: UCL Press)

Kirchheimer, Otto (1966) 'The Transformation of the Western European Party Systems', in 'Political Parties and Political Development', in Joseph La Palombara and Myron Weiner (eds), *Political Parties and Political Development* (Princeton, NJ: Princeton University Press.)

Kitschelt, Herbert (1990) 'New Social Movements and the Decline of Party Organization', in Russell Dalton and Manfred Küchler (eds), *Challenging the Political Order: New Social and Political Movements in Western Democracies* (Cambridge: Polity Press), pp. 179–208.

Kornhauser, William (1959) *The Politics of Mass Society* (New York: The Free Press).

Kriesi, Hanspeter, Koopmans, Ruud, Duyvendak, Jan Willem and Giugni, Marco (1995) *New Social Movements in Western Europe: A Comparative Analysis* (Minneapolis: University of Minnesota Press).

Lawson, Kay (1988) 'When Linkeage Fails', in Kay Lawson and Peter H. Merkl (eds), *When Parties Fail: Emerging Alternative Organisations* (Princeton, NJ: Princeton University Press), pp. 13–38.

Lehmbruch, Gerhard and Schmitter, C. Philippe (eds) (1982) *Patterns of Corporatist Policy-making* (London: Sage).

Lichtenburg, Judith (ed.) (1990) *Democracy and Mass Media* (Cambridge: Cambridge University Press).

Lijphart, Arend (1997) 'Unequal Participation: Democracy's Unresolved Dilemma', *American Political Science Review* 91(1): 1–14.

Lipset, Seymour M. and Rokkan, Stein (1967) 'Cleavage Structures, Party Systems, and Voter Alignments: An Introduction', in S. M. Lipset and S. Rokkan (eds), *Party Systems and Voter Alignments: Cross-National Perspectives* (New York: The Free Press), pp. 1–64.

Luhmann, Niklas (1969) 'Komplexität und Demokratie', *Politische Vierteljahresschrift* 11: 314–25.

Marsh, David (1983) *Pressure Politics: Interest Groups in Britain* (London: Junction Books).

Meyer, David and Tarrow, Sidney (eds) (1997) *The Social Movement Society: Contentious Politics for a New Century* (Boulder, CO: Rowman & Littlefield).

Michels, Robert (1962 [1911]) *Political Parties* (New York: The Free Press).

Milbrath, Lester (1965) *Political Participation: How and Why do People Get Involved in Politics?* (Chicago: Rand McNally).

Nagle, J.D. and Mahr, A. (1999) *Democracy and Democratization* (London: Sage).

Neidhardt, Friedhelm and Rucht,Dieter (1993) 'Auf dem Weg in die "Bewegungsgesellschaft"? ber die Stabilisierbarkeit sozialer Bewegungen', *Soziale Welt* 44(3): 305–26.

Norris, Pippa (2002) *Democratic Phoenix: Reinventing Political Activism* (Cambridge: Cambridge University Press).

Orloff, Ann Shola (1996) *Gender and the Welfare State* (Madrid: Instituto Juan March de Estudios e Investigaciones).

Parry, Geraint, Moyer, George and Day, Neil (1992) *Political Participation and Democracy in Britain* (Cambridge: Cambridge University Press).

Pateman, Carole (1970) *Participation and Democratic Theory* (London: Cambridge University Press).

Putnam, Robert D. (1995) 'Bowling Alone: America's Declining Social Capital', *Journal of Democracy* 6(1): 65–78.

Richardson, Dick and Rootes, Chris (eds) (1994) *The Green Challenge: The Development of Green Parties in Europe* (London: Routledge).

Richardson, Jeremy (1995) 'The Market for Political Activism: Interest Groups as Challenge to Political Parties', *West European Politics* 18(1): 116–39.

Rokkan, Stein (1997) *State Formation, Nation-Building, and Mass Politics in Europe* (Oxford: Oxford University Press).

Roller, Edeltraud and We els, Bernhard (1996) 'Contexts of Political Protest in Western Democracies: Political Organization and Modernity', in Fredrick Weil et al. (eds), *Extremism, Protest, Social Movements and Democracy. Research on Democracy and Society*, Vol. 3 (Greenwich/London: JAI Press), pp. 91– 34.

Rootes, Christopher (1999) 'Acting Globally, Thinking Locally? Prospects for a Global Environment Movement', in C. Rootes (ed.), *Environmental Movements: Local National and Global* (London: Frank Cass), pp. 290–310.

Rucht, Dieter (2002) 'The EU as a Target of Political Mobilisation: is there a Europeanisation of Conflict?', in R. Balme, D. Chabanet and V. Wright (eds), *L'action Collective en Europe. Collective Action in Europe* (Paris: Presses de Sciences Po), pp. 163–94.

Rucht, Dieter (2007) 'The Spread of Protest Politics', in Russell J. Dalton and Hans-Dieter Klingemann (eds), *The Oxford Handbook of Political Behaviour* (Oxford: Oxford University Press), pp. 708–23.

Rucht, Dieter (2010) 'Collective Action', in Stefan Immerfall and Göran Therborn (eds), *Handbook of European Societies: Social Transformations in the 21st Century* (New York: Springer), pp. 111–38.

Rucht, Dieter, Blattert, Barbara and Rink, Dieter (1997) *Von der Bewegung zur Institution? Alternative Gruppen in beiden Teilen Deutschlands* (Frankfurt/M.: Campus).

Schmitter, Philippe C. and Lehmbruch, Gerhard (eds) (1979) *Trends towards Corporatist Intermediation* (London: Sage).

Schmitter, Philippe C. and Streeck, Wolfgang (1991) 'Organized Interests and the Europe of 1992', in Norman J. Ornstein and Mark Perlman (eds), *Political Power and Social Change: The United States Faces a United Europe* (Washington, DC: American Enterprise Institute Press), pp. 46–67.

Schumpeter, Joseph (1966 [1942]) *Capitalism, Socialism and Democracy* (London: Allen & Unwin University Books).

Smith, Graham (2005) *Beyond the Ballot – 57 democratic innovations from around the world*, a report commissioned by 'POWER: An Independent Inquiry into Britain's Democracy' (a centenary inquiry established by the Rowntree Charitable and Reform Trusts).

Smith, Graham (2009) Democratic Innovations: Designing Institutions for Citizen Participation (Cambridge: Cambridge University Press).

Tarrow, Sidney (1994) *Power in Movement: Social Movements, Collective Action and Politics* (Cambridge: Cambridge University Press).

Tarrow, Sidney (1995) 'The Europeanization of Conflict: Reflections from a Social Movement Perspective', *West European Politics* 18(2): 223–51.

Topf, Richard (1995) 'Beyond Electoral Participation', in Hans Dieter Klingemann and Dieter Fuchs (eds), *Citizens and the State* (Oxford: Oxford University Press), pp. 52–91.

van Deth, Jan (ed.) (1997) *Private Groups and Public Life: Social Participation and Political Involvement in Representative Democracies* (Cambridge: Cambridge University Press).

Verba, Sidney, Norman Nie and Jae-on Kim (1978) *Participation and Political Equality: A Seven-Nation Comparison* (Cambridge: Cambridge University Press).

Visser, Jelle (1986) 'Die Mitgliederentwicklung der west-europäischen Gewerkschaften. Trends und Konjunkturen 1920–1983', *Journal für Sozialforschung* 26(1): 3–33.

We els, Bernhard (2003) 'Membership in Interest Organizations and Political Parties: the Development of Civil Society in the New Europe, 1990 and 2000', paper prepared for the conference 'Democracy and the New Europe', Paris, 13–16 November.

Williamson, Peter J. (1989) *Corporatism in Perspective* (London: Sage).

Chapter 7

Albert, M. (1991) *Capitalisme contre capitalisme* (Paris: Seuil). Translated as *Capitalism Against Capitalism* (London: Whurr, 1993).

Arnason, J.P. (1993) *The Future That Failed: Origins and Destinies of the Soviet Model* (London: Routledge).

Aron, R. (1962) *Dix-huit leçons sur la société industrielle* (Paris: Gallimard). Translated as *Eighteen Lectures on Industrial Society*. London: Weidenfeld & Nicolson, 1967.

Bailey, J. (ed.) (1992; 2nd edn 1998) *Social Europe* (London: Longman)

Balibar, Étienne (2004) *We, the People of Europe?: Reflections on Transnational Citizenship* (Princeton, NJ: Princeton University Press).

Beck, U. (1986) *Risikogesellschaft* (Frankfurt: Suhrkamp). Translated as *Risk Society: Towards a New Modernity* (London: Sage, 1992).

Beck, U., Giddens, A. and Lash, S. (1994) *Reflexive Modernization* (Cambridge: Polity Press).

Beck, U. and Grande, E. (2004) *Das kosmopolitische Europa*. Frankfurt: Suhrkamp. Translated as *Cosmopolitan Europe* (Cambridge: Polity Press, 2007).

Bell, D. (1987) 'The World and the United States in 2013', *Daedalus* 116(3): 1–32.

Berger, J. (1981) 'Changing Crises-Types in Western Societies', *Praxis International* 1(3): 230–9.

Bourdieu, P. (1970) *La reproduction*. Translated as *Reproduction in Education, Society and Culture* (London: Sage).

Bruter, M. (2005) *Citizens of Europe? The Emergence of a Mass European Identity* (Basingstoke: Palgrave Macmillan).

Budge, I. et al. (1997) *The Politics of the New Europe: Atlantic to Urals* (London and New York: Longman).

Castles, S. et al. (1984) *Here for Good: Western Europe's New Ethnic Minorities* (London: Pluto Press).

Checkel, J. and Katzenstein, P. (eds) (2009) *European Identity* (Cambridge: Cambridge University Press).

Coleman, D. (1996) *Europe's Population in the 1990s* (Oxford: Oxford University Press).

Crouch, C. (1993) *Industrial Relations and European State Traditions* (Oxford: Clarendon Press).

Crouch, C. and Streeck, W. (eds) (1997) *Political Economy of Modern Capitalism* (London: Sage).

Crozier, M. (1964) *The Bureaucratic Phenomenon* (Chicago: University of Chicago Press).

Delanty, G. (1999) 'Die Transformation nationaler Identität und die kulturelle Ambivalenz europäischer Identität', in R. Viehoff and R.T. Segers, *Kultur, Identität, Europa* (Frankfurt/M.: Suhrkamp).

Delhey, J. (2001) *Osteuropa zwischen Marx und Markt* (Hamburg: Kramer).

Einhorn, B. (1993) *Cinderella Goes to Market* (London: Verso).

Eley, G. and Suny, R.G. (eds) (1996) *Becoming National* (New York: Oxford University Press).

Elias, N. (1988) *Die Gesellschaft der Individuen*. Translated as *The Society of Individuals* (Oxford: Blackwell, 1992).

Eriksson, R. and Goldthorpe, J. (1992) *The Constant Flux: A Study of Class Mobility in Industrial Societies* (Cambridge: Cambridge University Press).

Eurostat (2009) *Europe in Figures: Yearbook 2009*, http://epp.eurostat.ec.europa.eu/portal/page/portal/publications/eurostat_yearbook_2010/previous_editions

Evans, P.B., Rueschemeyer, D. and Skocpol, T. (eds) (1985) *Bringing the State Back In*. Cambridge: Cambridge University Press.

Eyal, G., Szelenyi, I. and Townsley, E. (eds) (1998) *Making Capitalism without Capitalists: Class Formation and Elite Struggles in Post-Communist Central Europe* (London: Verso).

Favell, A. (2008) *Eurostars and Eurocities: Free Movement and Mobility in an Integrating Europe* (Oxford: Blackwell).

Fischer, M.E. (ed.) (1996) *Establishing Democracies* (Boulder, CO: Westview Press).

Giddens, A. (1991) *Modernity and Self-Identity* (Cambridge: Polity Press).

Gilroy, P. (1993) *The Black Atlantic: Modernity and Double Consciousness* (London: Verso).

Grundy, S. and Jamieson, L. (2005) '"Are We All Europeans Now?" Local, National and Supranational Identities of Young Adults', *Sociological Research Online* 10(3), http://socresonline.org.uk/10/3/grundy.html

Grundy, S. and Jamieson, L. (2007) 'European Identities: From Absent-Minded Citizens to Passionate Europeans', *Sociology* 41(4): 663–80.

Habermas, J. (1990) *Die nachholende Revolution* (Frankfurt: Suhrkamp). Title essay translated as 'What Does Socialism Mean Today? The Rectifying Revolution and the Need for New Thinking on the Left', *New Left Review* 1(183), September–October.

Hann, C.M. (ed.) (2002) *Postsocialism: Ideals, Ideologies and Practices in Eurasia* (London: Routledge).

Held, D. (1995) *Democracy and the Global Order* (Cambridge: Polity Press).

Herm, A. (2008) 'Population and social conditions', Eurostat 98, http://epp.eurostat.ec.europa.eu/cache/ity_offpub/ks-sf-08-098/en/ks-sf-08-098-en.pdf.

Hudson, R. and Williams, A.M. (1999) *Divided Europe: Society and Territory* (London: Sage).

Huntington, S. (1993) 'The Clash of Civilizations?' *Foreign Affairs* 72(3): 22–49.

Inglehart, R. (1977) *The Silent Revolution: Changing Values and Political Styles among Western Publics* (Princeton, NJ: Princeton University Press).

Inglehart, R. (1990) *Culture Shift in Advanced Industrial Society* (Princeton, NJ: Princeton University Press).

Judt, T. (2005) *Postwar: A History of Europe since 1945* (London: Heinemann).

King, R. and Donati, M. (1999) 'The Divided Mediterranean: Re-defining European Relationships', in Ray Hudson and Allan Williams (eds), *Divided Europe* (London: Sage), pp. 132–62.

Lane, C. (1989) *Management and Labour in Europe: The Industrial Enterprise in Germany, Britain and France* (Aldershot: Edward Elgar).

Lash, S. and Urry, J. (1987) *The End of Organized Capitalism* (Cambridge: Polity Press).

Laslett, Peter (1965) *The World We Have Lost* (2nd edn 1971; 3rd edn 1983, London: Methuen).

Lenoir, D. (1994) *L'Europe sociale* (Paris: La Découverte).

Mann, M. (1986, 1993) *The Sources of Social Power*, 2 vols (Cambridge: Cambridge University Press).

Marceau, J. (1977) *Class and Status in France* (Oxford: Oxford University Press).

Mendras, H. (1988) *La seconde revolution française, 1965–1984* (Paris: Gallimard).

Mendras, H. (1997) *L'Europe des Européens* (Paris: Gallimard).

Moore, B. (1966) *Social Origins of Dictatorship and Democracy: Landlord and Peasant in the Making of the Modern World* (Boston: Beacon Press).

Moore, B. (1978) *Injustice: The Social Bases of Obedience and Revolt* (London: Macmillan).

Nagle, J.D. and Mahr, A. (1999) *Democracy and Democratization* (London: Sage).

Offe, C. (1985) *Disorganized Capitalism* (Cambridge: MIT Press).

Oliver, C. (2008) *Retirement Migration: Paradoxes of Ageing* (London: Routledge).

Outhwaite, W. (2006) 'Europe after the EU Enlargement: Cosmopolitanism by Small Steps', in G. Delanty (ed.), *Europe and Asia Beyond East and West* (London: Routledge), pp. 193–202.

Outhwaite, W. (2010a) 'What is Left after 1989?', in George Lawson, Chris Armbruster and Michael Cox (eds), *The Global 1989: Continuity and Change in World Politics* (Cambridge: Cambridge University Press).

Outhwaite, W. (2010b) 'Legality and Legitimacy in the European Union', in S. Ashenden and C. Thornhill (eds), *Legality and Legitimacy* (Baden-Baden: Nomos), pp. 279–90.

Outhwaite, W (2010c) 'Europe at 21: Transitions and Transformations since 1989'. LEQS Paper No. 18, January, http://www2.lse.ac.uk/europeanInstitute/LEQS/LEQSPapers.aspx

Outhwaite, W. and Larry Ray (2004) *Social Theory and Postcommunism* (Oxford: Blackwell).

Roche, M. (2010) *Exploring the Sociology of Europe* (London: Sage).

Rogers, G. et al. (1995) *Social Exclusion* (Geneva: International Institute for Labour Studies).

Rosanvallon, P. (1981) *La crise de l'état-providence* (Paris: Seuil). Translated as *The New Social Question: Rethinking the Welfare State* (Princeton, NJ: Princeton University Press).

Ross, K. (1995) *Fast Cars, Clean Bodies: Decolonization and the Reordering of French Culture* (Cambridge: MIT Press).

Roy, O. (2010) 'When religion and culture part ways', 6 May, www.signandsight.com

Rumford, C. (ed.) (2007) *Cosmopolitanism and Europe* (Liverpool: Liverpool University Press).

Sakwa, Richard (ed.) (1999) *The Experience of Democratization in Eastern Europe* (Basingstoke: Palgrave Macmillan).

Saunders, P. (1995) *Capitalism: A Social Audit* (Buckingham: Open University Press).

Scharpf, F. (2009) 'The only solution is to refuse to comply with ECJ rulings', interview, *Social Europe* 4(1).

Schwengel, H. (1999) 'Europäische Sozialstruktur und Globaler Wandel' (University of Freiburg, http://www.zmk.uni-freiburg.de).

Seccombe, W. A. (1992) *A Millennium of Family Change: Feudalism to Capitalism in Northwestern Europe* (London: Verso).

Senghaas, D. (1982) *Von Europa lernen: Entwicklungsgeschichtliche Betrachtungen* (Frankfurt/M.: Suhrkamp). Translated as *The European Experience: A Historical Critique of Development Theory* (Leamington Spa: Berg, 1985).

Stråth, Bo (2002) 'A European Identity: To the Historical Limits of a Concept', *European Journal of Social Theory* 5(4):387-401.

Streeck, Wolfgang (1999) 'Competitive Solidarity: Rethinking the "European Social Model"', Max Planck Institute for the Study of Societies Working Paper 99/8 (Cologne: MPIfG).

Szelenyi, I. (1988) *Socialist Entrepreneurs: Embourgeoisement in Rural Hungary* (Cambridge: Polity Press).

Therborn, G. (1995) *European Modernity and Beyond: The Trajectory of European Societies, 1945–2000* (London: Sage).

Therborn, G. (2004) *Between Sex and Power: Family in the World, 1900–2000* (London: Routledge).

Therborn, G. (2011) *The World: A Beginner's Guide* (Cambridge: Polity Press).

Tönnies, F. (1955 [1887]) *Gemeinschaft und Gesellschaft*. Translated as *Community and Association* (London: Routledge, 1955).

Touraine, A. and Ragazzi, O. (1961) *Ouvriers d'origine agricole* (Paris: Seuil).

van de Steeg, M. (2002) 'Rethinking the Conditions for a Public Sphere in the European Union', *European Journal of Social Theory* 5(4).

Wagner, P. (1994) *A Sociology of Modernity: Liberty and Discipline* (London: Routledge).

Wallace, C., Datler, G. and Spannring, R. (2005) *Young People and European Citizenship* (Vienna: Institut für Höhere Studien).

Weiler, J. (2002 [2001]) 'Europe's *Sonderweg*', in K. Nicolaïdes and R. Howse (eds), *The Federal Vision: Legitimacy and Levels of Governance in the US and the EU* (Oxford: Oxford University Press), pp. 569–70.

Wessler, Hartmut et al. (2008) *Transnationalization of Public Spheres* (Basingstoke: Palgrave Macmillan).

Wiener, A. (1997) 'Making Sense of the New Geography of Citizenship: Fragmented Citizenship in the European Union', *Theory and Society* 26: 529–60.

Whyte, W.H. (1960) *The Organisation Man* (London: Penguin).

Chapter 8

Barbier, Jean-Claude (2008) *La Longue Marche vers l'Europe Sociale* (Paris: Presses Universitaires de France).

Cerami, Alfio and Vanhuysse, Pieter (2009) *Post-Communist Welfare Pathways: Theorizing Social Policy Transformations in Central and Eastern Europe* (Basingstoke: Palgrave Macmillan).

Cerny, Philip (1994) 'The Dynamics of Financial Globalization', *Policy Sciences* 27: 319–42.

Esping-Andersen, G. (1999) *Social Foundations of Post-Industrial Economies* (Oxford: Oxford University Press).

Esping-Andersen, G. (2009) *The Incomplete Revolution: Adapting to Women's New Roles* (Cambridge: Polity Press).

Eurostat (2010) http://epp.eurostat.ec.europa.eu/portal/page/portal/statistics/themes.

Hall, Peter A. and Soskice, David (eds) (2001) *Varieties of Capitalism: The Institutional Foundations of Comparative Advantage* (Oxford: Oxford University Press).

Held, David, Goldblatt, A. and Perraton, Jonathan (eds) (1999) *Global Transformations: Politics, Economics and Culture* (Cambridge: Polity Press).

Hollingsworth, J. Rogers and Boyer, Robert (1999) *Contemporary Capitalism: The Embeddedness of Institutions* (Cambridge: Cambridge University Press).

Huber, Evelyn and Stephens, John (2001) *Development and Crisis of the Welfare State: Parties and Policies in Global Markets* (Chicago: University of Chicago Press).

INSEE (1990) *Annuaire Retrospectif de la France: 1948, 1988* (Paris: Insee).

King, Desmond and Wood, Stewart (1999) 'The Political Economy of Neoliberalism: Britain and the United States in the 1980s', in Herbert Kitschelt et al. (eds), *Continuity and Change in Contemporary Capitalism* (New York: Cambridge University Press).

Maddison, Angus (1995) *L'Économie Mondiale 1820–1992, Analyse et Statistiques* (Paris: OECD).

Molina, Oscar and Rhodes, Martin (2007) 'Conflict, Complementarities and Institutional Change in Mixed Market Economies', in B. Hancké, M. Rhodes and M. Thatcher (eds.), *Beyond Varieties of Capitalism* (Oxford: Oxford University Press).

Nölke, Andreas and Vliegenthart, Arjan (2009) 'Enlarging the Varieties of Capitalism: The Emergence of Dependent Market Economies in East Central Europe', *World Politics* 69(4): 670–702.

OECD (2001) *Historical Statistics, 1970–1999* (Paris: OECD).

OECD (various years; 2009; 2010) Statistics online, http://www.oecd.org/statsportal/0,3352,en_2825_2935 64_1_1_1_1_1,00.html.

Orenstein, Mitchell (2009) 'What Happened in East European (Political) Economies: A Balance Sheet for Neoliberal Reform', *East European Politics and Societies* 23: 479–90.

Palier, Bruno (ed.) (2010) *A Long Goodbye to Bismarck? The Politics of Welfare Reform in Continental Europe* (Amsterdam: Amsterdam University Press).

Scharpf, Fritz W. and Schmidt, Vivien A. (eds) (2000) *Welfare and Work in the Open Economy. Vol. 1: From Vulnerability to Competitiveness; Vol. 2 Diverse Responses to Common Challenges* (Oxford: Oxford University Press).

Schmidt, Vivien A. (2002) *The Futures of European Capitalism* (Oxford: Oxford University Press).

Schmidt, Vivien A. (2009) 'Putting the Political Back into Political Economy by Bringing the State Back Yet Again', *World Politics* 61(3): 516–48.

Stopford, J. and Strange, S. (1991). *Rival States, Rival Firms: Competition for World Market Shares* (Cambridge: Cambridge University Press).

Streeck, Wolfgang and Yamamura, K. (2001) *The Origins of Nonliberal Capitalism: Germany and Japan* (New York: Cornell University Press).

Taylor-Gooby, Peter (ed.) (2004) *New Risks, New Welfare: The Transformation of the European Welfare State* (Oxford: Oxford University Press).

United Nations (1972) *Statistical Yearbook* (New York and Geneva: United Nations).

UN Economic Commission for Europe (2001) *Trends in Europe and North America, 2001* (New York and Geneva: United Nations).

World Competitiveness Yearbook (2000; 2009), http://www.imd.ch/research/publications/wcy/upload/scoreboard.pdf.

Chapter 9

Anderson, Jeffery J. (1995) 'Regional Policy and Politics in a United Germany', *Regional and Federal Studies* 5(1): 28–44.

Bache, Ian (1998) *The Politics of European Union Regional Policy* (Sheffield: Sheffield University Press).

Cornago, Noé (1999), 'Diplomacy and Paradiplomacy in the Redefinition of International Security: Dimensions of Conflict and Co-operation', *Regional and Federal Studies* 9(1): 40–57.

Davies, Norman (1996) *Europe: A History* (Oxford: Oxford University Press).

Eißel, Dieter et al. (1999) *Interregionale Zusammenarbeit in der EU* (Opladen: Leske & Budrich).

Gingrich, André and Banks, Marcus (2006) *Neo-nationalism in Europe and Beyond: Perspectives from Social Anthropology* (Oxford and New York: Berghahn Books).

Hrbek, Rudolf and Sabine Weyand (1994) *betrifft: Das Europa der Regionen* (Munich: C.H. Beck).

Judt, Tony (2005) *Postwar* (London: William Heinemann).

Keating, Michael (1998a) *The New Regionalism in Western Europe. Territorial Restructuring and Political Change* (Cheltenham: Edward Elgar).

Keating, Michael (1998b) 'What's Wrong with Asymmetrical Government?', *Regional and Federal Studies* 8(1): 195–218.

Keating, Michael, and John Loughlin (1997) 'Introduction', in M. Keating and J. Loughlin (eds), *The Political Economy of Regionalism* (London: Frank Cass), pp. 5–17.

Knodt, Michèle (1998) *Tiefenwirkung europäischer Politik. Eigensinn oder Anpassung regionalen Regierens?* (Baden-Baden: Nomos).

Kohler-Koch, Beate (1998) 'Europäisierung der Regionen: Institutioneller Wandel als sozialer Prozeß', in Beate Kohler-Koch et al., *Interaktive Politik in Europa: Regionen im Netzwerk der Integration* (Opladen: Leske & Budrich).

Loughlin, John (1993) 'Federalism, Regionalism and European Union', *Politics* 13(1): 9–16.

Loughlin, John (1996) '"Europe of the Regions" and the Federalization of Europe', *Publius: The Journal of Federalism* 26(2): 141–62.

Maiz, Ramon, Caamano, Francisco and Azpitarte, Miguel (2010) 'The Hidden Counterpoint of Spanish Federalism: Recentralization and Resymmetrization in Spain (1978-2008)', *Regional and Federal Studies* 20(1): 63–82.

Marks, Gary (1996) 'An Actor-Centred Approach to Multilevel Governance', *Regional and Federal Studies* 6(2): 20–8.

Mathias, Jörg (2004) *Regional Interests in Europe* (London and Portland, OR: Frank Cass).

Rydgren, Jens (2006) *From Tax Populism to Ethnic Nationalism* (New York and Oxford: Berghahn Books).

Sandford, Mark and McQuail, Paul (2001) *Unexplored Territory: Elected Regional Assemblies in England* (London: Constitution Unit, University College London).

Schöpflin, George (2000) *Nations, Identity and Power: The New Politics of Europe* (London: C. Hurst).

Wolff, Stefan (2003) *Disputed Territories: The Transnational Dynamics of Ethnic Conflict Settlement* (New York and Oxford: Berghahn Books).

Chapter 10

Asmus, R.D. (2010) *A Little War That Shook the World: Georgia, Russia and the Future of the West* (Basingstoke: Palgrave Macmillan).

Blair, T. (2001) 'Prime Minister Tony Blair Statement in Response to Terrorist Attacks in the United States – 11 September 2001', http://www.number-10.gov.uk/output/Page1596.asp: pp. 1–2, accessed 30 June 2004.

Burke, J. (2004) *Al-Qaeda: The True Story of Radical Islam* (Harmondsworth: Penguin).

Buzan, B. (1991) *People, States and Fear*, 2nd edn (Hemel Hempstead: Harvester Wheatsheaf).

Chomsky, N. (1994), *World Orders, Old and New* (London: Pluto Press).

Cronin, A.K. (2009), *How Terrorism Ends: Understanding the Decline and Demise of Terrorist Campaigns* (Princeton, NJ and Oxford: Princeton University Press).

Doyle, M (1986) 'Liberalism and World Politics', *American Political Science Review* 80(4): 1151–69.

EU (2010) 'Energy: Secure and Sustainable Supplies', http://europa.eu/pol/ener/index_en.htm, pp 1–2, accessed 23 March 2010.

English, R. (2009) *Terrorism: How to Respond* (Oxford: Oxford University Press).

Fukuyama, F. (1989) 'The End of History?', *National Interest* 16: 3–18.

Gaddis, J.L. (1986) 'The Long Peace: Elements of Stability in the Postwar International System', *International Security* 10(4): 99–142.

Hobsbawm, E. (1994) *Age of Extremes: The Short Twentieth Century, 1914–1991* (Cambridge: Cambridge University Press).

Huntington, S.P. (1996) *The Clash of Civilizations and the Remaking of the New World Order* (New York: Simon & Schuster).

IIFFMCG (2009) *Report by an Independent International Fact-Finding Mission on the Conflict in Georgia*, vol. 1, September, http//www.ceiigf.ch, accessed 1 February 2010.

IPCC (Intergovernmental Panel on Climate Change) (2007) *Climate Change 2007: The Physical Science Basis* (Geneva: IPCC).

Kaldor, M. (1999) *New and Old Wars: Organised Violence in a Global Era* (Cambridge: Polity Press).

Lucas, E. (2008) *The New Cold War: How the Kremlin Menaces both Russia and the West* (London: Bloomsbury).

Mearsheimer, J. (1990) 'Back to the Future: Instability in Europe after the Cold War', *International Security* 12(1): 5–56.

Medvedev, D. (2008a) 'Speech at a Meeting with German Political, Parliamentary and Civic Leaders', 5 June, http://eng.kremlin.ru/speeches/2008/06/05, pp. 1–2, accessed 12 May 2010.

Medvedev, D. (2008b) 'Interview given by Dmitry Medvedev to Television Channels, channel Russia, NTV', 31 August, http://www.kremlin.ru/eng/text/speeches//2008/08/31, pp.1–2, accessed 23 February 2008.

Morgenthau, H. (1978) *Politics Among Nations*, 5th edn (New York: Knopf).

Paris, R. (2001) 'Human Security: Paradigm Shift or Hot Air?', *International Security* 26(2): 87–102.

NATO Handbook (2001) 'The European Security and Defence Identity: NATO–EU Relations', http://www.nato.int/docu/handbook/2001/hb0403.htm, chapter 4, pp. 1–4, accessed 30 June 2004.

Peterson, J. and Pollack, M.A. (2003) *Europe, America, Bush: Transatlantic Relations in the Twenty-First Century* (London: Routledge).

Putin, V. (2005) 'Annual Address to the Federal Assembly, 25 April', http://www.kremlin.ru/eng/text/speeches/2005/04/25, pp. 1–9, accessed 27 April 2005.

Rogers, P. (2008) *Why We're Losing the War on Terror* (Cambridge: Polity Press).

Russian Ministry of Foreign Affairs (2009) 'European Security Treaty (Draft)', http://www.mid.ru/ns-dvbr.nsf/dveurope/065fc3182ca460dlc325767f003073, pp 1–5, accessed 23 February 2010.

Solana, J (2003) 'A Secure Europe in a Better World', European Council, Thessaloniki, 20 June, pp. 1–15.

Waever, O., Buzan, B., Kelstrup, M. and Lemaître, P. (1993) *Identity, Migration and the New Security Agenda in Europe* (London: Pinter).

Waltz, K.J. (1979) *Theory of International Politics* (New York: Random House).

World Bank (2002) *Globalization, Growth and Poverty* (Oxford: Oxford University Press).

Chapter 12

BBC (2009) *After Copenhagen*, http://news.bbc.co.uk/1/hi/sci/tech/8423822.stm, accessed 10 July 2010.

Beedham, Brian (1999) 'Special Report: The New Geopolitics', *Economist*, 31 July.

CIA (2010) *The World Factbook*, https://www.cia.gov/library/publications/the-world-factbook/geos/ch.html.

Delanty, Gerard (2010) 'The European Heritage from a Critical Cosmopolitan Perspective', *LDSE Europe in Question Discussion paper series*, http://www2.lse.ac.uk/europeanInstitute/LEQS/LEQSPapers.aspx.

Einhorn, Barbara (2006) *Citizenship in an Enlarging Europe* (Basingstoke: Palgrave Macmillan).

Elliott, Larry (2010) 'Masters of a Smaller, More Fragile Universe', *Guardian*, 1 February, p. 24.

European Centre for Disease Control (2010) http://ecdc.europa.eu/en/healthtopics/Documents/100119_Influenza_AH1N1_Situation_Report_0900hrs.pdf , 19 January, accessed 9 July 2010.

Ferrera, Maurizio, Hemerijk, Anton and Rhodes, Martin (2003) 'Recasting European Welfare States', in J. Hayward and A. Menon (eds), *Governing Europe* (Oxford: Oxford University Press).

Held, David, Goldblatt, A. and Perraton, Jonathan (eds) (1999) *Global Transformations: Politics, Economics and Culture* (Cambridge: Polity Press).

Held, David, and McGrew, Anthony (2001) 'Globalization', in J. Krieger (ed.), *The Oxford Companion to the Politics of the World* (New York: Oxford University Press).

Hurrell, Andrew, and Menon, Anand (2003) 'International Relations, International Institutions and the European State', in J. Hayward and A. Menon (eds), *Governing Europe* (Oxford: Oxford University Press).

Hutton, Will (2008) *The Writing on the Wall: China and the West in the 21st Century* (London: Abacus).

Interparliamentary Union (2010) *Women in National Parliaments*, 31 May, http://www.ipu.org/wmn-e/world.htm, accessed 12 July 2010.

Jacques, Martin (2009) *When China Rules the World: The Rise of the Middle Kingdom and the End of the Western World* (London: Allen Lane).

Judt, Tony (2005) *Postwar* (London: William Heinemann).

Mazower, Mark (1998) *The Dark Continent: Europe's Twentieth Century* (London: Allen Lane/Penguin).

Sakwa, Richard (2010) 'Russia and Turkey: Rethinking Europe to Contest Outsider Status', *Russie.Nei.Visions No. 51*, Paris, IFRI Russia/NIS Center (May), www.ifri.org.

Stevens, Anne (2007) *Women, Power and Politics* (Basingstoke: Palgrave Macmillan).

Taggart, Paul (2006) 'The domestic politics of the French and Dutch referendums', *Journal of Common Market Studies*, 44 (Annual Review): 7–26.

World Health Organisation (2006) *The World Health Report 2006: Working Together for Health* (Geneva, World Health Organisation), http://www.who.int/whr/2006/whr06_en.pdf

Zakaria, Fared (1997) 'The Rise of Illiberal Democracy', *Foreign Affairs* 76(6): 22–43.

Index

Page numbers in *italics* denote tables/maps
Page numbers in **bold** denote box and key figure entries